METACOGNITION

For
Katherine Rawson
and
Teal Eich and Margaret Metcalfe

METACOGNITION

John Dunlosky
Kent State University

Janet Metcalfe
Columbia University

Los Angeles • London • New Delhi • Singapore • Washington DC

For information:

SAGE Publications, Inc.
2455 Teller Road
Thousand Oaks, California 91320
E-mail: order@sagepub.com

SAGE Publications India Pvt. Ltd.
B 1/I 1 Mohan Cooperative
  Industrial Area
Mathura Road, New Delhi 110 044
India

SAGE Publications Ltd.
1 Oliver's Yard
55 City Road
London EC1Y 1SP
United Kingdom

SAGE Publications Asia-Pacific Pte Ltd
33 Pekin Street #02-01
Far East Square
Singapore 048763

Printed in the United States of America

Library of Congress Cataloging-in-Publication Data

Dunlosky, John.
Metacognition/John Dunlosky, Janet Metcalfe.
    p. cm.
Includes bibliographical references and index.
ISBN 978-1-4129-3972-0 (pbk.: alk. paper)
1. Metacognition. I. Metcalfe, Janet. II. Title.

BF311.D843 2009
153—dc22   2008011028

This book is printed on acid-free paper.

08 09 10 11 12   10 9 8 7 6 5 4 3 2 1

Acquisitions Editor:	Erik Evans
Editorial Assistant:	Lara Grambling
Production Editor:	Catherine M. Chilton
Copy Editor:	Taryn Bigelow
Typesetter:	C&M Digitals (P) Ltd
Proofreader:	William H. Stoddard
Indexers:	Leigha K. McFarren and Melissa Bishop
Cover Designer:	Candice Harman
Marketing Manager:	Stephanie Adams

Contents

Preface   vii

Acknowledgments   ix

1. Introduction   1

2. History   9
   Comte's Paradox and Turn-of-the-20th-Century
       Introspection   11
   Some Shortcomings of Introspectionism   15
   The Cognitive Renaissance   20
   The Return of Introspection and the Rise
       of the Metacognitive School of Psychology   26

Section 1. Basic Metacognitive Judgments   35

3. Methods and Analyses   37
   Metamemory: Measures and Questions   38
   Metamemory: Collecting, Analyzing, and Interpreting Data   44
   Overview of the Remaining Chapters on Basic
       Metacognitive Judgments   57

4. Feelings of Knowing and Tip-of-the-Tongue States   60
   Theories About Feeling-of-Knowing Judgments   61
   Tip-of-the-Tongue States   71
   Brain Bases of FOK Judgments   79
   Functions of Feelings of Knowing   81

5. Judgments of Learning   90
   Do All Monitoring Judgments Tap the Same Information?   91
   Variables Influencing JOL Accuracy   92
   Theories About Judgments of Learning   104
   Function of Judgments of Learning   110

6. Confidence Judgments   118
   Factors Influencing RC Accuracy   119
   Theories About Retrospective Confidence   129
   Function of Retrospective Judgments   139

7. Source Judgments   145
   Factors That Influence Source-Monitoring Accuracy   146
   The Source-Monitoring Framework   149
   Breakdowns of Source and Reality Monitoring   156
   Brain Bases of Source-Monitoring Judgments   164

Section 2. Applications   169

8. Law and Eyewitness Accuracy   171
   Confidence and False Memories   172
   Does Witness Confidence Matter to Jurors?   185
   Lying   187
   Hindsight Bias   191

9. Education   200
   General Models of Student Self-Regulated Learning   201
   Student Metacognition in Specific Domains   213

Section 3. Life-Span Development   233

10. Childhood Development   235
    Development of Theory of Mind   236
    Development of Metamemory   244
    Relationship Between ToM and Metamemory   260

11. Older Adulthood   264
    What Do Older Adults Believe About Memory?   267
    Aging and Memory Monitoring   272
    Aging and Control of Learning and Retrieval   284

References   293

Author Index   322

Subject Index   329

About the Authors   334

Preface

As I watch myself act I cannot understand how a person who acts is the same as the person who is watching him act, and who wonders in astonishment and doubt how he can be actor and watcher at the same moment.

—André Gide
Nobel Laureate for Literature, 1947

In this passage from *The Counterfeiters*, Gide's protagonist Edouard contemplates a mystery that inspires an entire area of inquiry on metacognition, "How can an individual both act and watch himself act at the same time?" By analogy, metacognition refers to thoughts about one's own thoughts and cognition. So for metacognition, instead of wondering how a person can watch himself act, an even more appropriate question is, "How can a person both think and *think about this thinking* at the same moment?" Although this ability to think about one's own thoughts does present many mysteries—which we explore throughout this book—such metacognitive acts are quite common. Every day, we think about our own thoughts and make decisions about how to act based on these metacognitions.

Over the past four decades, volumes of research have been conducted to explore people's metacognitions from various perspectives: Cognitive psychologists have sought to understand how people monitor and control their minds (two central components of metacognition), developmental psychologists have charted the growth of metacognition in childhood and its decline in late adulthood, and educational psychologists have sought to understand how students can take advantage of their metacognitive skills to improve their educational outcomes. Further excitement in the field arises from the relevance of metacognition to eyewitness testimony and legal procedures as well as the possibility that some nonhuman animals—for example, chimpanzees—are capable of monitoring their own thoughts.

Given the number of researchers now contributing to our understanding of metacognition within these and other domains, it would be difficult for any one textbook to survey the entire literature or even survey all the literature within a single domain. Accordingly, within this textbook, our main objectives were twofold. First, the textbook is meant to introduce students to the broad array of issues that arise in metacognitive research across multiple domains. We do describe some classic experiments in detail, but our focus is also on discussing general issues and themes that cut across domains. In this manner, the textbook will be ideal for courses designed for advanced undergraduates. Second, we discuss the methods and analyses that are typically used in metacognitive research, and our coverage in many areas highlights cutting-edge theory and debates that are pushing the field forward. Thus, the textbook will be ideal for graduate students and more seasoned scientists who want background knowledge about metacognition to extend their own interests and research.

Metacognition also has a variety of features that make it especially useful for the classroom and for the individual researcher. Each chapter ends with a set of discussion and concept questions and exercises to help students evaluate their understanding of the most important issues. Many chapters include "Mystery Boxes" that introduce an issue or debate that is being heatedly pursued in the field—that is, a mystery that researchers are trying to solve. Given that we describe many of the methods that can be used in helping to resolve these debates, our hope is that even advanced undergraduates can develop ideas on how to begin solving these mysteries using cutting-edge research designs.

We discussed the possibility of this textbook—the first one on metacognition—at Psychonomics in November 2002, after the inaugural meeting of the International Association for Metacognition. Our excitement for the project was stimulated by the accelerating interest in metacognition—both theoretical and applied—that is occurring worldwide. As the textbook moved from discussion to reality, many people have supported us. For feedback, advice, and materials, thanks go to Martin Chemers, Bridgid Finn, Doug Hacker, Reed Hunt, William Merriman, John Netfield, Joshua Redford, Bennett Schwartz, Keith Thiede, John Updegraff, and Tyler Volk. Many thanks to Katherine Rawson, who provided candid feedback on every chapter. Kate Guerini, Melissa Bishop, and Umrao Sethi provided critical assistance for completing a multitude of editorial jobs at Kent State and Columbia universities. And finally, thanks to all those at SAGE who were continually enthusiastic and supportive: Stephanie Adams, Jim Brace-Thompson, Cheri Dellelo, Lara Grambling, Anna Mesick, our copy editor, Taryn Bigelow, and cover designer Candice Harman.

—JD & JM

Acknowledgments

S age Publications would like to thank the following reviewers:

Margaret Anderson
State University of New York–Cortland

William M. Brown
Piedmont College

Erik De Corte
University of Leuven–Belgium

William G. Huitt
Valdosta State University

Michael McGuire
Washburn University

Patty Meek
University of Colorado at Denver

Bennett Schwartz
Florida International University

James P. Van Haneghan
University of South Alabama

David Whitebread
University of Cambridge

1

Introduction

Metacognition refers to thoughts about one's own thoughts and cognitions (Flavell, 1979). Although the term itself may seem mysterious, metacognitive acts are common. For instance, take some time to answer two questions. First, when was the last time you failed to recall someone's name, but were absolutely sure you knew the name? These frustrating events, called tip-of-the-tongue states, happen a lot and may increase in frequency as we grow older (Schwartz, 2002). They are metacognitive in nature because you are having a thought ("I'm sure I know the person's name") *about* a cognition (in this case, your thought is "that the person's name is *in your memory*"). Second, when was the last time you decided to write down lengthy directions, or perhaps even brief ones, and how often do you make a list of groceries to buy at the market? In such circumstances, you may realize that there is little chance of remembering important information, so you naturally rely on external aids—for example, lists, PalmPilots, or even other people—to ensure that you won't forget. Understanding the limits of your own memory also is a form of metacognition because it concerns your beliefs and knowledge *about* memory. What may also be evident from the rather common events illustrated above is that metacognition is not a single concept, but it is multifaceted in nature.

To illustrate further the facets of metacognition, consider the following scenario involving a college student who is preparing for an examination in Introductory Psychology on the biological basis of behavior.

Linda is diligently studying the *Introductory Psychology* textbook in her dormitory room, when her roommate turns on the TV. Realizing that the distraction will make it harder to memorize and understand the important facts, she grudgingly walks down to the study lounge. After securing the most comfortable couch, she continues studying by attempting to memorize the major parts of the brain. In doing so, she judges that in fact she knows most of them well, except that she keeps forgetting the lobes of the cerebral cortex. Thus, instead of spending more time on the other parts of the brain, she decides to invest her energy on the stubborn cortex. After repeating the lobes to herself multiple times, she still believes she won't remember them. To overcome this difficulty, Linda uses a simple strategy that she had learned from Mr. Bennett, her chemistry teacher in high school, which is to make up a meaningful phrase using the first letter of each lobe. With some diligent thinking, she comes up with "French Teachers Prefer Olives" to remember the Frontal, Temporal, Parietal, and Occipital lobes. After finishing the chapter, she also realizes that she doesn't quite understand how neurons communicate, and regardless of how hard she tries, she cannot seem to grasp the differences between action potential, resting potential, and graded potential. To cut her losses in wasted time, Linda decides to wait until the next class to ask some of her friends how neurons work.

This scenario illustrates three facets of metacognition that have been investigated extensively in the field: metacognitive knowledge, metacognitive monitoring, and metacognitive control. The definitions of these terms and other key concepts are presented in Table 1.1.

Metacognitive knowledge pertains to people's declarative knowledge about cognition. Declarative knowledge is composed of facts, beliefs, and episodes that you can state verbally (i.e., recall from long-term memory) and hence are accessible to conscious awareness (Squire, 1986), such as remembering that "dogs bark" or that "most cars have four wheels." By extension, metacognitive knowledge includes those facts and beliefs *about* cognition that you can state verbally. These facts may be general (e.g., "People who use images to learn lists of words often remember more than people who do not use images") or more specific (e.g., "I have difficulties solving Sudoku puzzles"). Linda demonstrated metacognitive knowledge when she recognized that distractions in the environment—for example, voices from the television—could interfere with her learning of classroom materials. Although Linda showed savvy knowledge about her cognition, metacognitive knowledge also may include incorrect beliefs. For instance, many students believe that studying the evening before an examination—popularly referred to as "cramming"—is an ideal way to retain new information, whereas decades of research indicate that spacing study of the same materials over longer intervals is a much more effective way of learning. Of course, if you haven't got it by the night before, by all means cram; what you learned might not last long, but if you are lucky, it will get you through the exam.

Table 1.1   Definitions of Important Concepts Relevant to Metacognition

Concept	Definition	Examples
Cognition	Symbolic mental activities and mental representations	Learning, problem solving, reasoning, memory
Metacognition	Cognitions about other cognitions	See examples in text
Metacognitive knowledge	Knowledge about a kind of cognition	• Knowledge about how learning operates • Knowledge about how to improve learning
Metacognitive monitoring	Assessing the current state of a cognitive activity	• Judging whether you are approaching the correct solution to a problem • Assessing how well you understand what you are reading
Metacognitive control	Regulating some aspect of a cognitive activity	• Deciding to use a new tactic to solve a difficult problem • Deciding to spend more time trying to remember the answer to a trivia question

Metacognitive monitoring refers to assessing or evaluating the ongoing progress or current state of a particular cognitive activity. To investigate metacognitive monitoring, researchers often ask experimental participants to explicitly judge a cognitive state. In Linda's case, monitoring was evident when she judged how well she had learned the major parts of the brain, and when she realized she did not understand how neurons communicate. Of course, if her judgments were inaccurate, she may have found herself in trouble. That is, if Linda actually *under*estimated how much she had learned, she may have spent too much time studying course materials that were already well learned and hence robbed herself of the opportunity to study materials that were less well-learned. Perhaps worse, she may have judged that she really knew the material well, and that she would remember it during the exam. Thus, if this judgment overestimated how much she had learned, Linda may have ended up with a poor grade, even though she was absolutely sure she understood all the material.

Metacognitive control pertains to regulating an ongoing cognitive activity, such as stopping the activity, deciding to continue it, or changing it in midstream. Linda's study behavior illustrates each of these forms of metacognitive control. She decided to stop studying the parts of the brain that she judged were learned well and instead focused just on the more difficult lobes of the cortex. In this case, she used monitoring to make a decision about how to allocate study time. To remember the lobes of the cerebral cortex, she controlled her studying by switching from a more passive rehearsal strategy to a more active strategy involving the generation of a meaningful phrase, in this case, that "French Teachers Prefer Olives." Metacognitive knowledge is important here in that she used her knowledge about strategies in the hope of overcoming her difficulty in memorizing important concepts.

Although this discussion and the corresponding definitions in Table 1.1 will be useful in grasping each of the concepts alone, a more analytic understanding about how they are related to one another and to cognition itself will prove important as well. Figure 1.1, which has been adapted from Nelson and Narens' (1990) influential article on metacognition, is a general framework about the relationship between metacognition and cognition. This framework includes two related levels, the meta-level and the object-level. The object-level can be viewed as the ongoing cognitive processes of interest, such as attention, learning, language processing, problem solving, and so forth. The meta-level also contains *a model* that is a person's understanding of the task they are performing and the ongoing cognitive processes that are engaged while they complete the task. This model is partly informed by people's monitoring of their progress on a task, but it also may be informed by their metacognitive knowledge. For instance, Linda may have constructed a model of her studying that included her goal to learn all the important biological concepts in the chapter she was studying as well as her belief that the best way to meet the goal was to study in a quiet environment and with effective study strategies.

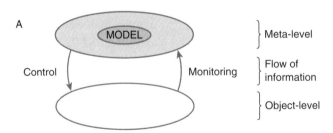

Figure 1.1   A framework relating metacognition (meta-level) and cognition (object-level) that gives rise to monitoring and control processes.

SOURCE: Adapted from Nelson, T. O., and Narens, L. (1990). Metamemory: A theoretical framework and new findings. In G. H. Bower (Ed.), *The psychology of learning and motivation* (Vol. 26, pp. 125–173). New York: Academic Press.

The interplay between the meta-level and the object-level defines the two process-based activities of metacognition—monitoring and control (for a generalization of this framework to more than two levels, see Nelson & Narens, 1994). In terms of this framework, metacognitive *control* is exerted whenever the meta-level modifies the object-level—more specifically, information from the meta-level acts to influence the ongoing activity at the object-level. Controlling the object-level, however, provides no information about the ongoing states of the object-level. Accordingly, you must monitor those object-level activities so that you can update your model of them (Nelson & Narens, 1990). In Figure 1.1, this process is metacognitive *monitoring*, which involves the flow of information from the object-level to the meta-level. This flow of information acts to update the model based on what is happening at the object-level. Examples of monitoring and control are presented in Table 1.1.

To help illustrate how this framework operates, Nelson and Narens (1990) offered a metaphor based on a telephone handset, which we expand upon here using a more contemporary example. Imagine that a friend calls you on the cell phone because she is excited to tell you about a movie that she just saw. Think of yourself as the meta-level and your friend as the object-level. Your goal is to understand your friend's message, and your model of this task may include numerous beliefs, such as that you probably won't understand your friend if you are both talking at the same time and that your friend hates being cut off while she talks. As you listen on your cell phone, you receive a flow of information from your friend as she speaks to you. Using the concepts from Figure 1.1, you are *monitoring* the ongoing message from your friend. At the same time, you can ask your friend to repeat anything you did not understand or hear well, or if you decide that you don't want the punch line of the movie ruined, you can ask your friend to talk about something else, or even hang up on her. In this way, you are controlling the conversation in the hope of meeting your own goals, and more specifically, what you are monitoring—the ongoing dialogue from your friend—is being used in the service of controlling the conversation. Of course, in terms of the framework in Figure 1.1, the object-level is not external to you—as in this example—but instead refers to any one of many cognitive processes that you could be monitoring and controlling.

Our leading scenario involving Linda also poses a mystery that we will explore in more depth throughout this book, namely, "How can people both think and think about themselves thinking at the same time?" That is, how can Linda both study and think about her studying as she is doing so? According to the framework in Figure 1.1, people become aware of their thinking when information from object-level thought processes is *represented by* the meta-level. The idea is that we can think about our thinking—or monitor thinking—by developing a higher-order representation (or model) of what cognitions are operating at the object-level. This particular answer to our question is similar to those posed by other philosophers and cognitive scientists (e.g., Rosenthal, 1998; Schooler, 2002). This framework is powerful because it is general: Any particular cognitive processes could be the object of meta-level processing. As important, the framework itself poses many empirical questions that will be explored thoroughly in this book, such as, How do people monitor ongoing thought processes, such as learning or problem solving? Is such monitoring accurate or does monitoring provide a distorted picture of people's cognitive activities? How is monitoring used to control ongoing cognitive activities, and when people control cognition, do they do so in an effective manner?

Throughout this book, we will describe key experiments and debates that have arisen in response to these, and many other, questions and mysteries about metacognition. In this brief introduction, we have defined some concepts that will appear throughout this volume. We conclude by describing the chapters and main sections of the book, and as important, we also provide suggestions on how to work your way through them.

Chapter 2 describes some of the historical origins of metacognition. Certainly, a metacognitive approach to psychology has not always been in good standing, especially during the peak of the behaviorist movement when many psychologists criticized using introspective methods to investigate the mind and even dismissed the need for the concept of consciousness in psychological science. In this chapter, we describe how modern metacognitive research has responded to early criticisms and give a brief overview of some events relevant to the rise of metacognition. We also introduce some of the pioneers of metacognition—such as John Flavell and Joseph Hart, among others—who were vital in promoting and shaping this area. Chapter 2 will be useful to those who want to become scholars of metacognition, although it is not essential for understanding subsequent chapters.

In the remainder of the volume, we review research that has sought to answer a variety of core questions about metacognition, some of which we introduced above. The book is separated into three major sections, each including a set of chapters on more focused topics. In each chapter within a section, we highlight issues and experimental data that have driven programs of research within an area. Although the massive amount of research conducted in each area precludes an exhaustive review in any chapter, we have attempted to touch upon a wide range of work by highlighting both seminal and cutting-edge research. As important, we discuss special topics and current mysteries in boxes throughout each chapter. The latter boxes document unresolved mysteries that new researchers in the area may find intriguing and exciting to explore, such as, "Do drugs impair your monitoring accuracy?" and "I'm in a tip-of-the-tongue state: How do I cure it?" Most chapters will introduce you to some of the influential leaders in the field, most of whom are still dedicated to pursuing programs of research aimed at solving mysteries in the field.

In Section 1, Basic Metacognitive Judgments, we entertain questions about how people monitor and control their memory, learning, and retrieval. In fact, much of this book examines issues that pertain to the metacognitive processes of memory—or metamemory—because the bulk of theoretical work relevant to monitoring and control processes has been conducted in this area. In Section 2, Applications, we discuss how metacognitive research has been applied to other tasks that are relevant to important real-world activities. These include the quality of eyewitnesses' confidence in memories of a crime as well as how metacognitive techniques have been used to improve student scholarship in educational settings. In Section 3, Life-Span Development, how metacognition develops and changes across the life span is of central interest. Monitoring and control processes are largely the focus of the first two sections, whereas in Section 3, we consider metacognitive knowledge in some detail, because it is here where scientists have wondered whether people's developing knowledge of cognition is a cause of cognitive development itself.

The chapters can be read in almost any order, although you may benefit by reading some before others. Because Chapter 3 describes the methods and analyses that have been used heavily in many disciplines in the field, we recommend reading this chapter before reading the others within that section or the chapters on Law and Eyewitness Accuracy, Childhood Development, or Older Adulthood. The remaining chapters can mainly be read independently of the others. With that said, our aim was to produce a volume in which each chapter builds upon issues and ideas within the previous ones, so paging through this volume chapter by chapter will likely lead to the most coherent and certainly most complete understanding of the principles of metacognition.

DISCUSSION QUESTIONS

1. In this chapter, the relationship between monitoring and control was illustrated with a metaphor involving two people speaking on cell phones, with one individual representing the meta-level and the other representing the object-level. Name as many different ways that the listener could *control* the input of this message. On one hand, why does this metaphor not actually represent a truly metacognitive system? On the

other hand, what metacognitive monitoring and control processes may be occurring within your own mind as you have a conversation with a friend? How might your inner metacognitive processes influence how you interact with your friend during this conversation?

2. Read the following sentence, and take a moment to reflect on how well you understand it: "The horse raced past the barn fell." If you are thinking, "I don't understand that sentence a bit," then you are similar to many others. Strangely, the sentence is grammatically correct. Here is a paraphrase to make it clearer: "The horse that was raced past the barn fell." Now, monitor your comprehension of this sentence. Any better? So, for comprehending sentences, people have some ability to monitor their understanding. Put differently, we are somewhat able to monitor the ongoing cognitive process of comprehension. Can you think of any cognitive processes that you would not be able to monitor? Why? (Just in case you still are concerned about the barn, the horse is the one that did the falling.)

CONCEPT REVIEW

For the following questions and exercises, we recommend that you write down the answers on a separate sheet in as much detail as possible, and then check them against the relevant material in the chapter. (For the reason why this trick will help you evaluate how well you have learned these concepts, see Dunlosky, Rawson, & Middleton, 2005.)

1. What is metacognition?

2. What is metacognitive knowledge?

3. Explain metacognitive monitoring and provide some examples of monitoring.

4. Explain metacognitive control and provide some examples of control processes.

2

History

Know Thyself

> —Inscription at the Oracle of
> Apollo in Delphi, Greece

The life which is unexamined is not worth living.

> —Socrates' rebuttal when
> found guilty of heresy

These famous quotes herald the importance of self-reflection and self-awareness, which place metacognition at the pinnacle of personal growth. And even though many people may not make time to seriously reflect on their lives, except perhaps on a birthday or an occasional New Year's Eve, almost every day of our lives, we do rely on our metacognitions. When we do, metacognition is typically used as a tool to deal with everyday problems—such as turning off a cell phone when traffic is extra heavy, or writing a note when it is absolutely essential to remember something. The importance of using metacognition to improve our daily lives is not at all limited to our contemporary world, but extends back to antiquity. In fact, the first documented success at controlling the mind to improve memory begins with a gruesome tale involving the poet Simonides (557–468 BCE), which was later told by Cicero in his *De Oratore* (Cicero, 2001).

According to Cicero (106–43 BCE), the famous poet-for-hire Simonides was attending a banquet given by Scopas, who was a rich nobleman. To honor Scopas, Simonides sang a poem that also included praise for Castor and Pollux. Sharing praise with the twins upset Scopas, who informed Simonides that he was to receive only half of his wage for the recital. Later, Simonides was called from the banquet to meet two young men who had asked to see him, but when he walked outside of the banquet room, he saw no one. While gone, the room collapsed, the roof fell, and all the partygoers were crushed to a point that they were not recognizable. Legend has it that the two young men were Castor and Pollux, who paid for their praise in Simonides' poem by saving him from certain demise. Most important for our story, to help the bereaved families identify their loved ones for burial, "It was reportedly Simonides who, from his recollection of the place where each of them had been reclining at the table, identified every one of them for burial. Prompted by this experience, he is then said to have made the discovery that order is what most brings light to our memory. And he concluded that those who would like to employ this part of their abilities should choose localities, then form mental images of the things they wanted to store in their memory, and place these in the localities" (Cicero, 2001, p. 219).

Thus, it appears it was Simonides who created this *method of loci*, which is a powerful mnemonic strategy that is used to improve memory. As Yates (1997) points out, in contrast to our modern world,

> In the ancient world, devoid of printing, without paper for note-taking or on which to type lectures, the trained memory was of vital importance. And the ancient memories were trained by an art which reflected the art and architecture of the ancient world, which could depend on faculties of intense visual memorization. (p. 20)

Simonides' story involves metacognitive activities in at least two ways. First, the method of loci involves visualization techniques that are internal mnemonics that involve people *acting on* their memories to control and improve them. Accordingly, these mental strategies reflect metacognitive activities and have been included in contemporary frameworks of metacognition (e.g., Nelson & Narens, 1990). Second, Simonides himself demonstrated that he had metacognitive knowledge, because he had learned that natural memory could be altered, as long as one spent the time developing images to train memory. This story (albeit tragic) also illustrates one way people can develop relatively subtle metacognitive knowledge about how memory operates.

Memory training in the Middle Ages often relied on complex mnemonics and external guides. One example is illustrated by the Abbey Memory System

(Figure 2.1), in which a series of objects (left panel) are to be memorized within locations of the abbey (right panel) to aid in enhancing memory.

These examples barely scratch the surface of the multitude of mental techniques that people have invented to control their minds and improve their memories. By doing so, people have developed a wealth of metacognitive knowledge and beliefs—beliefs about how memory operates and how it may be enhanced by mental mnemonics—and have used that knowledge to control the mind.

Comte's Paradox and Turn-of-the-20th-Century Introspection

Although sophisticated metacognitive knowledge has been evident in cultures since antiquity, only in the past 30 years have researchers begun to systematically investigate metacognition. Later in this chapter, we introduce some pioneers who blazed an experimental trail through this amazing capability of

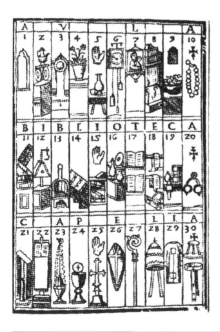
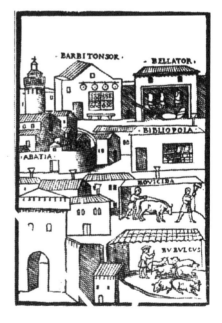

Figure 2.1   The Abbey Memory System.

SOURCE: Romberch (1553), as reprinted in Yates (1997).

human cognition—its ability to think about and control itself. Before we do so, however, we should consider a philosophical argument that questions whether human metacognition is even possible. This argument denies the reality of human introspection—a mental act that is synonymous with metacognitive monitoring. More specifically, Auguste Comte (1798–1857), a French philosopher who founded positivism, argued that

> as for observing . . . intellectual phenomena while they are taking place, this is clearly impossible. The thinking subject cannot divide himself into two parts, one of which would reason, while the other would observe its reasoning. In this instance, the observing and the observed organ being identical, how could observation take place? The very principle upon which [the introspection] is based, therefore, is invalid. (Brentano, 1874/1995, p. 32)

Nelson (1996) referred to this argument as Comte's paradox: "How [can] one and the same organ be the organ doing the observing and the organ being observed" (p. 104). Try to imagine this feat: How could your eye look at itself? Or most relevant for us, How could your mind look back at itself? Without a resolution to Comte's paradox, it would seem that metacognitive monitoring—or self-evaluation—is a mere illusion and potentially not privy to scientific enquiry.

To begin resolving this paradox, it will be worthwhile to take a much closer look at a popular technique, called *trained introspection*, that was used to investigate the mind in the late 1800s and early 1900s. As eloquently described by R. S. Woodworth (1921), introspection is the "observation by an individual of his own conscious action. . . . Notice that it is a form of observation, and not speculation or reasoning from past experience. It is a *direct observation of fact*" (p. 10, italics added). Wilhelm Wundt (1832–1920) was perhaps the most famous advocate of this introspective method. He argued that the subject of psychological science is immediate experience, which cannot be separated from the introspective method: "If the subject-matter is immediate experience, it is plain that the method is immediate experiencing" (Boring, 1929, p. 327). Introspection was not the exclusive method of psychology; many objective methods were also employed, and even Wundt himself rarely used introspection alone in the majority of his experiments. Nevertheless, many psychologists at the turn of the 20th century relied heavily on the introspective method, and E. B. Titchener—one of Wundt's most influential students—heralded introspection as the only method for psychology (for details, see Bolles, 1993, pp. 126–128; and Danziger, 1979). The "immediate experiencing"—or *concurrent introspection*—advocated by Wundt and others entirely sidestepped Comte's paradox, because it involved an introspector who indirectly and passively observed the mind "out of the corner of the mental eye" (Nelson, 1996, p. 104). Accordingly, Comte's paradox—that introspection could not occur because the observing organ and the observed organ were identical—was not a paradox at all, because for concurrent introspection to occur, just a portion of the mental organ was needed to look back upon itself. This argument resonates well with a contemporary resolution of Comte's paradox, which is based on neuropsychological evidence (see Box 2.1).

BOX 2.1
A Contemporary Rebuttal of Comte's Paradox

Comte's paradox was certainly taken as a potentially serious blow to using introspection for examining the contents of the mind; if the mind cannot observe itself, all monitoring and control of the mind is illusory. Our opinion, however, is that this paradox no longer poses a threat. A difficulty arises from an implicit assumption in Comte's argument, namely, that the organ for reasoning (the brain) consists of a single substance that cannot be subdivided. Just flipping through any modern text about the brain (and even not-so-modern ones) will reveal that it is composed of many neurological systems that work in unison.

Consider a situation in which you cannot readily recall the complete answer to an important question such as, "What are the names of all the Earth's continents?" You come up with some (e.g., North America, Asia, Europe, and Antarctica) but struggle with the others. In doing so, you introspect about your memory and decide that you could recognize the names of the other continents, even though you cannot recall them now. Comte would argue that this introspection is highly suspect, because how could your brain both introspect about your memory and at the same time attempt to retrieve memories? An answer to this question from neuroscientific research is that different systems of the brain are responsible for self-reflection and memory retrieval. At a molar level, the prefrontal cortex apparently plays a critical role in self-reflection, whereas the medial temporal lobe is critical for memory itself. So, a failure to retrieve the labels for some lobes of the brain that is based on disrupted medial temporal lobe dysfunction can still be reflected by intact functioning of the prefrontal cortex. Of course, the neurological analysis of self-reflection and memory is much more complex (for details, see chapters in Tulving & Craik, 2000). More important, what once was a burning paradox for philosophers and psychologists in the late 1800s is handled readily by current advances in our understanding of brain structure and functioning.

Nevertheless, other psychologists of the era believed that even if concurrent introspectionism (where one observes an ongoing mental activity *as* it occurs) were possible, it would be inadequate and misleading. Franz Brentano (1838–1917) argued that concurrent introspections are inadequate because people cannot observe intense emotions as they arise in the heat of the moment, and they are misleading because the act of observing inner processes may change them. For Brentano, concurrent introspection was out. Instead of concurrent introspection, he advocated *retrospective introspection*, in which one observes a mental process by recalling the events stored in memory that arose from that process.

To clarify the difference between these two kinds of introspection, consider this example: In searching for a bite to eat, you may struggle, but eventually decide to have Korean cuisine instead of Italian cuisine for dinner. To explore why you chose Korean cuisine, you can either monitor your thought processes as you make this decision (concurrent introspection), or you can make the decision first and then access the remnants of the information you used to make the decision that were stored in memory (retrospective introspection). Thus, for retrospective introspection, one presumably accesses the *products* of the mind's processes. Such retrospective introspection largely reduced the force of Comte's attack on introspection, as pointed out by John Mill (1806–1873):

> It might have occurred to M. Comte that a fact may be studied through the medium of memory, not at the very moment of our perceiving it, but the moment after: and this is really the mode in which our best knowledge of our intellectual acts is generally acquired. We reflect on what we have been doing when the act is past, but when its impression in the memory is still fresh. (James, 1920, p. 189)

Put differently, for a person to observe his or her own thought processes, the mind need not simultaneously be both the observer and the observed, but instead the "mind's eye" looks back at the products of the mind that have been stored in memory.

Some contemporary researchers would be unsatisfied with this memory solution to Comte's paradox because, according to current theory, both a percept and a memory are mental events that occur in the psychological present. Although a memory is *about* the past, the memory itself occurs in the present. That memory (just as much as if it were a percept) is what is occupying consciousness, attention, or is available in working memory. Kosslyn and colleagues (Kosslyn et al., 1993; Kosslyn & Thompson, 2000) have even shown that memory representations activate the same cortical areas as do percepts of the same content. If you *remember* a rod rotating, the same areas of the brain are activated as when you *see* a rod rotating. Thus, if it is paradoxical that an individual is able to monitor a percept and have a percept at the same time, it is equally paradoxical that an individual can monitor a memory and have a memory at the same time.

Despite this problem, at the turn of the 20th century Comte's paradox was not considered to present a real problem, and concurrent and retrospective introspection were commonly used to investigate the mind. In fact, numerous contemporary studies that we discuss in this volume use introspective techniques, such as when students are asked to evaluate their memories or when they are asked to report how they are solving a particular problem. Nevertheless, even though turn-of-the-century introspectionism relied heavily on metacognitive monitoring, it fell well short of producing a theory of human thought and action that relied on modern principles of metacognition. To understand why, we must turn to a more detailed analysis of introspection, which reveals its shortcomings that eventually led to its demise.

Some Shortcomings of Introspectionism

Perhaps the most important problem with turn-of-the-century introspectionism is that scientists of the era used introspection as a tool to discover the structure or functions of the mind. That is, these scientists were less interested in investigating people's introspections per se; instead, they used introspection as a tool—a virtual window into the mind. How introspection was used as a methodological tool is what undermined its ultimate success at providing a valid—or even consistent—description of the mind.

First, introspection was often believed to produce an accurate picture of the mind. That is, by using introspection in an appropriate manner, introspectors presumably reported accurately and completely about how their minds operated, such as reporting on the sensations produced by a stimulus or about the ongoing functions of an underlying mental process. Woodworth's (1921) definition (presented earlier) reveals the received view at the time that introspection involved the direct observation of fact, and even Brentano (1874/1995) assumed that when done retrospectively, such "inner perception is infallible and does not admit of doubt" (p. 35). Even if introspection were infallible and did not admit of doubt, it might still be largely inadequate if the mental processes that an experimenter wants to investigate do not produce mental images or sensations that are available to introspection. That is, the sensations and mental processes that are the focus of introspection must produce mental images that the introspector could perceive. If images are not always produced, then introspection could at best produce an incomplete—and hence not entirely accurate—depiction of thought. For instance, imagine trying to introspect about why you decided to have Korean food for dinner. If all the inner processes involved in this decision do not present themselves in your mind as images that you could "see with your inner eye," then introspection would not be useful in identifying these inner processes.

This raises the question, Do thought processes present themselves to us as images that can be the focus of the introspective method? Enter Oswald Külpe (1862–1915), one of Wundt's students. Külpe was a true believer in the introspective method—for a peek inside an introspectionist's laboratory, see Box 2.2. He wanted to use introspection to illuminate higher-order mental processes, such as the processes involved in decision making or those processes responsible for you thinking "13" when I tell you to add 6 and 7. Külpe and his dedicated students worked diligently on applying introspection to understand higher-order mental processes, and they consistently ran into difficulties. In a study by Karl Marbe, reported in 1901, participants lifted two weights and were instructed to decide which one was the heaviest—a standard task of psychophysics. The participants also used introspection to report what thoughts were in their minds immediately before they made this decision. Participants judged the weights but often failed in their introspections—the decision of which weight was heaviest seemed to mysteriously arise from nowhere. Similar experiments were conducted by Külpe and his students, and they repeatedly found that many thought processes were not accompanied by images. The repeated demonstration of such *imageless thoughts* suggested that either form of introspection—either concurrent or retrospective—was limited in what it could reveal about how the human mind operated.

BOX 2.2
Imageless Thought and the Würzburg School

What was it like to be a participant in a psychological experiment using introspection in the early 1900s? You can get a sense of the introspective approach and what it can tell you about your own mind by completing this simple demonstration. We will present some individual words below (e.g., "dog"), and you need to just say the first word that pops into your mind (e.g., perhaps "cat"). While you are playing this free-association game, you also need to use your inner eye in an attempt to introspect on the sensations or images that occur immediately before your response. For instance, when you read "dog," you may respond with "cat," but your main goal is to report any sensations or images that came to mind right before you said "cat." The hope is that your introspection will reveal the mental processes that were aroused by a given stimulus ("dog"), which in turn were responsible for eliciting your response ("cat"). Write down your introspections immediately after you generate each response; that is, we are more interested in your inner sensations and images that produce each response than the response itself. OK, let's give it a try. Get ready, because here's the first word for free association: party. That was not too difficult, was it? Now, take your time, and try out your introspective skills while generating a free association for a few more words: computer—football—chair. Look back at your introspections. What do they reveal? Did you have difficulties identifying the processes that produced your responses?

This demonstration is very similar to studies conducted by Külpe and his students, who made up the Würzburg School in Germany. Some of the first experiments were reported in 1901 by two of Külpe's students, Mayer and Orth (for a thorough description of introspective experiments from the Würzburg School, see Humphrey, 1951). Like the demonstration above, the experimenter would call out a stimulus word, and then the participant would report everything that bubbled up in consciousness until a response was made. Over 1,000 associations were obtained. Perhaps, like you, the participants did report some images and perceptions prior to making their responses. But another group of introspective reports occurred that could not be denied:

> The subjects frequently reported that they experienced certain events of consciousness which they could quite clearly designate neither as definite images nor yet as volitions. For example, the subject Mayer made the observation that, in the reference to the auditory stimulus-word "metre" a peculiar event of consciousness intervened which could not be characterized more exactly, and which was succeeded by the spoken response. (Mayer & Orth, 1901; taken from Humphrey, 1951, p. 33)

Maybe you had this same experience as well; that is, a response to "computer" may have come to your mind, yet you were not aware of any internal images or sensations that gave rise to your response. In this case, your responses—or thoughts—were not accompanied by inner images; these are the imageless thoughts that partly led behaviorists to mark introspection as an inadequate and misleading method. In spite of the presence of imageless thoughts, the Würzburg group continued to rely heavily on systematic introspection to investigate higher-order thinking. In fact, another Külpe student, Marbe, relied on reports from six introspectors to classify different forms of imageless thoughts. Suffice it to say that for these early psychologists, the accuracy of introspection was not often questioned. In contrast, among modern researchers of metacognition, the accuracy of introspection is questioned and systematically investigated by comparing people's introspections to objectively measured phenomena.

Of course, it would be unfair to dismiss the introspective method because it does not answer all the questions we may pose about the mind. Unfortunately, a second pitfall of the introspective method was even more devastating, because it did not meet an essential criterion of scientific methods—namely, that a method be reliable, producing the same results under the same experimental conditions. Perhaps to ensure reliability, participants in many of these studies were highly trained, and all aspects of the experiments were carefully controlled. Nevertheless, even with extensive training, introspective methods often supported different conclusions about the mind both within and across laboratories. Because introspection was not sufficiently reliable, many scientists began to question its worth as a scientific method.

The most well-known and outspoken critic of instrospection was John B. Watson (1878–1958), who defined behaviorism and established it as a prominent school of psychology. When Watson was a young psychologist at the University of Chicago, he taught courses on experimental psychology and had students analyze their minds using introspective techniques. But his research passions were focused elsewhere—namely, investigating animals that could not share any introspective ideas, even if they had them: "[Watson's] rats could not talk; they could not introspect to describe the contents of their minds. What they could do was behave. As early as 1904, Watson began to think that psychology should concern itself with behavior rather than with the mind" (Hothersall, 1995, p. 453). Just 9 years later, Watson (1913) published his clarion call for behaviorism in an article titled, "Psychology as the Behaviorist Views It." Merely three sentences into his behaviorist manifesto, Watson attacked introspection—a theme that he would take up with vigor throughout the article:

> Psychology as the Behaviorist sees it is a purely objective, experimental branch of natural science. Its theoretical goal is the prediction and control of behavior. Introspection forms no essential part of its methods, nor is the scientific value of its data dependent on the readiness with which they lend themselves to interpretation in terms of consciousness. (Watson, 1913, p. 158)

Watson argued strongly that consciousness could not be experimentally studied, so there was no need for introspective techniques, which he criticized as being a defective method. Thus, in one swoop, Watson would rid psychologists of consciousness and their means to study it through introspection. Watson's apparent disdain for other psychologists' interest in consciousness and introspection, which he believed was undermining progress in the field, is evident in his textbook on *Behaviorism* (1925):

> Literally hundreds of thousands of printed pages have been published on the minute analysis of this intangible something called "consciousness." And how

do we begin work upon it? Not by analyzing it as we would a chemical compound, or the way a plant grows. No, those things are material things. This thing we call consciousness can be analyzed only by *introspection*—a looking in on what goes on inside us.

As a result of this major assumption that there is such a thing as consciousness and that we can analyze it by introspection, we find as many analyses as there are individual psychologists. There is no way of experimentally attacking and solving psychological problems and standardizing methods. . . .

In his first efforts to get uniformity in subject matter and in methods the behaviorist began his own formulation of the problem of psychology by sweeping aside all mediaeval conceptions. He dropped from his scientific vocabulary all subjective terms such as sensation, perception, image, desire, purpose, and even thinking and emotion as they were subjectively defined. (pp. 5–6)

Even though metacognition was not a term used in the early 1900s, it is not a far stretch to assume it would have made Watson's short list of vocabulary to drop from psychology—metacognition may even have won the distinction of being the first on the chopping block, especially given that many metacognitive processes rely on our introspections. So if the mind is not fair game for Watson's behaviorism, then what is the object of psychological science? For Watson, its object was the study of observable behavior, with experimental analyses specifically leading to its prediction and control. This definition of psychology as the study of behavior was not altogether new when Watson offered it as a replacement for the "mediaeval conceptions," but his message was unambiguous and many psychologists were persuaded to pursue psychology as the behaviorist viewed it (Hothersall, 1995).

In the 1920s, behaviorism grew in its influence. Many prominent psychologists continued to explore mental processes throughout the mid-1900s, but behaviorism eventually would become the dominant school of American psychology, fueled by the innovative and influential work by Clark Hull, B. F. Skinner, and Edward Tolman, among many others. In fact, modern metacognitive research had to await the 1960s, which saw a resurgence in psychologists' interest in the mind and ultimately what is now considered the cognitive revolution. Our discussion here falls well short of providing a complete history of this revolution (for a thorough account, see Lachman, Lachman, & Butterfield, 1979), which Hunt and Ellis (2004) referred to more appropriately as the *Cognitive Renaissance* because the subject matter for modern cognitive psychologists is identical to the pre-behaviorist psychologists' subject matter in that both groups explored mental processes. Instead, we highlight some of the capstone achievements that were linked with this renaissance and, most important, that foreshadowed interest in a metacognitive approach to understanding human thought and behavior.

The Cognitive Renaissance

Behaviorism had a stranglehold on psychology for nearly 40 years and produced a wealth of data and theory relevant to how both human and nonhuman animals behave. So why did so many psychologists desert behaviorism in the 1960s? Two factors were involved: growing dissatisfaction with behaviorism as providing an adequate explanation for animal behavior, and a new approach to how to think about behavior in terms of mental processes (Hunt & Ellis, 2004). Concerning the former, behaviorists explained behavior in terms of stimulus-response connections that are developed through reinforcement. The presence of a stimulus was expected to trigger a learned response, much like a *reflex arc* in which an environmental stimulus (e.g., a puff of air on your eye) triggers a muscular response (i.e., blinking). The reflex arc was the fundamental unit of behavior, with new stimulus-response reflexes being learned through experience and reinforcement. Behaviorists viewed the stimulus-response connection—or reflex arc—as the building block of behavior because it presumably could be used to explain all behavior without recourse to mental processes.

No one experiment in particular was responsible for behaviorism losing its place as the leading school of psychology. Instead, the behaviorist stranglehold was gradually loosened by the discovery of many instances in which behavior could not be explained solely by stimulus-response connections. It was not until the 1960s that a large number of eminent psychologists turned from behaviorism toward a non-apologetic study of cognition, but troubling discoveries for behaviorism were readily available even in the 1920s (for extensive discussion, see Tolman, 1932). Tinklepaugh (1928) used a procedure to investigate monkeys' forgetting that elicited behavior that you may find quite understandable, but that would be utterly problematic for a staunch behaviorist to explain. A hungry monkey lingered over two cups, and a banana was placed under one of them; later in the experiment, the monkey could gobble up the banana if the correct cup was chosen. After the banana was placed, a screen was put between the monkey and the cups so that the monkey could not choose the correct one by simply keeping its eye on it. Then, after a certain amount of time had passed, the screen was lifted, and the monkey was given the chance to claim the delicious reward. Tinklepaugh also added an innovative twist to this procedure. On some trials, when the screen was blocking the monkeys' view of the cups, the banana was replaced with a piece of lettuce. His description of one monkey during this substitution trial is strikingly human: The monkey "extends her hand to seize the food. But her hand drops to the floor without touching it. She looks at the lettuce but (unless very hungry) does not touch it. . . . She has on occasion turned toward observers present in the room and shrieked at them in apparent anger. . . . The lettuce is left untouched" (Tolman, 1932, p. 73).

Perhaps you have some sympathy for Tinklepaugh's monkeys: They expected a banana and were upset when it was not there. What was difficult to reconcile with behaviorism, however, is that monkeys enjoy lettuce and will work to get it. They just enjoy bananas more than lettuce. As Tolman (1932) notes when discussing this experiment, even rats are disrupted when a more demanded food is replaced . . . by a less demanded food; it's just that "in the case of the monkey, this behavior exhibited lineaments more amusingly human" (p. 76). The point here is that monkeys—and even rats—were not necessarily learning stimulus-response connections (e.g., pick up the cup with a reward under it) but instead were learning what to *expect* from their responses. These expectations are cognitions that cannot be directly observed, and hence proposing that animals had expectations as well as being influenced by them most definitely was antithetical to the strict doctrines of behaviorism.

This kind of demonstration led some behaviorists, most notably E. C. Tolman (1886–1959), to advocate that not all behavior could be explained by strict stimulus-response behaviorism. According to Tolman, animal behavior is also influenced by motivational factors, such as the animal's drive to obtain reward and their incentive to do so. Although Tolman's views were certainly well regarded, they had little immediate influence in converting behaviorists into would-be cognitive psychologists. Nevertheless, many other demonstrations throughout the mid-20th century would uncover chinks in the armor of behaviorism and lead to its downfall as the dominant school of psychology.

A debate between B. F. Skinner and Noam Chomsky was significant historically in solidifying many psychologists' belief that behaviorist principles could not adequately explain all human behavior. Throughout his career, B. F. Skinner (1904–1990) argued persuasively for how the simple principles of behaviorism could be used to explain and control behaviors that had broad significance to humanity. One such instance included his attempt to use the principles of reinforcement to explain how people acquire and use language (Skinner, 1957). But could language arise solely from a collection of stimulus-response reflexes? Many linguists did not believe so, and in 1957, Chomsky forcefully rebuked Skinner's explanation of language as uninformative, if not utterly ridiculous. One argument can be illustrated with the following sentence: "His cat, Sophie, often annoyed him when she tried to curl up on his pillow to sleep, except on cold winter nights when Sophie would help to keep him warm." Certainly, you understood this sentence, even though you have never read it before and could not have learned it through the past association of single words. Now consider the immense number of sentences that you could possibly invent using your vast vocabulary. A person would need more than a lifetime to produce all of the possible sentences that could be created. For such feats of language generation and comprehension, an appeal to mental processes was necessary, and psycholinguists began to postulate the mental rules and syntax that were the basis of language acquisition, generation, and comprehension (for an excellent review, see Lachman et al., 1979).

Discontent about the explanatory power of behaviorist principles alone would likely not have led to the reemergence of cognitive psychology. Certainly, many believed an appeal to mental processes would be needed to explain animal behavior, but how were fledgling cognitive psychologists going to describe and investigate these mental processes? One answer to this question would be provided by computer science. The computer itself would be embraced as a leading model for the mind, because the computer as a model had a lot to offer: Computers rely heavily on programs, which are sets of rules that state how symbols can be manipulated to obtain a desired outcome. In this manner, a program *controls* the activities of the computer, which would become a core component of metacognitive models of human thought. Using the computer as a model also provided a language for cognitive psychologists to use in discussing the mind, which culminated in the information-processing model. As noted by Hunt and Ellis (2004),

> In the case of the information-processing model, one now could refer to the environmental energy as information rather than as a stimulus. The psychological processes of perception and comprehension could be thought of as coding, analogous to the coding operations necessary to transform the input to a computer into a form the machine can use. Memory could be described as storage and retrieval. Theories could be proposed based on the [computer] model and experiments designed to test those theories. (p. 21)

With a new model to guide the reemerging field, articles began to appear in the late 1950s and through the 1960s that would clearly mark the beginning of the Cognitive Renaissance. To name a few, Broadbent (1958) published his now-classic book on the bottleneck model of attention, Paivio (1969) investigated imaginal processes, and Mandler (1967) explored organizational processes in memory. Textbooks emerged that focused on exploring mental life, such as Miller's (1962) *Psychology: The Science of Mental Life* and Ulric Neisser's (1967) *Cognitive Psychology*. The latter volume was highly influential in fostering interest in cognition among teachers and would-be cognitive psychologists. These are just a few of many articles and books that have significantly contributed to the reemergence of cognition. For our history of metacognition, let's take a look at some early theories of mental processes that are notable because they included metacognitive processes that are being explored today.

In their book, *Plans and the Structure of Behavior* (1960), Miller, Galanter, and Pribram sought to replace stimulus-response descriptions of humans with a conception based on the relationships between internal images and the construction and use of plans in the control of behavior. According to these psychologists, "You *imagine* what your day is going to be and you make plans to cope with it. . . . A plan is, for an organism, essentially the same as a program for a computer" (pp. 6, 16). Miller et al.'s (1960) landmark book is worth reading today, partly because the authors discuss many concepts that are core to current theories of cognition, such as images, plans, and working memory.

For any student of metacognition, however, it was Miller et al.'s (1960) basic unit of analysis—which was to supplant the behaviorists' stimulus-response reflex—that is particularly germane. Illustrated in the left panel of Figure 2.2, their *test-operate-test-exit* (TOTE) unit is a feedback loop in which the outcome of a test informs (a) whether the desired state being tested for is present (congruity), in which case the loop is exited and the relevant operation is terminated, or (b) whether the desired state being tested for is not present (incongruity), in which case the operation continues. The TOTE is intentionally general, and depending on what flows across the arrows, such as neural energy or information, the TOTE can reflect the operation of a simple neural reflex or the operation of an information-driven mechanism. "In its weakest form, the TOTE asserts simply that the operations an organism performs are constantly guided by the outcomes of various tests" (Miller et al., 1960, p. 29). More concretely, consider the application of the TOTE unit to hammering a nail, which is illustrated in the right-hand panel of Figure 2.2. To hammer a piece of drywall onto a stud, the goal is to hammer a nail until its head is flush with the drywall. One tests the nail by examining whether it is flush. If it is not flush (incongruity), then one continues the operation of hammering. If it is flush, then hammering stops. Of course, this oversimplifies hammering, because to hammer, one must lift the hammer up and smack it back down. TOTE units can be designed to control this aspect of hammering as well. As shown in Figure 2.3, hammering a nail is described by a hierarchical plan based on the concatenation of TOTE units. Even the most complex behaviors can be explained by a hierarchy of TOTE units that control behavior from the planning stages (e.g., put up new drywall) to its implementation (e.g., drive in individual nails).

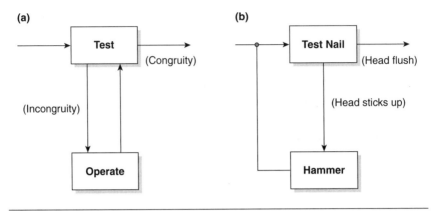

Figure 2.2   The test-operate-test-exit (TOTE) unit.

SOURCE: Miller, Galanter, and Pribram (1960).

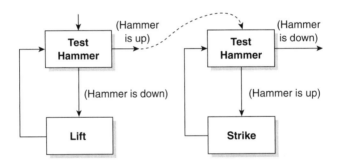

Figure 2.3   Complex human behaviors can be explained by concatenating two or more test-operate-test-exit (TOTE) units. In this illustration, two TOTE units are connected that could control the operations of hammering a nail.

SOURCE: Miller, Galanter, and Pribram (1960).

Hammering a nail is not a metacognitive act, per se, because the test involves monitoring the state of *external* stimuli. Nevertheless, the generality of the TOTE mechanism allows it to apply equally well in analyzing any human activity, including metacognitive ones. To convince yourself of this claim, flip back to Chapter 1 and compare the general metacognitive model

(Figure 1.1) introduced by Nelson and Narens (1990), which itself was inspired by the TOTE mechanism. For the metacognitive model, some process of the mind is monitored, which for the TOTE mechanism is analogous to testing an outcome. The outcome of such monitoring can then serve to control one's thought by either terminating that process (which is analogous to *exiting* the TOTE loop) or by continuing until some goal has been achieved (which is analogous to continuing the relevant operation engaged by the TOTE mechanism).

Although Miller et al.'s (1960) TOTE unit inspired many models of self-regulation that are described in this volume, it was not the only model arising early in the Cognitive Renaissance that implicated the central role metacognition played in controlling human behavior and thought. Let's consider two others that will help illustrate metacognitive processes involved in other forms of cognition: human memory and problem solving.

In 1968, Atkinson and Shiffrin proposed that human memory is a system composed of a series of stores. Information from the environment is copied into a sensory store, and when attended, is then transferred to a short-term store, which is limited in capacity. You can think of this short-term store as holding information of which you are currently aware, such as the meaning of this sentence. Once information resides in the short-term store, we can then operate on it by using a variety of *control processes*, such as rehearsing the information repeatedly or elaborating on the information in a meaningful fashion. People use these control processes all the time, such as when a waiter repeats a drink order in his head (i.e., in his "short-term store") until he has a chance to write it down. Most relevant for our history, these control processes are metacognitive in nature: The information in the short-term store (e.g., an order at a bar for drinks) is an object-level cognition and meta-level processing acts upon it, in this case by applying control processes (i.e., repeating the order) that increase the likelihood the information is transferred to the long-term store. For our waiter, the names of the drinks (e.g., Dry Martini, Bud Light, and Irish Whiskey) reside in his short-term store, and repeating them allows him to hold onto them in the short run and increases the chances that he will also remember them later as well.

In *Human Problem Solving*, Newell and Simon (1972) argue that problem solving can be understood as "a collection of information processes that combine a series of means to attain an end" (p. 91), and these means in general include choosing a goal for a problem, selecting a method to generate a solution, and evaluating the results of that method. These problem-solving processes are recursive in nature, so, for instance, if one realizes that a method has not produced the desired result, a new method may be chosen and applied to the problem. By now, it should be clear that these processes are partly metacognitive in nature, because they involve evaluating progress and using the outcome of such evaluations to make decisions about how to solve problems.

Despite these obvious references to metacognitive processes in early and influential theories of cognition, the overwhelming response of cognitive scientists was to investigate the cognitive components embedded in these models, such as by exploring the structure of the short-term store or by describing how people represent problems as they solve them. In contrast, an exploration of the metacognitive processes, such as how people monitor and control these processes, was largely ignored. Although speculative, this reluctance to investigate people's monitoring and control may be partly attributed to the great influence of behaviorists, who convincingly argued that the introspective method required to study these processes would not provide reliable and valid means for experimental analyses.

The Return of Introspection and the Rise of the Metacognitive School of Psychology

Lieberman (1979) eloquently argued for a limited return to introspection in the analysis of human thought and action. Although Lieberman concedes that introspection has limits as a method for understanding human thought and behavior, he rebukes the behaviorist tactic of completely dismissing introspection as worthless. Instead of rejecting introspection as totally unreliable and invalid, he argues that in deciding whether to use it as a scientific method, "the only reasonable criterion is an empirical one: whether or not introspective data help us to understand behavior" (p. 320). According to Lieberman, introspective data meet this criterion because they can produce invaluable evidence about how humans think. Here are two examples where introspection meets this empirical criterion. First, as we noted at the beginning of this chapter, as far back as the ancient Greeks, people reported that the method of loci is an effective technique for improving memory. These reports—which are introspective ones—had not been experimentally validated. In the early 1970s, several researchers demonstrated that memory performance was indeed superior after people used this mnemonic technique as opposed to when they were not instructed in how to study the to-be-learned materials, which confirmed the validity of the previous introspective reports.

Second, introspective data has been convincingly used to evaluate models of how the mind operates. For instance, Atkinson and Shiffrin's (1968) stage model of memory assumed that the more one rehearsed information in the short-term store, the greater the likelihood that information would be transferred to long-term memory and hence be remembered. To empirically test this assumption, Kroll and Kellicutt (1972) presented trigrams (sequences of three letters) to participants, who were later asked to recall them. The critical introspective addition to this method was that the participants were asked to report how often they rehearsed the letters by simply pressing a button during each rehearsal. Their data are presented in Figure 2.4, which plots recall as a function of the number of reported rehearsals across several conditions. The effects of the conditions (e.g., X3 versus X7 or Visual versus Auditory in Figure 2.4) are not of interest to us, but instead, our question is whether people's introspective reports of rehearsals were actually predictive of recall performance as predicted by Atkinson and Shriffin's model. The results shown in Figure 2.4 are consistent with their prediction, because in each of the four conditions (represented by the four symbols and lines in the figure), as people reported rehearsing more often (from 0 to 6), their recall performance steadily increased. As impressive, Kroll and Kellicutt (1972) also found that recall performance was better predicted by this subjective, introspective report of rehearsals than were other measures of rehearsal. These and other outcomes presented by Lieberman (1979) clearly establish the reliability of introspective reports, although he appropriately notes that "it would be foolish, of course, to claim that introspective reports would always be this reliable—The history of classical introspection has clearly shown that they are not. That same history, however, makes it equally clear that certain kinds of reports *are* useful" (p. 328).

Seemingly at odds with Lieberman (1979), Nisbett and Wilson (1977) argued that verbal reports—also known as "introspections"—are largely invalid because people cannot observe their cognitive processes. Moreover, even when people do make apparently accurate reports about how or why they are behaving in a certain way, such accuracy does not arise from their ability to validly introspect. Instead, the apparently valid introspections arise from the fact that people's educated guesses—or inferences—about how they behave are sometimes correct. Nisbett and Wilson (1977) offer numerous examples that support their main claim "that when people attempt to report on their cognitive processes . . . they do not do so on the basis of any true introspection" (p. 231). You can easily demonstrate one startling example, which takes advantage of the fact that most people have a preference for objects placed on their right. Grab four nylon stockings that are *identical*, and place them equally spaced on a table. Ask people who pass by to participate in a brief consumer survey—this would be easy to do in a dormitory or in a campus building. Simply ask each person the following question: "Which particular stocking do you like the best, and why?" When Nisbett

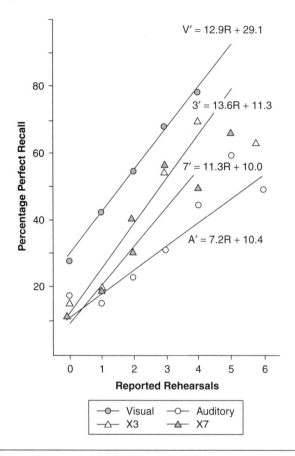

$V' = 12.9R + 29.1$

$3' = 13.6R + 11.3$

$7' = 11.3R + 10.0$

$A' = 7.2R + 10.4$

Percentage Perfect Recall

Reported Rehearsals

—●— Visual   —○— Auditory
—△— X3   —▲— X7

Figure 2.4   Percentage of correct recall of trigrams as a function of the number of rehearsals reported by participants. The four functions represent four conditions, which influenced the overall difficulty of the task. Note that regardless of condition, participants' instrospective reports are highly predictive of actual levels of recall performance.

SOURCE: From Kroll, N. E. A., and Kellicutt, M. H. (1972). Short-term recall as a function of covert rehearsal and of intervening task. *Journal of Verbal Learning and Verbal Behavior, 11*, 196–204.

and Wilson (1977) conducted this simple experiment, they found that the majority of people preferred the stocking on the right side of the table, yet no one mentioned that the reason for their choice involved the position of the nylon stocking!

How might the contradictory conclusions offered by Lieberman (1979) and Nisbett and Wilson (1977) be reconciled? That is, when will introspections be valid and when will they be invalid? In their classic article, "Verbal Reports as Data," Ericsson and Simon (1980) propose a theory of introspective reports, or verbal reports, that explains when introspections will be valid (under conditions described by Lieberman, 1979) and when they will not (under conditions described by Nisbett & Wilson, 1977). For this historical chapter, the theory is too complicated to cover exhaustively, but a sketch of it should suffice. Central to their theory is the stage model of memory (Atkinson & Shiffrin, 1968). In particular, when people introspect about some aspect of cognition, this aspect of cognition may reside in their short-term store during introspection, it may have resided in their short-term store at some point prior to the introspection, or it may never have resided in their short-term store. According to Ericsson and Simon's theory, people's introspections will be valid when they focus on information that is currently in the short-term store. In contrast, when people are asked to introspect about information not currently in the short-term store, the validity of their introspections may be hampered because they may no longer have access (e.g., due to forgetting) to the sought-after information. Finally, if the sought-after information never resided in the short-term store, the model predicts people's introspections will be largely invalid, unless of course they make a correct guess about what was going on in their minds.

Consider these different cases in terms of Kroll and Kellicutt's (1972) experiment, described earlier. When their experimental participants were studying trigrams for an upcoming test of free recall, they had to report how often they rehearsed each item by pressing a button. Note that repeating letters to oneself occurs in the short-term store, so it is not surprising that the participants' introspections were highly valid. In contrast, if the participants rehearsed the letters and then attempted to recall them, and only afterward were asked to report how often they had rehearsed the letters, these introspective reports would likely be less valid because the participants may have forgotten how often they had rehearsed each item. And finally, if Kroll and Kellicut asked the participants to report whether the presentation of each letter activated a particular part of the brain, their introspective reports would be highly invalid, because brain activity is not represented in the short-term store. Ericsson and Simon's theory has other dimensions that are relevant to fully understanding the validity of introspective reports, but for now the important point is that people's introspective reports can be valid under well-specified conditions (for details, see Ericsson & Simon, 1984).

BOX 2.3
Joseph T. Hart's Contribution to Reviving Introspectionism

"What city is the capital of Australia?" "Who wrote the book *The Old Man and the Sea*?" If you are not able to recall the answers to these questions, you may have the feeling that the answers are just out of your mind's reach—that they are on the "tip of your tongue." These tip-of-the-tongue (TOT) phenomenon are so common that psychologists have been interested in them for quite some time (for a review, see Brown, 1991). Even William James acknowledged this frustrating lapse of memory, and these tip-of-the-tongue states were investigated in the early 20th century. Unfortunately, the early research assumed that TOT states were real and valid; of course, the difficulty is that such TOT states are entirely subjective and based on introspective reports, so how can they be trusted? That is, just because you say that you are about to retrieve the capital city of Australia, how can we be sure your TOT state accurately indicates that the memory is just out of reach?

Joseph T. Hart (1965) answered these questions in a classic paper that predates the rise of contemporary metacognition research. This article and several others (e.g., Hart, 1966, 1967) were absolutely vital to the development of metacognitive research, because Hart introduced an innovative method to empirically test the accuracy of people's metacognitive experiences. Hart (1965) based his technique on the fact that people often recognize more answers than they can recall from memory. Based on this fact, he developed the now well-known recall-judge-recognition (RJR) method. People first attempt to recall answers to general-knowledge questions from memory. For answers they cannot recall, they then state whether they could recognize the correct answer. After making these judgments, participants receive a test of recognition, in which they are shown the correct answer along with multiple alternatives. If people's introspections about what they know (but cannot recall) are accurate, then their recognition performance should be higher for answers that they judged they would recognize than for those they judged would not be recognized. Time and time again, Hart demonstrated that in fact people's judgments were accurate. This research—which stemmed from his award-winning dissertation—was groundbreaking in multiple ways. First, his findings led to a perplexing question: How can you know something about your memory that in fact you cannot recall? We explore answers to this question in Chapter 4, Feelings of Knowing and Tip-of-the-Tongue States. Second, and most relevant to our history, in addition to establishing that people's introspections *can* be valid, Hart provided a rigorous methodology that allowed scientists to empirically test whether their introspections *were* valid. Thus, people's introspections no longer needed to be taken at face value in psychological research. Instead, scientists could systematically explore biases in people's introspections and develop techniques that were meant to debias their introspective judgments so that they more validly reflected the inner workings of the mind. For these reasons, much of the research on metacognitive monitoring discussed in this volume has been inspired by the seminal research of Joseph T. Hart.

By demonstrating how introspective techniques can validly reveal at least some aspects of cognition, Ericsson and Simon (1980, 1984) provided a cornerstone that was essential for the growth of a new school of psychology, the *Metacognitive School*. Even with this cornerstone laid, others were still needed before scientists would adopt a metacognitive perspective (including the methods, analyses, and explanations inspired by metacognitive principles) as a means to further understand human thought and behavior. To this end, the rise of the Metacognitive School would largely ride on the shoulders of several leaders in the field, who persuasively argued for the critical role of metacognition in understanding human behavior and development, and in doing so, offered a set of definitions, issues, and questions for others to rally behind.

Arguably, the most influential advocate for metacognition during its infancy was John Flavell, who coined the term *metamemory* in 1970. In this decade, the term *meta* began to arise in articles and conference papers, and much groundbreaking research in the area was conducted. For instance, Flavell, Friedrichs, and Hoyt (1970) asked preschoolers to study items until they were sure that they could recall them all. Many of the younger students said they were ready to be tested, when in fact they could not recall all of the items on the list. Similarly, Ellen Markman (1977) had elementary schoolchildren listen to a set of instructions that were incomplete, and they were supposed to report whether they had any difficulties understanding them. Many of the children did not detect the major error and claimed they had understood the instructions (for details, see Chapter 9, Education). Other instances of children's faulty metacognitions had also been demonstrated, and in 1978, Ann Brown published an overview of the new field in her chapter, "Knowing When, Where, and How to Remember: A Problem of Metacognition," in which she concludes that the "distinction between knowledge and the understanding of that knowledge [is] a valid and important distinction with great heuristic power" (p. 157).

These provocative demonstrations and growing interest in metacognition set the stage for Flavell's (1979) *American Psychologist* article, called "Metacognition and Cognitive Monitoring: A New Area of

John H. Flavell
Founder of modern
metacognitive research,
with major contributions
to our understanding
of theory of mind

Cognitive-Developmental Inquiry." This article was highly influential because it promoted the importance of metacognition, especially with respect to understanding cognitive development. Flavell (1979) defined *metacognition* as "knowledge and cognition about cognitive phenomena" (p. 906) and refined this definition by specifying classes of phenomena that constitute monitoring and control of cognition, such as metacognitive knowledge and metacognitive experiences. As defined in Chapter 1, *metacognitive knowledge* is a person's declarative knowledge or beliefs about how various factors influence the processes and outcomes of any given cognitive task. Flavell (1979) further subdivided this knowledge into three categories to reflect the fact that a given person may have knowledge (a) about how he or she processes information (person category), such as if you believe you are good at solving math problems but not chemistry problems; (b) about a specific cognitive task of interest (task category), such as that writing a class paper is difficult; and (c) about what strategies are effective (strategy category), such as that memory is often better served by using mental imagery than by merely repeating information over and over again. Metacognitive knowledge typically involves some combination of these three categories. As Flavell (1979) notes, "like any other body of knowledge children acquire, [metacognitive knowledge] can be inaccurate, can fail to be activated when needed, can fail to have much or any influence when activated, and can fail to have a beneficial or adaptive effect when influential" (p. 908). *Metacognitive experiences* are those cognitive or affective experiences that may occur as a person completes a cognitive task, and are most closely aligned with metacognitive monitoring as defined in Chapter 1. Flavell's article was particularly powerful in defining core components of metacognition as well as offering numerous testable hypotheses for how these components might develop throughout childhood, and in turn influence the success and progress of cognitive development itself. For any aficionado of metacognition, Flavell (1979) is a must read.

Although Flavell and his colleagues, most notably Henry Wellman, began to champion a metacognitive approach in the 1970s, the beginnings of this approach can be traced back to the 1960s, when Flavell (1963) was assimilating Jean Piaget's theory on child development in the landmark book, *The Developmental Psychology of Jean Piaget*. It was in the theoretical work of Jean Piaget and his colleagues that the notion of children having thoughts about thoughts clearly arose. These "thoughts about thoughts" were considered a pinnacle of child development in that they signified the presence of formal operations, which Flavell (1963) eloquently describes as "the crowning achievement of intellectual development, the final equilibrium state toward which intellectual evolution has been moving since infancy" (p. 202). Flavell goes on to emphasize that "the most important general property of formal-operational thought, the one from which Piaget derives all others (Inhelder and Piaget, 1958, pp. 254–255), concerns the *real* versus the *possible*. . . . Formal thinking is above all *propositional thinking*. The important entities which the adolescent manipulates in his reasoning are no longer the raw reality data themselves but assertions or statements—propositions—which 'contain' these data" (pp. 204–205). It seems likely that the theorizing by Piaget and his colleagues was directly responsible for inspiring Flavell to further consider the importance of "thoughts about thoughts" for early child development (Hacker, 1998a).

Thus, the 1970s saw the rise of the Metacognitive School of Psychology mainly from empirical research and theory construction in developmental psychology. Psychologists continued to refine what counted as metacognition (Brown, 1978; Flavell, 1979; Kluwe, 1982) and even debated the utility of these definitions in understanding human behavior (Cavanaugh & Perlmutter, 1982). Since then, a metacognitive approach has been adopted by researchers in many domains of psychology, including social, cognitive, educational, child and adult development, and clinical. The growth of metacognitive research within each of these domains has its own history. Some of these histories are lengthy, such as for cognitive and educational psychology, which began near the rise of the Metacognitive School of Psychology. In other domains, systematic exploration of metacognitive processes is just now catching on. Although we do not take the time here to trace out historical landmarks for each domain, in a way, the remainder of this book can be viewed as an extended history of metacognitive research. In each chapter, we will highlight the earliest groundbreaking articles within a domain or specific research area, so that you can trace the Metacognitive School from the germination of its seeds in the 1970s to its growth and expansion throughout psychological research.

Summary

The story of metacognition can be traced to antiquity, with Simonides heralding the power of his method of loci to control memory. Metacognitive processes played an especially important role for late-19th- and early-20th-century psychologists, who used introspection as a tool to discover the inner workings of the mind. Unfortunately, at the turn of the 20th century, introspective techniques were found to be somewhat inadequate and misleading—the findings did not always replicate across laboratories and many inner processes could not be revealed by introspection because they did not produce mental images. With much vigor, Watson banished introspection from psychology and the study of consciousness as the pursuit of psychological inquiry, and he offered behaviorism as a replacement.

Several decades later, many psychologists in turn found behaviorism inadequate, and they began to develop models of behavior that once again relied on mental processes. Even the earliest models of cognition included metacognitive processes. Nevertheless, metacognition itself did not become the object of systematic investigation until the late 1960s and early 1970s, when Joseph Hart gave us methods to investigate the validity of people's introspections and John Flavell persuasively argued that metacognitive processes were vital to child development and to human behavior in general.

DISCUSSION QUESTION

1. Imagine studying for an upcoming examination on this history chapter. You know you will have to answer some multiple-choice questions and some essay questions. Let's also assume that you want to make a very high score. How would you go about studying for the exam? Which processes involved in your studying are metacognitive and which ones are cognitive? As important, how would Miller, Galanter, and Pribram's (1960) TOTE mechanism describe your progress toward your learning goal?

CONCEPT REVIEW

For the following questions, we recommend you write down the answers on a separate sheet in as much detail as possible, and then check them against the relevant material in the chapter.

1. Compare and contrast early introspectionism (used by Wundt and others) with the use of introspectionism in modern metacognitive methods. What was the big advance in introspective research made by Joseph Hart?

2. What are imageless thoughts and why were they problematic for the use of introspection to explore the mind?

3. Most people do not realize that their decisions can be influenced by irrelevant stimuli, such as the position of items on a grocery shelf. According to Ericsson and Simon, why would we be unable to introspect accurately about such position effects?

Section 1

Basic Metacognitive Judgments

3

Methods and Analyses

Why all the excitement about metacognitive research? One answer is that metacognitive researchers are attempting to discover and understand aspects of human nature that may distinguish us from many other animals—our ability to think about our own thoughts, and our ability to use this thinking to control our thoughts and actions. These abilities pertain specifically to how humans—and perhaps some nonhuman animals (Terrace & Metcalfe, 2005)—monitor and control their minds. In the chapters in Section 1, we tackle some of the most fundamental questions about these core abilities of human metacognition within the context of metamemory research. Metamemory research concerns people's knowledge about memory and their monitoring and control of memory processes—from learning new materials to later retrieving them from memory.

There are numerous reasons to spend so much time discussing metamemory. Metamemory has a long tradition in psychological research, beginning in the 1960s with Joseph Hart's seminal work on feeling-of-knowing judgments. In fact, even before the term "metamemory" was coined, Tulving and Madigan (1970) enthusiastically endorsed the study of metamemorial processes in a popular passage:

> Why not start looking for ways of experimentally studying and incorporating into theories and models of memory one of the truly unique characteristics of human memory: its knowledge of its own knowledge. . . . We cannot help but feel that if there is ever going to be a genuine breakthrough in the psychological study of memory . . . it will, among other things, relate the knowledge stored in the individual's memory to his knowledge of that knowledge. (p. 477)

Many genuine breakthroughs have been made in the past 30 years, and systematic investigations of metamemory have supported the development of sophisticated hypotheses about how people monitor and control memory. In exploring metamemory, researchers have also created numerous methodologies that reveal its intricate nature. These methods have in turn been adopted to explore metacognitive processes in other domains, such as how metacognition changes across the life span and the role of metacognition in student scholarship. Thus, by understanding metamemory research, you will learn the basics about measurement, methodology, and theory that will appear in many chapters of this textbook.

Given the foundational nature of metamemory research, in this chapter we discuss general concepts and methods that are essential for thoroughly understanding the subsequent chapters on metamemory, which focus on monitoring and control of memory. Although investigations of metamemory *knowledge* certainly constitute a large portion of research in the field, this research has mainly focused on developmental questions. Thus, we hold our discussion of metamemory knowledge until Section 3 (Life-Span Development), and instead discuss basic issues pertaining to monitoring and control processes that will consistently arise in the chapters on Basic Metacognitive Judgments. The concepts in this chapter will be well-known to any expert of metacognition, but most important, they can be mastered by any student who is aspiring to expertise.

In the remainder of this chapter, we will guide you through some of the basics in metamemory research, including (a) standard methods used to measure monitoring and control of memory, (b) some major questions that drive research on monitoring and control of memory, and (c) analyses of metamemory data that are used to answer these questions.

Metamemory: Measures and Questions

Imagine studying for an upcoming test of your memory. Perhaps you are getting ready for a midterm exam in a French class. When you are studying, you can monitor and control your learning and retrieval as you proceed. To monitor your learning while studying French vocabulary, you may simply ask yourself, "How well have I learned the meaning of the term *"chateau"* (castle) for the upcoming test?" To monitor your retrieval during a practice test, you may attempt to retrieve the meaning of *"garçon,"* and when you finally retrieve the response, "boy," you may ask yourself, "Is 'boy' the correct response for *'garçon'*?" Having experimental participants answer questions like these as they study is the mainstay of metamemory research. That is, to investigate people's memory monitoring, researchers simply ask participants to judge their memory and retrieval.

Since Hart's (1965) seminal research, investigators have used subjective judgments to explore people's monitoring of many memory processes. Up until the late 1980s, however, much of this research was conducted in isolation; some researchers mainly focused on judgments of study, and others mainly focused on judgments of retrieval. Metamemory research was fragmented. In 1990, Nelson and Narens published a framework for metamemory that unified these seemingly disparate areas of research. Their framework allows an individual researcher to easily see how his or her own research on one aspect of metamemory fits into the larger body of work. For this reason, the framework has been highly influential and has historical significance in this subarea of metacognition.

Their framework organizes the different judgments of monitoring and measures of control into three stages of learning: acquisition, retention, and retrieval. The measures are presented in Figure 3.1 (adapted from Nelson & Narens, 1990), and their corresponding definitions are presented in Table 3.1 (adapted from Dunlosky, Serra, & Baker, 2007). Let's walk through these judgments in the context of a standard procedure for metamemory research. In this example, we introduce many of the measures presented in Figure 3.1, but, with some notable exceptions, typically only one measure has been investigated in any

Thomas O. Nelson (1942–2005): With Louis Narens, connected previously isolated areas of metacognitive research to unify the field

given experiment. First, consider the basic *memory* components of the research method, which involve acquisition (study) and retrieval (tests). In particular, a research participant may be asked to study 16 French-English translation equivalents, such as "*chateau*-castle" and "*garçon*-boy." After studying all the pairs, a recall test would be administered in which each cue is presented alone (e.g., "*chateau*-?"), and the participant's goal would be to recall the corresponding response (i.e., "castle"). After all the recall trials, the participant may then be asked to try to recognize all the pairs that she did not correctly retrieve during the recall test.

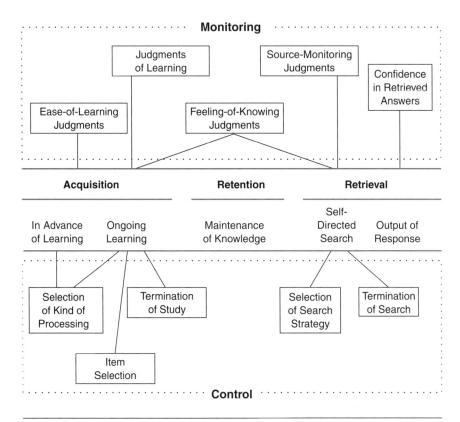

Figure 3.1   Monitoring judgments and control processes, and their relationships to the three stages of learning.

SOURCE: Adapted from Nelson, T. O., and Narens, L. (1990). Metamemory: a theoretical framework and new findings. In G. H. Bower (Ed.), *The psychology of learning and motivation* (Vol. 26, pp. 125–173). New York: Academic Press.

Now let's consider the measures of metamemory. To measure how people monitor memory (top panel of Figure 3.1 and top rows of Table 3.1), each participant would overtly judge each pair on a specific aspect of memory. For instance, after studying "*chateau*-castle," they might make a *judgment of learning*, which involves judging the likelihood of recalling the correct response on the upcoming test of recall. During the test, participants might also state their confidence that each response is correct. These are called *retrospective confidence judgments*. When the participants do not correctly recall a response, they may be asked to judge whether they will soon be able to recall it; that is, if the correct answer was currently on the *tip of the tongue*.

Table 3.1   Names and Common Definitions of Metacognitive Judgments (Monitoring) and Control Processes

Name	Definition
Metacognitive Judgments	
Ease-of-learning judgments	Judgments of how easy or difficult it will be to learn any given item
Judgments of learning (JOLs)	• Judgments of the likelihood of remembering recently studied items on an upcoming test • Immediate JOL: made immediately after studying an item • Delayed JOL: made well after studying an item
Feeling-of-knowing judgments	Judgments of the likelihood of recognizing currently unrecallable answers on an upcoming test
Source-monitoring judgments	Judgments made during a criterion test pertaining to the source of a particular memory
Confidence in retrieved answers	Judgments of the likelihood that a response on a test is correct (often referred to as retrospective confidence judgments)
Control Processes	
Selection of kind of processing	Selection of strategies to employ when attempting to commit an item to memory
Item selection	Decision about whether to study an item for an upcoming test
Termination of study	Decision to stop studying an item currently being studied
Selection of search strategy	Selecting a particular strategy for producing a response during a test
Termination of search	Decision to terminate the search for a response in memory

SOURCE: Adapted from Dunlosky, J., Serra, M., & Baker, J. M. C. (2007). Metamemory. In F. Durso et al. (2nd edition) *Handbook of Applied Cognition.* New York: Wiley

For these unrecalled pairs, they also might make a *feeling-of-knowing judgment* by judging the likelihood that they would recognize the correct response at a later time. For *source-monitoring judgments*, participants would be asked where they originally learned the vocabulary pair, such as whether it was one that had been studied in the textbook or one that had been heard from the teacher in class. Note that each of these judgments is made during a different stage of learning or retrieval, and each one closely corresponds to the kinds of judgment that people can make in their everyday lives.

In Figure 3.1, the judgments also differ with respect to how they may influence the control of learning and retrieval. More specifically, judgments of learning are closely linked to the termination of ongoing learning or the decision to continue studying, and feeling-of-knowing judgments are closely linked to the control of search during retrieval. The idea here is that monitoring is used to control various aspects of learning and memory. This general dynamic between monitoring and control processes was introduced in Figure 1.1, which can also be used to illustrate more specific instantiations of monitoring and control. For instance, Figure 3.2 illustrates the relationships between hypothetical constructs and measures for the termination of study. To understand this monitoring-control dynamic, imagine trying to learn a new concept, such as the definition for "metacognition." According to Figure 3.2, your decision to continue studying the definition is informed by your judgment of learning about how well you have already learned it. For instance, when you believe you have learned the definition, you may stop studying it. Of course, the model in Figure 3.2 is not highly refined, because even though it predicts that judgments of learning will be related to study times, it does not specify exactly how (or to what degree) these monitoring and control measures will be related. In upcoming chapters, we will describe more refined models for many of the control functions presented in the bottom half of Figure 3.1.

Extensive literatures have grown around the majority of judgment and control functions presented in Figure 3.1. Even though these literatures have often developed independently of one another, the questions that motivate this research are relatively few in number and relatively consistent across areas. Some of these questions have been listed in Table 3.2. Although these are not exhaustive of all those that have motivated metacognitive research, they do represent dominant questions that basic theoretical research has attempted to answer over the past three decades. Consider the first question: How do people monitor memory? Within each domain of memory monitoring, researchers have pursued answers to this question by investigating the relevant metacognitive judgment. As illustrated in Figure 3.1, if a researcher is interested in how people monitor their ongoing study of materials, then they may focus their efforts on investigating how people make judgments of learning. If a researcher is interested in how people monitor retrieval, then they may turn their attention to retrospective confidence judgments or feeling-of-knowing judgments.

In the chapters in Section 1, we will review psychological scientists' best answers to each of these questions. In each chapter, we focus on one metacognitive judgment that has garnered enough interest to provide relatively

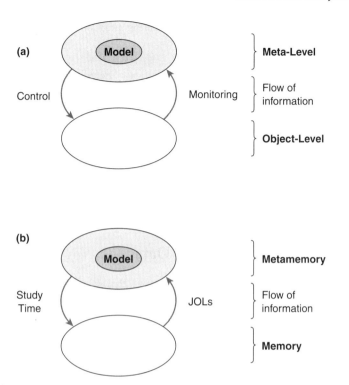

Figure 3.2   General model of monitoring and control relationships (Panel A)
and a specific instantiation of this model as it relates to the control
of study time (Panel B).

SOURCE: Dunlosky, Serra, and Baker (2007).

sophisticated answers to each question. When you are reading these chapters, do your best to compare answers to these questions across the various
judgments, such as judgments of learning and feeling-of-knowing judgments.
As you will find, although each literature focuses on a distinct aspect of
metamemory, answers to the core questions listed in Table 3.2 are strikingly
similar across the various judgments. Before immersing yourself in the specific literatures, however, you will need to understand the methods
researchers have used to explore memory monitoring and control. Thus, the
rest of this chapter provides a primer that describes how experimental psychologists have typically collected, analyzed, and interpreted data from
metamemory experiments.

Table 3.2   Core Questions About Monitoring and Control From Research
           About Adult Human Cognition

- How do people monitor memory?
- How accurate is memory monitoring?
- Can monitoring accuracy be improved?
- How is monitoring used to control?

SOURCE: Dunlosky, J., Serra, M., & Baker, J. M. C. (2007). Metamemory. In F. Durso et al. (2nd edition), *Handbook of Applied Cognition*. New York: Wiley.

Metamemory: Collecting, Analyzing, and Interpreting Data

As we mentioned earlier, people's monitoring and control processes are often studied by simply having them judge their memory—which measures monitoring—and by giving them free rein on how to allocate time on a memory task—which measures control. Let's work out the details with a standard method used in the field. As will be obvious as you read the remaining chapters in Section 1, this method has been creatively adapted by researchers to provide more and more sophisticated answers to the core questions listed in Table 3.2. Thus, if you fully understand the standard method and the analyses that are used, it will be much easier to grasp some of the more complicated methods we will discuss in later chapters.

Imagine that you are a participant in a metamemory experiment. You sit down in front of a computer, and you are instructed to learn 12 French-English translation equivalents—just like you would do to prepare for a foreign-language examination. During the first trial of this experiment, each French-English word pair is presented individually at a fixed rate, such as for 8 seconds a pair. Immediately after a pair is presented (e.g., *cerveau*-brain), you are asked to make the following judgment of learning: "What is the likelihood you will recall the English translation when later presented with the French word on an upcoming test?" Respond with any value from 0 to 100, where 0 means there is no chance you will recall the correct response, 20 means there is a 20% chance, . . . and 100 means you will definitely recall the correct response. During this initial trial, you study each French-English word pair and make a judgment of learning (JOL) for each as well. This trial is represented in the far-left column of Figure 3.3.

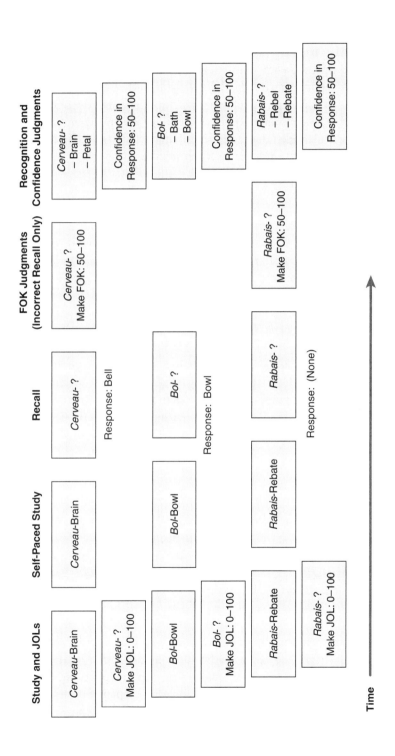

Study and JOLs

Cerveau-Brain

Cerveau- ?
Make JOL: 0–100

Bol-Bowl

Bol- ?
Make JOL: 0–100

Rabais-Rebate

Rabais- ?
Make JOL: 0–100

Self-Paced Study

Cerveau-Brain

Bol-Bowl

Rabais-Rebate

Recall

Cerveau- ?

Response: Bell

Bol- ?

Response: Bowl

Rabais- ?

Response: (None)

**FOK Judgments
(Incorrect Recall Only)**

Cerveau- ?
Make FOK: 50–100

Rabais- ?
Make FOK: 50–100

**Recognition and
Confidence Judgments**

Cerveau- ?
– Brain
– Petal

Confidence in
Response: 50–100

Bol- ?
– Bath
– Bowl

Confidence in
Response: 50–100

Rabais- ?
– Rebel
– Rebate

Confidence in
Response: 50–100

Time

Figure 3.3 Stages of a research experiment of monitoring judgments and control processes. Monitoring judgments include judgments of learning (JOLs), feeling-of-knowing (FOK) judgments, and retrospective confidence judgments; control processes include self-paced study times and retrieval times for recall. Example responses from a hypothetical participant for the majority of these measures are presented in Table 3.3.

45

After this initial study trial, you are then instructed that you will get another chance to study each word pair. During this self-paced trial, however, you are allowed to study each pairing as long as you would like. Each pair is then presented again individually, but now you study each pair until you decide to move on to the next, which you indicate by pressing the return key on the computer. The computer records how long you spend on each pair, which provides a measure of the termination of study time. Results from this self-paced trial (in seconds of study per item) are presented in the third column of Table 3.3.

Next, as advertised, you receive a test of your memory: Each French word is presented alone (e.g., *cerveau*-?), and you would attempt to retrieve the correct English translation equivalent. After this recall trial, you would then be asked to make a feeling-of-knowing judgment for each French word that you were unable to correctly recall the response. So, if you did not retrieve "brain" in response to "*cerveau*," you would be asked, "What is the likelihood that you will recognize the correct response when it is presented with other alternatives?" The rating scale for the feeling-of-knowing judgment is often constructed to reflect correct responding by guessing. For instance, assume that the recognition test involves presenting the correct answer with one other alternative: "What is the correct response to "*cerveau*": petal or brain?" If you did not know the answer, you would still have a 50% chance of responding correctly if you guess. For this recognition test, the feeling-of-knowing scale would range from 50% (which means you would not recognize the correct response and would be guessing) to 100% (which means you are absolutely sure you would recognize the correct response). Finally, during the recognition test, you might be asked to state your confidence in whether your answer was correct. These retrospective confidence judgments would be scaled in the same manner, with 50% meaning that you guessed to 100% meaning that you are absolutely sure your answer is correct. (Note that retrospective confidence refers to any judgment made about performance on a previous test of memory; thus, in Figure 3.3, participants could have also been asked to judge the likelihood that their responses on the recall test were correct.) These phases of the experiment are illustrated in the two right-hand columns of Figure 3.3. This simple procedure yields a wealth of data, which can provide answers to most of the questions listed in Table 3.2.

Now that you have a sense of the basic procedure, we will describe some standard analyses and how they relate to the core questions. The analyses begin by working with data from individual research participants, so we have included a hypothetical protocol from a single participant in the top part of Table 3.3. In this protocol, each pair is matched with outcomes from several dependent variables: a judgment of learning, a self-paced study time,

Table 3.3   A Participant's Data and Measures of Accuracy

Participant's Data

Item	JOL	Self-Paced Study (sec/item)	Recall	FOK	Recognition	Confidence
arcade-arcade	100	2.6	1	—	1	100
bol-bowl	40	3.2	1	—	1	100
caque-keg	60	2.8	1	—	1	80
parti-party	80	1.6	1	—	1	90
citron-lemon	20	5.4	1	—	1	80
glande-gland	80	2.8	0	80	0	90
cerveau-brain	60	4.2	0	60	1	80
chemin-path	0	5.8	0	50	0	60
rebais-rebate	40	6.0	0	70	0	60
singe-monkey	20	3.2	0	60	1	80
signe-sign	80	4.0	0	100	1	100
marc-mark	60	1.8	0	80	1	100
Mean	**53%**	**3.6**	**42%**	**71%**	**75%**	**85%**

Measures of Accuracy for Participant's Data

Kind of Judgment	Criterion Test	Relative Accuracy	Calibration
Judgment of learning	Recall	.24	11
Feeling of knowing	Recognition	.27	–4
Retrospective confidence	Recognition	.69	10

NOTE: For Recall, 1 = correct; 0 = incorrect. Relative accuracy = gamma correlation between judgment and performance on the corresponding criterion test. Calibration (bias) = signed difference score between mean judgment and mean criterion performance. See the text for other measures of judgment accuracy. Sec/item = seconds an item was studied during self-paced study.

a feeling-of-knowing judgment, and so forth. For instance, for the pair "*cerveau*-brain," this participant claimed that there was a 60% chance that she would correctly recall the item on the upcoming test (JOL), she used an extra 4.2 seconds studying the item during the self-paced study trial, and then she ended up not correctly recalling "brain" during the recall test (indicated by a value of "zero" under Recall). Subsequently, the participant made a FOK judgment of 60% for this item and then ended up correctly recognizing the correct response to "*cerveau*" on the recognition test. We now describe how such data can be used to answer the core questions in Table 3.2 about metacognitive monitoring-and-control processes.

How Do People Monitor Memory?

One way to analyze the data to answer this question involves computing a measure of central tendency of the judgments as a function of any independent variable that was manipulated during the task. For instance, take a closer look at the foreign-language vocabulary presented in Table 3.3: Six of the items were cognates (where the cue and target share much of the same orthography, e.g., *bol*-bowl), whereas the remainder of the items were not cognates. In this case, a mean judgment of learning (JOL) could be computed for cognates (Mean = 73) and for noncognates (Mean = 33). These values would be computed for everyone who participated in the experiment, and then those values would be subjected to standard statistical analyses, such as computing means across participants' values and performing an inferential test to evaluate whether JOLs significantly differ across levels of the independent variable. In the present case, JOLs would likely be higher for cognates than for noncognates (Metcalfe & Kornell, 2003), which provides one answer to our question, How do people monitor memory? Namely, people may judge their memory by looking for clues—in this case, physical similarity between words—that suggest some information is more likely to be remembered than other information (Koriat, 1997). Although this example may not seem exceptionally profound, in the next chapters, we will present evidence from numerous studies in which these straightforward analyses have led to insights into how people make various metacognitive judgments.

How Accurate Is Memory Monitoring?

In Chapter 2, we learned that in contrast to early introspectionism, we no longer assume that people's introspective judgments are perfectly valid and accurate. Instead, researchers explore the accuracy of judgments by systematically charting their distortions and by developing techniques to debias the judgments so that people can achieve high levels of accuracy at judging their memories. Toward these ends, data collected using the basic procedure allows researchers to estimate the accuracy of people's judgments and to examine conditions that may improve accuracy.

At the most general level, analyses of accuracy involve comparing a person's judgments with his or her performance on the relevant criterion task. So,

judgments of learning (which in our example involve predicting recall performance) would be compared to actual recall performance, and feeling-of-
knowing judgments (which in our example involve predicting recognition
performance) would be compared to actual recognition performance, and so
forth. What makes analyses of judgment accuracy somewhat complicated is
that there are two kinds of accuracy—relative accuracy and calibration—and
there are multiple ways to compute each kind of accuracy. We'll first contrast
the two kinds of accuracy and then consider some measures for each one.

Relative accuracy, which is also known as *resolution*, is the degree to
which a person's metacognitive judgments predict the likelihood of correct
performance on one item *relative* to another. Relative accuracy is relevant to
the following question: Are items more likely to be correctly recalled on the
final test when participants judge that they are more likely to recall the items
than when they judge that they are less likely to recall them? Put differently,
are a person's judgments across items positively correlated with the likelihood of correct test performance? In Table 3.3, as the participants' JOLs
increase from 0 to 100%, correct responses were more likely to be recalled.
Accordingly, the participant's JOLs show good relative accuracy.

Calibration, which is also known as *absolute accuracy*, is the degree to
which the level of judgment ratings corresponds to the actual level of performance. A person would have perfect calibration if the magnitude of his
judgments matched the actual level of performance, such as if she predicted
60% recall across items and then actually recalled 60% of the items. Our
hypothetical participant on average judged that the likelihood of recall
across items was 53% (i.e., mean JOL) but eventually recalled only 42% per-
cent of them—in this case, the absolute value of the participant's JOLs shows
(11%) overconfidence.

Relative accuracy indicates whether a person can *discriminate* between
differences in the memorability of the items, whereas calibration indicates
whether a person can estimate the *actual level* of test performance. Thus, to
investigate relative accuracy, the judgments can be made on any monotonic
scale, where increasing scale values indicate increasing confidence in memory.
For instance, in our example, judgments of learning ranged from 0 to 100%,
but they could have been made on a scale from 1 (low likelihood of recall) to
6 (high likelihood of recall) or on any other monotonic scale in which the
scale values increase with a person's subjective likelihood. In contrast, to
assess calibration, participants must make the judgments on a scale (e.g., *percentage* predicted recall) that is directly comparable to the scale used for test
performance (e.g., *percentage* actual recall). If participants make judgments
on a scale from 1 (low) to 6 (high), calibration should not be computed or
interpreted, because to which percentage of recall would a judgment of 2 or

3 (or any other value) correspond? There is no way to know. Thus, when designing an experiment to investigate calibration, one must make sure that participants predict performance on a scale that is directly comparable to how memory performance is measured.

In computing relative accuracy, a standard method is to correlate an *individual* participant's judgments with his or her corresponding test performance across items. Correlations range from –1.0 to +1.0. A correlation of zero indicates that the judgments have no accuracy in discriminating the performance of one item relative to another. As correlations increase from 0 to +1.0, judgment accuracy increases as well. For our hypothetical data, we used a nonparametric Goodman-Kruskal gamma to correlate judgments with test performance, partly because the gamma correlation has been a standard for the field (see Nelson, 1984, for a detailed rationale for using gamma). In fact, when we present results on relative accuracy throughout this volume, it will most often be based on the gamma correlation. Of course, relative accuracy could be estimated by computing any other correlation between each participant's judgments and recall, such as a Pearson *r* correlation, or other measures that are now being developed (for advanced discussions of the limitations of using gamma and for alternative measures of relative accuracy, see Benjamin & Diaz, 2008; Gonzalez & Nelson, 1996; Masson & Rotello, 2008). A critically important point to remember is that regardless of which measure one chooses to use in estimating relative accuracy, it should be computed across each *individual* participant's judgments and test performance. For our hypothetical data (Table 3.3), the relative accuracy of the individual's JOLs is .24, whereas the relative accuracy of the retrospective confidence judgments is .69. After a correlation is computed for each participant in an experiment, those individual values would be subjected to standard statistical analyses, such as computing means across participants' values and performing inferential tests to evaluate whether each group correlation is significantly greater than zero, which would indicate above-chance accuracy.

Calibration can be estimated in numerous ways. The signed difference score, which is a measure of *bias*, is arguably the most intuitive measure and involves computing the magnitude of the judgment and the corresponding magnitude of test performance for each participant. Next, subtract test performance from judgment magnitude, so that a negative value (judgments lower than test performance) indicates underconfidence and a positive value (judgments higher than test performance) indicates overconfidence. Our hypothetical participant had overconfident judgments of learning (53% – 42% = 11%) and slightly underconfident feeling-of-knowing judgments (71% – 75% = –4%).

Another standard method of analysis involves constructing a calibration curve, in which the mean level of test performance is plotted as a function of varying levels of judgment magnitude. Let's construct a calibration curve for JOLs from the hypothetical data in Table 3.3. First, for each level of JOL magnitude (0%, 20%, 40%, and so forth), compute the percentage of items that were correctly recalled. For instance, this participant made one JOL of 0% for the item "*chemin*-path," and she did not subsequently recall the item. Thus, the percentage correct for a JOL magnitude of zero is in fact zero. She gave a JOL of 20% to two items and subsequently recalled one of them correctly, so the percentage correct for a JOL magnitude of 20 is 50%. Continue to compute the percentage of correct recall for all JOL magnitudes. After you finish, plot the percentage of correct recall (on the *y* axis of your figure) as a function of JOL magnitude (on the *x* axis). Compare your figure to our rendition of this participant's calibration curve, which is presented in Figure 3.4.

Given that calibration curves almost always are represented with the judgment on the *x* axis (because they predict actual performance on the *y* axis), it is important to understand what constitutes perfect calibration as well as overconfidence and underconfidence. In any calibration curve, perfect calibration is represented by the solid diagonal line in Figure 3.4—that is, where the level of test performance exactly matches the judgment values. Values that fall *above* the diagonal represent *under*confidence because those data points represent situations in which judgments are lower than actual performance. For instance, for items in which you made JOLs of 20%, if actual performance were *above* 20%, it would indicate that you were underconfident. In contrast, values *below* the diagonal represent *over*confidence. That is, for items for which you made JOLs of 20%, if actual performance were *below* 20%, it would indicate that you were overconfident. Thus, interpreting calibration curves can be a bit confusing, because underconfidence is represented by having values over the line of perfect calibration, whereas overconfidence is represented by values under the line of perfect calibration. Finally, consider our hypothetical participant, who was certainly not perfectly calibrated. As we will find out next, this particular calibration curve is representative of actual calibration curves reported in the field.

A typical calibration curve for retrospective confidence judgments is presented in Figure 3.5, which was taken from Gigerenzer, Hoffrage, and Kleinbölting (1991). In contrast to Figure 3.4, which plots a curve for only one participant, in this case the calibration curve results from averaging across the curves from many participants. Most important, much more information is provided by calibration curves than by difference scores. In particular, the latter provides an estimate of how the judgments are biased collapsed across all items, whereas with a calibration curve, one can evaluate whether people are overconfident or underconfident across the entire range of the judgment scale. As shown in Figure 3.5, calibration curves for retrospective

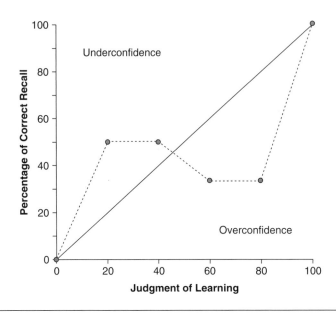

Figure 3.4   Calibration curve based on data in Table 3.3. Solid diagonal line represents perfect calibration.

confidence judgments often show that people are underconfident when making lower judgments but overconfident when making higher judgments, which has been called the *hard-easy effect*.

When calibration curves are presented, researchers may also report a calibration index (for comparison of various indices for calibration, see Keren, 1991; Lichtenstein & Fischhoff, 1977; Wallsten, 1996). Such indices provide a single quantitative estimate of how well calibrated people's judgments are. For instance, one calibration index involves computing the difference between the judgment magnitude and the corresponding level of test performance for each level of judgment. The absolute value of each difference is obtained, and these values are then weighted by the number of observations per cell. In particular, the formula is

$$1/N \sum_{t=1}^{T} n_t |r_t - c_t|$$

where N is the total number of observations, T stands for the number of judgment ratings, r_t is a given judgment rating itself, n_t is the number of times a person made a judgment of r_t, and c_t is the percentage correct for all items given a judgment of r_t. For our hypothetical participant, N = 12 and

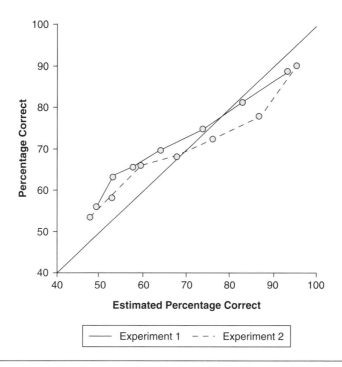

Figure 3.5   Calibration curves for retrospective confidence judgments.

SOURCE: Gigerenzer, G., Hoffrage, U., & Kleinbolting, H. (1991). Probabilistic mental models: A Brunswikian theory of confidence. *Psychological Review, 98,* 506–528.

T = 6 (i.e., 0, 20, 40, 60, 80 and 100, or 6 different judgment ratings). So, for t = 1, n_t = 1, r_t = 0, and c_t = 0, whereas when t = 2, n_t = 2, r_t = 20, and c_t = 50, and so on. This particular person's calibration index for JOLs is 25.2. This value represents the mean weighted difference between a given calibration curve and the line of perfect calibration, with larger values indicating worse calibration.

Of course, for either kind of judgment accuracy—relative accuracy or calibration—we often want to know whether it differs between various groups, because group differences in accuracy may mean that differences exist in how well the two groups can monitor memory. For instance, as we will discuss in the next chapter, relative FOK accuracy is impaired in people who have suffered damage to their frontal lobes as compared to control participants (Janowsky, Shimamura, & Squire, 1989). This intriguing outcome suggests that these patients are deficient in memory monitoring, and more interesting, that the frontal lobes are vital for humans to accurately monitor memory. Although this conclusion is reasonable, some pitfalls exist in conducting research where group differences in estimated accuracy can be definitively interpreted as indicating differences in monitoring ability per se. We explore some of these pitfalls in Box 3.1, which warns that one should think twice (by double-checking the research design) before interpreting group or individual differences in judgment accuracy.

BOX 3.1
Advanced Issue: Think Twice Before
Judging Differences in Judgment Accuracy

When investigating judgment accuracy, we're often interested in how it differs across individuals (or between groups of individuals), because these differences could reflect corresponding differences in monitoring ability across these individuals (or between the groups). For instance, you may find that people with Korsakoff disease have lower relative FOK accuracy than do individuals without the disease, or in conducting a meta-analysis of the literature, you may find that the calibration of FOK judgments tends to be greater when people are given more practice at making the judgments. The critical question is, Should you conclude that Korsakoff disease impairs memory monitoring, and that practice judging memory improves memory monitoring?

The answer to these questions is "yes," when a well-designed experiment is conducted, and this book is filled with such examples. Nevertheless, in some cases the answer will be a resounding "no," because some not-so-obvious problems with methodology can render any difference in judgment accuracy largely uninterpretable. Schwartz and Metcalfe (1994) described a variety of these potential problems, and we will consider two in some detail here.

First, when interpreting group differences in either calibration or relative accuracy, it is essential that the groups are equated in memory performance. The reason for equating performance rests on the fact that memory performance is involved in the computation of judgment accuracy. So, if the groups differ in memory performance, any differences in judgment accuracy may not be due to monitoring (as tapped by the judgments) but instead may have resulted from differences in memory per se. Not equating on memory performance is most problematic for interpreting group differences in calibration. For instance, the earliest research on aging in adulthood suggested that aging impairs monitoring accuracy because calibration of the JOLs was lower for 70-year-olds than for 20-year-olds. In contrast to their poor memory and their belief that their memories are failing, older adults' judgments actually appeared substantially overconfident. The difficulty, however, was that in these studies, memory performance was consistently much lower for older adults than younger adults. Once the two age groups were equated on performance, the age-related deficit in calibration vanished (Connor, Dunlosky, & Hertzog, 1997), which indicates that the age differences initially reported in this field did not reflect true age-related deficits in monitoring ability.

The second problem also has to do with memory performance. In this case, however, it concerns the form of the criterion test that is used to measure memory. The take-home point here is that differences in accuracy between two groups cannot be interpreted unambiguously if the criterion test differs across those groups. To better understand this point, consider research by Thiede and Dunlosky (1994), who were interested in how accurately students could predict their performance on a recall test versus a recognition test. The students made JOLs on paired associates (e.g., dog-spoon), and then were given either a recall test (e.g., dog-?, recall the correct response) or a recognition test (e.g., which pair is correct: dog-carpet or dog-spoon?). They reported that JOL accuracy was greater when people predicted recall than recognition, but does this indicate that people's monitoring is better when they judge whether items will be recalled than recognized? Although possible, an alternative explanation is that guessing on the recognition test reduces accuracy. To illustrate, assume a student is actually accurate in judging that she will not correctly remember "dog-spoon." On the recall test (dog-?), as predicted, she won't recall "spoon." On the recognition test, however, even if she does not remember the correct pair, she still has a 50% chance at guessing the correct response. Consistent with the possibility that correct guessing can inadvertently reduce accuracy, when Thiede and Dunlosky (1994) factored out "correct guessing" from the criterion tests, judgment accuracy no longer differed for predictions of recall performance versus recognition performance.

As dramatic, in a review of the FOK literature, Schwartz and Metcalfe (1994) examined how relative FOK accuracy was influenced by the number of alternatives on the recognition tests. In the example above, there are two alternatives, and hence the likelihood of correct guessing is 50%. As the number of alternatives increases, the likelihood of correct guessing decreases, so judgment accuracy should rise with the number of alternatives. Their findings were compiled across multiple investigations and are presented in Figure 3.6, which presents the relative accuracy of FOK judgments (gamma correlation) as a function of number of alternatives in the criterion recognition test. Each point on Figure 3.6 represents the outcome from a different study. As illustrated here, relative accuracy increases as the number of alternatives on the test increases. Moreover, when the criterion test was recall (far right on Figure 3.6), accuracy was the highest, presumably because correct guessing is unlikely during recall tests. The conclusion from Figure 3.6 is simply that all the differences in relative accuracy

(Continued)

(Continued)

across the studies do not indicate actual differences in monitoring ability. Instead, the differences can be attributed to the measure of relative accuracy being influenced by correct guessing on the criterion test.

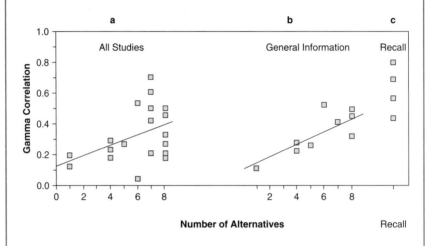

Figure 3.6   Relative accuracy of feeling-of-knowing judgments (as estimated by the gamma correlation) as a function of the number of alternatives on the criterion recognition test. Panel A includes all studies in this meta-analysis. Panel B includes the subset of studies that used general information questions as items. Panel C includes those studies in which the criterion test was recall.

SOURCE: Schwartz, B. L., and Metcalfe, J. (1994). Methodological problems and pitfalls in the study of human metacognition. In J. Metcalfe and A. Shimamura (Eds.), *Metacognition: Knowing about knowing* (pp. 93–114). Cambridge: MIT Press.

The points raised in this Advanced Issue box cannot be overemphasized. Namely, when you are considering the meaning of any measure of judgment accuracy, remember that if you find group differences, before concluding that the groups differ in memory monitoring, make sure that the groups do not also differ in memory performance. Moreover, think twice before you claim that a group is really bad at monitoring memory. Perhaps they're quite good, but it's just the criterion test of memory—such as one that allows a lot of correct guessing—that's making them look bad.

Although both kinds of accuracy have been used to explore the accuracy of almost all the metacognitive judgments represented in Figure 3.1, research on a given judgment has often heavily focused on just one kind. For instance, the bulk of the research on judgments of learning and feeling-of-knowing judgments has focused on relative accuracy, whereas for retrospective confidence judgments, calibration is almost exclusively investigated. Given that these two measures tell us something very different about how well people can monitor and evaluate their memories, as you read the upcoming chapters, pay special attention to which measure is being discussed.

As for our third core question in Table 3.2—Can monitoring accuracy be improved?—researchers have used a variety of manipulations and techniques in an attempt to improve the relative accuracy or calibration of people's monitoring judgments. In the chapters in Section 1, we'll touch upon some of the manipulations that have shown the most consistent success at helping people to more accurately monitor their learning and retrieval.

How Is Monitoring Used to Control?

To investigate how monitoring may be used to control memory processes, researchers often have examined the relationship between a given metacognitive judgment and its corresponding measure of control. For instance, as illustrated in Figure 3.1, judgments of learning made during study may be relevant to how people make decisions about whether to restudy a given item, and feeling-of-knowing judgments made after a recall test may be related to how long someone will persist at trying to retrieve a sought-after answer. Let's focus on the possible role of judgments of learning to control self-paced study. One typical analysis involves correlating a participant's judgments with subsequent self-paced study. For our hypothetical data (Table 3.3), this correlation was negative (–.57), which suggests that this person used judgments to control study by allocating more study time to items that were originally judged less well-learned than to those that were judged as more well-learned. This outcome suggests that a person's monitoring (as measured by metacognitive judgments) affects how she controls memory. Although such correlational analyses are straightforward, as you will discover in the upcoming chapters, they have successfully revealed the intricate nature of metacognitive control processes.

Overview of the Remaining Chapters on Basic Metacognitive Judgments

In the next four chapters, we review the extensive literatures that have arisen around some of the most highly investigated judgments about learning and retrieval: feeling-of-knowing judgments, judgments of learning, retrospective confidence judgments, and source-monitoring judgments. For each judgment, we address some of the most current answers to questions presented in Table 3.2. In doing so, we also point out gaps in our understanding. In some cases, these gaps signify heated debates and disagreement about how to answer a specific question, such as how people use their judgments of learning to control their study time. In other cases, however, the gaps represent a relative absence of empirical work about a particular question. Thus, our objective is to highlight what is currently known about how adults monitor and control their memories, as well as to reveal some limits in our current knowledge that will require scrutiny in future research.

DISCUSSION QUESTION

1. Many psychological scientists—and many people in general—are interested in what is responsible for the development of cognitive abilities. For instance, why are children better at memory tasks when they are 12 years old than when they are 6 years old? One hypothesis is that as we develop, our metacognitive monitoring and control processes improve, and in turn, learning develops as well. How would you design an investigation to evaluate this hypothesis with respect to monitoring of ongoing study while individuals are attempting to memorize a list of paired associates? What measures would you use, and what evidence would indicate the monitoring of learning improves as we develop in childhood? What evidence would indicate that the control of learning improves as we develop in childhood? (Hint: For some answers to these questions from the developmental literature, see Chapter 10.)

CONCEPT REVIEW

For the following questions and exercises, we recommend you write down the answers on a separate sheet in as much detail as possible, and then check them against the relevant material in the chapter.

1. What aspect of methodology distinguishes between the various metacognitive judgments—for instance, a judgment of learning versus a feeling-of-knowing judgment versus an ease-of-learning judgment?

2. Why are various metacognitive judgments linked more closely to different aspects of control? That is, why are JOLs linked to self-paced study whereas FOK judgments are linked to retrieval?

3. Compare and contrast relative accuracy and calibration of people's judgments.

4. If you had people make judgments of learning on a 6-point scale (e.g., 1 = will not recall to 6 = absolutely will recall), could you interpret a measure of relative accuracy? Could you interpret a measure of calibration?

5. Draw three calibration curves on the same figure. One calibration curve should be perfectly accurate, the other should demonstrate complete underconfidence and the final one should demonstrate complete overconfidence.

4

Feelings of Knowing and Tip-of-the-Tongue States

The first metacognitive judgment that was subjected to rigorous experimental scrutiny was the feeling-of-knowing (FOK) judgment. In 1965, a graduate student—Joseph Hart, at Stanford University—devised a method that he called the recall-judge-recognition paradigm, or RJR method for short. The experimental participants were individually given a number of general information questions to answer such as, "Who was the first person to set foot on the moon?" Questions that participants answered correctly were not considered further. However, for those questions to which participants gave an incorrect answer, or failed to produce an answer at all, they were then asked to make a FOK judgment that involved predicting whether they would choose the correct answer on a multiple-choice task. After making FOK judgments for all questions that were not answered correctly, a multiple-choice recognition task was administered, so that the accuracy of the judgments could be estimated. In summary, participants first attempted to *recall* answers, then they *judged* whether they would be able to recognize the correct answer to incorrectly recalled ones, and finally they tried to *recognize* the correct answers—hence, the recall-judge-recognize (RJR) method. The interesting and, at the time, surprising finding was that even though participants had just demonstrated that they were unable to come up with answers to many questions, their predictions concerning which answers they would later recognize were accurate. In particular, their recognition performance was higher when they predicted that they would later recognize the correct answer than when they predicted they would not.

What was so surprising was that people could accurately judge whether an answer was in memory even though they could not recall that answer. How we are able to do this posed a puzzle for the field that triggered a great deal of research on people's metacognitions—their ability to know what they know and what they do not know, which is a vital self-reflective process. In the remainder of this chapter, we discuss current theories about how people make FOK judgments, each of which also provides an answer to the question, Why do people's FOK judgments show above-chance levels of relative accuracy? (For a reminder on the meaning of "relative accuracy," refer to Chapter 3.) We also explore a related phenomenon, called a tip-of-the-tongue state, which vexes people almost daily. We then discuss the brain systems that give rise to FOKs, and we close the chapter by considering the functions of FOKs in controlling strategy selection and memory retrieval.

Theories About Feeling-of-Knowing Judgments

In the next two sections, we review scientists' best attempts to unravel the mystery of people's feelings of knowing; namely, how can we know that a memory is available in our minds when in fact we cannot recall that memory? We begin with the target-strength account, which was first posed by Joseph Hart, and then we move to more contemporary heuristic-based solutions to this intriguing mystery.

Target Strength Account

According to Hart (1967), FOK judgments directly tap how strongly a target is activated in memory. If you cannot recall the (target) answer to the question, "Who produced the first commercially successful electric guitar?," then your FOK is based directly on how strongly your neural representation of the target (in this case, "Fender") was activated when you were asked the question. According to this account, people will judge that they know a target answer that they cannot recall when the strength of the target falls below their recall threshold but above a FOK threshold. If the strength of a target answer in memory falls below this FOK threshold, then they will judge that they would not recognize the target. Because FOKs directly tap the actual strength of a target in memory, they should often show high levels of relative accuracy.

Despite its historical significance, the target-strength account has not received definitive support in the literature. Connor, Balota, and Neely (1992) provided relevant evidence in the following manner (see also Jameson, Narens, Goldfarb, & Nelson, 1990). First, they replicated an intriguing finding by Yaniv and Meyer (1987). Participants were asked to provide the sought-after target to definitions, for example, "What is a mythical figure, half-man, half-horse?" In this case, the target is "centaur." They then made a FOK judgment for each target that they did not recall. After this retrieval-judgment phase, a lexical-decision task was conducted, where the correct responses to definitions (e.g., centaur) were mixed with nonwords (e.g., gantean). During the lexical-decision task, these letter strings appeared, and participants had to decide as quickly as possible as to whether each one was a word or a nonword. Just like Yaniv and Meyer (1987), Connor et al. (1992) found that *more* lexical-decision errors were made for nonrecalled targets that received low FOK judgments than for those that received high FOK judgments. On first blush, this outcome appears consistent with a target-strength (direct-access) account: Presenting the definitions ("What is a mythical figure, half-man, half-horse?") is activating some targets in memory (but not others) and doing so increases the memory strength for the activated targets. This increased activation would then produce high FOKs for the targets and would also boost the accuracy of lexical decisions for them (Yaniv & Meyer, 1987).

A follow-up experiment by Connor et al. (1992), however, demonstrated that this interpretation was not appropriate. Participants first performed the lexical-decision task, and then a week later, they returned to the laboratory to answer the questions and make FOK judgments. In this case, because the lexical-decision task occurred *before* the questions were presented, priming would not occur for lexical decisions, so lexical decisions and FOKs should not be related. Surprisingly, they still found that more lexical-decisions errors were made for nonrecalled targets that received low FOK than high FOK judgments. A target-strength account cannot explain these data, because the definitions are presented *after* the lexical-decision task and hence could not have enhanced the activation of targets with high FOK judgments. Connor et al. (1992) offered the following explanation: "The [FOK] estimate reflects the subject's current assessment of the level of expertise he or she has in a topic, where the speeded lexical decision performance simply reflects speeded recognition of an item that falls into a category with which the subject is familiar" (p. 553). That is, FOK judgments do not tap the strength of a particular target directly, but instead are based on one's expertise—or familiarity—with a topic domain. Their domain-familiarity hypothesis is currently a leading, heuristic-based account of FOK judgments, which we explore in detail in the next section.

Heuristic-Based Accounts

In contrast to the direct-access accounts, heuristic-based accounts do not claim that people's FOKs directly tap the activation of some underlying target. Instead, a feeling of knowing arises because people *infer* the target's existence based on some relevant factor, such as familiarity with the cue for a question. Such a FOK judgment is said to be *heuristically based*, because using cue familiarity gives one a good and easy-to-use rule—or heuristic—about whether you will be able to recognize the correct answer. Let's consider two cues that could inform such a heuristic—cue familiarity and target accessibility—and how they could support accurate FOK judgments.

Cue Familiarity

Much research has suggested that people base FOK judgments on their quick assessment of the familiarity of a retrieval cue. Consider two situations: one in which you cannot immediately retrieve the answer to a question, and the other where you do not retrieve a name of an acquaintance. In particular, you may be unable to answer the question, "Who wrote the book *Atlas Shrugged?*" Or you may be unable to retrieve a person's name when you see him on the street. In these cases, however, you may have an unmistakable feeling that you would recognize the author or the person's name. In the former case, the *cue* is the question itself ("Who wrote the book *Atlas Shrugged?*"), and in the latter case, the *cue* is the person's face. According to the cue-familiarity hypotheses, you have a feeling of knowing because the cue itself is highly familiar. That is, a high feeling of knowing is not based on retrieval of the sought-after target, but rather on either (a) familiarity with the domain of the cue (e.g., you read a lot of literature, and you are familiar with authors' names), or (b) perceptual or conceptual familiarity with the cue (e.g., the cue seems familiar because you recently were exposed to the words "atlas" or "shrugged," or you have seen this particular person a lot, but cannot recall his name).

Because such cue familiarity tends to be predictive of what people will later recognize, this heuristic would produce accurate FOK judgments. Concerning sheer familiarity with the cue, if a person senses that he is familiar with the words in a cue (or a person's face), it is likely that the person has past experience with the word (or the person). Of course, words in a question often occur with their answer (when you see the words "*Atlas Shrugged,*" they often will appear with Ayn Rand), and a person's face often occurs with a name (when you saw the person in the past, you probably heard his name on more than one occasion). The idea here is that even when we cannot recall a sought-after target, the fact that we are familiar with the cue suggests that the actual target is lurking just below the surface of memory waiting to be retrieved. In these cases, high cue familiarity leads to high FOK judgments and a higher likelihood of correctly recognizing the target than does low cue familiarity, which would lead to low FOK judgments and a lower likelihood of recognition.

Now consider domain familiarity. If unable to immediately retrieve the name of the capital of Turkey, the frequent traveler would probably give a higher feeling-of-knowing rating than someone who rarely travels. The former would also likely have a better chance than the latter of choosing the correct response from the alternatives: BURSA, RIYADH, ISTANBUL, ANKARA, ASHGABAT, JEDDAH, MECCA, TABRIZ, MANAMA, MUS-CAT. But this frequent traveler might not be an art lover, and so when unable to retrieve the answer to, "Who painted *Two Tahitian Women?*," she should by the cue-familiarity heuristic give a low feeling of knowing (and should also be unlikely to correctly choose the target when given the alternatives). The idea is that if people are familiar with the domain of a question, they will be able to eliminate wrong answers fairly easily, and they should know they are likely to be able to do so. If they are unfamiliar with the domain, they will have much less luck. That is, with a bit of metacognitive smarts, they should know that they will be worse on those unfamiliar domains and will do much better on familiar ones. Thus, using either familiarity with a cue or familiarity with the domain the cue comes from as a heuristic to make FOK judgments would often support accurate judgments.

Much evidence favors the cue-familiarity hypothesis. For instance, while initially trying to retrieve an answer to a question, people can make different kinds of error, such as errors of omission (recalling nothing) or errors of commission (i.e., recalling a wrong answer, such as recalling "Margaret Atwood" instead of "Ayn Rand"). In the RJR method, people are often asked to make a FOK judgment after both kinds of error, and before doing so, the experimenter tells them that in fact they had just made an error. Examination of how FOK judgments relate to these errors suggests that participants are basing their judgments on cue familiarity. In particular, Krinsky and Nelson (1985) found that FOKs given to commission errors were higher than those given to omission errors. Commission errors tend to occur in domains with which people are more familiar (Butterfield & Mangels, 2003; cf. Koriat, 1993), so even when people make a commission error, their domain familiarity may nevertheless suggest that they have a good chance at recognizing the correct answer. Of course, this evidence is indirect, and although other relevant evidence also suggests domain familiarity influences FOK judgments (e.g., Connor et al., 1992; Costermans, Lories, & Ansay, 1992; Marquié & Huet, 2000), *experimental* evidence (where an independent variable is manipulated) is not currently available, partly because domain familiarity is a pseudo-experimental variable. Thus, further experimental research is needed to more closely scrutinize the influence that domain familiarity has on FOK judgments.

Even more convincing evidence for the cue-familiarity hypothesis has been offered by Lynne Reder (1987, 1988), who was a leader in demonstrating the centrality of this cue in the FOK judgment process. She argued that if FOK judgments were based on explicitly retrieved information, then one might expect that the time needed to make these judgments would be at least as long (or longer) than the time needed to retrieve information. In contrast to this prediction, she and her colleagues found that judgment reaction times were shorter than retrieval latencies. Most relevant to the cue-familiarity hypothesis, Reder also experimentally manipulated familiarity with the cue in the following manner. Participants first read a long list of words (some of which appeared in pairs) and rated how often they encountered certain pairs of words together in real life, such as while reading or listening. These *primed* words then appeared in half of the general-knowledge questions during the subsequent recall-judgment phase. For instance, "grape" and "wine" may have been rated for co-occurrence and would subsequently occur in a general-information question such as, "What grape is dominant in wines produced in the French region of Tavel?" Priming these words presumably would increase the familiarity of the cue (in this case, the question) and hence should increase people's FOK judgments. As expected, Reder (1987) found that FOK judgments were often higher for questions with primed pairs than for questions without them (see also Schwartz & Metcalfe, 1992).

Metcalfe, Schwartz, and Joaquim (1993) also used a paradigm in which they repeatedly presented the same cues across several trials (which did not improve retrieval of the target) or repeatedly presented the targets. More specifically, participants studied two lists of paired associates (e.g., pickle-lucky, where the first word, "pickle," is the cue, and the second word, "lucky," is the target). As shown in Table 4.1, the second list of paired associates was the same for all participants, and the first list differed depending on the group. The left-hand column refers to the general relationship of both lists, with AB, AB meaning that the same pairs appeared on both lists, and AD, AB meaning that the same cues (A) appeared on both lists, but they were paired with different targets on the two lists. Most important for now, note that the cues are repeated across both lists for the first two groups, but different cues are used on the two lists for the second group. Thus, when the cues (e.g., lucky-?) are presented for the FOK judgments, cue familiarity should be higher when the cues were repeated than when they were not. In this case, the prediction from the cue-familiarity hypothesis is that FOK magnitude should be higher for the AB, AB group and the AD, AB group than for the CD, AB group, which is exactly what was found (see the far-right column in Table 4.1).

Table 4.1   Percentage Recall and Feeling-of-Knowing (FOK) Judgments for Pairs Presented on List 1

Group	List 1	List 2	% Target Recall	FOK Magnitude
AB, AB	pickle-lucky table-picture butter-psyche	pickle-lucky table-picture butter-psyche	39	48
AD, AB	pickle-carpet table-maple butter-sandal	pickle-lucky table-picture butter-psyche	17	49
CD, AB	single-carpet fragrant-maple marble-sandal	pickle-lucky table-picture butter-psyche	19	38

SOURCE: Adapted from Metcalfe, J., Schwartz, B. L., & Joaquim, S. G. (1993). The cue-familiarity heuristic in metacognition. *Journal of Experimental Psychology: Learning, Memory, and Cognition, 19*, 851–861.

NOTE: FOK magnitude refers to the mean FOK judgment across pairs for a given group. FOK judgments were made on a 100-point scale, from 1 (no idea of correct response) to 100 (sure they would recognize the correct answer). The pattern of mean recognition performance was identical to recall performance.

In summary, much evidence indicates that people use their familiarity of a cue to make FOK judgments. This heuristic account provides one answer to our main question, Why do FOK judgments show above-chance relative accuracy? Namely, when we are familiar with a cue (and hence make a high FOK judgment), it's often because we have seen the cue and target in the past, so if the cue is familiar we likely have some lingering memory for the target as well and hence will recognize it on the criterion test. When we aren't familiar with a cue (and hence make a low FOK judgment), it's probably because we have rarely seen either the cue or target in the past, so we won't later recognize the correct target. Note, however, that even though relative accuracy is usually above chance (with judgment-recognition correlations being greater than zero), it also is often far from perfect, with correlations typically being below +.50. These mid-to-low levels of relative accuracy are also consistent with the application of a heuristic, because as explained by Metcalfe et al. (1993), "frequently our predictive ability is disappointing, as might well be expected given that we base these judgments on a heuristic rather than on some direct assessment of the . . . target itself" (p. 860).

Target Accessibility

Another heuristic basis for FOK judgments involves retrieving (or accessing) information relevant to the sought-after target. The idea is that when making an FOK judgment, we continue to attempt to retrieve the sought-after target, and some information may be retrieved. According to this *accessibility* hypothesis, when making an FOK judgment, accessing more information about a target (and accessing the information more quickly) will increase your confidence that you will later recognize the correct response (Koriat, 1993, 1995). As argued by Asher Koriat (1993), "the computation of FOK is parasitic on the processes involved in attempting to retrieve the target, relying on the accessibility of pertinent information" (p. 609). That is, a FOK judgment arises as a by-product of the retrieval process aimed at discovering the sought-after target. For instance, when asked to make a FOK judgment for the question, "Who wrote *Atlas Shrugged?*," you may readily retrieve that the author's last name begins with an "R" and that the author was a woman. In contrast, for "Who produced the first commercially successful electric guitar?," you may not retrieve anything when searching for the answer. According to this hypothesis, your FOK judgment will be higher for correctly recognizing the former target than for the latter one. Although the success of this retrieval process will rely on the strength of the target in memory, this view is not another version of the target-strength (direct-access) account. The target-strength account indicates that people have direct knowledge about target strength, whereas the accessibility hypothesis posits that people use the products of retrieval as a heuristic to *infer* target strength.

We have already described evidence relevant to this accessibility hypothesis. Reconsider data from Metcalfe et al. (1993), which is presented in Table 4.1. Participants who studied each paired associate twice (i.e., the AB, AB group) outperformed the others on the recall test (which preceded the FOK judgments). Accordingly, one could argue that overall, target access was greater for the AB, AB group, so a prediction is that this group should also have the highest FOK magnitude. In contrast to this prediction, FOK magnitude does not vary with target access but instead varies with cue familiarity, which indicates that at least in some circumstances cue familiarity is a dominant basis for people's FOK judgments. It is important to note, however, that these two heuristic accounts for FOKs—cue familiarity and accessibility—are not mutually exclusive, so both heuristics can jointly influence people's FOKs. And, as we'll see, accessibility does appear to have an important influence on FOK judgments.

According to Koriat's (1993) accessibility hypothesis (see also Schacter & Worling, 1985), FOK judgments are based on the total amount of information retrieved about the target, regardless of whether that information is correct or not. As a person recalls more and more, her FOK will increase too, even if all the information retrieved is incorrect. The idea here is simply that people are not good at evaluating the quality of information that is quickly accessed prior to making an FOK judgment, so all the information produces an FOK en masse. Note that this explanation naturally accounts for the above-chance relative accuracy displayed by FOK judgments. In particular, given that people often retrieve partial information about a target that is correct, being able to access some correct information (versus not being able to do so) would mean that the correct target is available in memory but just can't be recalled.

Asher Koriat has reported a great deal of evidence that is consistent with this proposal (for an excellent overview, see Koriat, 1994). In one experiment, participants studied a series of tetragrams—four-letter strings that were unfamiliar, such as FKDR, RFSC, and so forth (Koriat, 1993, Experiment 1). A participant studied a tetragram (FKDR) for 1 second, performed a distracter task for about 19 seconds, and then was asked to recall the tetragram. They were told that on each trial they would gain 1 point for each correct letter recalled but that they would earn no points if they recalled even one letter incorrectly. After this recall attempt, a FOK judgment was made for that tetragram. After these recall-judgment trials, a recognition test was given so that the accuracy of the FOK judgments could be assessed.

Two main questions arise from the accessibility hypothesis. Does FOK magnitude increase with the number of letters accessed? And, as important, Does FOK magnitude increase with letters accessed regardless of whether those letters were correct or incorrect? The results from this experiment are presented in Figure 4.1, where FOK magnitude is plotted as a function of partial information (PI) accessed—that is, the number of letters recalled from a tetragram—that was either correct (C) or wrong (W). Examine the left panel first. The data point at the top left-hand corner is the mean FOK rating for items in which four letters were recalled and they were all incorrect (PI-W = 4). Now compare this value to the one in the far right-hand corner, which is when all the letters accessed were correct (PI-C = 4). Note that the FOK magnitude is high and nearly identical for these two conditions. This comparison and several others from this figure illustrate that people judged they knew an answer if four letters were

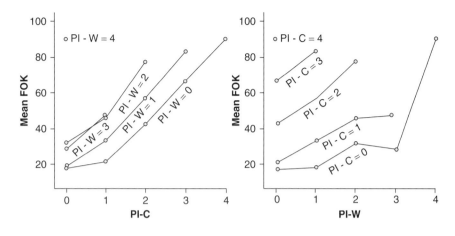

Figure 4.1   FOK magnitude as a function of amount of information accessed and whether the information was correct (C) or wrong (W).

SOURCE: Koriat, A. (1993). How do we know that we know? The accessibility model of the feeling of knowing. *Psychological Review, 100,* 609–639.

recalled, regardless of whether those letters were correct or incorrect. Moreover, in both panels of this figure, it is evident that FOK magnitude generally increases as more letters are recalled. FOK increases with PI-C (and PI-W), from 0 to 4. As important, when participants largely accessed correct information (PI-C) prior to making FOK judgments, relative FOK accuracy was well above chance, whereas when incorrect information was accessed (PI-W), their FOK judgments were not accurate at all. This and other evidence from Koriat's (1993, 1995) research provides support for the target-accessibility hypothesis.

At this point, you may be wondering: Which has a more potent effect on people's FOK judgments—cue familiarity or accessibility? Although such a question is reasonable and motivated early research on FOK judgments (e.g., for competing opinions, see Koriat, 1994, and Miner & Reder, 1994), the question does not deal with the fact that people may monitor both factors—cue familiarity and accessibility—when making a FOK judgment. Thus, we propose a more cutting-edge question about how people make FOK judgments in Mystery Box 4.1, which should motivate exciting research in the future.

Mystery BOX 4.1
Do People Monitor Multiple Cues
When Making a Feeling-of-Knowing Judgment?

Although we have focused on only three possible bases for people's FOK judgments, many others have been considered. In fact, Nelson, Gerler, and Narens (1984) compiled an extensive list of 12 factors that could influence people's FOK judgments, including those described in our text plus others, such as social desirability (i.e., saying one knows an answer so as to not be thought of as stupid) or actuarial information (i.e., saying one knows an answer because the question appears to be normatively easy). Certainly, it seems reasonable that any of these factors could in principle influence FOK judgments, which leads to a series of mysteries that future research must solve.

In particular, the steady growth of interest in how people make FOK judgments has typically rested on experiments that investigate either (a) the contribution of a given factor in isolation or (b) which of two factors (e.g., cue familiarity versus accessibility) has a larger influence under a given set of conditions. If more than one factor influences people's FOKs, however, it seems especially important to understand how people use multiple factors *jointly* in constructing FOK judgments. This venture is particularly critical if we want to understand exactly how people's FOK judgments reflect their monitoring of memory, which would require that we can isolate factors that do not reflect monitoring processes (e.g., social desirability). Many questions that remain without adequate answers today include: How exactly are two—or more—factors combined to make an FOK? If a given factor is available (e.g., target access), does it overshadow other factors that could increase the accuracy of FOKs (e.g., normative actuarial information)? And, when more than two factors influence FOK judgments, how can we estimate the separate influence of each factor on the judgments?

Almost no research has sought to answer these questions, with a notable exception. Koriat and Levy-Sadot (2001) investigated how two cues—cue familiarity and target accessibility—are combined (see also Benjamin, 2005). According to their interactive hypothesis, when a question is encountered (e.g., "What is the name of the largest kingfisher in the world?"), one first has an initial and quick preliminary feeling that is based on the familiarity of the cue (e.g., Miner & Reder, 1994). If the cue is not familiar, a search of memory will be brief if it occurs at all. In this case, because search for the target doesn't get started, the accessibility of the target will not influence FOKs. If the cue is immediately familiar, then a more thorough search for the sought-after target will occur. While searching, one may access information about the target, and in doing so, believe that the correct target could be recognized. Thus, only when the cue is familiar, and hence the search for the target persists, is target accessibility expected to influence FOK judgments. Across three experiments, Koriat and Levy-Sadot (2001) provided preliminary evidence that supported this interactive hypothesis.

Koriat and Levy-Sadot's (2001) ideas and experiments highlight an intriguing new avenue for research on FOK judgments, because we know a lot about which individual factors influence FOKs but very little about how they jointly influence FOKs. As you will find when we review the literature on other basic metacognitive judgments in the next chapters, research focusing on the joint effects of various factors on these judgments is also nearly absent. Certainly, a new wave of research will be required to solve the mystery of how people attend to, select, and combine multiple factors when judging their memories.

Tip-of-the-Tongue States

If you have played the game Trivial Pursuit—or some other game like it—then you are among many who love to challenge their memories about current and past events, trying to come up with answers to questions such as, "Who was the first man to set foot on the moon?" or "What team has won the most World Cup Championships?" Of course, for many of these questions, you may quickly retrieve the correct answer, yet for some others, you may struggle, feeling that you absolutely know the answer, if it would only bubble up to the top of your mind. Even if you have not played Trivial Pursuit, you probably have been frustrated by being almost but not quite able to recall something—for example, a person's name—that you are sure you know. Most of us actually have these *tip-of-the-tongue states* often; they arise when we are trying to recall someone's name, and they also arise more frequently as we grow older.

Given the ubiquity of such tip-of-the-tongue (TOT) states, and that they invoke emotional anguish in many of their victims, it perhaps is not too surprising that psychologists have been interested in understanding them for some time. In his classic textbook, *The Principles of Psychology* (1920), William James described TOT states in an often-quoted passage:

Suppose we try to recall a forgotten name. The state of our consciousness is peculiar. There is a gap therein; but no mere gap. It is a gap that is intensely active. A sort of wraith of the name is in it, beckoning us in a given direction, making us at moments tingle with the sense of our closeness, and then letting us sink back without the longed-for term. If wrong names are proposed to us, this singularly definite gap acts immediately so as to negate them. They do not fit into its mould. (p. 251)

James's description is eloquent and emphasizes the disturbing nature of TOT states, which pose as a "wraith" that teases us into believing we can remember something that we cannot. And often another word—a blocker, or "ugly stepsister," as some researchers call it—persistently comes to mind to torment us further (see Box 4.2 for more on blockers). These frustrating experiences are common. In his review of the literature, A. S. Brown (1991) concluded from diary studies that TOTs naturally occur about 1 to 2 times a week for younger adults, whereas the rate of TOTs is almost doubled per week for older adults.

BOX 4.2
Do Blockers Really Block
Our Access to Sought-After Memories?

So, you're daydreaming about this absolutely gorgeous classmate who you have a crush on. And who should appear, all alone, as you're standing in line to pay for your coffee? You're about to kiss the ground she walks on, and are wildly thinking of ways to impress her, when...oh, no! Not now! You're in a TOT state—of course you know her name, but you just can't retrieve it. To make matters worse, it's a *blocked* TOT. All that comes to mind—tormenting you, and turning you into a blithering idiot—is "Angelina." But you know her name is not Angelina. But what is her name, right there sparkling on the end of your tongue? You remember the professor mentioning her name, and even worse, you repeated her name, whistling, as you strolled across campus yesterday. But today, you're blocked. She's getting closer. She's interested. She breathes your name (oh, worse luck) in the most adorable husky tones. And you say: "Oh, hi, ah...uh...uh...uh...sputter."

The deep intellectual question, here, is whether poor old Angelina is really to blame? Does having a blocker come to mind really interfere with resolving the tip-of-the-tongue state? The blocking hypothesis—that retrieving a blocker hurts—is so widely accepted that some authors use the terms TOT and blocker synonymously. Kornell and Metcalfe (2006) addressed this question of whether blockers really block, experimentally, by giving definitions of words that were likely to induce TOT states, and then asking people whether they were in an unblocked TOT state or whether they were in a blocked state. To make sure people were actually in a blocked state when they said they were, they also had to state their blockers, and they had no difficulty in doing so. Moreover, people knew perfectly well that the blockers were wrong. They were annoyed by them and tried to get rid of them.

Smith and Blankenship (1989) had shown that giving people blockers that were made up by the experimenter, not self-generated, did interfere with people's ability to come up with the correct answer. But perhaps experimenter-provided interference and people's own, internal, blockers are different. Kornell and Metcalfe (2006) argued that if blockers really did block, then the way to get them to be less harmful would be to wait a while. Get them out of your mind, and then come back to the problem. This idea—to go away and do something else for a while, or, in other words, to incubate—is often evoked as a method to help people when they are stuck on solving insight problems. In this case, too, they're supposed to be blocked, and an incubation period away from the current dead-end (blocked) thinking is supposed to help.

To see whether waiting and allowing the blockers to be put out of mind would improve the resolution of blocked TOTs, Kornell and Metcalfe (2006) had a computer pick half of the blocked TOTs and half of the non-blocked TOTs to be thought about immediately. The other half of each category was separated out and presented later, and the person was given the same amount of time to work on them after the incubation period. If the blockers were really actively fighting off access to the target word, then waiting should have lifted the block (because the blockers were forgotten during the wait, and simply weren't there to block). The blocked TOTs should have benefited more from the incubation period than the originally nonblocked TOTs because the latter had nothing inhibiting their resolution in the first place. In contrast to this prediction, although the incubation period did help participants retrieve some of the sought-after targets, it helped such resolution by the same amount for the originally non-blocked TOTs *and* the blocked TOTs. The so-called blockers, apparently, were not blocking. So, although your blocked TOT dilemma, true to the observations of William James (1920), may have been frustrating, don't blame Angelina. In the meantime, if the classmate really likes you, why not just ask her what her name is—after all, asking someone for help is a great way to resolve TOT states.

Unfortunately, diary studies do not allow researchers to experimentally investigate the states in a manner that would lead to definitive answers to important questions such as, What causes a TOT state (but see Burke, MacKay, Worthley, & Wade, 1991)? To answer such questions, a laboratory analog for inducing TOT states was needed. Brown and McNeill (1966) developed the first one, which has been adapted numerous times to explore TOT phenomena. In particular, they presented a definition of a rare word, and experimental participants were asked to recall the word. While searching for these rare words, participants were also asked to report when they were in a TOT state, which was described as being unable to retrieve a word but having the feeling that the word was known and would soon be recalled. This procedure successfully elicited hundreds of TOT states. Moreover, when participants were in a TOT state, they were able to accurately recall some of the letters of the sought-after word and sometimes the number of syllables of that word. This evidence demonstrated that TOT states were accurate in that when people believed they were on the verge of recalling a sought-after target, the target was likely available in memory but just not currently accessible.

Further evidence for the accuracy of TOTs was discussed by Schwartz (1999, 2002), who described experiments modeled after the RJR method to explore FOK accuracy. In these experiments, participants first reported whether they were in a TOT state or not in a TOT state when they could not recall a sought-after target. After these judgment trials, a test of recognition was administered so that TOT accuracy could be estimated. Across multiple experiments from various laboratories, recognition performance was higher when people were in a TOT state than when they were in a non-TOT state (for complete details, see Schwartz, 2002). Again, these outcomes further establish that when someone complains about being in a TOT state, the actual target is more likely available in memory than when they aren't in a TOT state. This brings us to two questions: (a) What causes these frustrating states? and (b) How do explanations of TOT phenomena account for their accuracy?

Many answers have arisen for these questions, and like hypotheses for how people make FOK judgments, these answers can largely be separated into two classes: those implying that TOTs arise from a person having direct access to the strength of the sought-after target in memory, and those indicating that TOTs are inferential in nature. Direct-access accounts readily explain TOT accuracy, because when in a TOT state, a person allegedly has direct access to target strength, such as if a person directly monitors the neural activation of the semantic representation (i.e., its meaning) when the sought-after target cannot be retrieved (e.g., Burke et al., 1991). Burke et al. argued that people may, at least some of the time when they are in the TOT state, have essentially complete access to the conceptual meaning of words, but still be unable to retrieve the word's sound or phonemic representation. More generally, lexical access is thought to entail two or more successive, or possibly interactive, levels of processing. In Stage 1, a semantically and syntactically specified representation is accessed. In Stage 2, a phonological representation is accessed. The notion here is that the feeling of being in a TOT state can occur because there is complete access to the first level, but that the person may, nevertheless, be unable to produce the word because of an impairment, block, or problem at the second level. If this were so, then the person would be said to have complete semantic and syntactic access, but they might still be unable to recall the target. This model is thought to be most important in explaining the high rate of TOTs seen in older adults, but it may also apply to young participants in some instances.

To support the view that the problem in TOT states is phonological in nature, James and Burke (2000) preceded the definitions of words that commonly provoke TOT experiences by spoken primes that shared some of the phonology. For example, a TOT-provoking question would be "What word means to formally renounce a throne?" When one of the spoken-aloud primes given before the presentation of this question was the word "abstract," people were much more likely to answer the question (correct answer: abdicate), and they were less likely to be thrown into a TOT state, suggesting that at least some TOTs are not semantic but rather result from a lack of access to the appropriate phonology. Miozzo and Caramazza (1997), using the fact that Italian words have male and female gender as part of their syntax, showed that Italian speakers could tell, with above-chance accuracy, the gender of the words when they were in a TOT state as compared to when they said that they did not know. Thus, the syntax may be accessed.

Further support of the idea that at least some TOT states entail virtually complete access to the semantics of the lexical item that is sought, but a disconnect between that conceptual level of processing and the phonemic output, come from a study by Funnell, Metcalfe, and Tsapkini (1996). They reported on a patient who had production anomia, and who seemed constantly to be in a tip-of-the tongue state. This patient, H.W., was tested for the names of 150 words (50 nouns, 50 adjectives, and 50 verbs) that were specifically designed so that there was only a single word answer. An example would be: "When a person brushes butter on a turkey while it is cooking they are said to _____ the turkey." "Baste" is the only answer that works. H.W. was able to come up with only 1 of the 150 words. When he was given a recognition test for the words, however, he did better than college students from Dartmouth on choosing the correct alternatives. It would seem that this patient (and perhaps many people when in a TOT state) has essentially complete semantic access to the words when he is in a TOT state, yet he cannot access the appropriate phonology.

Thus, it would appear that there are cases in which people may be in a TOT state accompanied by complete semantic access to the target item. They may, however, also report being in a TOT state for other reasons, basing their TOT judgments on heuristics, such as the familiarity of the cue or partial, but not complete, access to information about the target word. Metcalfe et al. (1993) evaluated whether being familiar with memory cues could give rise to TOT states. The method used to do so was described above: Experimental participants studied lists of paired associates on two study-test trials, and sometimes both stimulus and response were repeated across lists (AB, AB), sometimes only the stimulus was repeated (AD, AB), and sometimes no words were repeated across lists (CD, AB) (see Table 4.1 for a refresher). Just like with FOK judgments, they found that TOT states were not elevated when the correct targets were strengthened through repetition, which cannot easily be explained by target-strength accounts. In contrast, TOT states occurred most frequently when the cues were repeated (AB, AB; and AD, AB) than when they were not repeated (CD, AB). Thus, it appears that people's TOTs partly arise from using the cue-familiarity heuristic.

According to the accessibility hypothesis, a person infers the presence of a target when any information (even partial information) is retrieved as the search for the target proceeds. As one retrieves more and more information about the target, the chances a TOT state will occur increases. Thus, if you cannot recall the answer to the question, "Which singer was known as Ol' Blue Eyes?," you may remember that the singer was male, he starred in *Ocean's Eleven* (the original), he was part of the Rat Pack, and his first name began with "T." Accessing so much information (regardless of whether it is correct or incorrect) may lead to a state where you absolutely know that you know the answer. Note that these products of the retrieval attempt will usually signify that a correct answer is stored in memory, so a TOT will often accurately indicate that the correct target (in this case, Frank Sinatra) is lurking somewhere in memory waiting to be discovered (even though some of the information retrieved, such as that his name begins with "T," was incorrect).

To evaluate this accessibility account, Schwartz and Smith (1997) used naturalistic materials developed by Smith, Brown, and Balfour (1991), which were drawings of make-believe animals along with their names, sizes, countries of origin, and diets. Figure 4.2 includes some *TOTimals,* and the format for the various conditions used in this experiment. For some TOTimals, only the name and country were presented (called the *minimum-information* condition); for other TOTimals, the picture was also included (*medium-information* condition); and finally, in the *maximum-information* condition, the name and country were presented along with the picture of the TOTimal, and its diet and size. Participants studied twelve TOTimals for 15 seconds each. During the subsequent test, the country of each TOTimal was presented as a cue (none of them originated from the same country), and participants were asked to recall the name of the corresponding TOTimal. If participants could not recall a TOTimal's name, they were asked to report if they were in a TOT state and also asked to report anything they could remember about the TOTimal. According to the accessibility hypothesis, participants were expected to report being in TOT states more often when they retrieved more information about the unrecalled target. Moreover, the maximum- and medium-information conditions were expected to lead to greater levels of access, so TOTs should arise more often in these conditions than for the minimal-information condition. The outcomes were consistent with these predictions (see Schwartz & Smith, 1997, Experiment 3).

In summary, TOT states likely arise either when people can access the sought-after target but cannot articulate it, or when they cannot recall a sought-after target yet find (a) the cue for the target (e.g., the question itself) to be highly familiar (as per the cue-familiarity heuristic), or (b) when other information about the target readily comes to mind (as per the accessibility heuristic). Research efforts aimed at an even better understanding of why TOT states occur will undoubtedly continue. Another avenue for research concerns discovering techniques to help people resolve a TOT state— that is, to retrieve a sought-after target when it eludes you. For more on resolving pesky TOT states, see Box 4.3.

Maximum-Information Condition

Panama-Yelkey
2
Berries

Medium-Information Condition

France - Rittle

Minimum-Information Condition
India - Merling

Figure 4.2   Examples of some TOTimals in all three information conditions used by Schwartz and Smith.

SOURCE: Schwartz, B. L., and Smith, S. M. (1997). The retrieval of related information influences tip-of-the-tongue states. *Journal of Memory and Language, 36,* 68–86.

BOX 4.3
I'm in a TOT State. How Do I Cure It?

Everyone finds themselves in a TOT state from time to time. TOT states arise naturally and are universal. In fact, in his survey of languages, Bennett Schwartz had native speakers of 51 different languages provide the saying that matched what English speakers mean when they say, "It's on the tip of my tongue." Speakers of 45 different languages used a similar metaphor, including Irish and Serbians who use "on the top of the tongue" and some Koreans who use the colorful phrase, "sparkling at the end of the tongue" (for details, see Schwartz, 1999, 2002). Those who *speak* language use this phrase, as well as individuals who use American Sign Language, which Thompson, Emmorey, and Gollan (2005) refer to as the "tip-of-the-finger" state. Similarly, it appears that we can experience the same frustration when we fail to retrieve the name of an odor (Jönsson & Olsson, 2003), which has been dubbed the "tip-of-the-nose" phenomenon.

Given that TOTs appear to be a truly universal problem, frustrating people around the globe, some form of therapy or intervention seems in order. How can we resolve these TOT states? The research on TOT resolution is relatively sparse, and no one is currently conducting systematic research to develop a set of "no fail" tactics to retrieve frustratingly elusive memories. Nevertheless, a handful of studies do offer some suggestions on how to increase the chances of resolving a TOT state. One suggestion comes from Beattie and Coughlan (1999), who reported that people resolved more TOT states when their hands were free to gesture than when they were instructed to make sure their arms were folded (for explanations for why gestures may help, see Schwartz, 2002, p. 93). So be sure to pull your hands out of your pockets and let them do some talking when you're in a TOT state.

In experiments by Brennen, Baguley, Bright, and Bruce (1990), participants were asked general-information questions in which the answer could be a famous person's name. When in a TOT state, participants were shown either the person's picture or initials of the sought-after name. Presenting the initials increased the likelihood of retrieving the name, which suggests the strategy of walking through the alphabet in hopes of coming across the correct first letter of the word you're looking for will trigger retrieval of the entire word. No doubt many people already use such an alphabet strategy when searching memory in TOT states.

Of course, another excellent way to resolve a TOT state is simply to ask someone else to help you come up with your lost memory. Just recently, an author of this textbook couldn't remember the name of the singer who wrote, "Where Is My Mind?" After some frustration, he walked to the next office, asked a friend who immediately chimed in with "Frank Black of the Pixies." Thus, searching for external aid—from a friend, from the World Wide Web, or from any other relevant source—is likely a worthwhile endeavor when you're in a pinch to relieve frustration and to find that lost memory.

Finally, remember not to get too frustrated when you are in a TOT state, because diary studies indicate that most TOT states are eventually resolved, partly through the use of some of the techniques described above. For instance, Burke et al. (1991) examined TOT resolution for three groups differing in chronological age. In a diary, participants reported when they were in a TOT state and whether they eventually found the sought-after memory. TOT states were often resolved, with the percentage rates of resolution being 92% for younger college-aged adults, 95% for middle-aged adults, and 97% for older adults. Other diary studies also leave room for optimism, showing that resolutions usually occur in 30 minutes or less (for an overview, see Schwartz, 2002). So when you do fall prey to a TOT state, don't worry or get too annoyed—you'll likely come up with that memory.

Brain Bases of FOK Judgments

The nature of the neural circuitry underlying memory monitoring is unknown. Many researchers have suggested that metacognitive monitoring largely relies on the frontal lobes, but very few studies have shown the critical nature of this brain region for monitoring. We'll consider some of the seminal research here along with the most recent attempts to image the brain's functioning as people make FOK judgments.

In a classic article that used the RJR paradigm, Shimamura and Squire (1986) demonstrated that different kinds of amnesia differentially influence memory and memory monitoring (as tapped by FOK accuracy). Most amnesiacs, while showing profound memory deficits, also showed *normal* relative FOK accuracy—that is, they could make FOK judgments as accurately as you or me, even though their recall was extremely impaired. They also studied patients with Korsakoff syndrome, which is caused by alcohol abuse along with thiamine deficiencies. Korsakoff patients were not only memory impaired, but their FOKs also showed impaired relative accuracy.

In keeping with the hypothesis that metacognitive monitoring might be frontally controlled, the Korsakoff patients are thought by some researchers to have frontal lobe damage, while the other memory impaired patients had no frontal damage. The difficulty Korsakoff patients have with memory and memory monitoring was explained by Metcalfe (1993), who proposed the first formal memory model (instantiated as computer simulations) that included memory monitoring and accounted for the accuracy of FOK judgments. In this model, when a particular memory cue was presented (e.g., "What is the capital of Australia?"), the familiarity of the cue was immediately computed, and the judgments were directly based on that familiarity. Thus, similar to Reder's proposals (e.g., see Miner & Reder, 1994; Reder, 1987), Metcalfe (1993, 1994) argued that FOKs arose from a preliminary familiarity check in which the system monitored the novelty of the memory cue. If this cue highly matched other information stored in memory, a person had an immediate feeling of knowing the answer, but if the cue did not highly match other information in memory, a person would have a feeling of not knowing. Metcalfe (1993) demonstrated how this novelty monitoring device was critical for controlling a neural model of memory. Most relevant here, the deficits shown by Korsakoff patients can be simulated if one assumes that this syndrome selectively disrupts a person's ability to monitor the familiarity—or novelty—of a memory probe (for details, see Metcalfe, 1993).

Unfortunately, with Korsakoff syndrome, reduced memory and impaired metamemory go hand in hand. That is, there is nearly always a connection between memory functioning and FOK accuracy, and hence we are unable to determine whether people's relative FOK accuracy is poor because they have so little memorial information on which to base those judgments, or whether damage to the *judgment process* itself might be responsible. This problem was sidestepped by Janowsky et al. (1989), who investigated FOK accuracy for three groups of participants: patients with frontal lobe damage, patients with temporal lobe damage, and normal controls. Participants first studied sentences and then sometime later they were shown the sentences again but the final word of each one was missing. They were asked to recall the final word, and if they couldn't, they made an FOK judgment. Janowsky et al. (1989) equated the groups on overall memory performance by manipulating the delay between when each group studied the sentences and when they were asked to make the FOK judgments (for why equating memory performance is crucial, see Box 3.1). Even though the groups were equated on memory, FOK accuracy was still impaired for the patients with frontal lobe damage. Thus, impairments in memory per se cannot explain some patients' poor FOK accuracy. Instead, the current evidence on patient populations converges on the conclusion that frontal functioning is vital for metacognitive monitoring that underlies FOK judgments (for further evidence, see Souchay, Isingrini, & Espagnet, 2000).

Recently, a group of researchers (Schnyer et al., 2004) tested patients with specific frontal lobe lesions on a FOK task. The results are striking and implicate the frontal lobes as a key contributor to accurate FOK judgments.

They hypothesized that the prefrontal cortex plays a critical role in accurate FOK predictions of episodic memory performance. Fourteen patients with a broad spectrum of damage to the frontal cortex and matched control participants read sentences and later were tested for recall memory and made FOKs (as in Janowsky et al., 1989). Frontal patients were impaired at recall and recognition memory, and as a group, they were markedly impaired in FOK accuracy. Lesion analysis of frontal patients with the most profound impairment in FOK accuracy revealed an overlapping region of damage in the right medial prefrontal cortex.

These results are qualified by two functional Magnetic Resonance Imaging (fMRI) studies on normals. The first study (Maril, Simons, Mitchell, Schwartz, & Schacter, 2003) implicates the left midlateral prefrontal cortex as being crucial to people's feelings of knowing. The second study (Kikyo, Ohki, & Miyashita, 2002) also points to frontal areas, but more diffusely. Given that FOK and recall levels are often related, a strength of Kikyo et al.'s (2002) study is that they attempted to localize FOK functioning separate from memory functioning. Brain scans were taken while participants performed a version of the RJR method, and then Kikyo et al. decomposed the neural correlates of FOKs into those areas that did (and did not) overlap with neural areas that were activated during recall. As expected, this decomposition revealed substantial overlap in the neural correlates for FOK and recall, as shown in the middle three panels of Figure 4.3 (shown inside the front cover). Most important, it was apparent that the left inferior frontal gyrus and the right inferior frontal gyrus were not recruited for recall itself but were recruited when participants had a FOK (far-left panel). These areas may have a privileged role in metacognition processes as distinct from memory processes.

In summary, only a few studies are available that use state-of-the-art imaging techniques to investigate the neural bases of FOK mechanisms (for a review of the neural bases of TOT states, see Shimamura, 2008). Even though there is not consensus about the most specific brain areas that are involved in making FOK judgments, the imaging evidence converges on the same conclusion as the behavioral research in this field. Namely, echoing Pannu and Kaszniak's (2005) conclusion from their comprehensive review, results from "neurological populations are consistent with the conclusion that the frontal lobes play a central role in the production of accurate metamemory judgments" (p. 122).

Functions of Feelings of Knowing

Imagine yourself reading a textbook and stumbling while reading the word *bucolic* because you do not immediately recall its meaning. What would you do? If you immediately realize that you are not at all familiar with the word, you may look it up in a dictionary. In contrast, you may sense an initial feeling of familiarity with the word, so instead of cracking open your Webster's, you spend some time searching your memory for the definition. In these cases, initial familiarity with the cue for memory (in this case, the word "bucolic") is used to choose a strategy—dictionary look-up or memory search. Your FOK may influence how long you search memory for an answer as well. If you decide to search memory and you find yourself in a tip-of-the-tongue state or have a high feeling of knowing for the definition, you may continue the search. Alternatively, your feeling of knowing may wane and hence you may terminate your search.

In both these cases, feeling of knowing plays a functional role in the search for an answer to the question, "What does bucolic mean?" In the first scenario, an initial FOK informs strategy selection, whereas in the second scenario, an ongoing FOK informs termination of retrieval. In the next two sections, we review research that highlights these functions of people's FOKs.

Strategy Selection

Lynne Reder and her colleagues have developed innovative methods to investigate whether a preliminary FOK drives strategy selection—much like in the example above (for a review, see Reder, 1988). The idea here is that when we are asked a question, we have the experience of an immediate feeling of knowing (or not knowing) that occurs before we begin to search for the answer. It is this pre-retrieval FOK that is then used to make decision about whether to begin a full-blown search for the answer or to use some other strategy to come up with one.

In her earlier work, Reder (1987) developed a game-show paradigm in which participants were shown a question, but instead of answering it, they had to respond as quickly as possible as to whether they knew the answer to the question—just like a typical game show, such as *Jeopardy* or *Family Feud*. After they made this quick FOK judgment, they then had time to answer the question, so that the accuracy of their judgments could be estimated. Control participants were presented with the same questions but instead of making an FOK judgment, they had to answer the questions as quickly as possible. Several outcomes are noteworthy.

Lynne M. Reder
Developed creative methods to systematically explore the bases of FOK judgments

First, for anyone who has watched (or played along with) game shows, it is not surprising that it took less time to judge whether one could answer the questions than it took to answer them. Moreover, the initial FOK judgments were accurate in predicting whether or not the answer could actually be retrieved. Thus, an accurate FOK judgment could be made quickly and before any answer had been retrieved, which demonstrates the plausibility that a preliminary FOK could influence the decision about whether to search for an answer. Perhaps most impressive, the total time needed for participants to make this judgment and to answer the question was equivalent to the time taken to retrieve the answer by the control group. This outcome suggests that even members of the control group (who were not asked to *explicitly* make a FOK judgment) also had a preliminary FOK stage before answering the question.

An alternative possibility is that people's decisions are actually based on a very quick evaluation about whether the answer to a question is stored in memory. For instance, perhaps people quickly recall a part of the correct answer (as per the accessibility hypothesis), which then produces an initial FOK. Although possible, Reder and Ritter (1992) used a version of the game-show paradigm to rule out this possibility and to further establish the importance of a preliminary familiarity-based FOK in driving strategy choice. They had participants answer novel arithmetic problems, such as 28 × 16 = ?). The procedure, which is illustrated in Figure 4.4, involves the game-show flare: A problem is presented on a computer screen, and then participants must quickly decide which of two strategies to use to arrive at the correct answer—they could either decide to retrieve it from memory or to calculate it. After they made this quick decision, then they either attempted to retrieve the answer or to calculate it.

Of course, without any practice, participants would not know the correct answers and hence would have to choose the calculate strategy. Participants had hundreds of trials (Figure 4.4 illustrates only a single trial), and many problems were repeated across these trials. The issue is whether participants would switch to a retrieval strategy as they memorized some answers during practice trials. In particular, as participants became more familiar with a problem and learned the correct answer, they should shift from using the calculation strategy to a retrieval strategy. Some critical results are presented in Figure 4.5, which plots the percentage of times participants decided to use the retrieval strategy as a function of how often a problem was repeated. First, consider the curve with filled symbols ("copies of training problems"), which represents problems that were repeated in their identical form (so, 28 × 16 = ? was presented multiple times). Note that the percentage of trials that participants chose the retrieval strategy increased as the problems were presented more often.

Although this outcome was expected, as mentioned above, it can be explained by two different mechanisms: Either the initial decision to retrieve is based on a preliminary FOK that is triggered by familiarity with the problem (i.e., cue familiarity) or the decision to retrieve was based on a quick retrieval of the actual answer. To distinguish between these competing hypotheses, Reder and Ritter (1992) incorporated an innovative twist to the method. In particular, the final exposure of some problems was altered. For instance, 32 + 14 = ? may have been presented 8 times during the initial trials. On its final trial, however, the operator was switched, so that instead of presenting it as an addition problem, the participants would see 32 × 14 = ? Such "switched operator" problems were entirely new—participants had never seen them before, so they did not know (and could not retrieve) the correct answer. Thus, if participants were making decisions based on an initial retrieval of an answer, because the answer was not known, they should choose to calculate the answer. In contrast, if participants were basing their decision on the overall familiarity of the cue, they might actually choose to retrieve the answer, because in fact the problem would look familiar. As shown in Figure 4.5, participants were more likely to choose to retrieve the answers to these switched-operator problems because the initial problem (e.g., 32 + 14 = ?) had been presented more often before the switch. These outcomes provide strong evidence that the preliminary FOK that drives strategy choice is based on cue familiarity and not on access to the actual responses (for a review, see Miner & Reder, 1994).

Termination of Retrieval

Do your best to answer the following questions, which pertain to information from the History chapter. "Who was the scientist that popularized the term 'metacognition' in psychological research?" "Who was the famous orator from antiquity who is given credit for developing the method of loci?" In both these cases, you may have failed to remember the correct answer, but in doing so, you may have also taken a lot of time trying to recall "Flavell" and very little time trying to recall "Simonides."

What is responsible for how long someone searches for an answer that he or she cannot retrieve? One answer to this question, of course, is that one's feeling of knowing for the correct answer is used to make decisions about how long to persist while trying to retrieve an answer. To illustrate, consider this intuitive rationale. For some questions, you may immediately be sure that you do not know the answer. For instance, I might ask you, "What is Britney Spears' telephone number?" Because it's implausible that you've ever

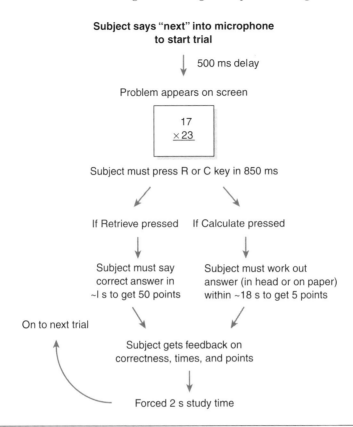

Figure 4.4   Illustration of a single trial of the game-show paradigm used by Reder and Ritter. Note that participants received more time to calculate if it was a multiplication problem than if it was an addition problem.

SOURCE: Procedure from Reder, L. M., and Ritter, F. E. (1992). What determines initial feeling of knowing? Familiarity with question terms, not with the answer. *Journal of Experimental Psychology: Learning, Memory, and Cognition, 18*, 435–451.

NOTE: s = second; ms = millisecond.

known her telephone number, you'd probably quickly say, "I don't know," without even searching your memory for the answer (Kolers & Palef, 1976). Thus, an immediate feeling of "not knowing" can lead to a quick termination of search. In contrast, if you were asked, "Who wrote *The Lord of the Rings?*," even if you can't recall the answer immediately, you may feel you know it, if you've read the trilogy or seen the movies based on them.

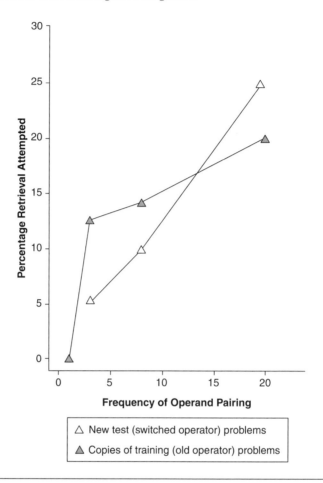

Figure 4.5   Percentage of trials in which participants attempted to retrieve an answer as a function of the frequency with which the problem was presented across trials.

SOURCE: Reder, L. M., and Ritter, F. E. (1992). What determines initial feeling of knowing? Familiarity with question terms, not with the answer. *Journal of Experimental Psychology: Learning, Memory, and Cognition, 18*, 435–451.

Based on this example, we would then expect to find a positive relationship between FOK and the duration of search, with higher FOKs leading to more time being used to dig up an answer from memory. Although the relationship between FOK and search duration has not received a great deal of attention in the field, the current evidence is consistent with the hypothesis that FOK affects how much time people use to search memory (e.g., Nelson et al., 1984; Reder, 1987). For instance, Nelson et al. (1984) used the RJR method in which participants first answered general information questions until they failed to answer 21 questions (Experiment 1) or 12 questions (Experiment 2). The latency of responding "I don't know" was recorded, which was the measure of how long participants persisted in searching for an answer before they gave up. They then made FOK judgments for these questions; afterwards, a criterion test was administered (e.g., multiple-choice recognition). In both experiments, Nelson et al. (1984) correlated the latency of incorrect recall, that is, how long it took for participants to say, "I don't know," with a variety of other measures, such as criterion test performance and FOK judgments. An impressive outcome was that latency of recall was not related to objective measures of memory, such as performance on the criterion tests. In contrast, in both experiments, the mean across individual participants' correlation between recall latency and FOK judgments exceeded +.35. Thus, as concluded by Nelson et al. (1984), these findings "suggest that the amount of time that people search for nonrecalled answers is determined not by what they know but rather by what they feel that they know" (p. 292).

Summary

Since Hart's (1965) seminal work on FOK judgments, researchers have sought to answer a variety of core questions about people's FOK experiences, including "Why do FOK judgments typically show above-chance relative accuracy?" and "What is the functional role of FOK in controlling human thought and action?" Concerning the first question, the original direct-access account proposed by Hart is no longer viewed as viable—people are not able to directly access the strength of items in memory. Instead, people appear to infer whether a nonrecallable memory is actually available in memory by using a variety of heuristics, such as cue familiarity or accessibility. As you'll find in the following chapters, such heuristic-based accounts are prevalent and have been successful at explaining both the accuracy and biases of other metamemory judgments.

Feeling-of-knowing judgments also appear to play a functional role in guiding people's strategy selection and retrieval. Concerning the former, a prominent view is that when people are presented with a problem to solve, a rapid feeling of knowing based on familiarity with the problem drives a decision about whether to retrieve the solution from memory or to compute the solution. Concerning retrieval, people appear to persist longer in attempting to retrieve a sought-after memory that does not immediately come to mind. At the extreme, when people are faced with a memory on the tip of the tongue, they may spend quite a bit of time searching memory and even resort to using external aids—for example, the Web or friends—to get relief from this frustrating experience.

DISCUSSION QUESTIONS

1. You find yourself with a friend in Hollywood, exploring some places where you think celebrities may be hanging out. After some deliberate searching with no luck, your friend tugs your shirtsleeve and quietly points across the way to a good-looking man in his 40s, who appears to be wearing an expensive outfit. She whispers, "I'm sure that guy over there is in the movies, but his name slips me. Do you know it?" In this scenario, describe all the metacognitive experiences (both monitoring and control) that your friend is having. Assuming that the gentleman in question is not a celebrity, why might she be having a strong feeling of knowing for his name?

2. Imagine a person who has a normal memory—this person's object-level memories are intact. Now imagine that this person also has no metacognitive experiences relevant to feeling of knowing. So, when she can't recall something, she never has any other experience than not being able to remember. How would this lack of metacognitive awareness influence her interactions with other people? Would she be great at games like Trivial Pursuit or *Jeopardy?* Why or why not? Even though her memory system is normal, would she appear to have normal memory? Do you think it would be more frustrating for her not to have an occasional TOT state than to have them like other people?

CONCEPT REVIEW

For the following questions and exercises, we recommend you write down the answers on a separate sheet in as much detail as possible, and then check them against the relevant material in the chapter.

1. Describe how scientists collect FOK judgments and how relative FOK accuracy is computed.

2. Describe evidence that indicates FOK judgments are based on (a) cue familiarity and (b) target accessibility.

3. Which brain areas do scientists believe are responsible for FOK experiences? Are these separate from those areas that serve memory itself?

4. What are tip-of-the-tongue experiences and how do they arise? Name two strategies to remember something that is currently on the tip of your tongue.

5. Describe the functions of FOKs.

5

Judgments of Learning

In the previous chapter, we explored in detail how people make FOK judgments and why we can make them with above-chance accuracy. A feeling of knowing itself requires almost no introduction because it is so common, such as when you struggle to remember a sought-after name when you feel you know it. You may persist at searching for the name, and when it seems to rest stubbornly on the tip of your tongue—frustration! In contrast to FOKs, other kinds of metacognitive judgment do not have such common and glamorous counterparts in everyday life. Nevertheless, they still are vital to how we use our memories in many important situations. To illustrate, consider the following vignette, which focuses on student scholarship in relation to memorizing new material for a class examination.

David had always wanted to learn another language, and so he decided to enroll in a beginner's course in French. Several weeks into the class, he faced an exam that involved learning vocabulary terms (e.g., *cheval*-horse) from several chapters. In preparing for the exam, David first examined all the materials and tried to judge how difficult they would be to learn, which are called *ease-of-learning* (EOL) judgments. He judged that it would be more difficult to learn verbs than nouns, so he decided to spend more time studying the verbs than the nouns. While studying, he also attempted to judge—or monitor—his ongoing progress. After studying each translation equivalent, he simply judged whether he had learned it well enough to recall it on the exam. He then used these *judgments of learning* (JOLs) to decide when to stop studying. Whenever David judged a vocabulary term as being well-learned, he dropped it from study, whereas he continued to study any that he believe he had not yet learned. Unfortunately, he often misjudged his own learning. Put differently, his JOLs were not very accurate. Thus, he ended up not spending enough time studying many of the terms that needed it.

This vignette highlights central questions about two metacognitive judgments—EOL judgments and JOLs. First, do people use these judgments to make decisions about how much time to devote to studying? In the present case, the answer is "yes," because David decided to devote the most time to those items he judged as least well-learned, which intuitively seems like a good thing to do. Second, how accurate are people at making these judgments? David's JOLs were not very accurate, and the effectiveness of his studying suffered for it. Like David, it turns out that people are often not very accurate at judging their learning, which leads to an important applied question: Can the accuracy of their judgments be improved?

In the present chapter, we will examine evidence relevant to each of these questions, which all have direct bearing on how well we can actually monitor memories as they are formed. Certainly, this monitoring skill can be useful, assuming of course our monitoring is accurate. After a brief comparison of FOK judgments to JOLs, we describe two factors—which are currently being explored extensively in the field—that dramatically influence the accuracy of JOLs. As important, we also critically examine various hypotheses for how people make these judgments, and end with a discussion of how people use monitoring of learning to control their study time.

Do All Monitoring Judgments Tap the Same Information?

Soon after Hart's (1965) groundbreaking research on FOK judgments, research on EOL judgments (Underwood, 1966) and on JOLs (Arbuckle & Cuddy, 1969) began. Although people's mysterious ability to accurately make FOK judgments has since garnered considerable attention, sustained devotion to understanding EOL judgments has been rather minimal and little is known about them. In the past two decades, however, JOLs have become one of the most intensely investigated kinds of metacognitive judgment. Thus, even though we touch on some intriguing results about EOL judgments, the bulk of this chapter is dedicated to describing developments in our understanding of JOLs and their use in regulating study.

Before we delve deeply into the research on JOLs, let's compare the three judgments that have received our attention up to this point: EOL judgments, JOLs, and FOK judgments. The reason for such a comparison is straightforward: If all of the judgments are highly interrelated, then they may be based on the same underlying processes and tap the same information. If so, everything we learned about FOK judgments in the previous chapter will readily generalize to these other metacognitive judgments. To evaluate this possibility, Leonesio and Nelson (1990) had college students study 20 paired associates (e.g., table-lake) and make all three judgments. Before studying the pairs, participants made EOL judgments in which they rated the items from least to most difficult to learn. Next, each item was presented individually for study, and then the items were tested by presenting each stimulus (e.g., table-?) and having the participants attempt to retrieve the correct response (i.e., lake). This study-test sequence was repeated until participants met different criteria for the items. Namely, half the items were studied until they were correctly recalled once (called *learned* items), and the other half were studied until they were correctly recalled four times (called *overlearned* items). After an item had reached its criterion, it was dropped from the study-test sequence. When all items had been dropped, participants made JOLs for items by rating them from most to least well learned. A 4-week retention interval occurred before the final phase of the experiment. During this final phase, participants received a criterion-recall test, made a FOK judgment for each nonrecalled item, and then had a criterion-recognition test for each non-recalled item.

This procedure allowed Leonesio and Nelson (1990) to compare the judgments because each participant made all three. Of most import now are the correlations among them. Correlations near +1.0 would suggest the judgments were based on the same underlying processes. Instead, the mean correlations across non-recalled items were small in magnitude: +.19 between EOL judgments and JOLs, +.12 between EOL judgments and FOK judgments, and +.17 between JOLs and FOK judgments. These low correlations suggest that the judgments are based on somewhat different processes or receive different kinds of input. For now, however, these outcomes indicate that some conclusions concerning FOK judgments covered in Chapter 4 may not entirely generalize to JOLs.

Variables Influencing JOL Accuracy

In the next two sections, we focus on two factors—number of study trials and the timing of the judgments—that have received a great deal of attention in the field because they have a dramatic effect on JOL accuracy. Many other factors have been explored, so our coverage here is meant to highlight some robust effects that have stimulated theory and debate. Before we introduce these factors in detail, let's consider some of the earliest JOL research, which initially demonstrated that people can accurately judge their memories for newly learned materials.

In the seminal work on JOLs, Arbuckle and Cuddy (1969) argued that if paired associates "differed in associative strengths immediately following presentation, subjects should be able to detect these differences just as they can detect differences in strength of any other input signal" (p. 126). They had college students study short lists of paired associates, and immediately after studying each one, they judged whether or not they would recall it. The likelihood of subsequent recall was greater for items that participants judged would be recalled than for those they judged would not be, which established that students had above-chance accuracy at predicting which items would be recalled. Seven years later, Groninger (1976) reported that people could accurately predict their recognition of individual words, and subsequent research in the next decade or so continued to demonstrate that people—and most commonly, college students—could accurately predict their test performance (e.g., King, Zechmeister, & Shaughnessy, 1980; Lovelace, 1984).

The bulk of this early wave of research, however, did not use measures of accuracy that indicated the *degree* to which the JOLs were accurate. In 1984, Nelson proposed that a gamma correlation be used to measure the relative accuracy of FOK judgments, and this correlation has become the standard for measuring the relative accuracy for all metacognitive judgments. Recall that relative accuracy pertains to the degree to which a person's judgments predict performance of one item relative to another. A correlation of zero indicates that relative accuracy is at a chance level; with this level of relative accuracy, an individual might as well just flip a coin to decide whether an item will be recalled or not. Increasingly positive correlations from 0 to +1.0 reflect better and better levels of relative accuracy. Ideally, the relative accuracy of JOLs would be near perfect (a correlation near +1.0), which would demonstrate that people are excellent at judging what they have learned (versus have not learned) during study.

So, exactly how accurate are people's JOLs? In the study by Leonesio and Nelson (1990) described above, the accuracy of the various judgments was also reported, and they found that the mean correlation between people's JOLs and criterion-recall performance was about +.30, which was reliably greater than zero. Other research reporting measures of relative accuracy in the mid-to-late eighties also demonstrated the same moderate levels of accuracy (e.g., Begg, Duft, Lalonde, Melnick, & Sanvito, 1989; Vesonder & Voss, 1985). The message from these experiments was clear both in its optimism and in its pessimism: People can accurately predict memory performance for simple materials, such as paired associates, but they have plenty of room for improvement.

Even though JOL accuracy does often tend to be rather poor, two factors have been discovered that influence it. The first factor discussed below—increasing the number of study-test trials—actually has different effects on calibration and relative accuracy, whereas the second factor—the timing of the JOLs—dramatically improves both.

Number of Study-Test Trials and the Underconfidence-With-Practice Effect

Everyone knows that the more often you study the better you will remember what you are studying. Although cognitive psychologists have discovered some intriguing exceptions to this apparent rule of memory, research on JOLs has focused on contexts in which extra study typically does improve memory. Of central relevance is whether improving memory also improves people's memory monitoring.

First, consider relative accuracy. Koriat (1997) examined the influence of multiple study-test trials on accuracy, where people studied items and made JOLs and then were tested on those items. This study-JOL-test procedure was repeated with the same items. As expected, test performance increased across trials, and so did relative JOL accuracy, with the accuracy being greater on the second trial than on the first trial. The cause of this improvement is straightforward. In predicting their performance after the first study trial, participants apparently based their JOLs on the outcomes of retrieval attempts on the preceding test trial, which are a potent predictor of performance on the next trial (e.g., Finn & Metcalfe, 2007; Vesonder & Voss, 1985).

Surprisingly, even though test experience boosts relative accuracy across trials, such experience has a different effect on calibration. In particular, Koriat, Sheffer, and Ma'ayan (2002) analyzed 11 experiments in which participants made JOLs during multiple study-test trials of the same items. As in Koriat (1997), relative JOL accuracy increased across trials. Moreover, the magnitude of JOLs also increased across trials, so JOLs did show sensitivity to learning. Most intriguing, however, was that the magnitude of JOLs underestimated the rate of learning across trials, which is illustrated in Figure 5.1. On the first trial (Presentation 1), people showed slight overconfidence, with the JOLs being somewhat higher than recall performance. On subsequent trials, people showed underconfidence in their JOLs, which Koriat et al. (2002) dubbed the *underconfidence-with-practice* (UWP) effect. The UWP effect is robust under numerous conditions, including ones in which participants are given feedback concerning the correctness of their answers during the test.

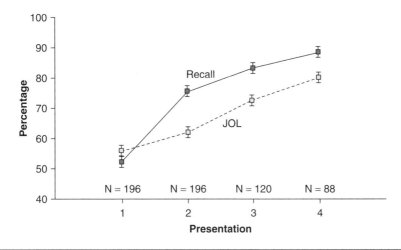

Figure 5.1   The underconfidence-with-practice (UWP) effect. Percentage of correct recall (solid line) and predicted recall (JOL, dotted line) plotted as a function of the number of study presentations. Values were computed by collapsing outcomes from 11 different experiments.

SOURCE: Koriat, A., Sheffer, L., and Ma'ayan, H. (2002). Comparing objective and subjective learning curves: Judgments of learning exhibit increased underconfidence with practice. *Journal of Experimental Psychology: General, 131,* 147–162.

BOX 5.1
Global Judgments: Predicting How Much You'll Remember

Many investigations about judgments of learning—as well as other metacognitive judgments—involve having people make item-by-item ratings, whether they involve rating memory for individual words, paired associates, or even text materials. In some real-world situations, however, individuals are more concerned with performance across all items and less so with performance on any particular one. When students prepare for final exams, they often are trying to achieve a certain grade (e.g., B or better). In this circumstance, students may make what has been referred to as a *global* (or aggregate) judgment, which involves predicting the percentage of items that they will answer correctly on an upcoming exam. Global judgments are receiving growing attention in the field, and some investigators now routinely examine the accuracy of item-by-item JOLs as well as global judgments.

(Continued)

(Continued)

Of course, because each participant typically makes only one global judgment, the relative accuracy of these judgments cannot be estimated. Instead, calibration here is computed by subtracting the global judgment (percentage predicted) from the actual performance (percentage correct). Recall that item-by-item JOLs often show overconfidence during a single trial. In contrast, Mazzoni and Nelson (1995) found that students' global judgment showed underconfidence after a single trial, perhaps because after studying a list of items, people realize that they will not remember many items from a long list. Moreover, Koriat et al. (2002) investigated whether global judgments would demonstrate the UWP effect. After studying the 60 critical items of the list, participants made a global judgment about how many of the 60 they would correctly recall. They made both JOLs and global judgments across four study-test trials of the same list. Not only did JOLs show the UWP effect as described earlier, the global judgments showed even more underconfidence across trials.

Of course, the global judgments in these experiments involved methods that students may not have experienced a great deal. In contrast, Hacker, Bol, Horgan, and Rakow (2000) investigated how accurate college students were at making global judgments for predicting performance on actual classroom tests. They were particularly interested in whether the students would become more accurate at making these global judgments across the semester. Students who performed the best in class did show improved predictive accuracy as they gained more experience taking the classroom exams. Unfortunately, the poorest performing students showed gross overconfidence in their predictions throughout the semester, which led Hacker et al. (2000) to conclude that "to help low-performing students become better self-regulators of their test preparation behaviors, their [global judgments of learning] may need as much attention as their knowledge deficits" (p. 169). We'll further discuss this research, which is directly relevant to student scholarship, in Chapter 9, Education.

In summary, the bulk of the evidence indicates that self-feedback from intervening test trials does benefit the relative accuracy of JOLs. Thus, retrieval practice can be an important basis of people's JOLs, which is a theme that we return to in discussing the timing of JOLs below. Even so, retrieval practice does not lead to perfectly sensitive JOLs, as demonstrated by the counterintuitive UWP effect. Although these effects have been replicated (Meeter & Nelson, 2003), the cause of this intriguing bias in JOLs is still being scrutinized. One leading hypothesis was offered by Finn and Metcalfe (2007), who speculated that people base their JOLs on the second trial on their memory for recall performance from the first trial. For instance, on the second trial, people will make very high JOLs for items that were correctly recalled on the first trial. In contrast, for items that were *not* correctly recalled on Trial 1, people presumably will make very low JOLs. A difficulty arises here because when people make low JOLs for the incorrectly recalled items, they do not entirely take into account that some of these items were learned on the second trial, which leads to underconfidence.

Furthermore, when Finn and Metcalfe (2008) manipulated how well people did on particular items on the first test, while equating performance on Trial 2, the second trial JOLs followed performance on the first, not the second trial. Differences in first trial test performance occurred because some items were repeated only once but some were repeated 5 times. Those items that received 5 repetitions on the first trial (and showed high levels on recall) received only 1 repetition on the second trial. Conversely items that had only 1 repeat in the first trial (and hence were poorly recalled) got 5 repetitions on the second trial. So, by the time people were making their JOLs on the second trial, memory had been equated. But people still relied on how they had performed on the particular items on the first trial test—that is, giving the poorly recalled items from the first trial low JOLs and the well recalled items from the first trial high JOLs. Although Finn and Metcalfe's (2007) explanation for the UWP effect is intuitively plausible and fits well with current evidence, research on this effect is in its infancy and will likely stimulate much debate on what is responsible for this metacognitive illusion. Certainly, discovering the causes of the UWP effect provides an important challenge for the field.

Timing of the Judgments and the Delayed-JOL Effect

As alluded to in the vignette that began this chapter, JOL accuracy is important with respect to how effectively individuals can allocate study time during relearning. Accordingly, a goal of research in this area has been to discover techniques to improve judgment accuracy. In 1991, Nelson and Dunlosky reported a relatively simple and intuitive technique that substantially improved JOL accuracy. They had observed that the majority of experiments investigating JOLs had done so by having participants make them immediately after study. These *immediate* JOLs were largely the basis of all conclusions described in the sections above. Nelson and Dunlosky compared them to *delayed* JOLs, which are illustrated in Figure 5.2. To estimate the relative accuracy of these judgments, college students studied 60 paired-associate items (e.g., dog-spoon). For half of these, they made immediate JOLs. For the other half, several minutes elapsed after an item had been studied before the delayed JOL was made, and this interval was filled with the study of other items. All judgments were prompted with only the stimulus of an item. So if "dog-spoon" had been studied, the prompt would be: What is the likelihood that you will remember the response for "dog-?" After all items had been studied and judged, a test of paired-associate recall was administered in which every stimulus was presented again (e.g., dog-?), and the participants were asked to provide the corresponding response.

As in previous research, the relative accuracy of immediate JOLs was low-to-moderate (mean across individual participant's correlations = +.38). In contrast, just a short delay between study and JOLs boosted their accuracy to +.90 (Nelson & Dunlosky, 1991). This *delayed-JOL* effect has been replicated many times with college students. Perhaps even more impressive, the delayed-JOL effect also occurs under diverse conditions and across many

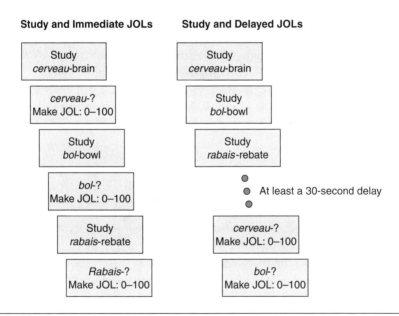

| Figure 5.2 | Illustration of immediate judgments of learning (JOLs) and delayed judgments of learning. For the latter, typically a 30-second delay (or more) occurs between the study and judgment for each item. In the present figure, the time between studying items and making delayed JOLs would be filled with studying other items (not shown). For both immediate and delayed JOLs, a test would occur (usually paired-associate recall, e.g., *bol-?*) after all items had been studied and judged. |

populations, such as for children and older adults (Connor et al., 1997; Schneider, 1998); for adults with traumatic brain injury (Kennedy, Carney, & Peters, 2003); and even for adults who are intoxicated (see Box 5.2 to learn more about judgments under the influence). To gain personal experience in making delayed JOLs, try out the "Minds-On Activity" on the delayed-JOL effect at the end of this chapter.

BOX 5.2
Do Drugs Impair Your Judgment Accuracy?

Many common intoxicants have dramatic and sought-after effects on consciousness. In moderation, alcohol produces a feeling of warmth and can decrease inhibitions and may also impair one's judgment. Nitrous oxide, which is often administered to minimize pain and memory for otherwise traumatic visits to the dentist, can produce a dreamlike state as well as mild auditory and visual hallucinations. Nitrous oxide also tends to dissociate one's perceptions from one's sensations. Benzodiazepines, such as lorazepam, are commonly used to reduce anxiety and insomnia. In contrast, caffeine offers a qualitatively different set of psychological effects, including a sense of heightened awareness and mental alertness. Each of these substances also influences cognitive performance. Alcohol, nitrous oxide, and benzodiazepines can have substantial deleterious effects on people's learning, whereas caffeine sometimes has a positive influence.

Although these substances apparently influence the phenomenology of ongoing experience, what will happen to JOLs for people under the influence? Given that alcohol, nitrous oxide, and benzodiazepine presumably dull the senses, will they also dull people's ability to monitor their learning. Will caffeine have the opposite effect? Using standard methods for collecting JOLs, researchers have answered these questions by comparing the accuracy of JOLs for people who were under a drug's influence versus JOLs for people who were sober—that is, they had taken some form of placebo. Perhaps surprisingly, not one of these drugs—alcohol, nitrous oxide, benzodiazepine, or caffeine—influenced the accuracy of people's JOLs, even though as expected they influenced memory performance (Dunlosky et al., 1998; Izaute & Bacon, 2005; Kelemen & Creeley, 2001; Nelson et al., 1998). This lack of effect on JOLs indicates that even when one's cognition is altered, one's metacognition can remain good.

Although the delayed-JOL effect is robust, it has some important boundary conditions where it does not occur that provide insights into why it occurs. Before we discuss one of these conditions, first take a moment to come up with some intuitive answers to the following: What might cause the delayed-JOL effect? Or rather, what are individuals doing when they make delayed JOLs? To answer these questions, it may help if you look again at the procedure for collecting delayed JOLs in Figure 5.2. One answer is simply that when participants are shown the prompt for the JOL (which is the stimulus of a pair), they attempt to retrieve the correct response and use the outcome from that retrieval attempt as a basis for the delayed JOL. When they retrieve a response, participants presumably make a high JOL, and when they don't retrieve one, they make a low JOL. The idea is that people's knowledge about memory (one aspect of metamemory) includes, "If I get it now, I'll get it later" and is used in making a delayed JOL.

Now let's see how this rudimentary explanation for the delayed-JOL effect can account for one failure to find it. Dunlosky and Nelson (1992) manipulated the kind of prompt for JOLs. As in their original work, everyone studied paired associates and made both immediate and delayed JOLs. Some participants were prompted to make JOLs with the stimulus alone. For a stimulus-alone JOL, the prompt for "cat-jury" would be: What's the likelihood that you will remember the word paired with "cat-?" when you are tested later? Other participants were prompted with both the stimulus and response of a pair. For example, the prompt for the pair "dog-spoon" would be: What's the likelihood that you will remember "dog-spoon" when you are tested later? As shown in Figure 5.3, the delayed-JOL effect was substantial for stimulus-alone JOLs, but it was not at all evident for stimulus-response JOLs. In this case, presenting the stimulus and response for the prompt undermines students' ability to attempt retrieval of the response, and hence the delayed-JOL effect vanishes.

What causes the delayed-JOL effect? Both the evidence above and intuition indicate that delayed attempts at retrieving the sought-after response are vital to the delayed-JOL effect. In fact, this *monitoring-retrieval assumption* underlies many of the hypotheses for the delayed-JOL effect. For instance, the monitoring-dual-memories hypothesis and the self-fulfilling-prophecy hypothesis both assume the delayed-JOL effect arises from retrieval attempts that occur prior to making the JOL. The difference between the hypotheses concerns *why* such retrieval attempts boost the accuracy of delayed JOLs. This critical question has essentially turned into a debate that is a recurrent theme of our discussion below: Do delayed JOLs increase relative accuracy by changing the underlying memory of items or by actually improving the *judgment process* itself that allows people to discriminate between items that are well-learned versus less well-learned? We briefly describe each hypothesis first, and then consider their status after a decade of empirical scrutiny.

Nelson and Dunlosky (1991) proposed the *monitoring-dual-memories* (MDM) hypothesis, which was inspired by the modal model of memory

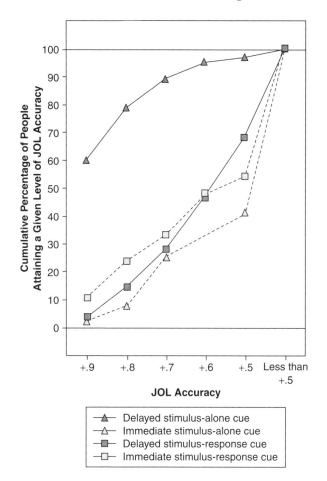

Figure 5.3   Relative accuracy for four kinds of judgments of learning illustrating the superior accuracy (for the majority of participants) of delayed JOLs cued by the stimulus alone.

SOURCE: Dunlosky, J., and Nelson, T. O. (1992). Importance of the kind of cue for judgments of learning (JOL) and the delayed-JOL effect. *Memory and Cognition*, 20, 373–380.

(Atkinson & Shiffrin, 1968). In making a JOL, an individual monitors information retrieved about the to-be-judged item stored in both short-term memory and long-term memory. For immediate JOLs, the to-be-judged item still resides in short-term memory, which interferes with an individual's ability to monitor whether the item is stored in long-term memory. By the time an individual makes a delayed JOL, the to-be-judged item no longer resides in short-term memory, so individuals will be able to monitor the degree to which the item is accessible from long-term memory. Because information about the item that is accessible from long-term memory will be a major basis of criterion test performance, the relative accuracy of delayed JOLs is high.

In contrast to the MDM hypothesis, Spellman and Bjork (1992) argued that the delayed-JOL effect was primarily a memory phenomenon. Their *self-fulfilling-prophecy* (SFP) hypothesis was based on the effects of retrieval practice on memory. A successful retrieval of a response increases the likelihood that it will later be successfully retrieved. As important, such an effect of retrieval practice would be minimal immediately after study (when all responses can be easily retrieved), but when a delay occurs after study, retrieval practice will have a much greater influence on long-term memory. Thus, assuming that people attempt to retrieve responses when making JOLs, successful retrieval will be a better predictor and greater cause of final recall performance for delayed JOLs than for immediate JOLs. The idea here is that the act of making a delayed JOL boosts the memory strength for retrieved items (and also leads to high JOLs) and hence artificially ensures good accuracy. Thus, the excellent accuracy of delayed JOLs is a self-fulfilling prophecy.

Empirical Evidence Relevant to Evaluating the MDM and SFP Hypotheses

Both of these hypotheses account for the delayed-JOL effect as well as for its absence when the prompt for JOLs is both the stimulus and response of each pair. The MDM hypothesis implies that people's monitoring improves across the delay because information in short-term memory does not interfere with monitoring what has been stored in long-term memory. In contrast, the SFP hypothesis claims that the delayed-JOL effect is primarily a memory phenomenon, and hence improved judgment processes contribute little, if any, to the effect (Kimball & Metcalfe, 2003). How have these hypotheses fared in the light of new evidence?

Unfortunately, a definitive evaluation of these two competing hypotheses has not yet been conducted, although the extant evidence in the field suggests that neither will provide a complete explanation of the delayed-JOL effect. Relevant to the SFP hypothesis, Kimball and Metcalfe (2003) showed that an extra study trial after JOLs are made can reduce JOL accuracy. Thus, consistent with the SFP hypothesis, accuracy can be influenced by changes in memory (e.g., from extra study or from making a JOL), but such memory-based influences will likely not account for the entire delayed-JOL effect (see Sikström & Jönsson, 2005, for relevant evidence and for a formal model of the delayed-JOL effect).

Evidence from Kelemen and Weaver (1997) challenges the MDM hypothesis. The prediction was based on how quickly an item becomes inaccessible from short-term memory. In particular, immediately after studying an item, the likelihood of successfully recalling it is near perfect. In the next 20 or so seconds after studying an item, the likelihood of successfully recalling it gradually decreases, which reflects losses in accessibility of the item from short-term memory across the brief time span. According to the MDM hypothesis, immediate JOLs are relatively inaccurate because input from short-term memory interferes with monitoring the contents of long-term memory. Therefore, as the interference from short-term memory declines, the accuracy of JOLs should increase.

To evaluate this prediction, Kelemen and Weaver (1997) manipulated the lag between study and stimulus-alone JOLs. As the lag moved from zero to a maximum of several minutes, progressively less interference should arise from short-term memory. They used the following lags: no delay (maximal interference as in immediate JOLs), 5-second delay, 15-second delay, 30-second delay, and a temporal delay of several minutes. All lags were filled with distracter tasks or the study of other items. As shown in Figure 5.4, JOL accuracy did not consistently increase with increasing lags as predicted by the MDM hypothesis. For instance, accuracy was no better after 30 seconds than after 5 seconds, and perhaps most telling, delaying JOLs by 30 seconds (when interference from short-term memory would be minimal) did not produce the full delayed-JOL effect. Based on this evidence, Kelemen and Weaver rejected the MDM hypothesis as an adequate explanation for the entire delayed-JOL effect. Given that short delays consistently improved accuracy (e.g., a 5-second lag versus immediate JOL), however, they also concluded that "clearly, [short-term memory] distraction moderately increases JOL accuracy" (p. 1404).

Although a number of investigations have been designed to evaluate specific hypotheses for the delayed-JOL effect, an obvious conclusion to date is that not one hypothesis has gained unequivocal support. Note, however, that the MDM and SFP hypotheses are not mutually exclusive, so a complete explanation of the effect may require inclusion of both short-term interference effects and the reactive effects of making JOLs on memory. Regardless of its ultimate explanation, everyone agrees that the substantial accuracy shown by delayed JOLs holds promise for applications involved in improving student learning. We explore this possibility further in the section concerning the function of JOLs later in this chapter.

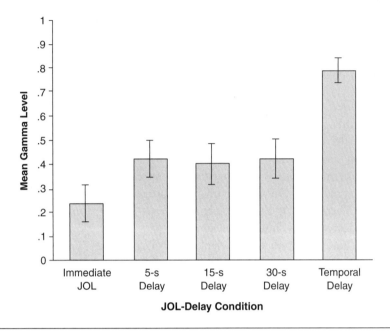

Figure 5.4   Relative accuracy of JOLs with increasing lags between study and judgments of learning.

SOURCE: Kelemen, W. L., and Weaver, C. A. (1997). Enhanced metamemory at delays: Why do judgments of learning improve over time? *Journal of Experimental Psychology: Learning, Memory, and Cognition, 23,* 1394–1409.

Theories About Judgments of Learning

The hypotheses described above were developed to account for the accuracy of JOLs and have largely been applied to understanding the delayed-JOL effect. Ironically, their focus on the delayed-JOL effect may undermine their power at accounting for the entire range of data concerning judgment accuracy. The difficulty lies in the monitoring-retrieval assumption, which is that people base stimulus-alone JOLs on the outcomes of retrieval attempts. This assumption has been questioned recently by Son and Metcalfe (2005), who have shown that people often produce very fast JOLs when they predict that they will not recall a response. These JOLs are made too quickly to be due to a retrieval attempt and are likely attributable to a failure to recognize the JOL prompt (see also Benjamin, 2005). But even assuming that people primarily rely on a retrieval attempt when making delayed JOLs, retrieval alone does not capture the multitude of ways that people can—and do—make JOLs.

Accordingly, in the next sections, we describe some hypotheses that pertain to how JOLs are made (for discussion of others not described here, see McGuire & Maki, 2001). Our review of these hypotheses will not only capitalize on some of the findings already described above but will introduce others that have been used in evaluating these hypotheses.

Ease-of-Processing Hypothesis

Begg et al. (1989) proposed that JOLs are based on the ease of processing an item immediately prior to making the judgment. A core idea is that this basis for JOLs is heuristic—a rule that may at certain times be valid whereas at other times it will be in error. For instance, in learning French-English vocabulary terms, you may attempt to come up with mnemonics to link the two words of each translation equivalent; for "*singe*-monkey," you may quickly imagine a monkey singing, whereas for "*cerveau*-brain," you may struggle to come up with an image to relate the two. Given that the first pair was easier to process at study than the latter pair, according to the *ease-of-processing* hypothesis, your JOL should be higher for "*singe*-monkey" than for "*cerveau*-brain." In this case, using ease of processing may lead to relatively accurate JOLs. But even if it does, processing ease can be misleading at times, because sometimes the items that are easy to process are the most difficult to remember. Begg et al. capitalized on this counterintuitive nature of processing ease by having participants study some words that are highly common (e.g., paper) and others that are rare (e.g., bucolic). The rationale was that processing would be easier for common words than for rare words, and as expected, JOLs were greater for common words. Criterion performance on a recognition test, however, was actually *better* for rare than for common words—the opposite pattern than was predicted for the JOLs. In this case, ease of processing apparently misled people's JOLs.

In their original experiments, Begg et al. (1989) did not directly measure the ease of processing, so perhaps some unknown third variable was responsible for its effect. Thus, Hertzog, Dunlosky, Robinson, and Kidder (2003) further evaluated this hypothesis by directly measuring processing ease. To do so, they instructed participants to study paired associates using interactive imagery. For instance, for the item "blossom-doctor," a participant might develop an image of a doctor eating a flower blossom. While studying, participants were also asked to press a computer key as soon as they had generated an image for an item. The latency between the presentation of an item for study and the participant's key-press was used to measure the ease of processing of that item. Shorter latencies reflected easier processing. Across three experiments, JOLs were negatively related to the latency of imagery generation: People predicted that they would more likely remember the pairs when they quickly generated images. Thus, the ease of processing at study apparently provides a potent cue for people's JOLs.

Retrieval-Fluency Hypothesis

The retrieval-fluency hypothesis also assumes individuals' JOLs are heuristic in nature. In this case, fluent retrieval of a response is a harbinger of good memory for an item. Benjamin and Bjork (1996) described several aspects of retrieval fluency. For instance, retrieval is more fluent (a) when sought-after information is retrieved more quickly as compared to when it is retrieved more slowly, and (b) when more information is retrieved than when less information is retrieved. This hypothesis is akin to Koriat's (1993) accessibility hypothesis for FOK judgments (see also Morris, 1990), because both assume that quick access to more information about a sought-after response will result in greater confidence in memory for it.

The effect of retrieval fluency on JOLs was demonstrated by Benjamin, Bjork, and Schwartz (1998). They adapted a method originally used by Gardiner, Craik, and Bleasdale (1973) to investigate the relationship between semantic and episodic memory. College students answered relatively easy trivia questions (e.g., "What gem is the color red?"), which tested their semantic memory for the correct responses. After answering each question, they predicted the likelihood that they would later freely recall the response in about 20 minutes. Put differently, they made JOLs for freely recalling the responses, which tested their episodic memory for those responses. The critical outcomes are presented in Figure 5.5. Consistent with the retrieval-fluency hypothesis, JOLs were highest for the most quickly retrieved answers. In contrast, free recall was actually greater for answers that had originally been retrieved more slowly than more quickly. Why did this seemingly counterintuitive result occur? Presumably, people may have thought they would be given the cues on the final test, and if the cues had been supplied, the JOLs would have been very accurate. But without the cues, those items recalled quickly may have been given little attention, and hence poor uncued (free) recall resulted. Thus, in this situation, using a fluency heuristic as a basis for JOLs actually led to poor relative accuracy. In fact, the correlation between JOLs and free recall was no different than chance.

A Cue-Utilization Approach for JOLs

The aforementioned hypotheses can each explain a subset of effects pertaining to JOLs, yet none of them can account for the entire host of effects

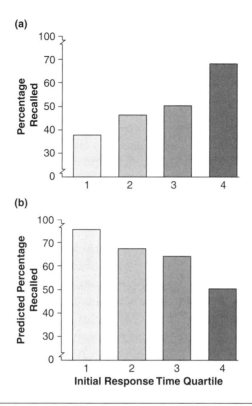

(a)

(b)

Initial Response Time Quartile

Figure 5.5   Free recall (percentage recalled) and judgment-of-learning magnitude (predicted percentage recall) as a function of the latency of cued recall. Latency (response time quartiles) is presented from fastest (1) to slowest (4) response times.

SOURCE: Benjamin, A. S., Bjork, R. A., and Schwartz, B. L. (1998). The mismeasure of memory: When retrieval fluency is misleading as a metamnemonic index. *Journal of Experimental Psychology: General, 127,* 55–68.

already discussed. For instance, the ease-of-processing hypothesis cannot readily explain the underconfidence-with-practice (UWP) effect. Of course, the hypotheses described above were not intended as general accounts of JOLs, so it is unreasonable to expect them to account for effects that extend beyond their particular domain of interest. Nevertheless, some common themes are evident, and one in particular was foundational to Koriat's (1997) cue-utilization approach for JOLs, which was the first general account of JOLs. This theme has already been introduced—both for JOLs and for FOK judgments. Namely, metacognitive judgments are assumed to be inferential in nature, being based on heuristics and rules about the likelihood of remembering items. According to the cue-utilization approach for JOLs, people use a variety of cues—for example, item relatedness, number of study trials, and so on—to infer whether an item will be remembered. In this way, high levels of JOL accuracy are not ensured but instead accuracy results from the correlation between the cues used to make JOLs and criterion test performance.

Asher Koriat Developed influential theories of monitoring and control of both encoding and retrieval

Any general account of JOLs should be able to explain the effect of different variables on JOLs. Let's briefly consider some of these effects here. First, item relatedness has a substantial influence on the magnitude of JOLs—in fact, the influence was just as large as it was on criterion test performance (Dunlosky & Matvey, 2001). In this case, JOLs are much greater for related pairs (salt-pepper) than for unrelated pairs (dog-chair). In contrast, whereas the number of study trials does influence JOLs, the effects of study trials are smaller on JOLs than on criterion test performance—which results in the UWP effect. Put differently, the effects of study trials on test performance are discounted by the JOLs. Finally, various factors also influence the relative accuracy of JOLs, such as intervening test trials and delaying JOLs, which should also be explained by any general account of JOLs.

To account for these and other effects, Koriat (1997) proposed a taxonomy of cues and how each kind of cue influenced JOLs. These cues were intrinsic cues, extrinsic cues, and mnemonic cues. *Intrinsic* cues refer to characteristics of the items that "are perceived to disclose the item's a priori ease or difficulty of learning" (p. 350). A prime example of an intrinsic cue is item relatedness. *Extrinsic* cues are those involving encoding operations or other conditions of learning not intrinsic to the items. A prime example here is using interactive imagery to study paired associates. Finally, *mnemonic* cues are those that are internal indicators based on subjective experience that suggest an item will be remembered. These include having the subjective experience of easily processing an item or fluently retrieving a response on a test. According to this cue-utilization approach, people's JOLs are differentially sensitive to the cues. For instance, Koriat (1997) proposed that JOLs will be less sensitive to the effects of extrinsic cues than to the effects of intrinsic cues. That is, extrinsic cues and intrinsic cues often have a substantial influence on memory performance, whereas extrinsic cues will have little influence on JOLs but intrinsic cues will substantially influence them. Evidence from the JOL literature is largely consistent with this prediction. Item relatedness, which is an intrinsic cue, has a major impact on JOL magnitudes and recall performance. In contrast, various encoding conditions (e.g., using imagery or levels-of-processing manipulation) and other conditions of learning (e.g., multiple study trials) have relatively small, if any, effects on JOL magnitudes. In fact, the UWP effect is yet another example of people's JOLs discounting the effects of an extrinsic cue.

Mystery BOX 5.3
Why Is Metacomprehension Accuracy So Low?

How good do you think you are at assessing your understanding—and memory—for text materials? When asked such a question, many believe that they would be excellent at judging how well they've comprehended what they've read. But is this self-assessment a delusion? Are we good at judging our comprehension? These intriguing questions cannot be adequately addressed by the majority of research described in this chapter, which pertains to students' JOLs for learning relatively simple materials—mainly paired associates. Although paired-associate research has fostered a better understanding of how people monitor learning, focusing only on these simple materials misrepresents the many challenges faced in school and other natural contexts that involve learning and comprehending difficult text materials. In the early 1980s, a new area of research arose to fill this gap, when Glenberg, Wilkinson, and Epstein (1982) and Maki and Berry (1984) began investigating how students assess their learning of text materials, an area that has been dubbed *metacomprehension*. Investigations of metacomprehension are conducted in a manner nearly identical to those concerning other kinds of metacognitive judgment. Experimental participants study multiple texts about various topics. After studying a given text, they make a metacomprehension judgment. This judgment typically involves predicting the level of performance on a test covering the content of the text. Of course, the participants are eventually tested, so that a measure of relative accuracy can be computed. In this case, relative accuracy is measured by the correlation between each participant's metacomprehension judgments and test performance.

So, how accurate are people's metacomprehension judgments? Since the genesis of metacomprehension research, people's ability to accurately judge

(Continued)

(Continued)

their memory and comprehension of text materials has been closely scrutinized (for reviews, see Lin & Zabrucky, 1998; Maki & McGuire, 2002). Such scrutiny has run head first into a seemingly impenetrable mystery that appears to defy the intuition that we can accurately judge when we comprehend what we're reading. In particular, the accuracy of people's metacomprehension judgments is usually poor, with correlations between the judgments and test performance usually being below +.40 and often closer to zero. Even experts in an area—for example, graduate students of physics reading texts on physics—show low levels of metacomprehension accuracy (Glenberg & Epstein, 1987). Is there anything that can be done to improve it?

Maki (1998) sought to improve accuracy by delaying people's metacomprehension judgments, a simple technique that greatly enhances the accuracy of JOLs for paired associates. In contrast to delayed JOLs, delaying the metacomprehension judgments did not improve their accuracy. A handful of techniques have been discovered, such as rereading and summarizing, that can markedly improve metacomprehension accuracy (for a review, see Dunlosky & Lipko, 2007). Why these techniques work is currently unknown, and even more germane, why metacomprehension accuracy is often so poor also remains an important mystery—one that when solved promises to foster student learning and comprehension of text.

In providing a unified framework for JOLs, the cue-utilization approach will help to organize a growing body of research. In doing so, it is inevitable that effects will be discovered that suggest deficits in the account. For instance, some extrinsic cues have just as large an effect on JOLs as they do on test performance (Begg, Vinski, Frankovich, & Holgate, 1991; Dunlosky & Matvey, 2001), which indicates that extrinsic cues are not always discounted by JOLs. At this time, however, it is too early to know whether these outcomes are only minor exceptions to Koriat's cue-utilization approach or foreshadow the need for a new approach to understanding how people judge their learning.

Function of Judgments of Learning

Functional Role of Judgments of Learning

An essential function of monitoring is to regulate behavior. Each kind of monitoring plays a particularly important role in controlling a specific aspect of learning or retrieval. As discussed in the previous chapter, FOK judgments serve in the control of retrieval, such as when you spend a long time searching for a person's name while you're in a TOT state. When people have a strong feeling of knowing, they often will use extra time searching for the sought-after response. The function of JOLs is in the control of learning in that people apparently use the output from monitoring study to guide which items to study and how long they will study them. An early investigation of this function of monitoring was conducted by Masur, McIntyre, and Flavell (1973), who reported that college students allocate more study time to items that they did not recall on a previous trial than to those that they did recall (for a historical review of this literature, see Son & Kornell, 2008). Nelson and Leonesio (1988) more directly investigated the potential influence of monitoring on the control of study by examining the relationship between ease-of-learning judgments and subsequent self-paced study time. EOL judgments were negatively correlated with self-paced study time, indicating that students spend more time studying items judged as difficult-to-learn than for those judged as easier-to-learn. In a review of the literature, Son and Metcalfe (2000) reported that the majority of outcomes correspond to this pattern, in which individuals devote more study time to more difficult than to less difficult items. That is, just as for our hypothetical participant discussed in Chapter 3, Methods and Analyses (see Table 3.3), mean correlations between JOLs and study time were often negative.

We will return to this negative JOL-study time relationship later when discussing theories of self-regulated learning. For now, however, let's consider the importance of monitoring accuracy to the control of study. In principle, given that metacognitive monitoring is used to control learning, the relative accuracy of monitoring is essential for effective self-paced study. In fact, the control function of JOLs is one of the most important reasons for discovering techniques to improve their accuracy because the more accurately individuals can make JOLs the more effectively they may be able to control their learning. To understand why this is the case, again consider the vignette that opened this chapter. David was relatively inaccurate at making his JOLs: Some vocabulary terms that he judged as well-learned had not been learned well at all, and some terms that he judged as not well-learned he had already learned. Accordingly, when deciding which terms to restudy—a kind of control process—he may often spend too much time studying well-learned items, and even worse, he may spend too little time studying what he hasn't learned yet. Instead of using immediate JOLs to assess his learning, imagine that David had used delayed JOLs, which are highly accurate. In this case, he could be much more effective at learning the vocabulary, because he could focus all his time on just those terms that he really needed to learn.

This hypothetical example is relatively intuitive, because it makes sense that being able to judge what you'll remember (and what you'll forget) will help you use study time more effectively. As important, this intuition coincides with recent experimental evidence. For instance, Thiede (1999) had college students study paired associates during multiple study-test trials: Each pair was studied and then a test of recall for each pair occurred; then this same set of pairs was studied and tested again. These study-test trials of the same pairs were repeated multiple times. During each study trial, the students were allowed to study a given pair as long as they wanted. When they finished studying an item, they merely pressed a key and proceeded to the next one. Moreover, students made JOLs during each trial. This kind of multi-trial experiment involving self-paced study yields a rich set of data, which many researchers have capitalized on to examine the control of study. In the present case, we're interested in whether JOL accuracy is related to learning. To address this issue, Thiede (1999) computed relative JOL accuracy by correlating each student's JOLs with recall performance, separately for each of the study trials. Those individuals with the highest levels of accuracy were the best overall learners, suggesting better JOL accuracy can support more effective self-paced learning.

This introduction to the final section on JOLs is intended to highlight two general conclusions: (a) that a function of JOLs—or memory monitoring during study—is to guide study, and (b) that this function is more effectively served when higher levels of JOL accuracy are achieved. In the next section, we further explore the function of JOLs by reviewing theory of self-regulated study, which has sought to explain exactly how we use memory monitoring in pacing study.

Theory of Self-Regulated Study

Students often set goals when attempting to learn new materials. You may decide that your Spanish class is not too important and hence set a goal to merely pass the class. You may believe that computer science is critical for obtaining a job after graduation, so you decide to try to master all the materials and concepts in the class. Such goals, which were dubbed the *norm of study* by Le Ny, Denhière, and Le Taillanter (1972), would be expected to have an obvious influence on how much time you study. In the example above, your norm of study is much higher for the computer science class than for the Spanish class, and all else being equal, you'd most likely spend much more time studying computer science. Perhaps not surprisingly, current evidence is largely consistent with the hypothesis that one's norm of study influences study time. For instance, in the study conducted by Nelson and Leonesio (1988) mentioned earlier, students were given one of two instructions prior to study. The *accuracy-emphasized* group was instructed to continue studying until they were absolutely sure they would correctly recall all the items, whereas the *speed-emphasized* group was instructed to spend just as much time as was needed to learn each item. The accuracy instructions would be expected to lead to a much higher norm of study, and in fact, the accuracy-emphasized group studied substantially longer than did the speed-emphasized group.

Although the norm of study is a central component to most theories of self-regulated study, an individual's goals alone cannot readily account for why people often spend more time studying items that they perceive to be difficult-to-learn than those they perceive to be easy-to-learn. More complex hypotheses will be needed to understand fully how students differentially allocate study time across materials.

The Discrepancy-Reduction Model

According to the discrepancy-reduction hypothesis, people's study time is in part based on the interplay between on-line monitoring of learning *and* their norm of study. More specifically, an individual monitors his current learning of an item and compares it to the norm of study. The individual continues to study until the perceived degree of learning meets or exceeds the norm of study. The idea is simply that one attempts to completely *reduce* the discrepancy between the perceived current degree of learning and the norm of study (Dunlosky & Thiede, 1998). This model naturally accounts for the modal outcome in which people spend more time studying difficult items, because more time will usually be required to reduce the discrepancy for more difficult items than for easier ones.

Nevertheless, Thiede and Dunlosky (1999) and Son and Metcalfe (2000) presented evidence that students are more sophisticated in allocating study time than is offered by the mechanistic account embodied by discrepancy reduction. Consider a situation in which students wait until the night before an exam to begin studying, which is unfortunately a commonly used strategy (see Taraban, Maki, & Rynearson, 1999). In this case, not enough time is left to master all the materials, so the most difficult material may not even be considered. That is, most of the limited time may be used to study the easiest material because students may realize that only this material could be learned before the exam. As a result, these students would spend more time studying the easier items than the most difficult ones, which is exactly counter to predictions from the discrepancy-reduction model. Both research teams independently evaluated this possibility, and both discovered circumstances in which students choose to spend more time studying easier materials over the more difficult ones. For instance, Thiede and Dunlosky (1999) had students select items for restudy when they had a very limited time to restudy the items, which is analogous to waiting until the night before to begin studying for an exam. Students who were given unlimited study time chose the more difficult items for restudy, whereas students who were pressured chose the easier items for restudy.

This *shift-to-easier-materials* (STEM) effect has been demonstrated across different materials and has been attributed to students developing a plan that involves trying to use restudy time in an efficient manner (Dunlosky & Thiede, 2004). Thus, the STEM effect cannot be explained by the discrepancy-reduction model and reflects adaptive decision making that can occur during the allocation of study time.

Region-of-Proximal-Learning Hypothesis

Metcalfe (2002) has also argued that discrepancy reduction does not adequately explain how people use monitoring to allocate study time. Moreover, if a discrepancy-reduction mechanism were controlling study, it would often lead to ineffective studying, because students governed by this mechanism would often likely spend way too much time on materials that they had little chance of learning. That is, students might waste too much time studying the hardest materials, which have the largest discrepancy. As an alternative, Metcalfe (2002) offered the region-of-proximal-learning (RPL) hypothesis, which states that study time is allocated to material in the region that is "just beyond the grasp of the learner and that is most amenable to learning" (p. 350). According to the discrepancy-reduction hypothesis, more time will be spent on items that have the largest discrepancy from being learned. In contrast, according to the region-of-proximal-learning hypothesis, after people eliminate the items that they already believe they know, they will first study the easier items (that are in their RPL) and then only if they have time will they move on to the more difficult items.

This RPL hypothesis was supported in many experiments reported by Metcalfe (2002; Metcalfe & Kornell, 2005). In one example, students with different levels of expertise studied Spanish-English translation equivalents of varying levels of difficulty. Students who already had experience with the Spanish language spent more time studying the more difficult items than the easier ones, because the former were in their region-of-proximal learning and the latter ones were already known. As important, novices who had little experience with Spanish spent more time studying the easier materials. A natural explanation is that the students allocated time according to their specific RPL, which included more difficult translation equivalents for the experts but included easier ones for the novices.

The two hypotheses described here—discrepancy reduction and region-of-proximal learning—pertain to how individuals may use on-line monitoring of learning to control their study choices and allocation of study time. Understanding the relationship between monitoring and control has been central to research on study regulation in the core cognitive literature and will continue to drive debate and exploration in the field. Nonetheless, other factors also may have a strong influence on how people allocate study time, such as individuals' personal sense of self-efficacy, their interest in the studied materials, their social interaction with peers, among many others. In studying new materials, people also make other choices that will influence the effectiveness of learning, such as deciding which strategy to use while studying or how to distribute their studying across time (see, e.g., Benjamin & Bird, 2006). Many of these factors are being rigorously investigated in cognitive and educational psychology and are central to theories of self-regulated learning (e.g., Nelson & Narens, 1990; Winne & Hadwin, 1998; Zimmerman & Schunk, 2001). A major challenge will be to continue developing general theories that describe how these and other factors jointly influence people's allocation of study time and their success at achieving personal learning goals.

Summary

Since Arbuckle and Cuddy's (1969) seminal work on JOLs, researchers have investigated how people monitor their learning. Conditions that allow individuals to monitor how well-sought-after information can be retrieved from memory—for example, delaying JOLs—have shown the most promise in enhancing the accuracy of JOLs. These and other effects can be explained by a variety of hypotheses. Although some of these hypotheses are viewed as antagonistic and competing, one assumption appears to provide a common ground for many of them. Namely, people infer how well they have learned new information from a variety of external and internal cues, and it is the quality of these inferences that to a large extent dictates JOL accuracy.

Judgments of learning also serve in the control of study time, which includes deciding which items to study and how long to study them. Often, people devote the most study time to items that have been judged as not well-learned—that is, people tend to study the more difficult items the most. In some circumstances, such as when little time is available for studying, a different strategy is used, and people allocate more study time to the easiest items. Presently, these relationships reflect a learner who is controlling study in a dynamic manner that is often effective, and current theories attempt to capture the adaptive nature of study time (Son & Sethi, 2006; Thiede & Dunlosky, 1999). Nevertheless, theory construction in this area is in its infancy, and we suspect future discoveries and debate will give rise to more powerful and comprehensive theories of how we regulate study time.

DISCUSSION QUESTIONS

1. Kelemen (2000) had college students study categories of related exemplars (e.g., kinds of fuel: alcohol, petroleum, butane, etc.). The category label (e.g., Kinds of Fuel) was shown along with its exemplars during study. To obtain JOLs, the category label (i.e., Kinds of Fuel-?) was presented alone and the students were asked to predict how well they would recall the corresponding exemplars. The students made both immediate JOLs and delayed JOLs, and surprisingly, the delayed-JOL effect did not occur; namely, relative accuracy was not better for delayed than immediate JOLs. Given the retrieval-monitoring assumption, can you think of any reason that making delayed JOLs did not produce very high relative accuracy? Can you think of any other contexts that may produce low levels of delayed-JOL accuracy?

2. When you are trying to learn something new—whether it be class materials, people's names, or even an on-the-job skill—do you ever monitor your learning? If you do, how do you do it? Based on current evidence, do you think your monitoring is accurate or misleading? How could you improve your monitoring skills? If you do not regularly monitor your learning as you study, how would you go about monitoring your learning to do so in the most accurate way?

MINDS-ON ACTIVITY: THE DELAYED-JOL EFFECT

The delayed-JOL effect is so robust, it is easy to demonstrate. So take a moment and give it a try. Quickly study each of the following pairs one at a time for about 4 seconds each (a partner can help you keep time). Immediately after you've studied each one, judge your learning about whether you will be able to recall the second word of each pair when you are shown the first word. Write a Y (for yes) in the brackets beside the pair if you think you will remember it, and write an N (for no) if you think you will not remember it.

arm-market [ ]	banner-nun [ ]	candy-prairie [ ]	lawn-book [ ]
cotton-doll [ ]	jail-coffee [ ]	grass-whale [ ]	pelt-brain [ ]
cat-jury [ ]	woods-chin [ ]	piston-dove [ ]	cellar-elbow [ ]

Next, wait 30 seconds and then, one at a time, make a judgment of learning for each one again below. Now your judgment is delayed.

arm-	[ ]	banner-	[ ]	candy-	[ ]	lawn-	[ ]
cotton-	[ ]	jail-	[ ]	grass-	[ ]	pelt-	[ ]
cat-	[ ]	woods-	[ ]	piston-	[ ]	cellar-	[ ]

Now, do not look back at the complete pairs and take a short break—for example, 5 minutes—before you continue. This would be a good time to complete the Concept Review below. After your break, with the full pairs still covered, go back and write down (in the space provided) the second word in each of the pair associates. Finally, score yourself by matching your responses to the correct responses.

How many words did you correctly recall? More important, did you show the delayed-JOL effect? To find out, examine whether you were more likely to recall the correct words when you said "yes" for the delayed JOLs than for the immediate JOLs? And were you less likely to recall the correct words when you said "no" for delayed than immediate judgments? What was your experience when you made your delayed JOLs? Did you expect they would be more accurate at predicting which words you would correctly recall? Why?

CONCEPT REVIEW

For the following questions and exercises, we recommend you write down the answers on a separate sheet in as much detail as possible, and then check them against the relevant material in the chapter.

1. Describe evidence that suggests JOLs and FOK judgments are not based on the same information.

2. People use various cues to make JOLs, such as by giving higher judgments to materials that are easier to process. What are three cues that people use in making JOLs, and how might using these cues actually *reduce* the accuracy of JOLs?

3. Why are high levels of monitoring accuracy important to effectively controlling study?

4. Some models of self-paced study explain how people use their monitoring to control study time. What are the differences (and similarities) between the discrepancy-reduction model and the region-of-proximal-learning model?

6

Confidence Judgments

Take a moment to recall the last time you answered any question. Perhaps it was while you were taking a classroom exam, playing a game of Trivial Pursuit, or even just telling a new friend the location of a local restaurant that you like. In many of these situations, we generate an answer as well as judge our confidence in whether the answer is correct. Such judgments are called retrospective confidence (RC) judgments, and much of the research highlighted in this chapter involves having people rate the likelihood that their answers are correct. Like other metamemory judgments, RC judgments also serve in the regulation of memory, because it turns out that the confidence we have in our beliefs and knowledge plays a central role in whether we will withhold or share an answer in addition to whether others believe the answers we give. In the courtroom, jurors are often persuaded by the testimony of an eyewitness who is highly confident in his or her memory of the accused. Certainly, a witness who states he or she is "absolutely certain that the defendant committed the crime" will be more influential than one who is just "kind of sure" that the defendant is guilty.

Unfortunately, people's confidence in their memories can be entirely inaccurate, yet they may also be entirely unaware that their extreme confidence in a memory is misplaced. Consider the case of Howard Haupt, which was described by Loftus and Ketcham (1991), who also present other captivating real-life examples of overconfidence by eyewitnesses to crimes. Haupt was accused of kidnapping a 7-year-old boy from a hotel in November of 1987. There were several witnesses to the kidnapping, but let's just focus on one of them, John Picha, who was working at the hotel at the time of the crime. Soon after the kidnapping, the police constructed a photo lineup, which included pictures of various suspects. At this time, however, Haupt was not among them. From this lineup, "eyewitness" Picha chose Spendlove, who also worked at the hotel, but who was subsequently cleared due to an alibi. Several days later, Picha identified another man (who also was not Haupt), and then claimed he was 90% confident that this suspect committed the crime. Nearly two months later, John Picha was shown another photo lineup, which this time included a picture of Haupt, who had been staying at the hotel when the kidnapping took place and bore some resemblance to the eyewitnesses' original descriptions. This time, John Picha identified Haupt as the culprit, but he said that he was not confident in his identification because he had already seen so many pictures of suspects. A month later, Picha was escorted to where Haupt worked and saw him in person. The next time Picha looked at the picture lineup, he identified Haupt with high confidence (9 on a scale of 1 to 10). Picha's inappropriate confidence was not unique, because, as explained by Loftus and Ketcham (1991),

> Each witness in this case originally identified someone other than Howard Haupt. As time passed and the witnesses were exposed to more pictures of Haupt, they eventually identified him as the man they had seen with the boy. With each succeeding identification they became more certain. . . . In the trial the prosecutor would emphasize [their final] confidence levels, leading [the jury] to believe the witnesses were always confident and thus adding greater weight to the identifications. (p. 171)

John Picha's extreme confidence was apparently produced in part by the repeated exposures to photographs of Haupt—who, for the record, was found "not guilty" after three days and 20 hours of deliberations by a panel of 12 jurors. This particular case stimulates many intriguing questions, such as what factors can lead an eyewitness to be overconfident in his or her memory? And, of course, are there techniques that can reduce any biases in eyewitness confidence? We will address some answers to these and other intriguing questions in Chapter 8.

In the current chapter, however, we will revisit some of the core issues relevant to theory of metacognitive monitoring. As in the previous chapters, we will describe factors that influence the accuracy of RC judgments. In contrast to research on FOK judgments and JOLs, research on RC judgments has put less emphasis on relative accuracy and instead has explored why these judgments often show poor calibration. Nevertheless, a similar set of key questions drives research on confidence judgments, such as why do people's RC judgments often show poor accuracy? Can their accuracy be improved? And what function do they play in the regulation of memory?

Factors Influencing RC Accuracy

In the next sections, we discuss the degree to which various factors influence the accuracy of RC judgments, and afterwards, we will outline leading theories that attempt to explain why these judgments often show poor calibration. Remember that calibration refers to how well the absolute level of the judgments for a set of answers matches the actual level of performance (for a refresher, see Chapter 3). For instance, let's say you were answering review questions about FOK judgments, which were provided at the end of the chapter. After answering each one, you made an RC judgment, and across all of the answers, let's say your confidence averaged 80%. The calibration of your RC judgments would be perfect if in fact you correctly answered 80% of the questions; your RC judgments would be overconfident if you correctly answered less than 80% of the questions, and underconfident if you answered more than 80% correctly.

Just a glimpse at the existing literature suggests that people's RC judgments are rarely perfect; instead, RC judgments often show systematic distortions toward over- or underconfidence. Two effects in particular—the overconfidence effect and the hard-easy effect—have captured the interest of researchers and have stimulated heated debates about what factors diminish the accuracy of RC judgments. The belief that people truly are poor at judging the quality of their memories—that their judgment ability is distorted—has also produced a small cottage industry aimed at improving RC accuracy. In the following sections, we describe these two effects and then proceed to discuss efforts to help people improve the calibration of RC judgments.

The Overconfidence Effect and the Hard-Easy Effect

In an influential review of the confidence literature, titled "Calibration of Probabilities: The State of the Art to 1980," Lichtenstein, Fischhoff, and Phillips (1982) reported data from four early studies that illustrate typical outcomes in the field (for other reviews, see Keren, 1991; McClelland & Bolger, 1994). In these studies, participants answered general-information questions (e.g., "What is the name of a dried grape? Raisin or prune?"), and then made a confidence judgment for each answer. Calibration curves from these studies are presented in Figure 6.1. As evident from this figure, participants were largely overconfident in the correctness of their answers. For instance, for answers that elicited extreme confidence (i.e., participants' responses were 1.0), the corresponding level of correct performance was below .85. Based on these and other outcomes, Lichtenstein et al. concluded that "the most pervasive finding in recent research is that people are overconfident with general-knowledge items" (p. 314).

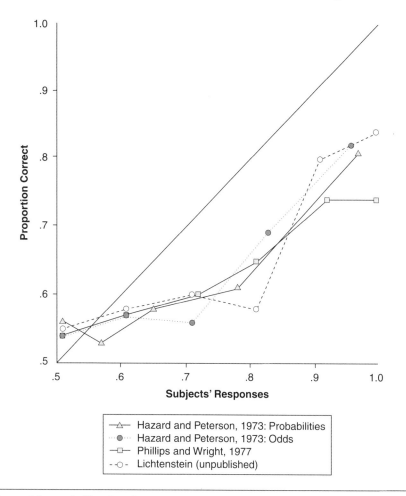

Figure 6.1   Calibration Curves.

SOURCE: Lichtenstein, S., Fischhoff, B., and Phillips, L. D. (1982). Calibration of probabilities: The state of the art to 1980. In D. Kahneman, P. Slovic, and A. Tversky (Eds.), *Judgment Under Uncertainty: Heuristics and Biases* (pp. 306–334). New York: Cambridge University Press.

BOX 6.1
Does Depression Promote Accurate Self-Assessment?

Most everyone gets a little down, at least sometimes. But when you are down, a bit blue, is it then when you have the most accurate understanding of who you are? When people are depressed, they may feel a bit inadequate, thinking that

(Continued)

(Continued)

they're not very good at almost everything. And in fact, people who are depressed often believe that they perform less well on tasks as compared to those who aren't depressed. Of course, these intriguing results beg the question: When people are depressed, are their beliefs about themselves accurate? They may judge that they are doing poorly, but are these judgments realistic? The answer to this question is "yes," according to the depressive-realism hypothesis, which states that those with depression are more realistic than those without it. The hypothesis is that nondepressives are simply overconfident and have unrealistic self-perceptions, which is supported by many of the findings described in this chapter. Moreover, the hypothesis proposes that "the perceptions and inferences of depressed individuals about self-referent events are more accurate and realistic, that is, they tend not to over- or under-estimate the subjective probability of events" (Fu, Koutstaal, Fu, Poon, & Cleare, 2005, p. 243). Thus, the depressive-realism hypothesis predicts that the accuracy of people's confidence judgments will be as good (and perhaps even better) for depressed individuals as for nondepressed ones.

Fu et al. (2005) also describe a competing hypothesis, which is that depressed individuals typically focus on negative aspects of their experiences and hence generally judge themselves more negatively than do nondepressed individuals. But how can this selective-processing hypothesis explain why nondepressives are overconfident whereas depressives often appear more accurate at judging their performance? The answer to this question is based on the fact that nondepressed people and depressed people can perform equally well on memory tasks. Thus, if a nondepressed person's RC judgments show overconfidence (e.g., mean RC judgment = 75%, and mean performance = 50%), his or her depressed counterpart may appear to show good accuracy (e.g., mean RC judgment = 55%, and mean performance = 50%). Note that in this case, both the depressive and nondepressive individuals achieved 50% correct performance, and hence the depressive individual's judgments were more accurate presumably because they just have lower expectations, not because they have more realistic beliefs.

Fu et al. (2005) developed an innovative technique to evaluate whether depressed individuals are realistic (as per the depressive-realism hypothesis) or whether they just consistently are less confident in their abilities (as per the selective-processing hypothesis). They had clinically depressed individuals and nondepressed individuals perform several tasks, such as answering general-knowledge questions and estimating the length of lines. Most important, after the participants performed a task, they estimated how many of their answers were correct. That is, participants made a global RC judgment about how well they performed each task. The innovation of this technique lies in that nondepressed people's global judgments can show pretty good accuracy. This fact allowed a comparison between the hypotheses. In particular, the depressive-realism hypothesis predicts that even in cases where nondepressed individuals show good calibration, depressed individuals should still be at least as good. In contrast, according to the selective-processing hypothesis, when nondepressed participants' judgments are not overconfident and accurate (e.g., mean RC judgment = 45%, mean performance = 50%), then depressed participants' judgments should be underconfident and inaccurate (i.e., mean RC judgment = 30%, mean performance = 50%).

Across the various tasks, it turned out that task performance was just about the same for depressed and nondepressed participants, although the latter group performed slightly better. Both groups' global postdictions somewhat underestimated performance on the task. Most important, calibration as measured by difference scores was slightly lower (although not significantly) for depressed participants (mean difference score = −21%) than for nondepressed participants. These findings led Fu et al. (2005) to conclude that "contrary to the depressive realism account, there was no evidence that the clinically depressed patients offered more realistic estimations of their performance. Indeed, the underestimation was, if anything, exacerbated (and clearly not reduced) in the depressed patients relative to the [nondepressed participants]" (p. 249). These findings and others (Hancock, Moffoot, & O'Carroll, 1996) certainly suggest that depression does not promote accurate self-assessment, at least in the domain of memory monitoring.

As important, however, Lichtenstein et al. (1982) also described a condition in which overconfidence does not occur. In particular, although overconfidence does appear most readily with questions (or tests) that are difficult, people's RC judgments are often *under*confident when questions (or tests) are relatively easy. This *hard-easy effect* was illustrated in Figure 3.5 in the chapter on Methods and Analyses.

What causes the overconfidence effect and the hard-easy effect? Are people truly that poor at judging the likelihood that their answers to questions are correct? Certainly, people are overconfident in many other domains, which suggests that perhaps we are just apt to be overconfident in our knowledge, beliefs, and decisions. In this case, perhaps cognitive biases systematically distort people's judgments. An alternative view is that people can be—and actually are—rather accurate at making RC judgments. According to this more optimistic perspective, the fact that people's judgments often are overconfident does not result from poor judgment but instead from how cognitive psychologists design their experiments. In this case, the overconfidence effect and the hard-easy effect are an artifact of experimental methods, which trick people and make them appear overconfident. These two perspectives lead to the questions: Do the methods used to examine these judgments actually make people look worse than they really are? Or, are cognitive biases responsible for people's poor judgment? Answering these questions has taken center stage in theorizing about RC judgments, and we consider some prominent answers to them when we discuss Theories About Retrospective Confidence later in this chapter.

Debiasing Overconfidence in Retrospective Confidence Judgments

Before turning to general theories of confidence judgments, we will discuss some attempts to improve their calibration. A potentially important distinction can be made between two classes of debiasing techniques (Keren, 1990). One class of techniques attempts to debias RC judgments by changing how the judge processes and represents the relevant information that will be the basis of the judgment. Such *process-oriented* modifications attempt to change the internal processing of the judged event (e.g., an answer to a general-knowledge question) in ways that will promote more realistic RC judgments. The other class of techniques attempts to debias RC judgments by directly influencing how the judge uses the rating scale for a particular task. For instance, if people are consistently 20% overconfident, they could simply be told to decrease their judgments by 20%. Such *response-oriented* modifications include warning people of overconfidence biases or even telling them not to use high ratings (e.g., don't use 100% on the rating scale) unless they are absolutely sure that an answer is correct. As Keren (1990) warned about such response-oriented modifications, the judge "is not necessarily forced to understand the internal structure of the problem and the source of the bias" (p. 527), so the effects of the modification may be limited.

Several debiasing techniques have been scrutinized, and many of these have shown some success at debiasing the overconfidence of people's RC judgments (for reviews of debiasing literatures, see Arkes, 1991; Fischhoff, 1982). In the following sections, we describe two techniques that have garnered popularity because of their promise for debiasing overconfidence. The first is an example of a process-oriented technique: Participants are required to generate reasons for their answers prior to making an RC judgment, which may debias judgments by modifying how the participants process task-relevant information. The second is an example of a response-oriented technique, which involves providing feedback that directly informs participants about the overconfidence of their RC judgments.

Generating Reasons for Answers: Does It Reduce Overconfidence?

Koriat, Lichtenstein, and Fischhoff (1980) proposed that when making an RC judgment, people are more likely to consider reasons—or arguments—that support their answers than arguments for why their answers may be incorrect. Such a bias toward confirming one's own answer, they posited, could contribute substantially to overconfidence. To evaluate this idea, Koriat et al. (1980) had participants answer standard two-alternative, general-knowledge questions, for example, "The Sabines were part of (a) ancient India or (b) ancient Rome." Before making an RC judgment for an answer, participants in one group generated an argument in support of their answer. Another group generated an argument against their answer. If people naturally tend to generate arguments in support of their answers, the former group would not show improved RC accuracy. In contrast, people generating arguments against their answer might become more realistic about their knowledge, and hence their accuracy might improve. As compared to a standard control group in which participants were not asked to develop arguments, providing arguments for one's answer had no influence on the accuracy of RC judgments. Providing arguments against one's answers, however, tended to reduce overconfidence.

Although these outcomes promote optimism that the calibration of RC judgments can be improved, more recent research suggests that arguments against one's answers may not always have a particularly strong influence on accuracy. First, other evidence has shown that generating arguments against one's predictions of future events has little influence on the accuracy of the judgments (Fischhoff & MacGregor, 1982). Second, and more germane to RC judgments, Allwood and Granhag (1996) had participants answer a series of two-alternative, general-knowledge questions and make RC judgments for each one. After answering a question, participants (a) merely gave an RC judgment (the *control* condition); (b) generated an argument against the answer (the *generate* condition), which was analogous to the method used by Koriat et al. (1980); or (c) were given an argument against the answer (the *given* condition). Being given an argument against one's answer, it was postulated, might improve accuracy, because the arguments were provided by a presumed authority (the experimenter) and because the participants tended to find the given arguments more compelling than the ones they had generated.

Nevertheless, the calibration curves—which are presented in Figure 6.2—illustrate that neither experimental condition produced better calibration than the control condition. Generating arguments (or being given them) against one's answers did not reduce the overconfidence effect. Allwood and Granhag (1996) speculated that "presenting an argument against the selected answer is too direct and it puts subjects in a position where they have a tendency to generate arguments or sentiments for their answer" (p. 118). Given that such speculation can be tested, more research on providing arguments will likely be useful in understanding the scope of their effect. Nevertheless, generating arguments apparently is not a panacea for reducing overconfidence.

Feedback and Debiasing RC Judgments

Feedback comes in different varieties and each kind may debias people's RC judgments in a subtly different manner (Stone & Opel, 2000). One kind involves giving direct feedback about the accuracy of people's judgments overall, which has been referred to as *performance* feedback. For instance, after completing a series of general-knowledge questions, if you are told that your RC judgments were highly overconfident, you may then reduce your confidence—and hence debias your judgments—when you complete another series of questions.

Lichtenstein and Fischhoff (1980) conducted an ambitious training program to evaluate whether performance feedback would debias people's RC judgments. Twelve subjects completed 11 one-hour test sessions. During each session, the participants answered 200 general-knowledge questions, each of which had two possible answers. After choosing an alternative, an RC judgment was made by assigning a probability from .50 to 1.0 that the

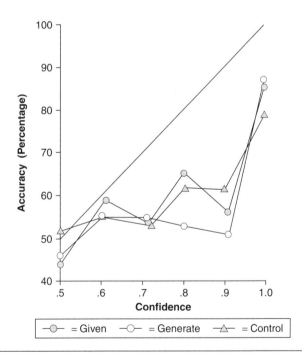

Figure 6.2   Calibration Curves.

SOURCE: Allwood, C. M., and Granhag, P. A. (1996). The effects of arguments on realism in confidence judgements. *Acta Psychologica, 91*, 99–119.

choice was correct. Following completion of the 200 questions in the first test session, participants received considerable performance feedback, which included various measures of calibration. Analysis of the results from the first session showed that the majority of participants demonstrated overconfidence in their RC judgments. In subsequent test sessions, however, most participants showed almost no overconfidence. In short, the effectiveness of performance feedback on debiasing RC judgments was evident after a single training session! In a follow-up experiment, overconfidence was again reliably improved after only one session of training. In the words of the authors, "These two experiments have shown that a single session of 200 items followed by intensive performance feedback is sufficient to teach people who are not initially well calibrated to be well calibrated" (Lichtenstein & Fischhoff, 1980, p. 167). The debiasing effect of performance feedback on calibration has been demonstrated in a variety of other domains as well (e.g., Adams & Adams, 1958; Stone & Opel, 2000).

BOX 6.2
Confidence of Groups: Are Two Heads Better Than One?

Late one evening, you find yourself with a group of friends playing Trivial Pursuit, and you split into two teams of three people. Someone on your team draws a card that has a simple question: "What is the capital of Australia?" You debate about the right answer and together are very confident that you have the correct one. We know from the research already reviewed, that when an individual is engaged in such a task—answering general-knowledge questions—there is a good chance that the RC judgments will be overconfident. With our game of Trivial Pursuit, however, would the power of having several heads reduce overconfidence and lead overall to more accurate judgments? That is, are "two heads better than one" when it comes to judging the correctness of answers? Intuitively, it seems that a group would outperform an individual, both in terms of the number of questions correctly answered as well as in the accuracy of RC judgments. Concerning the latter, better accuracy could arise because the group would engage in activities that can promote better accuracy, such as coming up with alternative answers and developing reasons for why a particular answer is wrong.

To examine these issues, Puncochar and Fox (2004) pitted groups against individuals in a classroom setting. Each week for 11 weeks, undergraduate students took a quiz that consisted of true-false and multiple-choice items. For any given quiz, each student first took it alone and made RC judgments for each answer. The judgments were made on a 0 to 100 scale, and chance performance

(Continued)

(Continued)

was indicated on each scale (e.g., for a multiple-choice question with four alternatives, 25% would be marked as "chance" on the RC scale). After students completed this task, the instructor arranged participants in groups of three or four. These groups then answered the same questions and filled out a group-confidence judgment for each answer as well. Following the third of these sessions, instructors provided feedback, which consisted of noting correct answers and highlighting over- or underconfidence in the judgments. Thus, the feedback could not have influenced performance on the first three quizzes.

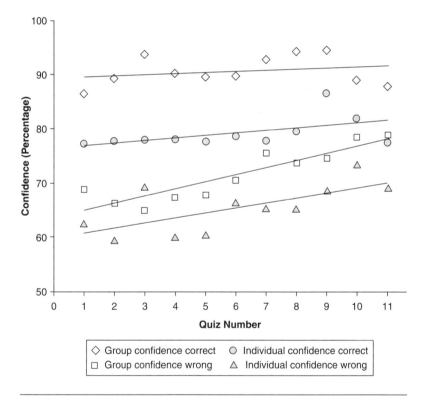

Figure 6.3   Mean percentage confidence for groups (open symbols) and individuals (closed symbols) for correct answers and for wrong answers.

SOURCE: Adapted from Puncochar, J. M., and Fox, P. W. (2004). Confidence in individual and group decision making: When "two heads" are worse than one. *Journal of Educational Psychology*, 96, 582–591.

As expected, performance on the quizzes themselves was reliably better for groups than for individuals, although the groups did only about 6% better. Most important, however, was Puncochar and Fox's (2004) key question: As compared to individuals working alone, will groups be more confident in their correct responses and less confident in their wrong ones? Their main results are presented in Figure 6.3, where the magnitude of RC judgments (confidence percentage) is plotted for correct and wrong answers. The groups were more confident when they responded correctly, and perhaps most surprising, they were also more confident when they responded incorrectly. In a follow-up study, Puncochar and Fox replicated these results and found that groups were more overconfident even when the students had read extensively about metamemory, overconfidence, and calibration—as you have done already with this textbook. Thus, in these experiments, "two heads were not better than one" when it came to judging the accuracy of answers. One explanation for these outcomes is simply that when the group arrives independently at the same answer—regardless of whether it is wrong or right—they have inflated confidence based on the intuition that "how could we all be wrong if we all came up with the same answer?" For instance, in the example at the beginning of this box, most people would say "Sydney" is the capital of Australia (which is wrong), and without any dissenters saying that the correct answer is "Canberra," a group might feel extra confidence that Sydney is in fact correct. Regardless of the explanation for Puncochar and Fox's findings, the take-home message is clear: Although group-think may sometimes improve final performance, it may also inspire undue confidence when what the group is thinking is erroneous.

Theories About Retrospective Confidence

Why are we so often overconfident in judging the quality of our knowledge? This question has stimulated a cottage industry of research and has fostered two relatively polar views, which differ with respect to how much people are to blame for their poor judgment accuracy (Jungermann, 1983). According to pessimists, people are inherently poor at judging internal states and are largely to blame for being over- or underconfident. In contrast, optimists argue that people are actually good at making these judgments, but psychological experiments are set up in a manner to make people look bad. These two camps are exemplified by various theories of RC accuracy. A leading example in the pessimist camp is Tversky and Kahneman's (1974) heuristics approach, which claims that people's decisions are irrational because they are based on heuristics that can systematically distort judgments. A leading example of the optimistic camp is Gigerenzer's probabilistic mental model theory, which claims that the tricky questions used by experimenters make otherwise good judges appear inaccurate.

Other theories of poor RC accuracy abound, such as Erev, Wallsten, and Budescu's (1994) error model and Ferrell and McGoey's (1980) partition model (for excellent reviews, see Dougherty, 2001; McClelland & Bolger, 1994). In the next sections, we explore the most prominent theories from the pessimist camp and optimist camp, and then we briefly consider approaches in which the two camps mingle in unified theories of judgment accuracy.

Heuristics and Biases

Take a moment to read the following vignette and make some judgments about it (from Tversky & Kahneman, 1982):

> Linda is 31 years old, single, outspoken, and very bright. She majored in philosophy. As a student, she was deeply concerned with issues of discrimination and social justice, and also participated in antinuclear demonstrations. (p. 92)

Now, rank the following statements based on how probable each one is, where 1 is most probable and 8 is least probable (from Tversky & Kahneman, 1982, p. 92).

a. Linda is a teacher in elementary school.   _8_

b. Linda works in a bookstore and takes yoga classes.   _2_

c. Linda is active in the feminist movement.   _3_

d. Linda is a psychiatric social worker.   _1_

e. Linda is a member of the League of Women Voters.   _7_

f. Linda is a bank teller.   _6_

g. Linda is an insurance salesperson.   _5_

h. Linda is a bank teller and is active in the feminist movement.   _4_

If you're like the majority of people, you stated that option "h" is more probable (gave it a lower number rank) than is option "f." That is, most people state that Linda is more likely "a bank teller and is active in the feminist movement" than she is "a bank teller." This particular outcome has multiple implications for how people judge uncertain events. Let's consider two implications here. First, when compared to rational judgment making based on the laws of probability, this particular ranking is irrational. In particular, based on the laws of probability, the likelihood of a given event, A, is always at least as high as the likelihood that A occurs along with another event, B. Put differently, the probability of A and B co-occurring is lower than (or equivalent to) the probability of A occurring alone, or $p(A \& B) <= p(A)$. When people rank "h" as more probable than "f," their judgments are at odds with this law of probability because they are endorsing that the conjunction of the two events (being a bank teller *and* being an active feminist) is more likely than the single event (being a bank teller). Tversky and Kahneman have demonstrated that people make this *conjunction fallacy* in numerous domains, including issuing medical judgments, predicting sports outcomes, and forecasting natural disasters. It may surprise you to learn that although the conjunction fallacy—i.e., judging $p(A \& B)$ as more probable than $p(A)$—is at odds with statistical rationality, even experts making judgments within their domain fall prey to this error.

The second implication leads us back to the role of heuristics in making judgments under uncertainty. Tversky and Kahneman (1974) argue that people's judgments are led astray by the use of the *representative heuristic*, which involves characterizing likelihoods on the basis of their similarity to a population or pattern. In the preceding vignette, a careful reading shows that it is constructed so that Linda's description is similar to (or representative of) an active feminist and unrepresentative of a bank teller. So, although it may seem unlikely that Linda is a bank teller, when the possibility that she is a feminist is added to the equation, the probability of the statement appears to be enhanced.

Other heuristics that may influence human judgment under uncertainty have also been intensely scrutinized (Gilovich, Griffin, & Kahneman, 2002), among them the *availability heuristic* and the *anchoring-and-adjustment heuristic*. In the case of the availability heuristic, an event is judged to be more probable when it is easier to retrieve instances of such an event to mind. Although this heuristic often leads to accurate judgments, it can also produce systematic bias when the ease of retrieval does not reflect the actual probability of occurrence. For instance, take a moment to answer this question: If you sample a word at random from the dictionary (with 3 letters or more), do you believe it is more likely that this word will begin with the letter "k" or that it will have "k" as its third letter? Because it is much easier to retrieve words that begin with "k," people judge that the chosen word is more likely to begin with "k" than to have "k" as the third letter, even though the opposite is true (for this and other examples, see Tversky & Kahneman, 1974). The use of such an availability heuristic has already been implicated in the accuracy of metacognitive judgments. In essence, the accessibility hypothesis for feeling-of-knowing judgments is a specific version of the availability heuristic.

The anchoring-and-adjustment heuristic refers to a situation in which people judge the likelihood of an event by beginning at an initial value and adjusting from this anchor to develop a judgment. An impressive demonstration of anchoring and adjustment was provided by Tversky and Kahneman (1974), who asked people to provide estimated answers for questions such as, "What is the percentage of African countries in the United Nations?" To obtain the anchors (or initial values), the researchers spun a wheel that was marked with percentages from 0 to 100. Once the anchor was determined, participants were asked (a) whether the actual percentage was higher or lower than the number on the wheel, and then (b) to estimate the actual percentage. The wheel stopped at different values (or anchors) for different participants, and these initial—and note, arbitrary—values had a marked influence on people's estimates. For instance, the percentage of African countries in the United Nations was estimated at 25 for participants receiving an anchor of 10 and was 45 for those receiving an anchor of 65!

Key to our concerns here, the anchoring-and-adjustment heuristic provides an intuitively appealing explanation for biases in the calibration of people's RC judgments. Consider the hard-easy effect, which is illustrated in Figure 3.5. According to Keren (1991), it seems reasonable that when making RC judgments, people begin with an anchor near the middle of the scale, because it seems unlikely that the experimenter would make the task outrageously easy or difficult. When an easy item is encountered, participants adjust their judgment upward, whereas when a more difficult item is encountered, they adjust downward. Given that such adjustments are usually insufficient (perhaps because participants are reluctant to use the extremes of the response scale), this anchoring-and-adjustment heuristic would lend itself to underconfidence for easy items and to overconfidence for difficult items.

In summary, the heuristics-based approach championed by Tversky and Kahneman (1974) has been highly influential. Of course, it is not without its critics. By focusing on biases, or cognitively-based illusions, the heuristic-based approach has been attacked for being overly pessimistic, because it is hard to believe that people are as irrational as they appear to be in these experiments. In fact, people often make fine judgments and decisions (as we've already discussed in previous chapters on judgment and control processes), so the heuristic approach may be overly negative. This critique, however, misses a major point of the heuristics approach (for details of other critiques and rebuttals, see Gilovich et al., 2002), because advocates of the heuristic approach are not denying that people's judgments can be good. In many cases, people use heuristics because they often produce quick and accurate judgments across numerous domains. The preponderance of biases highlighted in the literature does not mean judgments are always, usually, or even sometimes poor, but instead they result from the fact that the processes underlying people's judgments are most readily uncovered when those processes fail. Put differently, it is often easiest to understand how something operates when it fails to operate well than when it is running smoothly, and that is why the researchers who have explored the validity of the heuristic approach have often chosen methods that magnify the biases in human judgments. Thus, although the heuristic-based approach may be viewed as an important example of theory within the pessimist camp, advocates of this approach would not deny that human judgment can be highly accurate; it's just that their inaccuracy can be informative to understanding how we make judgments and decisions.

Ecological Approaches

Optimists argue that poor calibration of confidence judgments results from how scientists design their experiments. The scientists should not be viewed as devious, but instead optimists claim that scientists have inadvertently set up their experiments in a manner to make otherwise excellent judges look bad. According to ecological approaches, people are good, intuitive statisticians. People's difficulty apparently occurs because the experiments do not match either the real-world ecology of how people naturally judge uncertain events or the kinds of questions people usually encounter in everyday life. We consider both of these aspects of previous experiments—the format of the judgment and the materials—that may make even the most accurate judges look like they are irrational.

Making Probability Judgments Versus Frequency Judgments

One reason people may show poor judgment accuracy is that they are asked to judge the *probability* of a single event. For instance, you may answer the question, "What is the capital of Australia?" with "Sydney" and then judge the probability that this single answer is correct to be 75%. Note, however, that any single event is either correct or incorrect (or occurs or does not occur), so providing a probability that a single event will occur (other than 0 or 100%) seems inappropriate. Perhaps people are sensitive to the *frequency* of events in the long run, such as how often in the past you correctly answered Trivial Pursuit questions about the capitals of countries. The idea here is that if humans have adapted to make appropriate judgments (e.g., "Will I shoot par at golf today?"), it seems reasonable that these judgments are based on memories for the frequency of the event in the past (e.g., "How many times have I shot par on days like today?"). Using such frequency information as an input to making judgments holds many advantages over storing probabilities of occurrence; for instance, if one only stored event probabilities (e.g., "I've been 40% successful on days like today."), then it would be difficult to update the probability when new information is available (e.g., having 3 failures in a row). If frequency information is stored (e.g., "I've been successful about 4 times out of 10 on days like today."), then updating one's knowledge is rather straightforward (i.e., "Now I've had success 4 times out of 13."). Such a rationale led Cosmides and Tooby (1996) to the following bold claim:

> During their evolution, humans regularly needed to make decisions whose success could be improved if the probabilistic nature of the world was taken into account. They had access to large amounts of probabilistic information, but primarily or perhaps solely in the form of encountered frequencies. This information constituted a rich resource available to be used to improve decision-making. . . . Consequently, they evolved mechanisms that took frequencies as input. (p. 17)

Such a claim has important implications for understanding human judgment. Most important for our story, one implication is that if people naturally use frequencies to make judgments, then their accuracy should improve if the judgments refer to frequencies instead of probabilities. For instance, consider the Linda problem again, which was originally stated in the form of probabilities. Fiedler (1988) modified the original problem to focus on the frequency of occurrences in the long run instead of the probability of a single event. Just like in Tversky and Kahneman's (1974) original experiments, about 75% of the participants who were given the single-event version of the Linda problem fell prey to the conjunction fallacy. In contrast, only about 25% demonstrated this fallacy when given the frequency version of the problem. As with the Linda problem, Gigerenzer's (1991, 1994) reviews of this literature confirmed that many alleged errors in human reasoning—which were blamed on the use of fallible heuristics—apparently vanish when the problems are framed in terms of frequencies (see also Brase, Cosmides, & Tooby, 1998). Although impressive, recent evidence suggests that frequency formats do not always improve (and can sometimes hamper) people's judgments (e.g., Griffin & Buehler, 1999). Thus, whether the mind naturally uses frequencies is still a mystery to be solved.

Ecological Validity of Materials

Even so, an ecological approach to judgment and decision making—that people are tuned to the frequencies of events as they occur naturally in the environment—provides an intuitive account for the poor accuracy of people's RC judgments. In particular, Gigerenzer et al. (1991) proposed the *probabilistic mental model* (PMM) theory for how people judge confidence for general-knowledge questions such as, "Which city has the largest population, (a) Atlanta, Georgia, or (b) El Paso, Texas?" Answer this question and then provide an RC judgment about your answer, from 50% (guessing) to 100% (absolutely certain). According to PMM, confidence in one's answer may arise from two different models. A local mental model is constructed when people generate certain knowledge about the question, such as to rule in one alternative or rule out the other. For instance, perhaps you just heard on the radio that the population of El Paso is much larger than Atlanta's. When you can directly generate an answer, confidence will be 100%.

More interesting, is the case when one cannot generate a local mental model and must infer the correct answer. In this case, a probabilistic mental model is generated in which potentially relevant cues are generated, and the cue with the highest validity drives people's confidence. You may recall that Atlanta has a professional basketball team whereas El Paso does not. The validity of this cue—having a professional basketball team—is simply the probability that one city has a greater population than another city given that one city has a basketball team whereas the other does not. The cue validity of "having a basketball team" for predicting the larger city is relatively high. In particular, just taking the largest 50 cities in the United States, there is a 73% chance that the city with a basketball team will be larger than a city without one. According to PMM in the present case, if the best cue you retrieved is "has a basketball team," then you would choose Atlanta as your answer and give a confidence rating of 73%; that is, the validity of the cue used to infer the correct answer becomes one's confidence. It is important to note that when people generate a PMM, the confidence reflects the frequency of events as they encounter those events in the real world—for example, how often a city is larger than another one if one city has a basketball team and the other does not.

As pointed out by Gigerenzer et al. (1991), the general-knowledge questions used by experimenters to evaluate the accuracy of RC judgments are often misleading because they are chosen due to their difficulty. Misleading here means that the actual set of questions does not represent the target domains as they occur in the ecology. In the present example, assume you continued to use the "basketball" cue, yet the experimenter kept drawing "tricky" pairs of cities from the 50 largest cities in the United States, such as "Atlanta versus El Paso" or "Memphis, Tennessee, versus San Jose,

California." In both cases, you'd choose the incorrect answer (Atlanta and Memphis, because they have basketball teams whereas the other cities do not) yet would give a relatively high confidence rating. That is, your RC judgments would demonstrate overconfidence, which is a common outcome in prior studies that have included many "tricky" questions. In contrast, if the experimenter drew pairs of cities randomly from a list of the 50 largest ones, then your cue (choose the one with a basketball team) would work about 73% of the time, which would match your confidence level. Thus, a critical prediction from PMM theory is that when representative questions are used in confidence experiments, people should show excellent calibration.

To test this prediction, Gigerenzer et al. (1991) developed two sets of questions—one that concerned which of two German cities (from the largest 65) had the greater population, and a second set "selected" from typical questions used in previous studies, such as "Who was born first? (a) Buddha or (b) Aristotle." One might expect that the calibration would be greater for the (former) representative set of questions than for the (latter) selected set. The calibration curves (Figure 6.4) are consistent with this prediction. Moreover, to demonstrate that the difference in curves is not due to differences in content, Gigerenzer et al. (1991) also chose items from the representative set that matched the selected set in difficulty. As expected, this matched set (which was no longer representative) also showed poor calibration. Thus, people are not necessarily poor judges, and at least some of the poor calibration demonstrated in previous studies was an artifact of the experimental procedure (see also Juslin, 1993).

Hybrid Approaches to Understanding Confidence Accuracy

The ecological approach is optimistic about human judgment because it indicates that people can be excellent judges of the quality of their knowledge, as long as the questions used to test that knowledge appropriately reflect people's real-world experiences. Even with such optimism in mind, it seems unreasonable that human judgment would always be totally free from error. Accordingly, several investigators have proposed models of confidence accuracy that integrate ecological approaches with models that also account for the error in human judgment (e.g., Juslin, Olsson, & Björkman, 1997; Soll, 1996). Dougherty's (2001) approach is rather impressive, because his model incorporates the approaches mentioned above, as well as doing so in the context of a formal model of memory. Thus, his model integrates a formal theory of memory with compelling theories of judgment, which is relatively unique in the literature on metamemory.

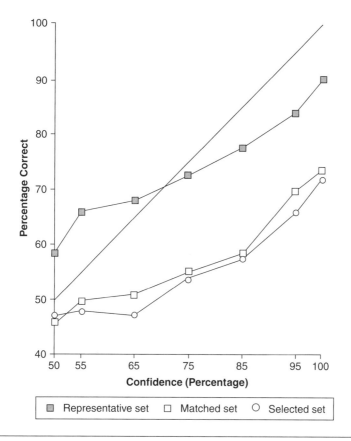

Figure 6.4   Calibration Curves.

SOURCE: Gigerenzer, G., Hoffrage, U., and Kleinbolting, H. (1991). Probabilistic mental models: A Brunswikian theory of confidence. *Psychological Review, 98,* 506–528.

Although these hybrid models indicate that at least some of the poor calibration of confidence judgments arises from faulty cognitive processes, the processes to blame are not faulty heuristics. Instead, the hybrid models indicate that poor calibration is partly due to *random error* that influences people's judgments (for details, see Erev et al., 1994). Nevertheless, given that these hybrid models combine the most compelling assumptions from the optimist and pessimistic camps, it is no surprise that they do an excellent job of explaining poor calibration.

BOX 6.3
Putting the "Meta" Into Theory of Confidence Judgments

In attempting to understand how people make RC judgments and why these judgments can be inaccurate, the various theories described in the text resort to forms of explanations that are prevalent in the metacognitive literature, such as that the judgments are inferential in nature or are critically influenced by the nature of the material being judged. What is surprisingly absent, however, is a clear recourse to metacognition, which pertains specifically to people's cognitions about their cognitions. Work by William Brewer and his colleagues, however, directly infuses the "meta" into theorizing about confidence judgments. They propose that when making RC judgments "individuals use the available sources of information (e.g., products of the memory process just carried out) along with metamemory beliefs about the relationship of these sources to memory accuracy to generate memory confidence" (Brewer & Sampaio, 2006, p. 541). The belief under scrutiny in their research (see also Brewer, Sampaio, & Barlow, 2005) is that when people are being tested, if they recall the study episode in which an item was originally encountered, they will have high confidence that the item was in fact studied.

To evaluate this proposal, Brewer and Sampaio (2006) played an experimental trick on participants. In particular, they had them study a series of sentences (e.g., "The bullet hit the bull's-eye") during a study phase, and afterwards, they presented these sentences again for a recognition test with RC judgments. That is, the participants would be shown "The bullet hit the bull's-eye," and the participants would state whether the sentence was originally presented, and how confident they were in their response. The trick was that during the recognition-confidence phase of the experiment, some of the new sentences (which had not been presented for study) were deceptive lures that were related to the gist of an old sentence. For the present example, a deceptive lure would be "The bullet struck the bull's-eye," where "hit" in the studied sentence was replaced with the word "struck." Brewer and Sampaio predicted that during the test, when seeing "The bullet struck the bull's-eye," participants would be likely to recall the word "hit" in place of "struck," and hence would incorrectly believe that this reconstructed memory was actually a true one. In this case, perhaps the participants would even recall the image that they had originally produced when reading "The bullet hit the bull's-eye." Accordingly, even though they had never studied "The bullet struck the bull's-eye," recalling the image from study and the gist of the original sentence would lead to high confidence in their response that the deceptive lure was in fact originally studied.

To test this prediction, participants made confidence judgments for both originally presented (old) sentences and for deceptive lures, and they also reported the reasons for their recognition decisions (e.g., "Why did you say that

'The bullet struck the bull's-eye' was an old item?"). Several outcomes were noteworthy. First, people frequently (and incorrectly) stated that deceptive items were in fact originally presented. Second, and as important, RC judgments were higher—indicating greater confidence—in their recognition decision when they claimed remembering a deceptive lure than when they claimed that a deceptive lure was in fact not originally presented. Moreover, when participants claimed a sentence was old, their confidence was highest when they also reported that they recalled the sentence from the study episode, regardless of whether the sentence was deceptive or nondeceptive. These outcomes support Brewer's metamemory hypothesis in which people's beliefs that recalling previous information about an item means that the item must be old. Unfortunately, this belief will lead people's judgments astray when such recall is incorrect and arises from deception that provokes people to inaccurately reconstruct the past.

Convergence and Divergence in Thinking About Confidence

Although debates continue about which approach—heuristic-based or ecological—best captures both the successes and failures of human judgment, the two camps do not entirely diverge. Even the ecological approaches assume that heuristics partly drive human judgment. For instance, according to the probabilistic mental model proposed by Gigerenzer et al. (1991), people presumably base their confidence judgments on the cue that has the highest ecological validity, which is a powerful heuristic (called the "take the best" heuristic) that simplifies the judgment process (because only one of many possible cues is used in constructing a judgment) and often leads to excellent calibration (Gigerenzer, Todd, & ABC Research Group, 1999). Nevertheless, whether people's overconfidence and inappropriate reasoning mainly arises from the use of fallible heuristics or from how experiments are designed will likely continue to be scrutinized for some time.

Function of Retrospective Judgments

Imagine taking a test in a college course on metacognition. The test consists of short-answer questions ("Who is known for conducting the first experiments on FOK accuracy?") and multiple-choice questions ("What factor is known to improve the relative accuracy of judgments of learning? (a) forcing a quick judgment, (b) delaying the judgment after study, or (c) having people generate reasons about why they may forget the to-be-judged item").

In both cases, you can exert a great deal of control over whether you answer the questions and how long you persist in answering them. Concerning the latter, in Chapter 4 we discussed how feelings of knowing drive how long people persist in trying to answer a question before terminating a search.

In this section, we'll largely be concerned with the former, that is, whether you actually elect to offer a particular response. For instance, for the short-answer question, a variety of answers (e.g., Hart, Flavell, and Brown) may come to mind, so how do you decide which one to report? And more important, would you decide to report any one of them, especially if there is a penalty for answering incorrectly? For the multiple-choice question, possible answers are provided, so how do you decide which to choose? When reviewing your answers, perhaps you decide to change one. Why would you do so, and if you did change a multiple-choice answer, would you actually increase your score? We'll touch on recent answers to some of these questions in this section as well as in the Education chapter. To foreshadow, your confidence in various responses plays an important role in whether or not you will volunteer a response. That is, one function of RC judgments is apparently to help us decide when we should offer our responses and opinions and when to keep them to ourselves.

Koriat and Goldsmith (1996) point out that in memory experiments conducted in the laboratory, research participants are often asked to recall as much information from a list as possible. So, for instance, if you study a list of 20 words (e.g., dream, sofa, pillow, bed, etc.), then you would often be instructed to "do your best to recall as many words as possible." What researchers are trying to determine is the quantity of information that has been stored in (and is subsequently accessible from) memory. In many real-world situations, however, it is not just the quantity of information that one recalls that matters, but the quality of that information. For instance, eyewitnesses testifying in front of a jury should certainly offer all they know about a certain event, but a premium is also placed on the correctness of their recall—that is, they need to "tell the whole truth, and nothing but the truth."

One of the most influential theories of the self-regulation of memory reports was the work of Koriat and Goldsmith (1996), who assumed that accurate memory monitoring and effective control are essential to the quality of people's reports. To understand the importance of these metamemorial processes, it will be useful to consider their model in more detail. As shown in Figure 6.5, Koriat and Goldsmith proposed that after people are asked a question ("Input Question"), they attempt to retrieve candidate answers from long-term memory. For the question above about who conducted the first FOK research, perhaps you retrieved "Hart," "Nelson," and "Flavell." As answers are retrieved, you would presumably evaluate their quality, such as by making a subjective confidence judgment for each one. Perhaps you feel that there is a .60 probability that "Hart" is correct, a .30 probability that "Nelson" is correct, and a .10 probability that "Flavell" is correct. These values are the assessed probabilities (Pa) in the model. If you don't retrieve any other candidates, you'd choose the best one—in this case "Hart"—from those you did recall. At this point, however, you do not necessarily report "Hart," because according to this model, you would first compare your assessed probability (Pa = .60) to a response criterion, which is Prc (for Probability of response criterion) in the model. Prc is a threshold and is presumably set so as to maximize gains in performance for reporting correct answers relative to any costs that may occur for reporting a wrong answer. Perhaps you are taking a test where the payoff for a correct answer is low and the penalty for an incorrect one is very high. In this case, you might set Prc at .70. If so, as indicated in the model, your comparison between Pa and Prc would lead you to decide not to report "Hart," because Pa (.60) < Prc (.70). Unfortunately, the overall quality of your recall output would be diminished (a negative sign under ACC, which here stands for quality of recall) because you would actually be withholding a correct response.

Although the model itself is simple, it has several implications. Let's consider an important one here. In particular, the relative accuracy of people's RC judgments is expected to influence the quality of responses. To illustrate, imagine that in fact your Prc was relatively low (.30), so you'd be willing to respond with any best-candidate answer with Pa > .30. In the example above, you'd report "Hart" and would be correct in doing so; in addition, the relative accuracy of your judgments would be excellent, because "Hart" (the correct answer) received a higher Pa than did the other two (incorrect) candidate answers. In contrast, if instead you believed that the probability of "Nelson" being correct was .90, then you would incorrectly respond with "Nelson" because your RC judgments showed poor relative accuracy.

Koriat and Goldsmith (1996) evaluated this prediction—that better relative accuracy yields higher quality of responding—in the following manner. First, participants were forced to answer general-knowledge questions, and for each answer, they provided an RC judgment. Participants were forced to respond so that the experimenters would know what each participant's best-candidate response was for each question, and the RC judgments were used as each participant's assessed probability (Pa) for each response. Second, the participants answered the questions again, yet during this round of questioning, they could elect to withhold responses; that is, they were not required to respond. This procedure can be used to evaluate implications of the model when various factors are manipulated, such as the costs for responding

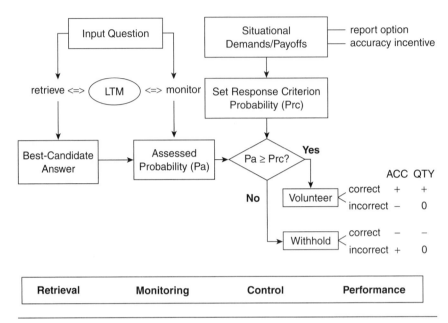

Figure 6.5   A model of the strategic regulation of memory reports.

SOURCE: Adapted from Koriat, A., and Goldsmith, M. (1996). Monitoring and control processes in the strategic regulation of memory accuracy. *Psychological Review, 103*, 490–517.

NOTE: LTM = long-term memory; ACC = quality of recall; QTY = quantity of correct recall.

incorrectly or the rewards for correct responses. To examine the role of relative accuracy, Koriat and Goldsmith (1996, Experiment 2) constructed two sets of general-knowledge questions—one that was standard and supported good relative accuracy, and another that included deceptive questions. The deceptive questions often elicited incorrect responses that were held in high confidence, so that relative accuracy would be low. For instance, when asked, "What is the capital of Australia?," many people will respond confidently that it is "Sydney" (when, in fact, Canberra is the capital).

Not surprisingly, performance during the forced-report phase was greater for the standard questions (27.9%) than for the deceptive questions (11.8%), which merely indicates that the latter questions were indeed deceptive. More important, however, is whether these differences disappear with the quality of recall during the free-report phase. According to the model, when people are not forced to report, their percentage correct (of those reported) will likely improve because in fact people can withhold incorrect responses. As expected, the percentage of accurate recall for free report for the standard questions was 75%, illustrating the expected improvement. In contrast, for the deceptive questions, free-report accuracy was only 21%, showing minimal improvement as compared to forced-report performance. Of course, the difficulty people were having with the deceptive questions is that their confidence judgments were inaccurate, so they failed to withhold incorrect responses that were held with high confidence.

Summary

A tradition of quality research on retrospective confidence judgments has arisen in the past several decades, and our review of the literature here admittedly only scratches the surface. Widespread interest in these judgments perhaps is not surprising, given that in everyday life, confidence in our beliefs and thoughts often arise naturally and lead us to make either well-founded or rash decisions. It is evident that at least in some contexts, people's confidence judgments can be inaccurate, and often overconfident. Several accounts have been proposed to explain such poor calibration, with leading explanations indicating that people's use of fallible heuristics are to blame or that the biased methods used to investigate people's judgments are to blame. Both explanatory traditions are backed by strong evidence and advocates, and we suspect that debates about why people's confidence judgments are often inaccurate will continue well into the future.

As important, retrospective confidence judgments function to influence people's decisions about whether to withhold or volunteer responses. We all have had experiences where we've withheld a response because we were not sure that we were correct and have eagerly volunteered our thoughts because we were sure that we were correct. Thus, obtaining high levels of both calibration and relative accuracy of RC judgments will be essential for the efficient regulation of retrieval. Given such insights, it is also evident why so much research has already focused on debiasing these judgments, and why programmatic research on them will continue to dominate the metamemory literature.

DISCUSSION QUESTION

1. You've been introduced to several of the most investigated metacognitive judgments: judgments of learning, feelings of knowing, and retrospective confidence judgments. You may make each one (either implicitly or explicitly) as you prepare for an upcoming test. How might each one either foster (or impair) your performance while preparing

and taking an exam? Although each judgment is made at a different time, they all may be influenced by heuristics. Describe a heuristic that may be used for each judgment. Under what conditions would these heuristics support excellent judgment accuracy? Under what conditions would they lead to poor accuracy?

CONCEPT REVIEW

For the following questions and exercises, we recommend you write down the answers on a separate sheet in as much detail as possible, and then check them against the relevant material in the chapter.

1. Describe two explanations for why people's retrospective confidence judgments often demonstrate overconfidence.

2. Given the importance of accurately judging confidence in your answers, what are some techniques that you could use to improve your accuracy as you take a test?

3. Why might two people show more overconfidence when they answer questions (and judge the quality of their answers) as a team than when they answer them individually?

4. Describe the functions of retrospective confidence judgments.

7

Source Judgments

We have, up until this point, considered the metacognitive judgments—feeling of knowing, judgments of learning, confidence judgments—that are commonly thought to define the field. Metacognition, however, involves, by definition, *any* reflection or judgment made upon an internal representation such as a memory. The judgment process needs to involve reflection on an *internal* representation to qualify. As such, all attributions that people make about their memories or cognitions are metacognitions—not just the big three stated above. You can think of many other kinds of commentaries about memories that would qualify: How long ago was the last time I drank a glass of champagne (referred to as *judgments of recency*)? How often did I work out in the last month (*judgments of frequency*)? How pleasant was my memory of visiting Europe last year? Answering any of these questions will require reflecting upon a mental representation, and hence they are metacognitive in nature.

One of the most interesting of the self-reflective attributions, and one that has been intensively studied, is a *judgment of source*. These judgments involve remembering the source of a memory or the context in which a memory originally occurred. So, if you remember that you should not be eating grapefruit (the content of memory), did you hear it from your doctor or your mother (source memory) or did you originally hear it in a hospital or in your own home (context memory)? A fascinating spectrum of possibilities is nested under source judgments. Did the memory itself occur in your hometown or on vacation in New York? Were you the source of the memory or was someone else? Did the event actually happen to you, or was it something you saw in a movie, or merely imagined?

Source monitoring includes the processes involved in making attributions about the origins of thoughts and memories (Johnson & Mitchell, 2002). Errors in source memory, while common, can have extreme consequences. For example, Dan Schacter (1996) recounts a real-life story about Donald Thomson, an Australian psychologist who was known in part for being the coauthor of a classic paper on the encoding specificity principle (Tulving & Thomson, 1973). As a world-renowned researcher on eyewitness memory, Thomson testified frequently in his native land, and he often did television interviews about the foibles of human memory. He was doing such an interview, focusing on how people can improve their memories, on the night a rape occurred many miles away from the TV studio. The rape victim accused Thomson. Fortunately, the television interview was live, and so he had a perfect alibi. But in a sense, Thomson had been in the room with the victim— as an image on her television screen. Presumably the victim had made a source-monitoring error: She confused Thomson's image from the screen with that of her assailant. Her memory was not altogether faulty: She had seen Thomson that night. But the context was radically different, and the consequences of this source-monitoring failure were potentially disastrous.

In this chapter, we will explore the vast literature on source monitoring. We'll begin by discussing some factors that influence the accuracy of people's source monitoring, such as the degree to which the sources are similar or whether the source itself provokes an emotional response. Afterwards, we'll introduce a popular theory of source monitoring, which indicates that people rely on both recollection and familiarity of an episode to infer its source. Finally, we'll consider the mysterious psychopathologies of schizophrenia and mirror sign (which underscore the perils of disrupted source monitoring) and describe the neurological underpinnings of source memory.

Factors That Influence Source-Monitoring Accuracy

The consensus view of the mechanisms underlying source judgments, as with other metamemory judgments, is that they are based on heuristics. When asked to assess a source, people use what information comes to mind to decide the source of a memory. For instance, if you wondered whether you had *imagined* the teacher yelling at another student or actually had *heard* it, you may rely on the fact that you can recall the tone of the teacher's voice to decide that you actually had heard it. If you only recalled a vague image of the event, you might instead infer that you had imagined it. The information that is used in making a source judgment can vary radically depending upon a number of factors, including how similar the sources were, whether the source was salient during initial encoding, and whether people are explicitly told to be careful about the source while making their judgments.

Similarity of the Sources

The similarity of the sources has a marked effect on the accuracy of source judgments. If two potential sources of a memory are highly *similar* to each other, the origin of the memory will be highly confusable and making the judgment will be more difficult and error prone (Ferguson, Hashtroudi, & Johnson, 1992; Lindsay & Johnson, 1991). If they are quite different from each other, the task is easier. So, if one has to say whether Mary or Lynn said a particular sentence, if Mary is female and Lynn is male, the task is much easier than if both speakers are female.

BOX 7.1
Measuring the Accuracy of Source Judgments

In a typical experiment on source memory, participants are asked to remember a variety of items that have different sources. For example, the items may be individual words (e.g., dog, pencil, bowl, and so forth) that are spoken by one of two voices (e.g., a male voice says half of the words aloud and a female voice says the other half). What we are mainly interested in is the degree to which participants can accurately discriminate between items that came from one source (perhaps the male voice) versus the other source (i.e., the female voice). Accordingly, measures of source-monitoring accuracy are most closely aligned with measures of relative accuracy for the more standard metamemory judgments, such as FOK judgments and JOLs.

Another aspect of source memory makes measuring its accuracy tricky. In particular, researchers will often investigate a factor to answer the question, Does this factor influence the accuracy of people's source judgments? So, one might investigate whether grade-school and college students are equally accurate at making source judgments. Likewise, one might be interested in whether presenting items multiple times during study (versus only once) improves people's memory for source. In these cases, however, a difficulty arises, because the factor in question may also influence item memory: Recognition for the originally presented items will likely be better for college students than grade-school students and will also be better when the items are presented multiple times during study. Thus, even if the accuracy of source judgments is

(Continued)

(Continued)

better for college students (or after multiple study attempts), how can we be sure that this difference in source accuracy does not merely reflect a difference in the memory for the items themselves?

Much effort has been put into answering this question, which highlights the importance of distinguishing between one's memory for the items (or content of an event) and their source. In fact, throughout this chapter, we will continue to make the distinction between item memory (or item recognition) versus source memory (or source monitoring). Murnane and Bayen (1996) reviewed a variety of measures of source memory and concluded that although some measures do not conflate item memory and source memory in some circumstances, "none of the empirical measures examined provides a valid measure of source identification in all circumstances" (p. 417). The bottom line is that all measures—including using techniques such as multinomial modeling to estimate item memory versus source memory (Bayen, Murnane, & Erdfelder, 1996)—are based on various assumptions, which if not met, will lead to invalid estimates of the accuracy of source judgments. Nevertheless, various measures often support the same conclusions about which factors influence the accuracy of source memory, and it will be evident from our review that the vast literature has led to some intuitively plausible and consistent conclusions about the accuracy of people's source judgments.

Similarly, if the two sources are spatially discrete, once again the task is easier than if they are overlapping. If the background colors are very different (for a judgment of context), the judgments are easier than if the backgrounds are difficult to distinguish. If two rooms in which events occur are very different, source judgments are easier. If they are very similar, the judgments are more difficult. It follows that when a large number of events occur in the same environment, pinpointing the exact event or source becomes difficult. Physical differences of this sort that contribute to the goodness of source judgments have been well documented, are systematic, and conform very nicely to one's intuitions.

Emotion and Imagery in Source Monitoring

A person's level of emotional arousal has an impact on source judgments that is selective. In a study by Mather et al. (2006), participants were shown a series of four different pictures. Each picture was flashed individually in a different location on a computer screen. After presentation of the fourth picture in the series and a brief delay, participants were asked where on the computer screen a given picture had appeared. Pictures in the trials were selected specifically to provoke high arousal, medium arousal, or low arousal. As people's arousal level increased, their memory for where the pictures appeared on the computer screen decreased. Furthermore, the locations of pictures that evoked higher levels of arousal were especially poorly remembered by participants who had high depression scores. The impact was less pronounced in nondepressed people. Thus, both the content of the materials (stressful or not) and the person's individual makeup (depressed or not) had an impact on whether they remembered the source of the pictures, in this case the location of a given picture on the computer screen. An unfortunate conclusion is that people's ability to make accurate source judgments may be lost just when they need it most—during stressful situations.

Other personal factors can affect whether sources of memories will be confused. Our mental capabilities and the way in which we put these capabilities to use also play a part. Suppose you are presented with items, some of which are words that are read aloud and some of which are pictures, and you later have to say whether a given target was read or presented as a picture. If you readily develop a vivid mental image when a word is read to you (e.g., if the item is "turkey," you envision a colorful turkey strutting), then a later source judgment about whether you heard the word or saw an image of the item might be difficult. In either case, you might recall a vivid image of a turkey. Consistent with this idea, people with less-developed imagery capabilities (versus those with superior imagery abilities) actually do better on this kind of source judgment (Johnson, Raye, Wang, & Taylor, 1979). Similarly, if people are told to imagine words spoken in a particular person's voice, it will be more difficult for them to remember later whether that word was imagined or spoken by that person (Johnson, Foley, & Leach, 1988). Thus, the vividness of a person's imagination can have a dramatic effect on whether things that actually happened are confused with those that were only imagined.

The Source-Monitoring Framework

What is evident is that sometimes we accurately remember the source of a memory and sometimes we do not. Johnson and Raye (1981; see also Johnson, 1983; Johnson, Hashtroudi, & Lindsay, 1993) have formulated a model, called MEM, for multiple-entry modular memory system framework, which can explain our successes and source errors as well as many other findings from the source literature. According to MEM, people do not have labels indicating the sources of memories. Instead, we make attributions of source based on characteristics of our mental experiences at retrieval, such as perceptual, contextual, semantic, and emotional information relating to the event, as well as on our memory for the mental operations that we employed when encoding an item. According to their *source-monitoring framework*, retrieving these characteristics

> results in mental experiences that can range from general feelings of familiarity or strength to memory for specific features such as perceptual details (e.g., color, shape), spatial and temporal information, semantic information, affective details (e.g., emotional reactions), and the cognitive processes engaged (e.g., elaboration, retrieval of supporting information). Different types of acquisition processes (e.g., reading, thinking, inferring) and different types of events (e.g., movie, newspaper, dream) tend to produce memorial representations that are characteristically different from one another. (Mitchell & Johnson, 2000, p. 180)

Thus, imagine that you are studying a list of concepts, some of which are presented as color photographs (e.g., pictures of a dog and a car) and others that are spoken (e.g., a male voice says "cup" and "book"). Later, you are shown a word (e.g., "dog") and asked whether it was presented as a picture or was spoken aloud. In this case, a detailed image of a dog may come to mind that includes perceptual details (brown fur) and depth (hind legs behind front ones). If so, you would infer that the concept "dog" was presented as a photograph, because encoding of a photograph often leads to memorial representations that are perceptually detailed. When presented with the word "car," however, little may come to mind except for a general sense that the word is familiar. Accordingly, because the characteristics that you recalled are not perceptually detailed, you would (incorrectly) infer that "car" must have been spoken aloud.

The idea here is simply that we have expectations about what should come to mind if a particular memory came from a given source. So, if an item was presented as a picture, one later expects to have a perceptually detailed memory for that item. If an item does not have those distinctive properties during the test, then we are likely to say that it was not presented as a picture (see, e.g., Dodson & Schacter, 2002). Likewise, when we are asked if a particular idea was imagined versus presented by someone else, we may rely on our memory for the mental operations that occur when we generate ideas. So, if we remember struggling mentally to generate an idea, we would likely say that in fact we had originally generated it. Of course, errors in source memory can arise because the actual representations for various sources are not entirely distinct: Sometimes items presented as pictures do not produce representations that are perceptually detailed and hence lead us to believe that they were originally spoken, and sometimes items that we merely hear provoke mental images and hence make us believe that we originally imagined them versus heard them being spoken.

In the next section, we discuss some intriguing findings in which people do not attempt to recollect attributes of a memory that could reveal its source. Instead, people over-rely on the familiarity of an event, and in so doing, are led to believe that uncommon names are really those of famous people.

Becoming Famous Overnight: The Negative Consequence of Familiarity

Jacoby, Woloshyn, and Kelley (1989) distinguished between familiarity with an item and specific recollection of an item via retrieval of its characteristics or attributes. As with the source-monitoring framework described above, recollecting specific attributes is what source judgments are usually based upon. As demonstrated in a clever experiment by Jacoby, Woloshyn, and Kelley, not using recollections to judge source can lead to very poor source monitoring. The researchers presented students with a list of 40 non-famous names that included, for example, the name Sebastian Weisdorf. Could the students be made to believe that such non-famous people as Weisdorf were really famous? Participants were subjected to a *fame test*, which was administered either immediately after the list of names was presented or the day after. They were asked to distinguish between non-famous names and famous ones, some of which were also embedded in the test list. On the day-after test, participants were explicitly reminded that all of the names on the list they had seen were non-famous. Thus, if they remembered a name from that list, they should say it was not famous.

When the fame test was given immediately after participants had read the non-famous names, their source memory was good. That is, when asked whether Sebastian Weisdorf was famous, they could use their retrieval of the source of that memory (i.e., the source was the list) to correctly state that Weisdorf was not famous. When participants were tested a day later, however, they tended to claim that the names on the previous day's list were those of famous people. Sebastian Weisdorf had become famous overnight! Presumably, the participants' source memory after the one-day delay was not good enough to allow them to eliminate the names as having been presented to them the day before. At the same time, the familiarity of those names was increased from reading them the day before. Together, the increase in familiarity and the decrease in source memory caused the students to make a misattribution of fame.

In this case, people would likely make the correct inference if they had appropriate source information about the presence of the name on the previously studied list and used it. But this may not be how we normally make fame judgments—instead of going through the effort of trying to recall why an individual is famous, we may often make these judgments on the basis of mere familiarity. Of course, doing so will not reveal the specific memories needed to accurately judge source. For instance, one might ask, was a particular name familiar because the person gave a guest lecture in an Introduction to Chemistry class or because she was a famous politician whose name was often mentioned in the newspapers? Without detailed source memory, and the appropriate evaluation of it, people are liable to attribute such familiarity to fame.

People use familiarity to make other attributions as well. Lindsay and Johnson (1989) also showed that people over-rely on familiarity to make a judgment of whether a target occurred in a particular scene, rather than retrieving the specifics of the scene. In fact, they may use mere familiarity even when they are specifically asked about the source. In Lindsay and Johnson's experiments, participants first viewed a complex picture. They were then given a description of the picture, but the description also included some objects that had not appeared in the picture (but which would be plausible in that context). These objects were the critical items. When the participants were required to say whether an object actually appeared in a picture, they claimed that some of the critical items (which were not actually in the pictures, but were mentioned later) were there. However, when they were asked whether the objects had occurred (a) in the picture only, (b) in the description only but not the picture, (c) in both the picture and the description, or (d) in neither, their source memory performance was much improved. Put differently, they were able to say that objects that had appeared *only* in the description had not been in the picture. Lindsay and Johnson argued that when people made the (less detailed) yes/no recognition judgments, they simply used the familiarity of the object as the basis of the judgment. They did not make further efforts to check that the source was correct. Thus, people *could* make source judgments fairly accurately, if so required, but if not pressed to do so they often defaulted to making their judgments based on mere familiarity.

The Role of Conscious Recollection in Source Memory

For many decades, researchers have argued that past events may alter behavior either (a) because we consciously recollect them or (b) because their influence is implicit; that is, the change is familiarity-based and may occur without conscious awareness of the inducing event (Tulving, Schacter, & Stark, 1982). The distinction between these two kinds of memory (i.e., explicit and implicit, or recollection-based and familiarity-based) may ultimately be captured by people's source judgments.

The process-dissociation methodology developed by Larry Jacoby (1991) underscores the importance of distinguishing between *recollection* and *familiarity* in source attributions. Jacoby developed a procedure to allow researchers to tease apart conscious recollection from unconscious memory processes based on familiarity by setting them in *opposition* to each other. In particular, he distinguished between recollection and familiarity, where recollection is taken to mean that an individual is consciously retrieving the source of an item. If people can recollect an event, they should be able to recognize that it actually happened, and so a conscious process underlies some recognition judgments. However, some recognition can be done on the basis of mere familiarity. Such familiarity-based recognition purportedly entails a fast and automatic process that does not include retrieval, does not require conscious access to the remembered event, and hence does not access source information.

So, how could we estimate how much these two processes—recollection and familiarity—contribute to people's attributions about their memories? Imagine that we conduct an experiment in which people read an article from *The New York Times* and one from *Rolling Stone*. Each article includes various facts (some similar, some different) about the 2008 presidential campaign in the United States. After people read each one, you test them by presenting a fact and asking them about its source. More specifically, to measure the extent to which the source (e.g., *Rolling Stone*) is recollected or inferred based on familiarity, they are given a recognition memory test that includes

Larry L. Jacoby
Championed creative techniques to explore the theoretical basis of memory judgments

new facts, facts only from *The New York Times*, and facts only from *Rolling Stone*. Participants are given one of two sets of instructions, as follows: (a) *inclusion instructions:* Say "yes" to any fact that was in either *The New York Times* or in *Rolling Stone*. These are called inclusion instructions because you are told to include facts from both stories (as opposed to new facts that were not in either story); or (b) *exclusion instructions:* Say "yes" to any facts that were in *The New York Times*, but say "no" to any new fact or any fact that came from *Rolling Stone*. These are called exclusion instructions because you are told to exclude new facts and all facts from *Rolling Stone*.

Under the inclusion instructions, participants would say "yes" to a fact regardless of whether they consciously recollected which source it came from or whether it was merely familiar, because most of the recently "read" facts should be more familiar than new facts (which, after all, were presented for the first time on the test). In contrast, under the exclusion instructions, participants would still say "yes" to facts that were familiar, unless they were able to recollect that the source was *Rolling Stone*, in which case they would reject it. Armed with the results of such an experiment, a researcher can use probabilities to estimate the contribution of recollection and familiarity to source performance (for equations and detailed discussion, see Jacoby, 1998). Other techniques, such as multinomial modeling (Batchelder & Riefer, 1990; Bayen et al., 1996) and analyses of receiver operation characteristics (Yonelinas, 1994), also provide estimates of how much these two processes influence source memory. Most important, all of these techniques generally yield the same conclusion: Recollection and familiarity both influence people's recognition performance and source judgments.

Mystery BOX 7.2
Source Monitoring: Two Processes or Just One?

In a provocative paper, Slotnick and Dodson (2005) argue that recollective processes do not contribute to the accuracy of people's source memory. They conclude that "the all-or-none process of memory retrieval (as assumed in the multinomial model and the recollection component of the dual-process model), although intuitively appealing, should be reconsidered as a viable description of memory retrieval" (p. 169). Counterintuitive though this may seem, they are actually arguing that when a friend asks you, "Did your doctor or your mother tell you not to eat grapefruit?," your source judgment is not at all based on whether or not you recall the source. But if recalling the past episode in which the event occurred is not responsible for our ability to make a source judgment, then what is?

In contrast to the two-process models (described in our text) that involve both recollection and familiarity, some theorists are putting forth the possibility that two processes are one too many and that familiarity alone—a one-process model—can explain how we make source judgments, among other judgments once believed to rely on recollection (e.g., Rotello & MacMillan, 2006; Siegfried, 2004). For the single-process models, familiarity varies along a continuum of strength, with the lowest strength indicating little or no memory for the correct source and the highest strength indicating perfect memory for the correct source. So, if you're asked whether the source was your doctor or your mother, your answer will be based on which source (doctor or mother) has the greatest amount of familiarity when presented with "Which one told you not to eat grapefruit?" Although this single-process model may not be highly intuitive, note that in the case presented in the text (and with the bulk of experiments on source memory), both sources are presented during the source judgment. That is, participants are asked which source was connected with this particular item, Source A or Source B? In such cases, source memory boils down to recognizing the correct source, which may entice participants to rely on the mere familiarity of each source in the context of the item.

The debate about whether conscious recollection is involved in source memory (or whether familiarity alone will suffice) is ongoing, and it is evident that researchers on both sides of this debate are unlikely to concede their positions without further exploration and discussion. On one hand, some data from source-monitoring experiments are apparently better fit by single-process models than by two-process models (for a review, see Slotnick & Dodson, 2005). Add to these demonstrations the fact that single-process models are more parsimonious, and one has a relatively solid argument for concluding that familiarity alone drives source memories. On the other hand, evidence from neuroimaging studies suggests that different brain regions are activated during some source-memory tasks as opposed to item-memory tasks. Moreover, these brain regions appear to be differentially associated with recollection and familiarity (e.g., Woodruff, Hayama, & Rugg, 2006). Certainly, with staunch advocates on both sides of the debate, we must consider this mystery to be one of the most important to solve in the literature on source monitoring. In particular, does one process (familiarity) or two processes (both recollection and familiarity) underlie source memory? And if it is the latter, under what circumstances does recollection play a role?

What is particularly powerful about these techniques is that they allow investigators to estimate how a particular factor influences source memory. For instance, as we grow older, our memory for source tends to decline (for details, see Chapter 11). Put differently, memory for sources is often worse for adults in their 70s than for those in their 20s. Using the process-dissociation procedure, Jacoby and his colleagues have shown that aging appears to cause deficits in people's recollection of sources, whereas aging leaves the more automatic familiarity-based processes intact. Other factors also appear to improve source memory by improving people's recollection of source, such as studying longer and fully attending to stimuli and their sources (for a review, see Kelley & Jacoby, 2000). From this evidence, it appears that our abilities to recollect the past—that is, consciously retrieve the characteristics of previous memories—play a critical role in our ability to accurately judge the source of a memory.

Breakdowns of Source and Reality Monitoring

Reality monitoring, which is the ability to correctly assess whether some event is the result of your imagination or whether it occurred externally to you, is a special case of source monitoring. One real-life question that speaks to reality monitoring is, Did you think up that new brilliant idea or was it something that a friend told you? Answering this question incorrectly may represent *cryptomnesia*, which refers to unconsciously plagiarizing someone else's work (Marsh & Bower, 1993). Cryptomnesia can have dire effects, such as when George Harrison—of the Beatles—was sued and found guilty for plagiarizing his major hit, "My Sweet Lord." Harrison evidently was unaware of plagiarizing from the Chiffons' hit "He's So Fine." In fact, the lawyer who tried the case said that it was obvious that Harrison had no idea that he had plagiarized the song, even though the two songs were virtually identical (for a discussion of this case and the literature on cryptomnesia, see Perfect & Stark, 2008). Whereas even normal college students are not perfect at making reality judgments, patients in whom there is a breakdown in this metacognitive capability are especially fascinating.

BOX 7.3
Trips to Outer Space and My Life With Two Wives

If you were talking to an uncle and he was telling you how last evening, right after dinner, he was abducted by an alien spaceship and took a trip to outer space, you might think he was lying to you. Unfortunately, however, individuals who have some forms of amnesia make up relatively far-out stories while they are having a conversation. Such confabulation is not always outlandish (and may be just an ordinary false memory about what they had watched on TV the previous evening), and as important, they are not lying. At least, most confabulators do not realize that they are confabulating.

Confabulation was initially thought to be a gap-filling process that is not qualitatively different from the constructive processes found in normal individuals, except that the confabulating individual is amnesic and so the gaps are more severe and require more reconstruction. Although this is a plausible hypothesis, it appears to be incorrect. When normal people's memory declines, they recall less, and what they do recall is more stereotyped, and certainly does not resemble the extreme forms of confabulation seen in some amnesiacs. As Alba and Hasher (1983) have noted, there is a lack of intrusion in the recall of normal people. Also, many amnesiacs do not confabulate. It appears in only a subset of amnesiacs, and with a particular kind of amnesiac—namely, those with Korsakoff amnesia, which results from a lifetime of alcohol abuse. Whitty and Lewin (1957) found a striking tendency of patients who had undergone anterior cingulectomy to spontaneously confabulate, though only for a few days following the operation. Strangely, these same patients often had an awareness of their deficit, saying, for example: "My thoughts seem to be out of control, they go off on their own—so vivid. I am not sure half of the time if I just thought it or it really happened" (Whitty & Lewin, 1957, p. 73).

Confabulation arguably results from a failure of reality monitoring. Consistent with this possibility, most confabulating patients have been shown to have damage to their frontal lobe. For example, a reduplicative paramnesia patient reported by Stuss (1991) doubled his family on returning home from the hospital. He claimed to have two wives (who were remarkably similar in age, build, appearance, and temperament) and 8, rather than 4, "matched" children, with children in each family spaced a year apart, which was roughly the amount of time the patient had been away from home in the hospital. The patient had frontal damage. Damasio, Graff-Radford, Eslinger, Damasio, and Kassel (1985) described a patient who had an aneurysm of the anterior cerebral artery. He claimed he was a space pilot and believed that Anwar Sadat had visited him in the hospital. Unfortunately, there are many such cases. Such breakdowns in reality monitoring nearly always show frontal damage, as indicated by a meta-analysis conducted by Johnson, Hayes, D'Esposito, and Raye (2000). Thus, a breakdown in metacognitive awareness—due to damage to the frontal lobes—apparently contributes to this debilitating dysfunction.

Schizophrenia

A common symptom of schizophrenia is auditory or visual hallucinations, and more generally, a difficulty distinguishing events that are internally generated from those that are externally produced. Such symptoms invite an interpretation that a core factor in schizophrenia is severe impairment in reality monitoring. Bentall (1990) reviewed 175 cases of patients who had described auditory experiences and concluded that hallucinators make hasty and overconfident judgments about the sources of their perceptions and have a bias toward inappropriately attributing their perceptions to external sources. They fail to recognize that some internal stimulation, with voicelike qualities, can be internally generated. If, for example, they believe that they control their own thoughts, and yet have an intrusive thought, a schizophrenic may not attribute that thought to the self and instead will think that it came from the outside.

The source-monitoring framework indicates that rather than attaching inside-outside markers to different sources, the judgments are made heuristically, based on information present in the memory or in the event. There are two independent source-monitoring processes: (a) heuristic source monitoring, that is, a comparison of the perceptual, temporal, semantic, and affective characteristics with what the individual expects from either an internal or external source, and (b) systematic source monitoring, that is, reasoning about the plausibility of a memory's source given the person's prior beliefs. Do schizophrenics use both of these processes—or criteria—as they evaluate the origins of a voice? Relevant to this question, Garrett and Silva (2003) investigated a sample of clinical patients, looking at the phenomenology underlying the belief that the voices were real, and that this error constituted a critical part of the psychotic illness seen in schizophrenia. Consider some of their findings. First, consistent with the heuristic criterion, many of the characteristics of an external source were present in the patient's reports about their hallucinations. The hallucinations were universally spoken in a clear voice, usually gendered, and nearly always involved back-and-forth conversation. Second, however, some clear violations arose in terms of the second criterion, systematic source monitoring. For example, more than 75% of the patients knew that other people could not hear these voices. One might expect that this would provide some clue that the voices came from inside, rather than being external, but this knowledge did not shake the patients' beliefs that the voices were produced externally, as the source-monitoring framework might predict. Furthermore, the observation that the voices came in dreams, and that they could predict the future, might also indicate the voices were not real, but they were interpreted by the patients to the contrary, as proof positive of their reality.

Blakemore (2003) has provided an alternative framework for explaining deficits in reality monitoring. She argues that there are specific brain circuits that allow people to evaluate when they are doing something themselves as compared to when it originates in the external world. Such a circuit is necessary if an individual is to gauge the effect of his own actions. That is, you must know that it is *your* actions that are affecting the world and not just accidental happenings or changes due to someone else's actions. Presumably, before we act, we set up an action plan, and then do the actions specified. Thus, the efferent feedback that results from one's own actions is different from such feedback from actions that are initiated by others, because (a) the motor feedback is different, but also because (b) the plan that is set up in advance of the movement and the expectations about what one's own motor actions are like are different.

Blakemore (2003) has proposed a framework for how this kind of internal monitoring is done, and why schizophrenics fail to realize that they themselves are doing things; that others are not doing them. According to the framework illustrated in Figure 7.1, when a person has a goal, it gives rise to a model that is similar to a rough sketch of their intentions about achieving the goal. Then, a motor plan, called the *forward model*, gives the specifications about what the muscles need to do, on-line, to achieve the goal. The forward model is a detailed expectation of what should happen and it runs in real time simultaneously with the person's actual motor actions. The forward model can evaluate feedback on a moment-to-moment basis, to allow correction of the motor movements. Such on-line feedback is extremely useful in allowing fine motor control of all kinds of action. To allow this feedback, a comparison is made between (a) what the person predicts (though not necessarily consciously) about what feedback should be received from the sensory system as a result of the forward model, and (b) what the actual result of the motor action is. If the expectation and the outcome are the same, the comparator registers no difference or a null result. This means that the person's intentions are in perfect synchrony with what happens. The lack of discrepancy means that the person himself is doing something, and it is running smoothly according to plan. The result of this comparator is taken as the source of people's attributions about the source of an event as being from themselves as opposed to being external. The attribution to the self comes from a lack of discrepancy between one's own expectations and what happens. So, when the comparator indicates nothing that means it's the person himself doing it. What about when there is a large discrepancy? That indicates that something or someone else was doing the action: It is not one's own intentions that are being actualized, but someone or something else's. Furthermore, Blakemore has proposed that it is impairments in this circuit that may be responsible for schizophrenics' errors in reality monitoring.

Suppose, for example, that the internal feedback from one's own actions was distorted. Suppose that because of this distortion the predicted state was wrong. The necessary match between what an individual intended to do and what actually happened might not be good enough for him to consider that he in fact controlled the action. He might, therefore, think someone else was moving his hand (as some schizophrenics do), or that someone else was speaking, when it was really self-initiated. Indeed, Knoblich, Stottmeister, and Kircher (2004) have shown that schizophrenics do have impairment in monitoring the fine-grained effects of their own actions. The researchers had

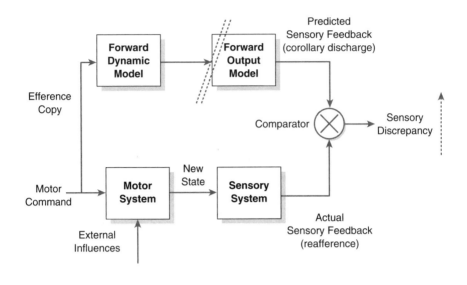

Figure 7.1   The Forward Model.

SOURCE: Blakemore, S.-J. (2003). Deluding the motor system. *Consciousness and cognition*, *12*, 647–655.

schizophrenics and normal participants follow a dot on a computer screen that was moving at a particular rate. Their only job was to say when they had to increase their speed to keep track of the dot. At a certain point, the dot was speeded up. Both normals and schizophrenics sped up to keep the dot in track. Their motor actions were appropriate. But the normals were much quicker and more accurate in saying when they had to make this change. The schizophrenics changed, but did not know that they had done so for a considerable lag—as would happen if they had poor monitoring of their own actions.

How might this apply to schizophrenics hearing voices? It would seem that the voices that schizophrenics "hear" and monitor as having been presented from the outside world are self-generated (Kinsbourne, 1995). Brain imaging studies of hallucinating patients have shown activation in the auditory cortex (Bentaleb, Beauregard, Liddle, & Stip, 2002), although areas implicated in monitoring are also activated (Shergill, Brammer, Williams, Murray, & McGuire, 2000). But if the *expected* outcome of the speech action does not match what the person "hears," then she may say that hearing this voice is not like hearing one's own voice speaking (where that monitoring is intact) but rather more like hearing an external voice.

One tantalizing bit of evidence favoring the forward model as applied to schizophrenia comes from an application of the model to an analysis of the mechanism underlying our sense of being tickled. Have you ever wondered why it is that other people are able to tickle you senseless, but no matter how hard you try, you are unable to tickle yourself? The forward model provides a coherent answer to this deep question. Consider what happens in the forward model when you try to tickle yourself. Your intention feeds through its loop in the model, instantiating a motor plan in imaginary-hypothetical space that is simultaneously carried out as your actual motor movement. These two brain streams meet at the comparator, and are compared. Nothing happens. They are the same. No discrepancy, no tickle. But when someone else tickles you, the comparator registers a large discrepancy, and voilà—a tickle. Now for the big question. Can schizophrenics tickle themselves? In fact, schizophrenics who suffer from auditory hallucinations can tickle themselves (for a review, see Blakemore, Wolpert, & Frith, 2000)! Score the forward model a big success.

Mirror Sign: Who Is That Person in the Mirror?

Perhaps the strangest self-monitoring deficit comes from a handful of case studies in which patients have a selective deficit in what is called the *mirror sign*. Normally, children, starting at about the age of 2, are able to recognize themselves in mirrors, and all normal human adults know that the image that they see in the mirror refers to them. We do not mistake the source of our reflection. Feinberg and Shapiro (1989) tested SM, who was a 77-year-old deaf woman. Having been deaf since she was 5, she was able to sign. When she would look in the mirror, she apparently did not realize that the person reflected was herself, and she would sign and claim to be communicating with "the other" SM. According to the patient, this other SM was virtually identical to her in age and physical characteristics but was someone else. Sprangenberg, Wagner, and Bachman (1998) described an 82-year-old woman who would look in the mirror and would report seeing a young girl looking out at her. This young girl would follow her around, reflecting at her from shop windows. Shown her own picture at the hospital, Sprangenberg's patient said, "That girl! What is she doing here? I thought she was only back at home!" That girl was, apparently, very much like the patient herself but younger. Despite efforts, the patient could not be taught or coached that the person in the mirror or in the picture was really her own image. Interestingly, like all other patients showing this syndrome, she understood that other people's reflections referred to the other people. But she could not understand or accept that her own reflection referred to herself.

Breen, Caine, and Coltheart (2001) evaluated two patients with mirror sign. The first was an 87-year-old man, who reported that another person followed him around. This other person was visible when he looked in the mirror. The patient also incorporated his wife into his mirror delusion, saying that the woman who was sometimes in the mirror was the wife of his own self-delusion. The second patient, TH, was a 77-year-old man who thought that his mirror other was a dead ringer for himself. He would talk to the person in the mirror. In addition, he elaborated something of a life for the delusion, believing that the person he saw when he looked in the mirror lived in the apartment next to his. Like other patients, TH could identify others in the mirror, but not himself. All of these patients had damage in the right frontal cortex. Mirror sign represents a profound source-monitoring deficit: A person sees an image in a mirror, yet fails to recognize the source of this image! As we'll discuss next, however, even individuals without deficits—like schizophrenia or mirror sign—can demonstrate surprising deficits in reality monitoring.

Reality-Monitoring Deficits in Normal Individuals

Distortions in reality monitoring are not the exclusive domain of psychiatric patients. Even college undergraduates are easily duped. Wegner and his group at Harvard have conducted a series of experiments in which they show that people will often assume responsibility for actions that actually were done by someone else, and the reverse. For example, Wegner, Sparrow, and Winerman (2004) had participants sit in front of a mirror dressed in a smock, with another person, a confederate of the researchers, behind the participant. The confederate's hands extended out of the smock where the participant's hands normally would have appeared (see Figure 7.2). The hands performed a series of movements. When the movements were preceded by spoken instructions as to what the hands were to perform (so the participant heard a plan in advance of the action that was then carried out), participants felt as though they were controlling the other person's hands! In contrast, when the instructions came after the movements, participants did not feel that they were controlling the confederate's hands, which is consistent with the forward model discussed above.

Our great (great) grandparents may have believed that they were communing with spirits when they used such parlor games as Ouija boards. Many of us today shake our heads in disbelief at their gullibility. Surely a gross failure of reality monitoring had overtaken them! But before we scoff too loudly, consider an experiment from Wegner and Wheatley (1999).

Figure 7.2   Setup for study illustrating reality distortions in "normal" subjects. The setup involves a participant and a confederate who is working for the researcher. In the mirror, the participant can see only the confederate's hands (left panel), as she is hidden behind the participant (right panel).

SOURCE: Wegner, D. M., Sparrow, B., and Winerman, L. (2004). Vicarious agency: Experiencing control over the movements of others. *Journal of Personality and Social Psychology, 86*(6), 838–848.

Although not implicating spirits from the dead, this experiment shows how easy it is for even normal college students to misattribute agency. The researchers had two students—a participant and a confederate—sit across from each other and jointly move a mouse to direct an arrow on a computer screen (Figure 7.3). The screen displayed images of 50 tiny objects, such as a dinosaur, a swan, a car, and so forth. The students were told to stop moving the mouse every 30 seconds, and then evaluate who was responsible for the stop, with responses ranging from "I allowed the stop to happen" to "I intended to make the stop." While moving the mouse around, music and words were played in the participant's ears via headphones. The words primed items on the screen (e.g., one of the words spoken in the headphones might be "swan"). The confederate did not hear music or words on her headphones, but she did receive instructions. On some critical trials, she was in complete control of the mouse and was told to move the arrow to a particular object. At the same time, on these critical trials, the object to which the confederate moved the mouse was sometimes primed for the participant, and sometimes it was not. The researchers found that when the object was primed well in advance (30 seconds) of the stop, the participants did not take responsibility for stopping the mouse. However, when the prime occurred between 1 and 5 seconds before the stop, the participants thought they had done it. Thus, having a plan in one's head (even if one did not generate that plan) can make even normal college students think that they caused an event to happen when, in fact, they had no control over it!

Even normal individuals without any psychopathology can make astounding—and almost unbelievable—errors in their source monitoring. Indeed, psychopathologies like schizophrenia are on a continuum with normal functioning, with the diagnosis itself having much to do with the magnitude of the distortions, their persistence, how disturbing they are to the individual, and whether they keep the person from functioning in society and in personal relationships. Thus, a small slip in monitoring should not be taken as evidence of dysfunction. Rather, we might hope that our sympathy for people who have serious breakdowns may be heightened by our realization of the fragile nature of our own reality monitoring.

Brain Bases of Source-Monitoring Judgments

Many researchers are now attempting to isolate the brain regions responsible for one's memory for an item versus memory for its source. For example, Mitchell, Johnson, Raye, and Greene (2004) found selective prefrontal cor-

Figure 7.3   Setup for demonstrating that people who plan an action can have a sense of control even if they were not responsible for the action. A participant and a confederate jointly move a mouse to direct an arrow on a computer screen. In this case, the participant's sense of controlling the mouse is illusory.

SOURCE: Wegner, D. M., and Wheatley, T. (1999). Apparent mental causation: Sources of the experience of will. *American Psychologist, 54*, 480–492.

tex (PFC) activity, particularly left lateral PFC activity, when people were recollecting specific source information (either the format or location of an originally presented item) as compared to when remembering could be based on mere familiarity.

Whereas most researchers agree that the monitoring functions are related to activation in the prefrontal cortex (although exact locations of particular kinds of monitoring functions—source, frequency, recency, feelings of knowing, judgments of learning—are still being determined), they also affirm a role for the medial temporal lobes in binding parts of a memory together (see Kroll, Knight, Metcalfe, Wolf, & Tulving, 1996). Such binding processes, in which an event and its source are associated, seem to be critical for accurate judgments of source. Thus, insofar as the source needs to be bound to the content to inform accurate judgments of source, it would seem necessary that the medial temporal lobes would also be involved in these particular metamemory tasks.

Consistent with this possibility, Davachi, Mitchell, and Wagner (2003) demonstrated that the frontal lobe and the medial temporal region of the brain were involved in item and source memory. As can be seen in Figure 7.4 (shown inside the front cover), the hippocampus (often thought to be implicated in binding) and the posterior parahippocampal cortex were selectively activated when people were retrieving the source of a memory. In contrast, when people were making simpler familiarity judgments (i.e., attempting to recognize the items themselves and not their sources), the perirhinal cortex was activated. Although the circuitry between these various brain regions remains to be fully specified, this study goes a long way in illuminating what is probably a selective interaction among multiple brain regions in supporting source memory.

Moreover, neuropsychological research has also weighed in on the debate about whether recollection and familiarity-based processes may contribute independently to memory judgments. In particular, using functional Magnetic Resonance Imagery (fMRI), Yonelinas, Otten, Shaw, and Rugg (2005) demonstrated that within the prefrontal cortex the anterior medial region was related to recollection, but lateral regions (including the anterior and dorsolateral prefrontal cortex) were related to familiarity. Ranganath et al. (2003) also showed that familiarity and recollection were dissociable within the medial temporal lobes. They found that recollection was associated with hippocampal and posterior parahippocampal activation, whereas familiarity revealed selective activation in the rhinal cortex. It is interesting that the regions that some researchers have isolated as being those that underlie recollection (as opposed to familiarity) are the same regions that other research teams have isolated as being responsible for source judgments as opposed to item recognition. Thus, these brain imaging studies, like the behavioral studies, suggest that two different systems are involved in these two kinds of memory processes.

Summary

Our ability to remember the source of a memory can often be as important as having an accurate memory itself. In fact, if you misremember that you heard that an upcoming exam was rescheduled from your teacher in class rather than from your teacher in a dream, you might find yourself unprepared on exam day. Although such extreme disruptions of source memory might seem unlikely, it is apparent that people of all sorts can suffer from deficits in source memory.

As with other metacognitive judgments, such deficits (and successes) in source monitoring arise from the heuristic nature of the judgments themselves. That is, people use a variety of cues from memory to *infer* the source of a memory. According to the source-monitoring framework, errors in source monitoring partly arise when the characteristics retrieved about a memory incorrectly match what we expect to retrieve about a different source. So, in the example above, perhaps your dream was vivid, with many perceptual characteristics (hearing the teacher's voice and seeing him dressed in his typical manner) and emotional ones (remembering how relieved you were when he said the test date was moved). Remembering such characteristics of the dream may persuade you that it did in fact happen. As the cognitive and brain bases of source monitoring are further understood, perhaps techniques can be devised that will consistently and dramatically improve the accuracy of source judgments for normal individuals and those with psychopathologies.

DISCUSSION QUESTIONS

1. Imagine four friends sitting around a Ouija board and having fun trying to obtain answers to some of life's most intriguing questions such as, "Will I be rich when I grow older?" Or, "Is global warming really going to cause a problem for our children?" As they're playing this game, two friends are convinced that the planchette (the indicator with the arrow that everyone touches) is moving on its own and is in fact controlled by spirits revealing the truth about these questions. Assuming that they actually believe that the planchette is moving on its own (versus being moved by the other friends), why might they make this (somewhat hilarious) error in source attribution?

2. In the fame task, non-famous names that are presented a day prior to the test phase are erroneously judged as being famous. The difficulty people have here is that the earlier

presentation of the names makes them familiar and people fail to remember that the source of that familiarity is their previous exposure. How could such techniques be used by politicians to implant false beliefs in voters? How might advertisers use them to make consumers believe their product is better than others, when in fact all the competing products are virtually identical? As a voter and consumer, how could you potentially side-step being inappropriately persuaded? That is, how could you more accurately evaluate the truthfulness of politicians' statements or the overblown claims of advertisements?

CONCEPT REVIEW

For the following questions, we recommend you write down the answers on a separate sheet in as much detail as possible, and then check them against the relevant material in the chapter.

1. What is the difference between source memory and item memory?

2. According to the source-monitoring framework, how do people judge their source of an item? Why are we sometimes inaccurate at judging sources?

3. Which brain areas do scientists believe are responsible for the recollective processes that underlie source judgments?

4. According to the forward model, how can we explain that schizophrenics may confuse an inner voice with an external source? That is, why might they have auditory hallucinations?

5. What is "mirror sign" and how does it represent a source-monitoring error?

Section 2

Applications

8

Law and Eyewitness Accuracy

Do you swear to tell the truth, the whole
truth, and nothing but the truth?

Such a simple question that people so often "swear" to, yet how easy is it to live up to telling the "whole truth, and nothing but the truth"? Certainly, for eyewitnesses who are reporting on their memory of a crime, telling the whole truth (and nothing but the truth) requires accurate metacognitive monitoring and control—to sift out incorrect memories or fabricated ones to get to just the valid ones. From what you've already learned from this textbook, you know that it is likely impossible for anyone to meet this standard—telling nothing but the truth—in any but the simplest of scenarios. Moreover, the perception that people can achieve this standard in the courtroom is just one of many examples of how metacognition is relevant to law and eyewitness testimony. People's beliefs about their own and other people's memories—their confidence that others are remembering correctly, their beliefs with respect to suppressing or disregarding evidence and their ability to do so, and their evaluations about the veracity of other people's reports—are crucial metacognitive phenomena of particular relevance to courtroom proceedings and the judicial system.

In Chapter 8, we review some findings on the relation of people's confidence to the correctness of their memories, on people's assessment of the truth of witnesses' memories based on their expressed confidence, and on people's abilities to detect lies. Finally, we will explore the pernicious influence of a phenomenon called hindsight bias or the "I knew it all along" effect. Experiments show that even though people have a good ability, for example, to assess whether testimony should be admissible, this "knew it all along" effect thwarts their ability to control their decisions about guilt or innocence accordingly. As we shall see, this particular kind of mental time travel—back to a naive state—is extraordinarily difficult for people to do. Before we get to that, however, let us begin our exploration of the role of metacognition and the law with people's feelings and expressions of confidence.

Confidence and False Memories

If people are given misinformation about an event that they experienced or witnessed, they may later believe that the misinformation is true and actually happened. For example, imagine watching a film in which a car goes through a stop sign, and then you receive the suggestion that it actually had been a yield sign. Later, when you are asked whether it was a stop sign or a yield sign that you saw, you may well say it was a yield sign (Loftus, Miller, & Burns, 1978). Even *how* you are asked about what happened during an event can influence your memory of it. After witnessing a car accident on video, people can be asked how fast the cars were going when they "smashed" into each other, or instead, how fast the cars were going when they "hit" each other. When the question is framed in terms of "smashing," people are likely to remember the speed as being faster than if the question is framed as "hit." They also may report that they saw broken glass at the scene of the accident, even though no windows were broken (see Loftus & Hoffman, 1989, for these and other examples). Moreover, when an inaccurate event (e.g., you saw a yield sign) is suggested repeatedly (versus just a single time), people are even more likely to claim that the event actually happened, and their confidence in this false memory is greatly enhanced (Zaragoza & Mitchell, 1996). In all of these situations, people come to inaccurately judge that an untrue memory about an event is actually true. People's metacognitive monitoring is failing, and unknowingly, they do not tell "nothing but the truth."

Perhaps the most famous research involving completely implanted misinformation is a study by Loftus and Pickrell (1995) in which the experimenters implanted a person with the "memory" of having been lost in a shopping mall. We describe this experiment in detail below, but an important point here is that the implanted memory had emotional content. By some views, emotional memories should be difficult to mistake. Indeed, some therapists and lay people believe that emotional memories simply cannot, by their very nature, be false, and that reported emotional memories of abuse, such as those that frequently surface during therapy, are necessarily true. In contrast to this view, the possibility that some disturbing memories might be attributable to suggestion, to imagination, or to having been inadvertently implanted by therapists trying to help the victim, need not indicate that the victims are not reporting what they remember in good faith (or, indeed, that the therapists were not trying to help). It is conceivable that a person might genuinely believe that a false memory is true. Whether or not this happens, however, is an empirical question.

High confidence is frequently taken to mean that a memory is true. But, as we saw in the chapter on confidence, people, at least in laboratory situations, are frequently overconfident. Are people in the real world also overconfident? When people swear they are telling the truth, can they be mistaken? The answer to both questions is "yes." And, in the next sections, we'll consider some answers to more specific questions that arise in the literature: First, could a person show high confidence about remembering an event that never happened? Second, what underlies people's confidence, and does this confidence normally provide a reliable index of which memories are true and false? Third, can confidence be manipulated? If so, how? And, fourth, are there any special circumstances—such as when a memory is of a traumatic event—in which a person's confidence in his or her memory is infallible?

Can We Have High Confidence, Even for an Event That Never Happened?

The study introduced above by Loftus and Pickrell (1995) addressed our first question. They conducted a case study in which they tried to implant a nonexistent memory into the mind of a 14-year-old boy named Chris. He was given descriptions of three true events that had happened in his childhood along with one false event that had never happened. The false memory was introduced in a paragraph reminding Chris that when he was 5 he had been lost in the University City shopping mall in Spokane, Washington, where the family often shopped. He was crying loudly when rescued by an elderly man, and reunited with his family. Chris wrote about the four events every day for 5 days, providing all of the descriptions he could remember of each, but being told that if nothing more came to mind he could write "I don't remember." On the final day, it was evident that the false event that had been initially suggested to Chris had become a vivid memory. He remembered that the man who rescued him was "cool," that he was scared he would never see his family again, and that his mother scolded him.

He remembered that the man wore a blue flannel shirt, that he was "kind of bald on top," and that he had glasses.

But surely, even though he could imagine such details, he did not believe that this completely confabulated event had actually happened? When asked to give his confidence about these four memories on a scale from 1 (low confidence) to 11 (high confidence), the ratings for the true memories were 1, 5, and 10, for a mean of 5.3. He gave an 8 to the false memory, and provided rich details about his thoughts at the time it had occurred. Clearly, his confidence was misplaced, because the event never happened (for other provocative examples, see Loftus, Coan, & Pickrell, 1979/1996).

An equally famous experimental study—the so-called Sam Stone study— was conducted on young children by Leichtman and Ceci (1995), who investigated how 3- to 4-year-olds and 5- to 6-year-olds remembered events that had never happened and how such "memories" might play out in a courtroom trial. Their study, like many others that asked the question of whether we should invariably believe children's testimony, was conducted hard on the heels of a number of real-life incidents in which young children had falsely accused adults of wrongdoing. Before we describe the experimental evidence, we'll highlight two—of many—cases in which children's false accusations have had a devastating effect on everyone involved.

In the Kelly Michaels case, a minor incident (one of the children, after having had his temperature taken at a pediatrician's office, said that his teacher had done that as well) led to repeated and very leading interrogations of all of the children in the Wee Care Nursery School. Of course, the parents were alarmed and outraged. The "memories" of the children suddenly started revealing all manner of abuse by Kelly Michaels. The escalation of the hysteria over what was apparently completely confabulated memory on the part of the children eventuated in Michaels being charged with 131 counts of sexual abuse against 20 children. All of these charges were made solely on the children's alleged memory of abuse. Michaels evidently committed these 131 heinous acts without provoking the notice of any other teacher (even though the memories of the children included things like Michaels dancing naked on top of a piano). No physical evidence was available. Michaels was convicted of 115 counts of sexual abuse of preschoolers, and was sentenced to 47 years in prison. Eventually, with the help of two investigative reporters (Dorothy Rabinowitz and Debbie Nathan), an attorney who took up her case (Morton Stavis), and a brief by 45 cognitive and clinical psychologists, the verdict was overturned and Michaels was released. But not before she had served 5 years in prison, 18 months of which were in solitary confinement (for her own safety). In a similar and equally outrageous case (the "Christchurch Crèche case" in New Zealand), Peter Ellis served his full sentence for alleged satanic abuse for which there was absolutely no evidence except the children's often wildly impossible testimony. Ellis refused to be released early on parole because the condition for doing so was that he admit his guilt.

Leichtman and Ceci's (1995) experimental study was an attempt to investigate such extreme examples of memory contagion in a controlled manner. Unlike most real-world events where it isn't possible to know (for sure) what really happened, the original events in the experiment were documented and allowed careful analyses of the boundary conditions of children's memory and confidence. The experiment takes its name from its central character, Sam Stone. Before he visited the nursery school, the children were told, repeatedly, that Sam was clumsy and tended to break things. When he actually visited, Sam stayed for only 2 minutes, and interacted amicably with the children. He broke nothing. The next day, however, the children were shown a soiled teddy bear and a torn book, and were asked whether, perhaps, Sam had done it. About 25% of the children said that perhaps he had done it, but none claimed to have seen him do it. Over the next 10 weeks, however, they were repeatedly asked things like, "I wonder whether Sam Stone was angry when he tore the book?" "I wonder whether he got the teddy bear dirty on purpose or by accident?" This questioning was considerably more benign, by the way, than the interrogations endured by the children in the Kelly Michaels case. Nevertheless, by the end of the 10-week period, when the children were asked to describe Sam Stone's visit to an outsider who hadn't been there at the time, 72% of the 3- to 4-year-olds said that Sam Stone had ruined one of the items, and fully 45% of them said they had actually seen him do it—indicating a high-confidence memory. The older children were a little better than the younger ones, with only 11% claiming to have actually seen him do it (but 11% is enough to convict!). The children who claimed to have seen him do it embellished these false memories with perceptual details that, according to Johnson and Raye's (1981) framework of source monitoring (see Chapter 7), would be convincing to both the children and to outside onlookers. So, if you confidently remember seeing the event (versus just believing you saw it), and you can describe some detail as to how it happened, it seems natural to believe the event could have happened.

False memories might be thought to be a phenomenon specific to children. Children have difficulty with reality monitoring, as is illustrated in Box 10.1 in the developmental chapter. Indeed, children have, until recently, been excluded from testifying in the U.S. legal system, in part, because of the notorious false accusations and memories of the children of Salem, Massachusetts, in 1692. Twenty-nine people were convicted and 19 were hanged because children remembered seeing them doing acts of witchcraft.

Although false memories may, in fact, be more common in children, false memories are certainly not the exclusive domain of children. Susan Clancy (2005) has interviewed more than 50 people who believe, with great conviction, that they have been abducted by aliens. This is a claim that most of us would agree is a false memory, despite the interviewees' high confidence. It would seem, then, that it is entirely possible for someone to have a high-confidence memory about something that never happened.

So, does high confidence in a memory count for nothing? We will explore the mechanisms underlying confidence in the next section.

What Underlies People's Confidence?

Given that people's confidence is based on the amount, speed, or clarity of what comes to mind, as well as the surrounding details indicating that the event was real and happened to them, one might expect that confidence would be a good indicator of correctness. Indeed, there are a host of confidence studies that begin with people being presented with a list of words. On a later test, they are shown each word again, along with new words that they did not study, and they indicate whether each word was presented earlier. They also make a confidence judgment about whether each recognition decision is correct. Most relevant here, the relative accuracy of people's confidence judgments is high. Higher confidence ratings almost inevitably mean that the item had been previously presented. Low ratings correlate very well with the items being new.

And, in the real world, too, when a person says, "I saw the person clearly and have high confidence that this is the culprit" as compared to someone who says, "Well, it was kind of fast and pretty much a blur and I think that maybe it was this person but I'm not sure," most people readily believe the person with high confidence and not the one with low confidence, and with good reason. Indeed, when people have been given factual questions to answer, followed by their confidence judgments about the correctness of their answers, their confidence judgments are highly accurate. Data from Butterfield and Metcalfe (2006), for example, showed that when people expressed confidence in the highest third of the confidence range, they were correct 70% of the time. In contrast, they were only correct 16% of the time when their confidence was low. And when people find out they have made a high-confidence error, they are surprised. Butterfield and Mangels (2003) have used event-related potential (ERP) techniques—in which electrodes measuring brain activity are attached to the scalp—to show that a particular "surprise"-related brain wave called the p300 occurs in these cases. Thus, under conditions in which confidence is not manipulated, an individual's confidence is likely to be a good marker of whether he or she is right or wrong. The problem is, as we will see shortly, that confidence can be readily manipulated, so that it does not accurately discriminate between true and false memories.

Even so, several studies have shown that people's confidence can be used as a barometer for determining whether a memory is true or false, at least to a limited extent. Read (1996; also see Roediger & McDermott, 1995), for example, conducted a study in which people saw the words "slumber, tired, rest, night, dark, comfort, sounds, eat, bed, snore, dream, and awake." When asked to recall the items from the list, 65.9% of the participants falsely recalled that "sleep" had been on the list. But was it? Look back. It's not there. Moreover, the same percentage recalled words that actually had been presented, so percentage of recall did not indicate whether the memory was a true memory or a false one (for a demonstration of this powerful effect, see the Minds-On Activity at the end of this chapter). People's confidence, however, does. In particular, in the study by Read (1996), retrospective confidence judgments were higher for words that actually had been presented (4.55, where 5 = extremely confident that the word was presented to 1 = no confidence) than for the seductive lures (e.g., "sleep") that had not been presented (3.0). Furthermore, when participants were asked whether they actually *remembered* hearing the presented words (e.g., slumber, tired, and rest), as compared to sleep, the proportion of "remember" responses was greater in the former case than in the latter (.73 and .46, respectively). But is the glass half empty or half full? That is, people believed in a false memory 46% of the time! So, although the confidence judgments do show some accuracy, people still do make metacognitive errors.

Some data indicate that a different metacognitive measure—people's source judgments—can sometimes be used to determine whether a memory is real, due to actually witnessing an event, or merely the result of a suggestion (Hicks & Marsh, 1999). Although people's fast familiarity recognition judgments may lead them to wrong conclusions about past experiences, being asked for more refined source judgments allows the elimination of some of the errors. For example, Lindsay and Johnson (1989) showed that sometimes people initially claim to have seen something that had only been suggested to them. If they were pressed further, however, to determine the source of the memory, people were better able to identify those items that were actually seen as compared to those only suggested. Use of this careful kind of source monitoring of memories could be invaluable in extracting accurate testimony from witnesses (see Box 8.1, The Cognitive Interview). Later, in Chapter 11, we will discuss how older adults who were trained to adopt more stringent standards to evaluate their memories were able to overcome one kind of memory illusion (Multhaup, 1995). It would appear that if metamemory processes are adequately engaged, people may be in a better position to sort out real memories from confabulations or implanted memories (Lane, Roussel, Villa, & Morita, 2007).

BOX 8.1
The Cognitive Interview

In the United States, more than 200 people have been convicted for committing a crime they did not commit and later have been exonerated by DNA evidence—after serving an average 12 years in prison. Cassel (2000) pointed out the great concern over such wrongful convictions. These, and other cases, led the U.S. Department of Justice to issue national Guidelines for Eyewitness Evidence, and to a nationwide effort to improve the methods of eliciting information from witnesses to avoid the production of false memories.

The Virginia case of Tommy David Strickler is an example of why such guidelines are needed. Strickler was convicted of capital murder, abduction, and robbery in the death of Leanne Whitlock. In 1991, he was sentenced to death. The case was appealed on the grounds that police evidence that might have discredited the testimony of the central eyewitness—who, at trial, convincingly gave a compelling and confident narrative filled with vivid detail—had not been made available to the defense. The prosecutor had said in his closing argument, "We are lucky enough to have an eyewitness who saw [what] happened out there in that parking lot. [In a] lot of cases you don't. A lot of cases you can just theorize what happened in the actual abduction. But Mrs. Stoltzfus was there, she saw [what] happened." The eyewitness, Anne Stoltzfus, publicly credited her vivid trial account to her "exceptionally good memory" and to her "very close contact with [the petitioner that] . . . made an emotional impression" on her. She said she had "absolutely no doubt" about seeing Strickler abduct Whitlock.

There was much, however, that the jury had not heard. For example, during her first interview with police two weeks after the crime, Stoltzfus had been unable to identify the victim, Leanne Whitlock. She identified Whitlock two weeks after her first meeting with Detective Daniel Claytor, and only after spending time with Whitlock's boyfriend "looking at current photos" of Whitlock. Early in the investigation, she also could not identify the alleged perpetrators. In a letter written to the detective three days after their first interview, she admitted that she had not remembered even being at the mall, but that her daughter had helped "jog" her "vague memory." In another early note to the detective, she only vaguely described the victim's car and she failed even to mention the license plate number that she claimed she dictated to her daughter, a passenger in her car at the scene of the abduction. At trial, however, she recalled both the car and the license number in detail. Finally, in a letter to Detective Claytor, she thanked him for his "patience with her sometimes muddled memories" and noted that "it would have been nice if I had remembered all this at the time and simply gone to the police with the information. But I totally wrote this off as a trivial episode of college kids carrying on." Further, as Cassel (2000) noted, in a letter to the Harrisonburg *Daily News-Record,* Stoltzfus said (all unbeknownst to the jury), "It never occurred to me that I was witnessing an abduction. In fact, if it hadn't been for the intelligent, persistent, professional work of Detective Daniel Claytor, I still wouldn't realize it. What sounded like a coherent story at the trial was the result of an incredible effort by the police to fit a zillion little puzzle pieces into one big picture." Strickler eventually lost his appeal on the basis that there was sufficient evidence, other than Stoltzfus's testimony, to justify his conviction and the imposition of the death penalty.

Police departments don't want to present questionable testimony that could discredit them or have verdicts overturned (or have questionable verdicts upheld). Accordingly, even many years before the Department of Justice guidelines were issued, police departments throughout the United States had been collaborating with psychologists to improve the way they interviewed witnesses to decrease the chances that they would implant false information. Ideally, interrogators want to extract more information from witnesses, without increasing errors. In response to this need, Ronald Fisher, a professor at Florida International University, along with Ed Geiselman, a professor at UCLA, developed the *cognitive interview*, a procedure now used by many police departments in the United States (Fisher & Geiselman, 1992).

The cognitive interview guides a witness through four memory-enhancing procedures: (a) thinking about the context, including the physical surroundings and their personal emotional reactions at the time of the event; (b) reporting everything that comes to mind, regardless of how fragmentary or inconsequential it seems; (c) remembering the events in several different sequences—from beginning to end, but also in reverse order, and from highly memorable points as well as from points of low salience; and (d) recalling the events from different perspectives, such as from a different person's point of view, or from above the scene. In its modified form, the cognitive interview also concentrates on building rapport with the witness, and getting the witness to actively participate in the interview rather than just responding to questions. It encourages the witness to tell the story in his or her own words without interruption before asking the witness to return to the memories from different perspectives and to examine the memory images in as much detail as possible. What the cognitive interview does not do is make suggestions of any sort about the content of what is remembered. Most important, studies have shown that this method increases the amount of correct information the witness recalls (often by 30 to 40%), and it does not increase the amount of incorrect information.

Can Confidence Be Manipulated?

Recall the Howard Haupt case, from Chapter 6. Haupt was mistakenly accused of kidnapping. He was not one of the original suspects in the case, but he had been staying at the hotel where the victim was kidnapped, and he had appeared in a photo lineup shown to the witness who later identified him. It was after the photo lineup, and after the witness saw Haupt in person, that he identified Haupt in another photo lineup as the kidnapper, with high confidence. That is, after multiple exposures to Haupt, the witness became familiar with him and began to believe that in fact he had committed the crime. Presumably, the witness had mistaken the origin of his familiarity with Haupt: Instead of saying "Haupt seems familiar because I recently saw him in a photo lineup," he instead attributed his familiarity to Haupt's having been the kidnapper. In this example, increased confidence appears to have resulted from exposure.

There is now good evidence that confidence can be influenced by the mere presentation or repetition of information, whether that information is diagnostic or not, and even whether the information is true or not. In a seminal study on spurious confidence, Oskamp (1965) had three groups of participants—licensed clinical psychologists, psychology graduate students in training, and undergraduates—who were briefed about the case of Joseph Kidd (a pseudonym). The experimental participants received four installments of material about Kidd in an effort to simulate the increased knowledge that therapists might acquire over sessions, as they got to know a client better. The first stage contained only demographic information as follows: "Joseph Kidd is a 29-year-old man. He is white, unmarried, and a veteran of World War II. He is a college graduate, and works as a business assistant in a floral decorating studio." The second stage consisted of $1\frac{1}{2}$, single-spaced, typed pages about Kidd's childhood; the third stage was 2 pages about his high school and college years. The fourth stage, $1\frac{1}{3}$ pages, went through his army experience and his life up to age 29.

After reading each stage of Joseph's case, the participants answered 25 questions, such as

> During college, when Kidd was in a familiar and congenial social situation, he often
>
> (a) Tried to direct the group and impose his wishes on it.
> (b) Stayed aloof and withdrawn from the group.
> (c) Was quite unconcerned about how people reacted to him.
> (d) Took an active part in the group but in a quiet and modest way.
> (e) Acted the clown and showed off.

The correct answer is (e).

The other questions were similar to this one in that they tapped into Kidd's customary behavior patterns, attitudes, interests, and typical reactions. They were based on either factual data or well-documented conclusions from the actual case. The experimental participants were expected to follow the usual procedure in clinical judgment in making their assessments by forming a personality picture of Kidd on which to base their conclusions—in much the way a juror is expected to amass knowledge and draw inferences. None of the questions, however, were rote memory questions from the materials presented. The judge-participants made a confidence judgment on each of their answers, with a value of 20% indicating chance performance.

The data were similar across groups except that the more experienced clinicians were, perhaps surprisingly, somewhat less confident by stage four than were the other groups. The data (collapsed across the various groups of participants) are shown in Figure 8.1. Test performance did not improve as the evaluators were given more and more information. Mostly, the questions were answered incorrectly—none of the performance data are above chance levels (which was 20% given that each multiple-choice question had five alternatives). What did increase, and dramatically so, was people's confidence in their answers. Whereas the participants were only slightly overconfident after reading the demographic information alone, their ratings were wildly overconfident by the end of stage four. It seems that even information that is unhelpful in increasing accuracy (in this case, additional information provided about Kidd across the four stages) has a large and unwarranted effect on people's confidence.

Along similar lines, Shaw and McClure (1996) showed that merely asking questions several times increased people's confidence in their answers, even though the answers themselves did not improve. In their experiment, they staged an interruption in a classroom, and then questioned the students about the event 5 times over the next 5 weeks, with some of the questions being repeated and some not. Although the accuracy of their answers did not improve over the 5-week interval, their confidence in those answers did. Studies in which people's confidence increases with the sheer volume of information, or from mere repetition, rather than with the quality of the information have implications for courtroom confidence. A standard practice in preparing witnesses for trial is to rehearse the witnesses in the story that they will tell. The grooming that goes on to prepare witnesses in high-stakes trials approaches that done for presidential candidates, and the result, when successful, is the same. The witnesses become highly confident, but sometimes for the wrong reasons. The pernicious aspect of this drilling

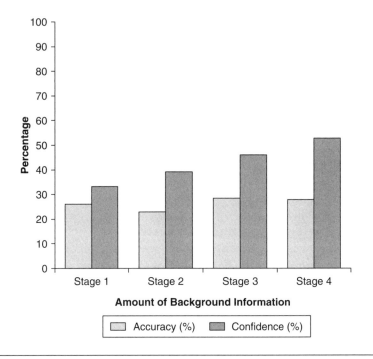

Figure 8.1   Percentage correct (accuracy) on the tests and the percentage confidence in answers on the test across four stages in the spurious confidence study.

SOURCE: Oskamp (1965).

procedure is that the witnesses become confident, and exude that assured aura, whether what they are remembering is true or not.

Is People's Confidence in Their Memories Ever Infallible?

Surely the inaccurate confidence judgments given in the above cases are mere quirks. Perhaps we do need to be wary of what young children say with high confidence—their frontal lobes are not yet well developed, and their metacognitive judgments of all kinds may be fragile. And laboratory studies with adults may be questionable as well, because the stakes are typically low. Perhaps Chris's high confidence in his false memory of being lost in the shopping mall resulted, in part, because it didn't really matter whether or not he had been lost in the shopping mall. Perhaps Oskamp's participants also knew that it really didn't matter, so why work that hard to be accurate?

What if it did matter? What if the events were emotional? Life threatening? What about cases where the memory is one of a trauma, as, unhappily, is often the case in criminal investigations? When a person is tortured or abused, our folk knowledge is that the victim's confidence about the identity of the perpetrator will be high and that he or she will be right. These are the excruciatingly painful situations that can't be ousted from memory, in which people could *never* forget a face, much as they might wish to. But is this folk knowledge correct?

Few studies of eyewitness memory have been conducted under conditions of traumatic stress, for obvious reasons—extreme trauma is not something that can be easily produced in the lab. Studies in which people are shown violent films are often used to study whether stress enhances memory or not, and whether people's confidence is appropriately enhanced. The American Academy of Pediatrics (2001) has estimated that by age 18, the average person in the United States will have viewed 200,000 acts of violence on television alone. It seems likely that we have habituated to filmed violence, and at least for some people, it is not really that stressful. Indeed, one of the most violent films to date (*The Shining*) to which a hormonal stress response has been measured showed that stress levels, while somewhat elevated, were well within normal diurnal variation (Hubert & de Jong-Meyer, 1989). So films are unlikely to tap into situations where people would "never forget that face." But it is extremely difficult to test people in real-world traumatic situations.

Unfortunately, there is now plenty of real-life evidence that extremely confident witnesses have been mistaken, with dire consequences. These cases are invariably ones in which there is no physical evidence, but a witness confidently "tells the truth" about who committed some heinous crime, such as assault, robbery, or murder. Based on the witnesses' confidence in their memory, the jury votes to convict and the alleged criminal wastes away in jail, on death row, or worse. Later, DNA evidence saved from the scene of the crime has shown—without any doubt—that the alleged culprit was innocent. In a recent case, Charles Chatman served nearly 27 years of a 99-year sentence for aggravated sexual assault before he was released based on the outcome of DNA tests. In the past decade, over 30 cases like this one led to the exoneration of inmates based on the outcome of DNA tests—in the state of Texas alone. For more facts about misplaced confidence that led to wrongful convictions (that were later overturned by DNA tests), go to the Innocence Project on the World Wide Web.

We were able to find one study that experimentally investigated eyewitness identification of the perpetrator in a truly traumatic situation, where it was known with certainty what had actually happened and who the "aggressor" was. This study tapped a very special situation—soldiers' training in a simulated prisoner-of-war camp. Morgan et al.'s (2004) investigation of eyewitness identification and people's confidence in that identification was made under conditions that, as evidenced by the extremely elevated levels of cortisol, were at trauma levels equivalent to those experienced by people undergoing open heart surgery or combat. Cortisol is a stress hormone that is released in response to either a physiological stressor, or, in the case of humans, a psychological stressor. Levels of cortisol give some grounding to our assessments of how stressful a situation is. Cortisol levels are normally quite low. A scary movie may cause the levels to triple—but this is still fairly low. The same increase occurs if people are asked to do spontaneous public speaking during which their intelligence will be evaluated. (This frightening task makes many people's stomachs turn over just to think about it, and is called the Trier Social Stress Test, or TSST.) Such situations are about the limit for normal psychological investigations, but these do not come close to producing the levels of cortisol seen in real trauma. The levels of cortisol in Morgan's study, however, were roughly 10 times higher than these already inflated levels, and so give a very good approximation of the condition one would experience, physiologically, during trauma.

The study site was a mock prisoner-of-war camp designed to train U.S. soldiers how not to capitulate should they be captured. The army trainers were realistic in the stresses to which they exposed the men, including subjecting them to situations modeled after those that American prisoners of war reported after the Korean War. According to Morgan et al. (2004), after some classroom style training,

> participants are confined in a mock prisoner of war camp (POWC). This phase is designed to offer one of the most challenging training experiences that active duty participants will ever experience while in the military. In the POWC, each participant is placed in isolation and then subjected to various types of interrogation. These interrogations are designed to test the limits and abilities of the participants to withstand "exploitation by the enemy." (p. 266)

The exact procedures used are classified information, so the authors were unable to offer more details, except that people undergoing this training exhibited levels of stress hormone beyond anything seen in everyday life. They also showed astonishingly high levels of dissociative symptoms, such as out-of-body experiences and psychotic-like behavior.

During the effort to extract information from the trainee in the prisoner-of-war situation, there were two interrogators: the high-stress interrogator, whose job, in part, was "physical confrontation" with the participant, and the low-stress interrogator, who did not threaten at all, and indeed, "befriended" the participant (but who did, at the same time, try to trick the participant into giving away information). The duration of exposure between these people was more than just a brief glimpse, as sometimes happens in experiments on eyewitness identification. Each of the two interrogators had 40 minutes of face-to-face contact with each participant.

One might suppose that the 509 participants would never forget the high-stress, violent interrogator (though they might possibly forget the unthreatening one). Just the opposite was found. Three methods of eyewitness identification were used: (a) a live lineup, (b) a photo lineup with all potential interrogators shown simultaneously (a simultaneous lineup) and the participant choosing from the group, and (c) a photo lineup with each potential interrogator shown individually (a sequential lineup) and the participant stating whether each photo was an actual interrogator or not. The likelihood of correctly identifying the interrogator (i.e., the proportion of hits) is presented in Figure 8.2, which clearly shows that participants had better memories for the low-stress interrogator than for the high-stress interrogator, with hit rates for the latter being astonishingly low. Thus, the victims identified the interrogator very poorly when the event was traumatic. But when they did correctly identify him, did they do so with extremely high confidence, as folk knowledge suggests? The answer is no. The mean confidence ratings about the accuracy of their reports (made on a scale from 1 to 10, with 10 being highest) were 6.2 for the high-stress interrogator and 7.9 for the low-stress interrogator.

Does Witness Confidence Matter to Jurors?

Perhaps the jury ultimately doesn't care about the witnesses' confidence. Unfortunately, given the evidence that a clever attorney can easily manipulate confidence and that it is undiagnostic, that does not appear to be the case. As in daily life, other people's confidence is taken by jurors to be of prime importance in evaluating the reliability of a witness and in making their decisions. A number of studies have investigated people's responses to other people's confidence.

Cutler, Penrod, and Dexter (1990), for example, conducted a mock-jury study to examine juror sensitivity to eyewitness identification evidence. Participants were eligible and experienced jurors from Dane County, Wisconsin, who viewed a videotaped trial that involved an eyewitness identification. The responses of experienced jurors were also compared to those of undergraduates, but differences between the undergraduates and

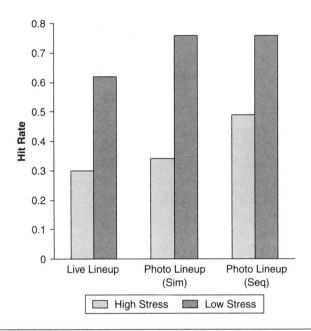

Figure 8.2   The probability of correctly identifying an interrogator during a live lineup, a photo lineup where all photos are presented simultaneously (Sim), or a photo lineup where all photos are presented sequentially (Seq).

SOURCE: Data adapted from Morgan et al. (2004).

the eligible jurors in their sensitivity to eyewitness evidence were negligible. Ten factors associated with the crime and the identification were manipulated—such as whether or not the perpetrator was disguised as well as what the witnesses' confidence was in their memory of the crime. The result of main interest was that the confidence of the eyewitness was a more powerful predictor of the verdicts people returned than any of the other nine factors!

Brewer and Burke (2002) constructed a mock-jury situation in which they manipulated both the consistency of the testimony given by a witness and his or her confidence. Surprisingly, consistency mattered little, but confidence, once again, had a strong influence on jury decisions. As disturbing, Fox and Walters (1986) showed that eyewitness confidence had a strong impact on jury decisions, even in the face of conflicting expert testimony.

There are, however, some boundary conditions. Tenney, MacCoun, Spellman, and Hastie (2007) showed that although confident witnesses are deemed more credible than unconfident ones in general, should such a confident witness be caught in a mistake, less-confident witnesses might appear more credible than more-confident ones. Thus, although mere confidence does have an effect, juries are not entirely insensitive to other factors that indicate the credibility of a witness. The problem, of course, is that in most courtroom situations, jurors do not know what is accurate. Thus, the many studies showing the overwhelming impact of confidence on the verdicts that juries return, makes the unreliability and the manipulability of this metacognitive judgment highly worrisome.

Lying

In all of the above discussion of metacognition in the courtroom, we have assumed that people were acting, remembering, and judging in good faith— that they were trying to be honest. But what if they weren't? What if they were lying? Despite perjury laws, there are, of course, many reasons that a person might lie. In this section, we will examine several aspects of lying relevant to the courts.

Deception is an act that is intended to foster in another person a belief or understanding that the deceiver considers false. It consists of both a communication of information and a metacommunication about the sincerity of the message, that is, the message is false, but the communicator intends to instill the belief that it is true. The recipient hears the message and also makes a judgment about its truth. Thus, lying and detecting people's lies will draw upon people's metacognitive abilities. The first question we address is whether people are able to detect when other people are lying.

Can People Detect Lying?

Ekman and Friesen (1969) refer to behaviors that give away a falsehood as *deception cues*, and those that reveal the true information, *leakage cues*. In some intermediate cases, it is not clear that the situation is one of deception, such as self-deception, intentionally transparent lies (where the sender wants the receiver to ascertain that the communication is a lie), and mistaken lies (where people think they are telling a lie but it really is the truth, or vice versa). Here, we will exclude consideration of these complicated cases and focus only on what is considered barefaced lying. When people engage in such lying, are there clues that give them away, such that a jury, or an experienced investigator, might be able to tell?

It has turned out to be notoriously difficult to determine when a person is lying. The folk wisdom is that people can control their verbal but not their nonverbal behavior. If true, one should study body language and voice characteristics, not the words that are spoken. Many people think (and there is some empirical support) that lies can be detected with tics of the body, more so than the face, presumably because the body is less controllable. But there are also facial clues that provide a giveaway, although it is not the large expressions, which tend to be controllable by the liar. Rather it is the facial microexpressions—very fast muscle movements—that are inconsistent when a person is lying. Such microexpressions, however, can generally only be seen with a slow-motion replay (although some people can detect them). In addition, the voice is particularly difficult to control. Thus, a good lie detector may pay particular attention to the manner of speaking rather than the content of the speech.

Because lying is apparently more cognitively demanding than telling the truth, people often pause more when they are lying. In some studies, brow furrowing has been correlated with lying, as have speech errors, and shrugs (Zuckerman, DePaulo, & Rosenthal, 1981). Although all of these factors have some relation to lying, their diagnosticity is hardly overwhelming. An early study by Zuckerman et al. (1981) showed that the correlation between people's confidence in the accuracy of their own ability to detect lies and their actual accuracy had a median value of .06, which was not different from zero. The inescapable conclusion is that although liars may show subtle signs of lying and most people think they can detect these, they can't.

The folk view of lying also favors some blatant misconceptions. Surveys indicate that people (both lay people and police) believe that liars avert their gaze and fidget (Akehurst, Köhnken, Vrij, & Bull, 1996). This notion is promoted in Inbau, Reid, Buckley, and Jayne's (2001) interrogation manual, a source that has been widely used by police departments across the United States and by other interrogators. As Mann, Vrij, and Bull (2002) have shown, however, police officers who endorse this view are among the worst at detecting liars, because the cue is simply undiagnostic: Liars don't fidget any more than do truth tellers.

Some studies (e.g., DePaulo & Pfeifer, 1986; Köhnken, 1987; Kraut & Poe, 1980) have reported that people in general have no ability to detect deceit. But can *anybody* reliably detect when someone else is lying? Ekman and O'Sullivan (1991) investigated individual differences in lie detection. They looked at the performance and the confidence of secret service observers, federal polygraphers, robbery investigators, judges, psychiatrists, special interest participants (who were taking a course on lie detection, but before they had explicit instruction on diagnostic factors), and college students. Although it might be thought that several of these groups would be especially good at this skill, only the secret service participants were accurately able to detect liars.

All of the groups in Ekman and O'Sullivan's (1991) study were asked twice to rate their ability to detect lies, first before seeing the videotapes that constituted the test, and then afterwards, when they were specifically asked about how well they had done. The correlation between metacognition of general ability and actual performance was not different from zero: Overall, their perception of how well they would do was not related to how well they did do. Similarly, overall retrospective confidence about performance also had a zero correlation with performance. Across all of the groups, then, people's metacognitive assessments of their ability were undiagnostic.

Some group differences, however, were embedded in this overall zero correlation. The federal polygraphers' initial metacognitive ratings of their general ability to detect lies were positively correlated with their actual ability to do the task. Perhaps they had had enough feedback in their jobs to know whether they were good at detecting or not. Perhaps even more interesting, however, was a negative correlation in the secret service group. Within the one group of experts in this study who (as a group) could do the task, the metacognitions were backwards: secret service officers who thought they couldn't detect deception were better at detecting it than secret service officers who thought they could.

Lies Become Truth, or the Frequency-Validity Relation

Although people have great difficulty determining whether or not other people are lying, they might still be able to determine whether particular statements are true or not. And, of course, when a statement is entirely implausible, people will know that it is false, at least some of the time. Most research on this question has addressed statements in the murky middle, where most people do not know for sure whether statements are true or not. It was first empirically demonstrated by Hasher, Goldstein, and Toppino (1977) that the mere repetition of statements that were untrue could result in people coming to believe that they were true. This failure reflects a metacognitive deficit because when people encounter the false statement, their familiarity with it makes them judge it as true.

In the Hasher et al. (1977) experiment, participants rated the truthfulness of 60 statements. The statements themselves came from knowledge domains of politics, sports, religion, the arts, and so forth. The statements were along the lines of "Lithium is the lightest metal" or "The total population of Greenland is about 50,000 people." Some of them were true and some of them were false, but people were unlikely to know for sure. Validity ratings were made by participants after the tape-recorded presentation of each statement. There were three sessions in the experiment. The twist was a simple one: Over the three sessions, some of the statements were repeated whereas others were not. The results showed that the true statements were rated as more true, when they were repeated. Unfortunately, so too were the false statements. Whereas the false statements, on the first repetition, were close to the "uncertain" boundary, with a rating of 4.18 (on a 7-point scale, with 7 = definitely true, 4 = uncertain, and 1 = definitely false), by the third session (after multiple repetitions) they had crept up half a point to 4.67.

This result has now been replicated many times, with a variety of researchers showing what has come to be known as the "frequency-validity" relationship. In response to concerns about the external validity of laboratory findings using college students to "real people in the real world," Gigerenzer (1984) telephoned people in Schwabing, a community on the outskirts of Munich, Germany, and asked them to answer questions, similar to those of Hasher et al. (1977)—giving their validity ratings—over the phone. The results were the same as other researchers have found with laboratory studies. Reber and Schwarz (1999) showed that by increasing the perceptual fluency of statements, by having them be easy or difficult to read against the background, they were also able to alter people's judgments of their truth. Those statements that were easier to read were assessed as being truer. And there are many other examples of these kinds of surprising, and arguably distressing, effects—that is, where increasing the familiarity of a (false or true) statement enhances its believability. For instance, lies that are repeatedly told about political candidates during campaigns (e.g., she's a flip-flopper or he's in bed with corporate criminals) are eventually believed by many people who hear them but never attempt to evaluate whether they're true.

Whereas many studies have shown that lies may become truth with repetition, the final study we mention in this section showed that liars may also come to be perceived as truth tellers, with repetitions. Brown, Brown, and Zoccoli (2002) showed that the more times people saw a photograph of a person, the more credible they found the person to be. The credibility increase was comparable for both judgments of honesty and judgments of sincerity at short (2-day) and long (14-day) intervals. The effect depended on repetition, but not explicit recognition that the faces had been seen before. So, the more often you see liars tell lies, the more likely it is you will believe them.

Hindsight Bias

The final topic that we will touch on in this chapter is *hindsight bias,* or what is sometimes called the "knew it all along" effect. This effect has profound implications for the criminal justice system, for issues as wide-ranging as whether jurors are able to disregard testimony that has been ruled inadmissible, or whether medical practitioners are liable for adverse outcomes in malpractice suits. Baruch Fischhoff was first to report this phenomenon in 1975. As we will see, one of the explanations for this phenomenon is considered metacognitive. But before we get into that, let's first take a look at what Fischhoff did that created such a stir.

In a seminal experiment that has generated hundreds of subsequent studies in a wide variety of domains, Fischhoff simply informed his experimental group about the outcome of an event and then asked them to say what they thought the outcome would have been if they had not known already what the outcome was. The targeted event, in Fischhoff's original experiment, was the 19th-century war between the British and the Gurkhas. Of course, people who actually knew the outcome had to be eliminated, but there were few such people. The subject was chosen for just that reason—to be something that people wouldn't know much about. (Notice that this situation is also true for jurors hearing cases. People who know or think they know a lot about a case are excluded. If a crime occurs in your neighborhood, or if you know people involved, you will probably not be allowed on ·the jury.) Fischhoff developed four possible outcomes (e.g., Gurkhas won, or the British won), and—in a counterbalanced manner—he told different participants that each of these four possible outcomes had been the actual outcome. In the control condition, no outcome information was given. After giving (or in the case of the control condition, not giving) the outcome information, he asked all participants to estimate a probability for the likelihood of each of the four possible outcomes, but to do so retrospectively, *as if they did not know the outcome.* The result was that people were unable to keep from biasing their responses about the probabilities in favor of what they "knew" to be the actual outcome. That is, they judged the outcome they had been *told* was the actual outcome to be more likely than it actually was (as indicated by the control condition).

An example of hindsight bias in the real world comes from a study by Bryant and Brockway (1997), who made use of the notorious O. J. Simpson case. They asked the participants, 2 hours before the verdict, 48 hours after the verdict, and 1 week after the verdict, to indicate the chances that the jury would find Simpson (a) guilty of first-degree murder, (b) guilty of second-degree murder, or (c) not guilty. In the post-verdict sessions, participants were asked about their knowledge of the verdict (100% of the participants knew that he had been acquitted) as well as whether they believed that Simpson was guilty (83% said yes) or innocent (17% said yes). Then, participants were asked for their retrospective judgments of the jury's vote. (The researchers did not constrain the participants to make these three outcomes add up to 1.) The results are shown in Figure 8.3. People were much more likely to judge that Simpson would be acquitted in the post-verdict sessions (and hence after they knew that he had been acquitted) than before they knew the verdict in the case.

Why Does Hindsight Bias Occur?

The hindsight-bias effect has been explained from three viewpoints: the personal needs view, the memory view, and the anchoring view. The first explanation—the personal needs view—is based on the idea that people like to be right. But for some people this need to be right, and to have been right, is stronger than it is for others. In an early study, Campbell and Tesser

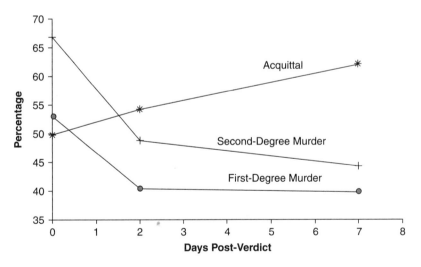

Day 0 = 2 hours before the verdict.
Day 2 = 48 hours after the verdict.
Day 7 = 1 week after the verdict.

Figure 8.3   Estimates of the chances of conviction and acquittal in the O. J. Simpson criminal trial, over time.

SOURCE: Bryant and Brockway (1997).

(1983) found that people with certain personal needs and personality characteristics were more prone to claim that they "knew it all along." The researchers first attained people's scores on the Rokeach Dogmatism Scale—a questionnaire that measures people's intolerance for ambiguity. The more participants could not tolerate ambiguity, the greater their hindsight bias.

Other researchers have shown similar effects. For example, Musch (2003; also see Musch & Wagner, 2007, for a review) showed that people who were high on field dependence showed greater hindsight bias than did field-independent people. He also showed that a tendency toward favorable self-presentation, as well as rigidity or the need for predictability—both variables similar to those measured by Campbell and Tesser (1983)—were also related to greater hindsight bias. There is also a tendency for children and older adults to show stronger hindsight bias than young adults (Bayen, Pohl, Erdfelder, & Auer, 2007). The age-related differences, however, may or may not be due to personal needs or personality variables, because the cognitive variables such as memory, which we will discuss below, are also different for children and older adults as compared to young adults. In any event, whereas personality differences do have an effect on hindsight bias, they cannot be the whole story. Given that the effect is found even in people lacking the kinds of personal needs that have been thought likely to bias their outcomes, cognitive factors are implicated in the explanation of the effect.

The second explanation is purely cognitive—based on the idea that different sources of information in memory may be blended together. As a number of researchers have pointed out, the structure of the hindsight-bias situation is similar to that of the memory-based misleading-information paradigm. People see or witness an event, and then, afterwards, are given information about that event. In a classic example of the memory paradigm, people see a blue car and are later given the suggestion that it was green. When they are asked to choose the color of the car, they choose blue-green (Loftus, 1977). In the hindsight situation, people are given a question such as, "How many countries are there in Africa?" Perhaps they think it is 45. Then they are told that the actual answer is whatever the experimenter chooses—say 59. When asked about their initial estimation, they give a compromise somewhere between 45 and 59—maybe 52. The memory explanation postulates that in both cases the memory for the original event is blended with that of the later information or that there is some sort of interference or distortion from the later information that may impair accurate retrieval of the earlier information.

The third explanation of the hindsight-bias effect is that it is an anchoring effect. The anchoring explanation of hindsight bias is simple—it says that the outcome (e.g., you are told that O. J. Simpson was acquitted) serves as an anchor, and later estimates of the probabilities of events are pulled toward this anchor. Anchoring effects in general (i.e., the tendency of a given quantity or entity to become a beginning point for later judgments) have been shown to be pervasive in human judgment and decision making. This explanation is viewed as metacognitive in nature, because it emphasizes how anchors unduly influence people's evaluations of their memories about their original beliefs.

Tversky and Kahneman (1974) have shown how numbers exert anchoring effects even when participants see researchers spin a wheel of fortune, leaving no doubt that the number provided is random. Some savvy real estate brokers and car dealers use this ploy regularly—showing clients an expensive house or car at the outset to get the customer to pay a higher price; that is, enticing customers to opt to buy a more expensive house (or car) or pay more for the same one.

The second and third explanations are difficult to tease apart. Indeed, McCloskey and Zaragoza (1985) have proposed that the effects found in the misleading-information paradigm in memory might really be due to a bias or anchoring effect, rather than being a memory effect. Pohl and Gawlik (1995) have attempted to distinguish the two cognitive explanations of hindsight bias by using a Markov model that proposes different processes for the two explanations. Even they admit, however, that the data in the two paradigms look remarkably similar, and that the distinction between them may be model dependent and not robust. Thus, we do not know whether what happens is that people's memory is changed by the outcome information, or the outcome information exerts a bias or pull on a decision process. Nevertheless, the empirical result itself is rock solid: Knowing the outcome of an event has an irreversible effect on what people think they would have believed had they not known the outcome. This "knew it all along" effect has legal consequences, some of which will be reviewed in the next section.

Confessions, Inadmissible Evidence, and Hindsight Bias

One of the most interesting hindsight situations occurs in cases of coerced confession. A famous case, relevant to this issue, was the murder trial *Arizona v. Fulminante*, in which Fulminante confessed. The confession was entered into testimony. But it was later ruled that the confession had been coerced. A coerced confession is, of course, inadmissible. Circumstantial evidence suggested that he had committed the murder, but, even so, confession has an enormous impact upon a jury. The issue was whether the circumstantial evidence alone would have resulted in a conviction had the confession not been presented. This case went to the Supreme Court, which ruled that the introduction of the confession constituted a "harmless error," and let the verdict stand.

In some states, rather than having a judge in a pretrial hearing assess whether or not a confession was coerced, the jury members are asked to hear the evidence and make the judgment. They are then supposed to disregard the evidence if they determine that the confession was coerced. This raises two questions: First, can people make accurate judgments about whether a confession was coerced? This is a fairly standard question about people's metacognitions, although one about the circumstances surrounding someone else's behavior rather than about their own learning or memory. Second, can people use their metacognitions to appropriately control their memory, and ultimately, their verdict?

An experiment addressing these issues was conducted by Kassin and Sukel (1997), using mock jurors who were given a confession that was elicited under low or high pressure. The mock jurors correctly realized that the high-pressure confession was coerced, and they remembered the (mock) judge's admonition to disregard it. But even though they said they would disregard it in their judgments, their conviction rates indicated otherwise. People who were on the mock juries in which no confession was given turned in a conviction rate of 19%. The conviction rate was 63% in the low-pressure (admissible confession) condition. In the high-pressure inadmissible confession condition, the conviction rate was lower than it was with the admissible confession, but it was still 44%—much higher than the rate given when no confession had been heard. Thus, although people knew that the testimony was inadmissible and they thought they could disregard it and, indeed, they thought that they *had* disregarded it, they were unable to do so.

Malpractice, Liability, and Hindsight Bias

By now you can probably infer the implications of hindsight bias for medical malpractice. Once a person suffers a negative medical outcome, anyone assessing the situation will think that the doctors involved should have known that there was a high likelihood of it occurring, so if only they had taken the proper steps, it could have been avoided. Malpractice. In medical circles this bias is known as the retrospectoscope! Many think that hindsight bias is largely responsible for many malpractice claims and for the runaway costs of physicians' medical-liability insurance.

Retrospective blame can also be an issue for mental health professionals. Consider the following case. In the late 1960s, Tatiana Tarasoff and Prosenjit Poddar dated several times. When Tarasoff began to date other men, a distraught Poddar sought counseling. He divulged his intention to kill Tarasoff to his therapist, who had him detained by police. Poddar, however, was released after he agreed not to pursue Tarasoff. Later, Poddar tracked down Tarasoff and stabbed her to death. No one had been warned that Poddar posed a threat to her life! Subsequently, the 1974 Tarasoff decision established that therapists have a duty to warn potential victims that a patient may be dangerous. If therapists do not use reasonable care in such situations, they may be liable for negligence. When a patient becomes violent, the perceived probability of violence shifts from the time of the assessment by the therapist to the time of the assessment by the judge hearing the case. The law—not taking hindsight bias into account—says the therapist should have known. LaBine and LaBine (1996) have documented many instances of this phenomenon. Similarly, people blame their financial woes on auditors: They should have known, and they may face liability suits for not having said so. The evaluative judgments of auditors' performance, however, may be due to hindsight bias (Anderson, Lowe, & Reckers, 1993).

Other Examples of Hindsight Bias

We have focused, in this chapter, on the implications of hindsight bias for decisions made in the courtroom. We would be remiss, however, to close without noting that the effect is pervasive. Once people know the answer to anything, they think that it was obvious. After (but not before) solving an insight problem, people think that it was easy. They may even think that a student who is still struggling to find the answer—as they did—is deficient in some way.

And woe to the brilliant individual who makes a new discovery. In science, such a true discovery is too often belittled by naysayers who claim that it's obvious. Obvious in retrospect! To thwart such naysayers, one can make them state *their* predictions before revealing one's discoveries. Unfortunately, however, hindsight is likely to distort even their memory of what they predicted. Similarly, in politics, once the outcome of an election is known, those pundits who (by accident, perhaps) said the "right" thing only look normal and rational. They don't look like prophets, because everybody knew it all along. But those who, with the same evidence, made a different assessment have egg on their faces.

Several researchers (Ofir & Mazursky, 1997; Sanna, Schwarz, & Small, 2002) have begun an effort to look at situations in which people claim not "I knew it all along," but rather "I *never* would have known that." We applaud this new line of research. But we are nevertheless willing to bet that once the answer about "we *never* would have known *that*" is finally known, most of us—the colleagues of these brave explorers—will say that we knew it all along.

Summary

People often confidently believe in their memories of past events. Such high confidence in memory is often not misplaced. In our everyday lives, many of our memories are valid and we should be confident in them. Unfortunately, memory can too easily be altered in numerous ways: You may remember that a person was present at a crime scene because you later saw the person walking down the street. You may recall an event that was merely suggested to you during repeated interviews with police. You may come to believe that an event represents a true memory because you were forced to confabulate that memory. In many of these cases, people will be highly confident in their false memories and may stick tenaciously to them even though hard physical evidence suggests otherwise.

Perhaps worse, misplaced confidence in invalid memories—as well as hindsight bias that people have difficulties escaping from—can have dire consequences in many settings. These consequences are perhaps most evident in the judicial system in which confident witnesses are readily believed (even without physical evidence to support their testimony). Society as a whole is largely ignorant of how mere repetition can lead to false memories—that is, most people lack the metacognitive knowledge about how their minds operate and how easily they can be tricked. Besides introducing some general issues relevant to metacognition and the law, we hope this chapter will make you think twice before you swear "to tell the truth, the whole truth, and nothing but the truth," or fully believe that the testimony you are considering—even if from a witness testifying in good faith—must be true.

DISCUSSION QUESTIONS

1. In this chapter, we discussed a variety of situations in which people were led to develop a false memory of the past: People remembering a yield sign (after one was suggested to them) when in fact they saw a stop sign, and a child being led to believe he was lost

at a mall when in fact he never was lost. Do you believe that people can be made to believe that *any* kind of event happened to them? Which kinds of event do you think would be difficult to implant, and for what kinds of people?

2. Morgan et al. (2004) reported what you might consider to be a rather surprising finding: When people were interrogated, their ability to later identify the interrogator was much worse with an interrogator who evoked a lot of stress than with an interrogator who evoked little stress. One might expect that people would remember the stressful interrogator, as if the stress would focus their attention on the person who was being abusive. Think of several explanations for why people might have difficulty remembering a stressful interrogator. How could you evaluate (using an experiment) your explanations for why stress can impair memory?

MINDS-ON ACTIVITY: IMPLANTING FALSE MEMORIES

Using a simple method (Roediger & McDermott, 1995), it is relatively easy to make people recall words that they did not originally hear. In many cases, the victims are surprised to learn their memories are not valid. To demonstrate this false-memory effect, you will probably only need one participant—such as a friend or family member—although the demonstration can be attempted with multiple people at once. Here's what you need to do. For each list below, read one word at a time (for about 3 seconds a word), and tell your participants to try to remember them for an upcoming test. After you've finished reading each list, have them count backwards from a 3-digit number (e.g., 475 or 899) by threes for 30 seconds or so. This rehearsal-prevention task will ensure that they just can't repeat back the final few words on the list. After 30 seconds of counting backwards, have them (a) write down every word they can remember, and (b) make a retrospective confidence judgment for each word that they recalled (e.g., from 0 to 100, where 0 means they have no confidence that the word was on the list and 100 means they are 100% confident it was there). Now, repeat for the other lists.

When you're finished, check to see if they recalled the seductive lures: sleep (for List 1), needle (List 2), and sweet (List 3). Were they just as confident in their memory of the words that were on the list as they were for the seductive lures? How might you help people to reduce the likelihood of recalling the seductive lures? If you have ideas, try your experiment again (but with new participants) to find out if your technique actually reduces false memories.

List 1	List 2	List 3
bed	thread	sour
rest	pin	candy
awake	eye	sugar

tired	sewing	bitter
dream	sharp	good
wake	point	taste
snooze	prick	tooth
blanket	thimble	nice
doze	haystack	honey
slumber	thorn	soda
snore	hurt	chocolate
nap	injection	heart
peace	syringe	cake
yawn	cloth	tart
drowsy	knitting	pie

SOURCE: Lists are a subset from Roediger and McDermott (1995).

CONCEPT REVIEW

For the following questions and exercises, we recommend you write down the answers on a separate sheet in as much detail as possible, and then check them against the relevant material in the chapter.

1. How has DNA evidence been informative with respect to showing that witnesses' extreme confidence in their memories can be entirely misplaced?

2. What is hindsight bias, and what are the most prominent explanations for it?

3. How accurately can people detect when other people are lying? Why might lie detection be so difficult?

4. Describe evidence that indicates that in fact jurors are influenced by the confidence of eyewitnesses' testimony.

9

Education

Students are under pressure to learn enormous amounts of course content in usually very little time. With the No Child Left Behind Act in place, even more pressure is being placed on students to meet statewide standards in key content areas. Thus, although education offers incredible rewards, to reap them, students, their teachers, and parents will need to successfully meet many challenges, which begin in early grade school and continue through college and sometimes beyond. To meet these challenges, education research seeks to understand how students learn and reason as well as how to improve their learning and reasoning. Of course, such research has led to the discovery of many techniques that can improve student scholarship. Moreover, given the promise of metacognition for supporting student learning, it is perhaps not surprising that hundreds of articles have addressed metacognition and student education. In the present chapter, we will touch on only a small subset of these studies, with the hopes of illuminating how metacognition can influence student learning.

Recall our student, David, who was introduced in Chapter 5 as he was preparing for an examination in his French class. David's progress was partly explained by how well he could monitor and control his learning. In this vignette, we illustrated the importance of accurate monitoring and effective control of learning, but we did not capture other metacognitive processes that can contribute to David's, or any student's, success. Successful students may have more knowledge about effective strategies and tactics to employ as they study, and they also may believe that they can successfully meet challenges from demanding course content. For instance, even if David can accurately monitor, he may have difficulty learning the foreign-language vocabulary if he does not know about effective strategies for linking associates, and perhaps worse, if he does not believe he can learn the vocabulary in time for the test, he may not even try.

General Models of Student Self-Regulated Learning

Fortunately, a great deal of theory in education research attempts to provide a broader picture of all the competencies that can influence student scholarship. Theories include many processes that are not metacognitive in nature, such as motivation, goal setting, and goal orientation, among others. Nevertheless, metacognitive processes—such as self-reflection and control of learning—represent the core of many of these theories (Zimmerman, 2001). Although many general theories of self-regulated learning are available (for reviews, see Boekaerts, Pintrich, & Zeidner, 2000; Zimmerman & Schunk, 2001), we will organize our review of the extensive literature on metacognition and education around Winne and Hadwin's (1998) model, because it emphasizes the monitoring-and-control processes that are at the center of self-regulatory behavior.

Winne and Hadwin (1998) proposed that a complete understanding of students' self-regulated learning would include four stages: task definition, goal setting and planning, enactment, and adaptation (see also Pintrich, 2000; Zimmerman, 2000). For *task definition*, students decide their task for studying, and then *set goals* for the task and *make plans* to achieve them. *Enactment* involves using numerous strategies to accomplish the plans, and then students may *adapt* any aspect of their learning process based on their experiences during learning. If you had an upcoming test over the chapters on Basic Metacognitive Judgments in this text, you might decide that your task is to understand the theories about how people monitor their memories and how this monitoring is used to control learning and retrieval. Realizing that you have left little time for study, your goal may involve trying to really understand the theories of monitoring and to not worry about the sections on memory control. To accomplish this goal, you may plan to read each chapter, but to focus most carefully on the theories of monitoring by taking notes on the key points. After taking the exam, you may realize that the note-taking strategy was not enough and decide that in the future you will adapt by allowing more time for studying and by supplementing note taking with developing review questions as you read.

According to Winne and Hadwin (1998), these four stages all are driven by the same cognitive architecture. In particular, during each stage, five factors interact in producing a desired outcome for that stage: Conditions,

Operations, Products, Evaluations, and Standards. These factors can be remembered by noting their acronym, which is how a student C-O-P-E-S with self-regulated learning. So, for a given stage, a student may note the conditions in which studying occurs, perform operations (e.g., using strategies) that yield products, and then evaluate those products by comparing them to standards. The product of each stage literally defines it, in that the product of task definition is the task definition itself, and the products of goal setting are goals. Each of these products is reflected in the standards that a student attempts to achieve. Standards are specific expectations (or goals) that students want to meet while they study. They can be multifaceted, in that while studying for a test, you may decide that you need to learn at least 80% of the key materials (one standard) but that you must do so in one evening (another standard).

Their model is presented in Figure 9.1, which lists the various stages in terms of their products (bottom right of figure) and depicts how COPES interact to drive student performance. To illustrate, imagine yourself preparing for a brief talk that you will be giving about models of self-regulated learning in a seminar on metacognition. As a motivated student yourself, you first consider that you have about two hours to prepare (Task condition: time) and will be able to use PowerPoint during your talk (resources). You also know a lot about these models (Cognitive condition: domain knowledge) and hence have very high self-efficacy (motivational factor) for being able to develop an excellent talk. Based on these conditions, you set the following standards: complete preparation for talk in two hours, use PowerPoint to support your talk, and make sure that the core principles of self-regulated learning are emphasized and illustrated with real-world examples. To accomplish these goals, you choose to outline your talk, set up the PowerPoint presentation, and then practice your talk at least twice. At this point, you engage in developing your presentation by applying your strategies and monitoring your progress.

Most important for our focus on metacognition are the monitoring and control operations that appear in the middle of the figure. Monitoring serves the purpose to compare the products of strategic behavior against one's standards. Such comparison yields a set of cognitive evaluations (one for each standard) that provides feedback on how to proceed. A generic example is embedded in the figure. In particular, this student has developed five standards (A thru E) for the task at hand—so, desired performance for B is greater than for C, which in turn is greater than for A. By comparing these standards to the products of strategies, this student realizes that A is right on target, whereas performance for C is too low and for D is too high. In this case, the student may elect to choose a different strategy to promote performance on C; alternatively, the student may believe that the standard for C cannot

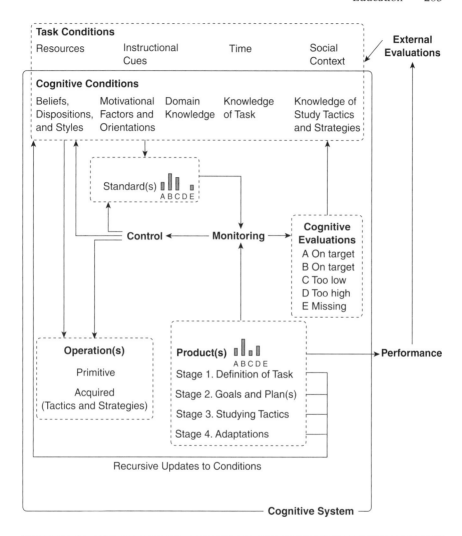

Figure 9.1   The COPES model of self-regulated learning.

SOURCE: Winne, P., and Hadwin, A. (1998). Studying as self-regulated learning. In D. J. Hacker, J. Dunlosky, and A. C. Graesser (Eds), *Metacognition in Educational Theory and Practice* (pp. 249–276). Hillsdale, NJ: Lawrence Erlbaum.

be obtained and hence terminate studying altogether. In terms of developing your talk in the example above, you may monitor ongoing time and stop after two hours (first standard met), but although your PowerPoint presentation is finished (second standard met), you have only practiced the talk once (final standard not met). At that point, you may spend a little more time practicing or decide that once was enough.

The model itself is inherently complicated, because so many factors can interact to influence students' activities and their performance. It becomes even more complex when one realizes that self-regulated learning is not linear, but in fact the processes are recursive in nature. As noted by Greene and Azevedo (2007), "with monitoring and control functioning as the hubs of regulation within each [stage], Winne and Hadwin's model can more effectively describe how changes in one phase can lead to changes in other phases over the course of learning. This allows the model to explicitly detail the recursive nature of [self-regulated learning]" (p. 338). For instance, after one hour of developing your talk, you may realize that the other standards were too ambitious, so you may go back to the task definition stage and develop a new set of study goals.

In the remainder of this section on General Models, we will briefly highlight education research that is relevant to student metacognition (for a comprehensive review of Winne & Hadwin's (1998) model, see Greene & Azevedo, 2007). Of course, the research from cognitive psychologists described in the chapters on Basic Metacognitive Judgments are relevant to understanding some of these processes and how to improve them. For instance, as discussed in Chapter 5, cognitive psychologists have investigated the mechanisms that produce the delayed-JOL effect in which students are rather accurate at monitoring their learning of simple associates if monitoring is delayed some time after study. Although the distinction between cognitive research and educational research in these domains is fuzzy, cognitive research tends to be laboratory based and focuses on the minute analysis of the underlying mechanisms involved in monitoring and control. In contrast, education research is often—but not always—conducted within classrooms using representative materials and seeks to investigate the relationships between metacognition and student achievement.

We will consider some of the metacognitive components of general models of self-regulated learning next. In doing so, we will discuss some representative education research about each component. Afterwards, we will survey some of students' metacognitive capabilities within specific domains of education that are foundational to student learning: reading, writing, and mathematics.

Self-Efficacy

Self-efficacy pertains to people's beliefs about their ability to successfully complete a given task (Bandura, 1977, 1997). Given that self-regulated learning is a largely goal-directed endeavor, students' perceptions about whether they can successfully achieve those goals can be just as influential on their performance as their actual abilities. Why this may be the case is revealed by the model in Figure 9.1, because self-efficacy (a beliefs and motivational factor under "Cognitive Conditions") can influence both the standards students set when studying and what strategies they select while studying. Concerning the former, students who don't believe they can achieve an A-level understanding of physics may set much lower goals than students who believe they can master it. Concerning strategies, students may not choose to use a relatively effective strategy if they do not believe the strategy will help them meet their goals—such as they think it will take too much time to use or they cannot perform it well.

Research with students has clearly demonstrated the importance of self-efficacy to achievement (for a review, see Pintrich, Marx, & Boyle, 1993). Consider an investigation by Chemers, Hu, and Garcia (2001), who examined students' adjustment in their first year in college. Prior to beginning their first year, students filled out a questionnaire that measured their academic self-efficacy, which included eight questions about their confidence in their ability to succeed academically. If you want to assess your own academic self-efficacy, check out their questionnaire in Table 9.1. Chemers et al. (2001) reported that students who had higher academic self-efficacy (measured before attending college) also had greater expectations for success, and most important, had higher levels of academic performance in their first year of college. In a review of the literature on self-efficacy, Robbins et al. (2004) surveyed 109 different studies to estimate the degree to which academic self-efficacy was related to cumulative grade point average. They compared self-efficacy to other factors, such as academic skills, perceived social support, and how committed students were to their particular college. They found that academic self-efficacy was highly related to cumulative grade point average (GPA) in college, and moreover, it was more highly related to GPA than were the other factors. Evidently, believing you will succeed is an important ingredient for success in school.

Such findings demonstrate the potential importance of self-efficacy to classroom performance, and they also suggest that improving students' self-efficacy will boost their performance. The idea here is simply that students with higher self-efficacy are more likely to self-regulate learning in an effective manner. If you believe that you can achieve, you will set more specific (and more demanding) goals for achieving and will use more effective strategies while attempting to achieve. Students who don't believe they can pass a chemistry course may never even take one, whereas others who believe they can do well in chemistry may take one, set high goals, and keep adapting

Table 9.1   Academic Self-Efficacy Scale

For each statement below, indicate how accurately it captures you on the following scale:

1	2	3	4	5	6	7
Very untrue						Very true

1. I know how to schedule my time to accomplish my tasks.

2. I know how to take notes.

3. I know how to study to perform well on tests.

4. I am good at research and writing papers.

5. I am a very good student.

6. I usually do very well in school and at academic tasks.

7. I find my university academic work interesting and absorbing.

8. I am very capable of succeeding at the university.

SOURCE: Chemers, Hu, and Garcia (2001).

NOTE: Higher values indicate higher levels of academic self-efficacy.

their strategies (and time spent studying) so as to excel. Numerous studies have demonstrated these links between self-efficacy and effective self-regulation (for a review, see Schunk & Ertmer, 2000)—believing one can succeed in school enhances motivation to regulate learning and in turn increases one's chances of academic success.

Metacognitive Monitoring

How Accurately Do Students Monitor Their Performance for Classroom Tests?

As evident in Figure 9.1, monitoring and control are central to effective self-regulated learning and performance. As we have emphasized throughout this textbook, accurate monitoring of learning and performance is critical, because if students are consistently overconfident in their knowledge, they may understudy, use ineffective strategies, and underachieve. The idea here is simply that the calibration of students' monitoring is related to effective self-regulated learning (Stone, 2000).

Numerous classroom studies are now available that demonstrate this link. Consider a study by Hacker, Bol, Horgan, and Rakow (2000) in which undergraduate college students were asked to evaluate their progress while enrolled in educational psychology courses. Prior to each exam, the students predicted the percentage of items that they would correctly answer. After taking the test, the students were divided into five groups that pertained to their actual level of performance on the in-class exams, from the students who had the best scores (Group One) to those who had the worst scores (Group Five). They then plotted students' predicted scores from each group with that group's actual score on the examination. In Figure 9.2, students' actual performance for each group is plotted against their predicted performance (open squares). So, for Group One, the students predicted that they would score about 83% on the exam, whereas they actually scored about 86%. The poorest performers (Group Five) predicted that they would score about 76% on the exam yet only scored about 45%. What is most striking in this figure is that the poorest performers were also the most overconfident! As noted by Dunning, Kerri, Ehrlinger, and Kruger (2003), "This lack of awareness arises because poor performers are doubly cursed: Their lack of skill deprives them not only of the ability to produce correct responses, but also of the expertise necessary to surmise that they are not producing them" (p. 83).

This effect has been termed "unskilled but unaware" (Kruger & Dunning, 1999), and it appears rather commonly across many settings. Nevertheless, two caveats should be noted. First, Hacker et al. (2000) also had people postdict their performance after they had taken an exam. Students' postdictions were accurate (see filled circles on Figure 9.2), even for the two groups of poorly performing students (although the poorest performers were overconfident). Thus, the unskilled are not always unaware of their level of ability. More important, the fact that students can accurately postdict their performance raises an interesting question: Can students use their postdictions to perform better on a test by changing their responses when they have little confidence in their initial answers? For an answer to this question, see Box 9.1.

Second, as discussed in Chapter 3 (Box 3.1), given that by definition poorer students are poorer performers, the exact interpretation of "unskilled but unaware" can be difficult to pin down. In the present case (Figure 9.2), for instance, note that all students predicted they would score about 70 to

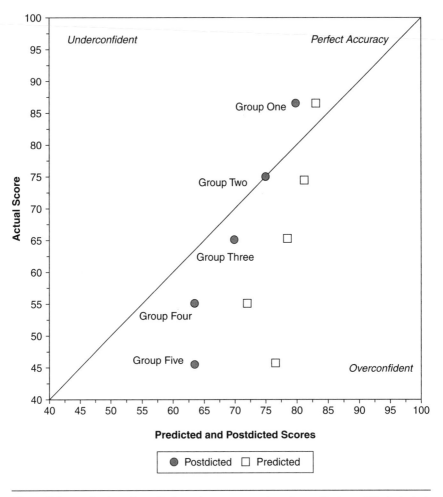

Figure 9.2   Students' predictions (open squares) and postdictions (filled circles) as a function of student performance on the first examination of the semester.

SOURCE: Hacker, D. J., Bol, L., Horgan, D. D., and Rakow, E. A. (2000). Test prediction and performance in a classroom context. *Journal of Educational Psychology*, 92, 160–170.

80% on the test. Perhaps all groups were largely unaware of their actual abilities and hence they all provided a reasonable guess about how well they would perform—somewhere in the B to C range. If so, poorer performers are almost destined to demonstrate overconfidence in their judgments because in fact they perform so poorly.

BOX 9.1
Should I Change My Mind (and My Answers)
When Taking a Test?

Testing is now becoming a high-stakes endeavor. Students take standardized tests throughout grade school and high school, and their scores can have a major influence on the funding for their schools and on their own progress. High school students take standardized exams to help them gain admittance to college, and then they take even more exams in hopes of getting into the graduate school of their choice. Of course, earning that cherished high score will largely result from a number of factors, such as diligent preparation (studying and self-testing) for the exams, and students' general intelligence and motivation. Any edge a student can obtain, however, can be worthwhile, which leads us to our main question here, Should students change their answers after they initially respond to a multiple-choice question? Folklore—and most people's intuition—answers this question with a resounding "no." You should stick with your initial answer because any wavering between answers likely means you're confused, so why not stick with your first "gut hunch"?

In this case, however, folklore and intuition are most certainly incorrect. In their review of this literature, Benjamin, Cavell, and Shallenberger (1984) revealed some consistent findings. First, although most students (but not all) tend to change answers, typically a student will change only a few answers on a given test. Second, and most important, even though some correct answers are changed to incorrect ones, the majority of the time answers are actually changed from incorrect to correct. Thus, in general, changing answers on multiple-choice tests will produce an increase in test performance. It seems unlikely that students will benefit if they change answers based on any whim, and in fact, some students do not gain from changing, because as noted above, some answers are changed from correct to incorrect.

So, how do you know when to change an answer versus when to leave it alone? One answer to this question is to trust your feelings of confidence in your answer. Consider a study conducted by Shatz and Best (1987). Students took a multiple-choice exam for an Introductory Psychology course. Immediately after taking the exam, it was scored and given back to the students. As the exam was discussed, students were asked to mark any answer that they had changed and to provide their reason for changing the answer from a list of alternatives, such as they accidentally marked the wrong answer, they initially misread the questions, or they had originally guessed and hence decided to change their answer. As in previous studies, very few of the answers (4.4%) were changed, and the majority of changed answers went from incorrect to correct. Most relevant here

(Continued)

(Continued)

is that when people said they had initially guessed and then changed their answer, only 35% of the time did answers move from incorrect to correct. In contrast, for any other reason given, about 72% of the answers changed from incorrect to correct. Thus, you should definitely consider changing answers on multiple-choice tests, but if your initial confidence judgment indicates that you were merely guessing, you may be better off sticking with your initial gut hunch.

Given these caveats, a more interesting question is, With experience taking examinations across a semester, do students' predictions become better calibrated? That is, after receiving feedback on multiple tests throughout the semester, will students show greater judgment accuracy on the final test? Hacker and colleagues (2000) were able to answer this question because they had students make predictions for all examinations throughout the semester. The answer to these questions was both "yes" and "no." At the end of their 15-week course, the accuracy of all students' predictions on the third examination did improve. These improvements, however, were enjoyed only by the students who performed well on the tests across the semester; the poorest performers were no more accurate in predicting their final exam performance than they were at predicting performance on the first exam. That is, even after all the previous test experience, the most poorly performing students did not recalibrate their judgments.

Although few studies have been aimed at improving the accuracy of students' judgments of their test performance within the classroom, two studies provide some optimism that accuracy can be enhanced. Both focused on improving the calibration of retrospective confidence judgments during a class test. Schraw, Potenza, and Nebelsick-Gullet (1993) investigated whether giving students incentives to make accurate judgments would enhance their accuracy. Students enrolled in an introductory class on educational psychology took two tests—one that tapped comprehension and the other that tapped math skills. After answering each question on the tests, the students rated their confidence in the accuracy of their response. Most important, incentives were manipulated across students: Some students were told that they would receive extra credit if they performed well on the tests, and some were told that they would receive extra credit if their judgments were highly accurate. As expected, calibration (on either test) was superior for students who received incentives to make accurate judgments.

Schraw et al. (1993) provided an important demonstration that calibration can be improved. However, given that many teachers may be unwilling to award credit to students if they make accurate judgments (which should be a means to an end and not the end itself), it would be worthwhile to discover other ways to improve judgment accuracy. Perhaps if students were given explicit training and practice judging their performance, their judgment accuracy would improve. To evaluate this possibility, Nietfeld, Cao, and Osborne (2006) trained students to more accurately make confidence judgments across an entire semester. At the end of every class period, the students were engaged in brief exercises to improve their monitoring skills. In particular, they rated their confidence in understanding the content for that day and described which concept from the class that they had particular difficulty understanding. These students also received practice questions about the course content, which they answered and then provided confidence judgments for their answers. As they reviewed their answers, the students were asked to reflect on the accuracy of their confidence judgments. The key outcome measure was calibration of the confidence judgments on each of four exams that were administered across the semester. Most important, calibration for the students who received training in monitoring skills was compared to that of students who did not receive training. On the first exam, calibration was identical for students who received training and for those who did not receive training. As the class progressed, however, the training began to substantially benefit students' judgment accuracy. In fact, by the second exam and throughout the remainder of the class, calibration was consistently one standard deviation greater for the trained students than for the untrained ones. Even more important, Nietfeld et al. (2006) reported that improvements in calibration across the semester were predictive of higher scores on the final test. So, as expected from theories of self-regulated learning (Figure 9.1), improving monitoring skills also led to better performance.

Although students' monitoring accuracy in the classroom has only recently begun to be investigated (for a review, see Hacker, Bol, & Keener, 2008), it is evident from the studies discussed above that at least some students can evaluate their classroom performance with acceptable levels of accuracy. Furthermore, students' monitoring skills can be improved and when it does, so does their learning. Many questions remain for future research such as, What is the best way to train students? How long will the effects of training last, and will the benefits of training on judgment accuracy in one class transfer to other classes?

Metacognitive Control

As we've discussed in previous chapters, the function of monitoring is to allow people to effectively control their cognitive processing. In terms of education, students may use monitoring to control many aspects of their activities to promote their achievement. In preparing for tests, students may monitor their performance on one exam, and depending on their evaluations, they may prepare differently for the next exam. For instance, they may decide to increase their efforts in hopes of improving their performance or even decrease their efforts to obtain the same level of performance but with less time. Let's take a look at one monitoring-based intervention that was designed to improve middle-school students' regulation while solving logic problems.

Delclos and Harrington (1991) had fifth and sixth graders play a problem-solving game called Rocky's Boots. In this game, students build a simulated electronic circuit (on a computer) that will "boot" specific targets off the screen—when the correct targets are "booted," the students earn the most points. Targets are specified by logic gates. For instance, the students might be told that they should boot all "Green Diamonds" but nothing else. In this case, the student should set up a "green sensor" and a "diamond sensor" and connect them with an AND gate. In this case, only objects that are Green AND Diamonds will be booted from the screen. The students can use three kinds of gates (AND, OR, NOT) to solve problems, which become more complicated as they require more (and a greater variety of) gates to solve. A main question posed by these researchers was, Will training students to monitor their progress and success during practice phases help them to better regulate their problem solving?

To answer this question, some students received no training (i.e., the comparison or control group), one group of students received general problem-solving training (e.g., reading the problem carefully and thinking about similar problems), and the monitoring group received this problem-solving training along with a series of questions to help them monitor their performance. These questions had students reflect on each aspect of problem solving such as, Have you looked at the problem carefully? Did you look for clues that would help you solve this problem? How many points did you score? According to Delclos and Harrington (1991), these questions "forced the individual to attend to the problem-solving processes being used, providing a built-in metacognitive component to their problem-solving practice" (p. 36). After training, the monitoring group outperformed the other two groups on the most difficult problems, and as impressive, they used less time to solve the problems. One explanation for the benefits of monitoring training was that forcing students to reflect on their problem solving encouraged them to use more strategies (Delclos & Harrington, 1991). Put differently, as reflected in models of self-regulated learning (e.g., Figure 9.1), students who monitored their activities were more likely to effectively control them, which in turn improved their performance.

Student Metacognition in Specific Domains

In the present section, we survey literature devoted to investigating the contribution of metacognition to student performance within three specific domains: reading, writing, and mathematics. Explaining self-regulated learning (SRL) within each domain is a major goal of the general models mentioned above—and, in fact, many studies introduced in this section could be discussed in relation to Winne and Hadwin's (1998) model and to other general models of SRL. We chose to highlight these domains separately because they are especially central to student education and have received a great deal of attention in the field.

Reading

Literacy is arguably the foundation of education: If you cannot read and write, you will not be able to grasp many other essential domains of education, such as science, history, and literature. Given the importance of proficient reading to education, it perhaps is not surprising that some of the first work on metacognition was conducted in the domain of reading. Consider the groundbreaking work by Ann Brown (which is showcased in Box 9.2) and by Ellen Markman. Markman (1977) evaluated whether first- and third-grade students could detect major omissions in a set of instructions. Without the omitted detail, the students could not know how to proceed. The question was, Could the students monitor that they could not understand how to proceed? More specifically, in one task, the experimenter dealt four cards (with one letter on each card) upside down to herself and to the student, and said that they would both turn one card over at a time, and whoever had the special card each time would win the cards. Which card was special was never mentioned. Most third graders detected the problem, whereas the first graders did not. Markman (1977) concluded that the first graders did not internally enact the instructions and hence could not evaluate whether their understanding would allow them to obtain the goal of winning the game.

As one of the first psychologists to investigate metacognition, Markman (1977; 1979) has had a major impact on the field. She introduced a method to investigate comprehension monitoring—detecting inconsistencies and errors in instructions and text—that has been widely used and has provided much insight into why people often have difficulty monitoring their comprehension of text. We'll return to error detection later, but first we'll describe a general metacognitive model that will help to put self-regulated reading into a larger perspective.

BOX 9.2
Ann Brown's Contribution to Metacognition and Education

Some students seem more gifted at learning, whereas others appear to be relatively slow. Why? In the mid-1970s, many scientists assumed that slow learners
had inferior memory capacities, which would undermine their success in the
classroom. Ann Brown, along with her collaborator Joseph Campione, championed another view (Brown & Campione, 1996). In particular, Brown argued that
slower learners had deficits in metacognition. In her classic chapter, "Knowing
When, Where, and How to Remember: A Problem of Metacognition," Brown
(1978) introduced many researchers to the concept of metacognition and to its
potential importance for understanding child development. The strength of
Brown's conviction is evident in her claim that

> My bias is that the processes described as metacognitive are the impor-
> tant aspects of knowledge, that what is of major interest is knowledge
> about one's own cognitions rather than the cognitions themselves. Just
> as fever is a secondary symptom, an epiphenomenon of disease . . . so the
> outcome of intelligent evaluation and control of one's own cognitive
> processes are secondary symptoms of the basic underlying processes of
> metacognition. (p. 79)

Ann Brown and her colleagues adapted (and developed) rather novel methods for exploring and improving students' monitoring of their comprehension
while learning classroom content from text. Let's just consider two of her numerous articles, which bear directly on metacognition and text learning. Brown and
Smiley (1977) investigated whether students—from 8 to 18 years old—had critical knowledge about the structure of text materials; namely, that some ideas
were more important to the meaning of a text than were others. Students read
the texts and were later told that the ideas differed in their importance; some of
them were so unimportant that they could be deleted without compromising the
main theme of the text. They then had the participants judge the importance of
the idea units by first removing the least important quarter of the ideas, then by
removing the next least important quarter of ideas, and so forth. The youngest
participants (8- and 10-year-olds) did not distinguish between what were normatively the most (versus least) important ideas in the text, whereas older participants did. An implication of this developmental trend is that the younger
students would be unable to strategically focus on the most important ideas
when reading.

Palinscar and Brown (1984) reported two studies that were meant to foster
comprehension and comprehension monitoring by having seventh graders engage
in several activities, such as summarizing their reading, developing questions

about the content, and having them predict what the future content of the text would include. Palinscar and Brown selected these activities "because they provide a dual function, that of enhancing comprehension and at the same time affording an opportunity for the student to check whether it is occurring" (p. 121). As important, they introduced reciprocal teaching as a means to train students to use these activities in which the teacher and the student would take turns leading a discussion about various portions of each text. The teacher would at first model the key activities (listed above) and then the students were encouraged to participate in these activities as much as possible. Their intervention was a huge success: The students showed large improvements on the criterion tests of comprehension, and as important, they used the trained activities on new tasks in which they had not been trained. Since the publication of their landmark paper, the use of reciprocal teaching to foster comprehension and comprehension monitoring has been shown to be effective by numerous investigators (for a review, see Rosenshine & Meister, 1994).

Ann Brown was an innovator in the history of metacognition. She defined and promoted a metacognitive perspective for understanding child development and improving student achievement. In 1995, four years before her death, Ann Brown received the Distinguished Scientific Award for the Applications of Psychology from the American Psychological Association (1996) "for outstanding contributions to the study of cognitive development, learning theory, and educational practice. Her work on metacognition brought the idea into common use among educators... her educational wisdom is unparalleled" (p. 309). Certainly, Brown's research and wisdom will continue to have an impact on education and metacognitive research.

As you've learned from previous chapters, any metacognitively regulated activity—such as reading—is conceptualized as having both monitoring components and control components. For reading, the former may include evaluating one's understanding of a text or evaluating whether a text is inconsistent with one's prior knowledge of a domain, and the latter may include using monitoring to guide restudy or to apply various strategies to support learning and comprehension of text materials. In general, these metacognitive components of reading are captured by Hacker's (1998b) model of comprehension monitoring (Figure 9.3), which is partly based on Nelson and Naren's (1990) general framework of metacognition (see Figure 1.1). Several aspects of this model are noteworthy. First, it highlights that a student's goal is often to develop an internal representation of a text, which includes representing the textbase of a text (i.e., the words and sentences explicitly stated in a text) as well as representing the meaning of the text (i.e., comprehension that goes beyond the textbase and may involve integrating the explicit text material with one's previous world knowledge; Kintsch, 1988). Second, students may adopt a standard with which to evaluate ongoing reading, such as that they want to fully comprehend all aspects of a text or perhaps that they merely want to memorize the most critical concepts in it. In this manner, the model in Figure 9.3 can be viewed as a specific instantiation of Winne and Hadwin's (1998) general model of self-regulated learning (Figure 9.1 above).

Third, and most relevant to metacognition, this model highlights that monitoring and control functions to help students achieve their learning goals. For reading, a skilled reader may engage in the following phases: (a) preparing to read, which may involve developing reading goals and skimming a text to evaluate its structure; (b) constructing meaning from the text, which can involve focusing on the most important aspects of a text, identifying the main ideas, making inferences, interpreting the text, and monitoring comprehension; and (c) reflecting on reading, such as by asking questions and summarizing (Paris, Wasik, & Turner, 1991). These phases are recursive and do not need to occur in any strict order. All of these activities may involve monitoring and control: Students may evaluate whether their goal will meet a teacher's expectations and change their goals accordingly (phase 1); while reading, they can evaluate whether they have actually identified the main ideas and whether their inferences are accurate, and then look back at parts of text to correct any potential misunderstanding (phase 2); and the final phase focuses largely on metacognitive activities. Based on their analysis of skilled reading, Pressley and Afflerbach (1995) demonstrated that skilled readers actively engage in all of these cognitive and metacognitive activities. They proposed that skilled readers engage in *constructively responsive reading*, which involves reading with a sense of purpose and actively constructing meaning from a text.

Given the central role of metacognitive skills, monitoring and control processes can contribute to students' comprehension and memory of text. If monitoring or control failures occur, students may also fail to fully comprehend or remember a text. The literature on metacognition and reading has investigated the degree to which readers of all ages and abilities effectively regulate their learning across all these phases, and accordingly, the literature is immense. Thus, in the remainder of this section, we briefly describe some representative research that has explored how well students monitor and control their reading. For more comprehensive reviews of this literature, see chapters in Israel, Block, Bauserman, and Kinnucan-Welsch (2005).

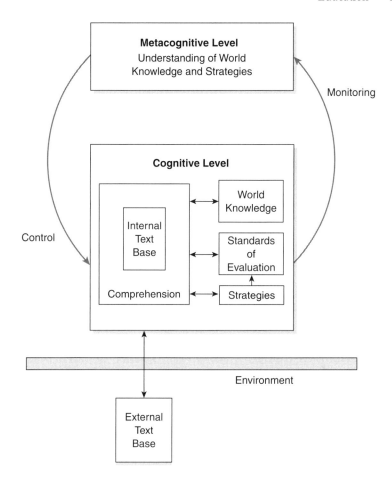

Figure 9.3   Model of reading comprehension that highlights both cognitive and metacognitive components.

SOURCE: Hacker, D. J. (1998). Self-regulated comprehension during normal reading. In D. J. Hacker, J. Dunlosky, and A. C. Graesser (Eds.), *Metacognition in educational theory and practice* (pp. 165–191). Hillsdale, NJ: Lawrence Erlbaum.

Monitoring the Learning and Comprehension of Text

As implied by the model in Figure 9.3, students' monitoring of their learning and comprehension of texts may fail for many reasons. Young readers may lack strategies (or not spontaneously use them) that are needed for comprehension monitoring, such as constructing a representation of a text that can be checked for incompleteness (Markman, 1977). At times, comprehension itself may be so demanding that mental resources are not available for monitoring also to be successfully engaged. Moreover, students may not have or use appropriate standards of evaluation when attempting to monitor their progress toward a goal. For instance, students may use a standard "Do I understand individual sentences?" when monitoring their comprehension instead of using a broader standard that is more appropriate for monitoring comprehension such as, "Do I understand the gist of the text that arises across sentences?" (Brincones & Otero, 1994).

To investigate these issues, researchers have mainly used variations on three standard methods that reveal students' ability to evaluate their learning and comprehension of texts. One method is to have students judge their learning and comprehension of a text after they have read it. As discussed in Mystery Box 5.3, research in this area—called *metacomprehension*—has largely demonstrated that people of all ages have difficulties accurately judging their text learning and comprehension. Researchers have also relied on having people report their thoughts as they read (called *think-aloud* protocols), which can reveal how students monitor and control their reading as well as improve their text comprehension (Kucan & Beck, 1997; Pressley & Afflerbach, 1995). Another frequently used method—which was introduced above—involves having students read texts that include errors to determine who detects the errors versus who does not (for a review, see Otero, 1998). Surprisingly, even adults may miss apparently obvious inconsistencies in text, including explicit contradictions. To end this section, let's consider how normal reading may actually contribute to such failures in comprehension monitoring.

Read the following text, which is adapted from Otero and Kintsch (1992):

> Superconductivity is the disappearance of resistance to the flow of electric current. Until now it has only been obtained by cooling certain materials to low temperatures near absolute zero. That made its technical applications very difficult. Many laboratories are now trying to produce superconducting alloys. Until now superconductivity has been achieved by considerably increasing the temperature of certain materials. (p. 230)

Did you notice anything wrong about this text? When Otero and Kintsch (1992) had 10th- and 12th-grade students read four critical texts like the one above, many students did not notice any difficulties. Now look again: The second and final sentences contradict each other—just like in their other critical texts. Otero and Kintsch (1992) argued that one reason people have difficulties in detecting contradictions in text is that the internal processes involved in constructing an understanding of a text may decrease the like-lihood that a contradiction will be represented in long-term memory. Ironically, then, normal reading processes (which at times will lead to correct error detection) would explain why many people fail to notice the contradictions. In particular, if people overweigh the initial sentences of the text—which often set the stage for the remaining sentences—then the subsequent "incon-sistent material will simply be overlooked" (Otero & Kintsch, 1992, p. 229). In this way, processing at the cognitive level (Figure 9.3) is providing incom-plete information for monitoring processes that occur at the metacognitive level. A prediction from their hypothesis was that students who did not detect the inconsistencies would be less likely to remember the contradictory sentences. They had the students recall the text content, and as shown in Figure 9.4, those who did not notice the contradiction were much less likely to remember the final sentence.

In summary, people may fail to accurately monitor their learning and comprehension of text for many reasons. As researchers continue to discover the reasons for these failures, we suspect that techniques can be developed to further help everyone sidestep their monitoring problems and further improve their learning and comprehension.

Control of Learning and Comprehension of Text

Students can benefit by applying appropriate reading strategies while they work toward their learning goals. Certainly, some students (espe-cially as they get older and their reading skills improve) do report using an arsenal of strategies to support their reading. In one of the first stud-ies on this topic, Myers and Paris (1978) explored second- and sixth-grade students' knowledge about reading. Many second graders may just be developing their language skills, so it is not surprising that they were unaware of many important parameters of reading. According to Myers and Paris, second graders "were not sensitive to task dimensions or the need to invoke special strategies for different materials and goals. They reported few strategies or reasons for checking their own understanding" (p. 688). Moreover, they reported that poor sixth-grade readers—as com-pared to better readers and comprehenders—were less likely to use a vari-ety of monitoring and reading strategies. And in a study by Hare and Smith (1982), sixth-grade students reported using a variety of strategies while reading: rereading parts of texts, summarizing texts, slowing down when reading difficult passages, and attempting to develop relationships across various portions of a text. Thus, by sixth grade, many students—although perhaps not all—are using a variety of strategies to read texts.

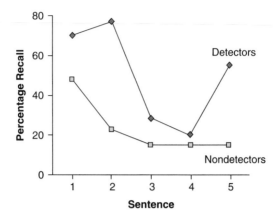

Figure 9.4   Percentage correct recall of sentences. The contradictory sentences are numbers two and five.

SOURCE: Adapted from Otero, J., and Kintsch, W. (1992). Failures to detect contradictions in a text: What readers believe versus what they read. *Psychological Science, 3*, 229–235.

To investigate college students' control of their reading, Baker and Anderson (1982) capitalized on the error-detection paradigm. The students read texts that included inconsistencies: Some occurred in sentences that included the main point of a passage, whereas others were embedded in sentences that included details. Some sentences contained no inconsistencies. The texts were presented one sentence at a time, and students could control their reading by allocating as much time as they wanted to read individual sentences as well as by rereading (or looking back to) previously presented sentences. If students were detecting inconsistencies and regulating their reading, they should spend more time reading (and rereading) sentences with inconsistencies. Their results are presented in Table 9.2. As expected, students allocated more time when sentences contained inconsistencies (embedded in a "Main Point" or "Detail") than when they did not ("None"), and they were more likely to reread the first sentence in an inconsistent pair. These results indicate that students can monitor their comprehension and use their monitoring to strategically regulate their reading.

Although studies like these indicate that many students are strategic readers, for a variety of reasons, students may not be strategic and hence fail to

Table 9.2   Time Allocated (Seconds) and Proportion of Rereading

Location of Inconsistency	Kind of Sentence	
	Main Point	Detail
Time Allocated		
Main point	10.7	7.8
Detail	6.8	9.2
None	7.4	6.3
Proportion of Rereading		
Main point	.90	.58
Detail	.51	.74
None	.57	.58

SOURCE: Adapted from Baker and Anderson (1982).

effectively control their learning and comprehension of texts. Like the second graders in the study by Myers and Paris (1978), students may not know how to resolve some problems that arise during reading. Even if they do have appropriate strategies, they may not know when to use them. Moreover, motivation, time constraints, and available processing resources may also undermine students' effective regulation of reading. From their review, Paris and Paris (2001) conclude that

> Students who were able to discuss their work with awareness of the psychological characteristics that affect performance were more likely to be able to identify reading strategies that would enhance the comprehension and learning. Thus, the ability to assess one's work is linked to the ability to evaluate literacy strategies. This suggests that metacognitive abilities are necessary for both [comprehension and learning]. (p. 96)

Given that such metacognitive abilities can enhance students' comprehension, many researchers have developed interventions to improve student reading that are based on metcognitive principles (e.g., Cummins, Stewart, & Block, 2005; Donndelinger, 2005). These interventions show much promise—and are often successful—for promoting student literacy.

BOX 9.3
Explain Yourself! Does Self-Explanation
Improve Student Performance?

Most of us talk to ourselves from time to time. We may ask ourselves why we said something, talk to ourselves about what we want to do later in the day, or even reminisce about how well the past week has gone. Such inner thought at times may be distracting, but if you talk to yourself in the right way, it can benefit your performance on many tasks. The key to reaping these benefits is doing it the "right way."

Michelene Chi and her colleagues were among the first to herald the potential benefit of thinking to oneself while solving problems (e.g., Chi & Bassok, 1989; Chi, Bassok, Lewis, Reimann, & Glaser, 1989). In their highly influential article, "Self-Explanations: How Students Study and Use Examples in Learning to Solve Problems," Chi et al. (1989) compared good and poor students' thoughts as they studied worked-out examples of various mechanics problems. Worked-out examples are often incomplete, so that students will need to fill in the blanks by explaining why a particular step was taken. If students spontaneously explained what they were doing as they studied a problem, Chi et al. thought that those students would fill in the blanks toward a deeper understanding of the problem. In particular, the authors argue that "explaining is a mechanism of study that allows students to infer and explicate the conditions and consequences of each procedural step in [an] example, as well as apply the principle and definition of concepts to justify them" (p. 151). Such self-explanation is metacognitive in that students need to monitor and explain their progress and understanding as they work on a problem.

To demonstrate the benefits of self-explanation, Chi et al. (1989) had students first study worked-out problems, and while they were doing so, the students also had to think aloud. Next, the students solved problems on Newtonian mechanics, and they were separated into "good" and "poor" students based on their performance on these problems. In the analyses of the students' think-aloud protocols, one fact was striking: As compared to the poor students, good students spent more time explaining the content of the worked-out example, which "consisted of inferences about the conditions, the consequences, the goals, and the meaning of various mathematical actions described in the example" (p. 168). The better students monitored difficulties in their comprehension, and they were more likely to use this monitoring to control their learning by attempting to make inferences that would resolve the miscomprehension. These results indicate that the right way to think while solving problems is to explain your understanding of a problem as you proceed.

Siegler (2002) has also done some particularly interesting work on self-explanation. In one study (described in Siegler, 2002), he investigated learning of the Piagetian concept of conservation with 5-year-olds who did not yet know how to do these tasks. Children were shown two rows each with the same number of objects (7, 8, or 9) arranged in one-to-one correspondence. Then the experimenter would do things like spread out one of the rows, or add or subtract one object or more from one of the rows, while at the same time saying what he was doing. Then the children were asked whether they thought the transformed row had the same, more, or fewer objects than the untransformed row. In the training phase, one group of children was given straightforward feedback about their answers. A second group was asked to explain their reasoning ("Why do you think that?"). These children—especially those who gave elaborate reasons for why they "thought that"—tended to learn quickly. Siegler also had a third group, the "explain the correct reasoning" group. In this group, the children were told what the experimenter thought, and they were asked to explain the experimenter's reasoning: "How do you think I knew that?" This third group did extraordinarily well across training sessions, as is shown in Figure 9.5.

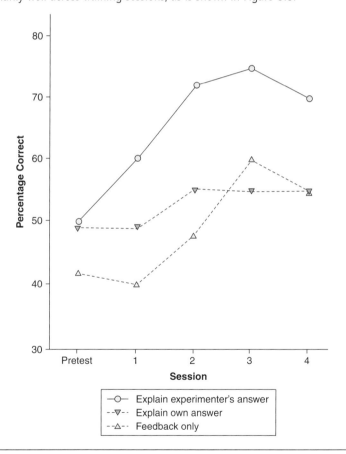

Figure 9.5   Percentage correct on pretest and training sessions of number conservation task.

SOURCE: Siegler, R. S. (2002). Microgenetic studies of self-explanations. In N. Granott and J. Parziale (Eds.), *Microdevelopment: Transition processes in development and learning* (pp. 31–58). New York: Cambridge University Press.

(Continued)

(Continued)

Perhaps not surprisingly, self-explanation has been investigated extensively, and researchers have demonstrated that it can benefit students' performance in numerous tasks, which include solving mathematics problems (Wong, Lawson, & Keeves, 2002), solving problems that involve the use of analogical reasoning (Neuman & Schwarz, 1998), and comprehending science texts (Ainsworth & Burcham, 2007). In his review of general research on verbalization and problem solving, Dominowski (1998) concluded that self-explanation improves student performance because the metacognitive thoughts it elicits "promote a different kind of problem-solving approach, a more reflective strategy that subjects continue to use even when answering questions [and self-explanation] is no longer required" (p. 40). Indeed, a report of the Department of Education's Institute for Educational Sciences, the 2007 Practice Guide on "Organizing Instruction and Study to Improve Student Learning," strongly encouraged teachers to help children learn using this method. So, if you're stuck attempting to perform a difficult mental task, you may consider talking to yourself—it can help, as long as you don't just mindlessly repeat your inner thoughts, and instead focus on explaining what you are doing. So, when in doubt, don't forget to Explain Yourself!

Writing

Writing and reading are highly interrelated, with an obvious connection being that students who are writing read their prose to evaluate and revise it, which would involve many of the same processes involved in comprehension and comprehension monitoring. The first models of writing that attempted to describe its processes were informed largely by think-aloud protocols, where writers of various abilities would describe what they were doing as they wrote. One of the most popular of these models, by Hayes and Flower (1980), captures the three majors processes engaged by expert writers: planning, translating, and reviewing. For *planning*, writers may set goals, generate ideas to meet them, and organize the ideas into a coherent structure. *Translating* involves taking one's ideas and translating them into a written document. And *reviewing* involves reading the written document and evaluating whether the initial goals had been met. As important, this model (shown in Figure 9.6) also highlights the central role of metacognitive monitoring in writing at every phase, although it is perhaps most evident during the reviewing phase.

In their landmark book, Bereiter and Scardamalia (1987) conducted numerous studies to identify differences between novice and expert writers. Their analyses uncovered two different styles of writing. In particular, novice

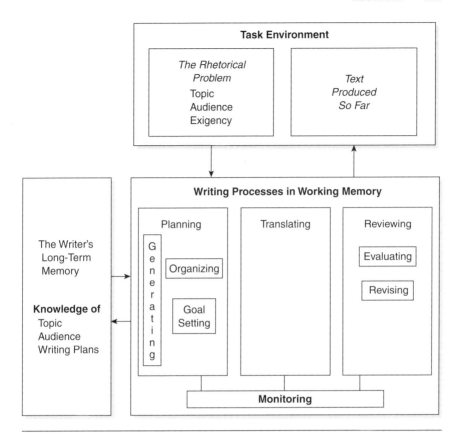

Figure 9.6   Hayes and Flower Model of Self-Regulated Writing

SOURCE: Hayes, J. R., & Flower, L. (1980). Identifying the organization of writing processes. In L. W. Gregg and E. R. Steinberg (Eds.), *Cognitive processes in writing*. Hillsdale, NJ: Lawrence Erlbaum.

writers were more likely to merely list all they knew about a topic, with writing being complete when they had finished describing what they knew. Such *knowledge telling* was indicative of young writers (e.g., 10 years old and younger). In contrast, expert writers were more likely to be *knowledge transforming*, where the writer's knowledge is transformed to tell a more coherent story. In terms of the Hayes and Flower (1980) model, writers who engage in knowledge transforming are more likely to plan their writing and evaluate their progress. As children rise through the ranks of early grade school, their writing changes from knowledge-telling to a more mature knowledge-transforming style (Bereiter & Scardamalia, 1987). As Sitko

(1998) noted in her review of writing research, "What distinguishes these more mature patterns is that they involve conscious control over parts of the process that are ignored by the less mature writer" (p. 97). Such conscious control is quintessentially metacognitive in nature, with mature writers reflecting on and reworking their writing.

As important, students who more often plan and monitor their writing produce better essays (Conner, 2007), which again establishes the link between using metacognitive strategies and obtaining good scholastic outcomes. Although a lot of research has focused on improving student writing (for reviews, see Fitzgerald & Markham, 1987; Sitko, 1998), the general approach has been to train students on multiple aspects of expert writing at the same time, including planning, structuring good sentences, and using feedback to improve revision. This approach is certainly sensible if one's main goal is to enhance the quality of student writing by incorporating what we know about expert writing into interventions. Unfortunately, however, even though the interventions often involve training some metacognitive skills, the degree to which improvements in metacognition (versus some other process involved in writing) contribute to overall gains in the quality of writing is typically unclear.

Moreover, writing research has received less attention than reading. One reason for this disparity may simply be how difficult and time-consuming it is to objectively grade students' lengthy prose. Fortunately, new technologies are being developed to grade students' writing online. For instance, Summary Street (Wade-Stein & Kintsch, 2004) is an automated system that evaluates whether a students' summary of texts meets objective standards and provides immediate feedback on multiple dimensions (e.g., adequate coverage of content and redundancy), which students can use to reconceptualize and revise their writing. Such automated tutors show much promise in supporting research efforts to investigate students' self-regulation of writing, as well as in providing external scaffolds (e.g., focused feedback) for improving student writing. Certainly, given that writing itself is foundational to thinking and to student scholarship throughout all levels of education, an important research agenda will be to continue developing techniques to help students become expert writers.

Mathematics

Can you solve the following equation for "y"?

$$x^2y + 2xy + x - y = 2$$

Or, can you find the largest triangle that can be inscribed in a circle? Without any training, solving these problems (from Schoenfeld, 1987) and others like them would be nearly impossible. Perhaps surprisingly, what Schoenfeld (1987) found was that even students who knew enough mathematics to solve the problems had difficulties. As he observed in videotapes of students solving these kinds of problems, they would often spend time struggling with the solutions— they were "on a wild goose chase. They had ample opportunity to stop during that time and ask themselves 'Is this getting us anywhere? Should we try something else?' but they didn't. And as long as they didn't, they were guaranteed not to solve the problems" (Schoenfeld, 1987, p. 193). In his influential work on mathematical problem solving, Alan Schoenfeld (1985) reported that students too often would choose a solution for a math problem and stick tenaciously to it, even though doing so meant that they would not explore other options and potentially discover the correct solution.

The students spent plenty of time trying to solve the problems but very little time in thinking about the problems and where they were proceeding. For comparison, Schoenfeld (1987) also observed how mathematicians solved difficult geometry problems. The mathematicians spent a great deal of time thinking about the problems; in contrast to the students, the experts analyzed the problems and planned how to proceed. The mathematicians demonstrated another hallmark of expert problem solving, in that they frequently monitored their progress, asking themselves questions such as, "Am I making progress?" If the mathematicians decided one approach was not working, then they tried another one. As concluded by Schoenfeld (1987), "with the efficient use of self-monitoring and self-regulation, [mathematicians] solved a problem that many students—who knew a lot more geometry than [they] did—failed to solve" (p. 195). Thus, metacognitive skills and knowledge are an important factor leading to successful problem solving in mathematics (Carr & Jessup, 1995).

Of course, many other factors are important as well, and based on analyses of math expertise, De Corte, Verschaffel, and Op 'T Eynde (2000) recommend that students develop a disposition for mathematics that involves developing mastery of various aptitudes, such as (a) domain-specific knowledge, including knowing facts and rules of mathematics; (b) general strategies for problem solving; (c) knowledge about one's own cognitive functioning (i.e., metaknowledge); and (d) self-regulatory skills. As De Corte et al. (2000) conclude, "From the perspective of self-regulated learning, it is important in this respect to stimulate in students the development of attitudes toward and skills in assessing their own mathematical learning processes and performances" (p. 691). It is important to notice that like the models of self-regulated reading and writing, monitoring one's progress is core to self-regulation in mathematics. Accordingly, this leads to a key question: Can students be taught how to monitor and regulate their mathematical problem solving in a manner that improves their self-regulation and performance?

The answer is a resounding "yes," and multiple techniques have been used to improve students' self-regulation in this area (e.g., Desoete, Roeyers, & De Clercq, 2003; Kramarski, Mevarech, & Arami, 2002; Schoenfeld, 1985; for a review, see De Corte et al., 2000).

In a large-scale intervention by Fuchs and colleagues (2003), more than 350 third graders (from six different schools) participated in a project to help them learn to foster their self-regulation skills, including goal setting and self-monitoring, in hopes that doing so would improve their mathematical problem solving and promote transfer. More specifically, across training sessions (two per week over 16 weeks), students independently attempted to solve a problem and then were trained to engage in monitoring activities: They scored their problem and then plotted their daily score from zero to the maximum score for that problem. During the next session, they were encouraged to beat their previous score, set a goal for solving the problem for that day, and attempt to solve the new problem, then score themselves again. Outcome measures included performance on several transfer problems and questionnaire measures of metacognition, including math self-efficacy and self-monitoring. This self-regulation group—which also received transfer training in math problem solving—was compared to groups that received transfer training only and a control group that did not receive any training. Prior to training, all groups were equally good at solving problems; after training, however, the self-regulation group consistently outperformed both the transfer-training group and the control group. Moreover, the students who were trained to set goals and monitor their progress had higher math self-efficacy and reported engaging in more self-monitoring when they solved math problems. These outcomes from Fuchs et al. (2003) are promising: Interventions aimed at improving students' metacognitive skills can enhance their efficacy, self-monitoring, and most important, their performance while solving math problems.

BOX 9.4
Does Intelligence Reign Supreme, or Does Metacognition
Also Influence Student Achievement?

Everyone knows students who seem really smart—quick to raise their hand in class and adept at the toughest, most analytic subjects, like mathematics and physics. Certainly, these students often are at the top of their class. But is having the highest IQ (intelligence quotient) the only means to achievement in school? The answer to this question is certainly "no." According to evidence from systematic research by Veenman and his colleagues (Prins, Veenman, & Elshout, 2006; Veenman & Beishuizen, 2004; Veenman, Kok, & Blöte, 2005), students' metacognitive skills also contribute to their overall success.

Intelligence in part refers to one's basic ability to reason and solve problems (e.g., Horn, 1989), so it's not surprising that a student's intelligence would be related to how well they perform in school, which often requires sheer reasoning and problem solving. Thus, one possibility is that intelligence itself is the dominant means to achievement. If so, students' intelligence per se would itself foster better metacognitive skills, and in this way, the rich would get richer. That is, they would have the raw problem-solving abilities and the best metacognition, but metacognition itself would not contribute to achievement independently of intelligence. Another possibility is that intelligence and metacognition contribute independently to achievement—if so, even students with a somewhat lower IQ could find themselves performing well by compensating through the appropriate use of their metacognitive skills.

To evaluate these and other possibilities, Veenman et al. (2005) had 12- and 13-year-olds solve several math problems, and they also obtained the students' grade point average for math. A key question was, Will students' metacognitive skills predict their performance (both solving math problems and their GPA) when intelligence was factored out? To measure these constructs, the students took a standardized intelligence test, and their metacognitive skills were assessed as they solved the math problems. In particular, the students were told to "think aloud" while solving the problems, and their think-aloud protocols were analyzed for signs of 15 different metacognitive activities. These activities included planning, keeping an overview of solutions to create opportunities for checking outcomes, checking and reflecting on answers, and reflection that was relevant to learning from earlier experiences. The use of these metacognitive strategies was positively correlated with performance: Students who used more of them performed better. Moreover, this relationship was still significant after the students' intelligence scores were factored out. Perhaps most impressive, these on-line measures of metacognitive skills were correlated with overall math GPA (.40), and this correlation remained significant (.30) even when individual differences in intelligence were taken into account.

These researchers have also shown an independent contribution of students' use of metacognitive strategies to performance relevant to reading comprehension (Veenman & Beishuizen, 2004) and to inductive learning (Prins et al., 2006). The latter work demonstrated that metacognitive skills were particularly important when students were solving problems just at the boundaries of their knowledge and abilities. Thus, although intelligence does matter, metacognitive skills are also valuable for students' success in school.

Summary

Much of the groundbreaking work in metacognition was conducted by researchers who desired to understand whether young students could effectively monitor and regulate their learning, reading, writing, and mathematical problem solving. General models of self-regulated learning—which have largely grown from an educational perspective—attempt to capture all aspects of students' activities and their environment that may contribute to student scholarship. Accordingly, educational psychologists are interested in students' basic cognitive abilities, along with the integration of these abilities into a framework that highlights goal setting, self-efficacy, domain knowledge, motivation, and other factors. The core of these general models, however, is most often constituted from the two powerhouse concepts in metacognition: monitoring and control.

In the present chapter, we surveyed the immense literature on metacognition and education. Our survey was far from exhaustive. We only touched on a handful of the studies conducted within the domains we covered. Moreover, we were not able to highlight many other domains in which researchers' use of a metacognitive perspective has led to insights, such as in note taking (Pressley, Van Etten, Yokoi, Freebern, & Van Meter, 1998), learning with hypermedia (Azevedo, Cromley, Winters, Moos, & Greene, 2005), and student emotion and metacognition (Efklides & Chryssoula, 2005), to name only a few. We hope that our survey demonstrated the promise of a metacognitive approach to improving student scholarship as well as serving as a bridge to the vast literature for young scientists interested in education.

DISCUSSION QUESTIONS

1. As students prepare for an exam in Introductory Psychology, they may regulate their learning in numerous ways. In the context of Winne and Hadwin's (1998) model, how might metacognitive monitoring play a critical role in helping students prepare for the exam? As important, discuss how each component of self-regulated learning could lead to suboptimal performance—that is, a poor grade—if it was either not engaged while learning or failed to be engaged in an appropriate manner. According to this model, why might a student believe she is ready for an exam, when in fact she has not adequately learned the material to achieve a passing grade?

2. Research on education and metacognition arguably represents one of the most active and extensive areas in metacognitive research. Accordingly, we were unable to cover all student behaviors that have been of interest to the field, such as note taking and

asking questions in class. For each of these domains, develop a list of metacognitive processes that might influence the quality and quantity of work within that domain. For instance, based on your understanding of student metacognition, how might specific metacognitive processes contribute to good versus poor note taking, both in the quantity of notes a student takes in class as well as in the quality of the notes. Do the same for asking questions in class. How would you empirically investigate the contribution of these metacognitive processes to student success in these domains?

CONCEPT REVIEW

For the following questions, we recommend you write down the answers on a separate sheet in as much detail as possible, and then check them against the relevant material in the chapter.

1. Why might students fail to recognize that their prior knowledge about a topic (such as how the heart works) is inconsistent with what they are reading in a textbook?

2. What is self-explanation, and how might it improve student learning?

3. What is self-efficacy and why might it be related to student achievement? According to Winne and Hadwin's (1998) model, what are different ways self-efficacy can improve student learning?

4. What is the difference between knowledge telling and knowledge transformation? How might students monitor their writing differently, depending on whether they are a knowledge teller or a knowledge transformer?

5. How can metacognition contribute to students' ability to solve math problems?

Section 3

Life-Span Development

10

Childhood Development

All of us were children, and many of us will be lucky enough to live long, fulfilling, and happy lives into late adulthood. Throughout the life span, people change in many ways: As children, we become more competent at many cognitive activities, such as learning, problem solving, and communicating with others; as adults, many continue to develop expertise in areas of interest, and eventually, begin to show signs of decline in some competencies that developed earlier in life. Developmental psychologists are concerned with understanding these changes, which involve growth, stability, and decline in people's behavior and mental capabilities from birth until death. A life-span approach to psychology involves describing and understanding our competencies as they improve from birth to young adulthood and then stabilize (and sometimes decline) as we grow older. For present purposes, our interest is in how development across the life span influences various aspects of metacognition, such as metamemory knowledge, monitoring and control processes, and strategic behavior. Are some of these aspects of metacognition influenced by maturational processes whereas other are not, and do metacognitive processes in development account for changes that occur in cognition across the life span?

In the next two chapters, we will discuss the developmental trajectories that occur in many metacognitive abilities in childhood (Chapter 10) and in older adulthood (Chapter 11). Our plan is to describe some of these trajectories, as well as to consider how the development of metacognitive abilities may foster changes in other aspects of cognition. In the present chapter, we first touch on some highlights of the immense literature that focuses on the beliefs—or theories—that children develop about how their own and other people's minds work. Then we survey the literature on the development of metamemory, with special emphasis on children's knowledge and use of strategies to accomplish various cognitive tasks. In the present chapter, we also entertain whether nonhuman animals—such as apes and dolphins—demonstrate the precursors of human-like metacognition. Humans may not be the only animals who can think about their own thoughts.

Development of Theory of Mind

Theory of mind (ToM) refers to our ability to attribute mental states to ourselves and to other people. Children's theory of mind itself is multifaceted and includes how well they understand a variety of mental states and beliefs, such as false beliefs, emotions, and desires. A sophisticated theory of mind may involve understanding that people can hold beliefs that are not identical to one's own beliefs, or understanding what it means "to know" or "to forget." Thus, you may attribute to yourself any number of emotions, desires, and beliefs, and at the same time, also attribute these (or other) mental states to other people, even if they conflict with your own. So, for instance, you may attribute to yourself the mental state that "I desire to go to the soccer game tonight" and similarly that "My roommate does not desire to go to the game tonight." As we've discussed throughout this volume, an accurate understanding of your own mind can help you both judge and effectively control your own cognition and behavior. Beyond this self-control, a sophisticated theory of mind that involves an understanding of other people's minds—and that mental states such as belief need not reflect reality—also has an important functional role in allowing us to predict other's thoughts and behavior. This functional role of theory of mind is evident from Aristotle's practical syllogism (Perner, 2000) in which our understanding of "desire" and "belief" allows us to predict how someone is likely to behave. To illustrate, consider this scenario: "Emma wants (or desires) to play with her new dollhouse." And, "Emma believes that her dad just moved the dollhouse to the basement." In this scenario, you may accurately predict that Emma will look for the dollhouse in the basement, assuming of course, that you have an appropriate theory about how other minds operate. Without such an understanding, children would have difficulties understanding how others think and why they behave the way they do, which in turn could lead to inappropriate and ineffective social interactions.

Accordingly, developmental psychologists have spent a great deal of energy attempting to understand when and how our theory of mind develops.

In the next sections, we briefly consider two issues that have received massive attention in the field (for reviews, see Flavell, 2004; Perner, 2000; Sodian, 2005): When do children begin to demonstrate an explicit theory of mind in which they represent their beliefs and the mental states of others? And what are the mechanisms that underlie the development of this theory of mind?

Time Course of the Development of Theory of Mind

To document the time course of ToM development, scientists needed to devise methods to measure it. Groundbreaking research on theory of mind was presented by Premack and Woodruff (1978), who asked, "Does the chimpanzee have a theory of mind?" They found that chimpanzees could correctly choose solutions for problems for another actor (e.g., an actor who was trying to unlock a door, and the chimpanzees correctly chose "keys" from a group of pictures offering alternatives). Based on this evidence, they concluded that in fact chimpanzees do have some ability to impute mental states to other agents; in this case, that the actor desired to open the door (for an extensive review of this literature, see Suddendorf & Whiten, 2001). Other researchers questioned the strength of their conclusions, because it was possible that the chimpanzees were solving the problems based solely on how they represented the problem and did not necessarily have to represent the mental state of the actor.

False Beliefs and Deception

Several rebuttals to Premack and Woodruff's (1978) conclusion included the argument that to convincingly demonstrate that people (or other animals) have a theory of someone else's mind, they must demonstrate an understanding that someone can have a false belief that does not match reality. The idea is that if you understand that a friend *falsely* believes that your favorite TV show comes on at 8 p.m. in the evening (even though you heard that it had been moved to 9 p.m.), you must understand that someone else's mind can represent the world independently from reality. In this case, you know the state of the world (the show is on at 9 p.m.), and hence your understanding that your friend has a false belief (believes that the show is on at 8 p.m.) demonstrates that you represent your friend's mind as separate from the actual state of the world. Based on this kind of rationale, Wimmer and

Perner (1983) developed a method to investigate children's understanding of false beliefs, which has had an enormous impact on the field. Consider the structure of one of the problems the children had to solve (illustrated in Figure 10.1, shown inside the back cover) and the rationale for why solving it correctly indicated they understood false beliefs: Max puts chocolate into a green cupboard and then he leaves the kitchen to go outside to play. While he's gone, Max's mother takes the chocolate from the green cupboard and places it into the blue cupboard. When Max comes back to the kitchen, where does he look for his chocolate? Answering this question taps into children's theory of mind because they can only answer it correctly when they are able to represent Max's wrong belief (that the chocolate is in the green cupboard) as different from what they know is correct (i.e., that the chocolate is really in the blue cupboard when Max returns to the kitchen). Across multiple experiments (Wimmer & Perner, 1983), children from 3 to 5 years of age were led through several versions of the scenario above, and the central measure was whether they would correctly indicate that Max would look in "the green cupboard" for the chocolate. None of the 3-year-olds correctly passed this test, whereas some of the 4-year-olds and the majority of 5-year-olds did correctly pass.

Some 25 years after Wimmer and Perner's (1983) landmark research, hundreds of studies have investigated children's ability to pass false-belief tasks of all sorts. In a review of this literature, Wellman, Cross, and Watson (2001) conducted a meta-analysis of 178 distinct studies, and the outcome of this analysis yielded a clear picture: Performance on false-belief tasks demonstrated a developmental pattern in which the youngest preschool children had below-chance performance, whereas performance improved as children became older. Moreover, this developmental pattern was found across different countries and across a variety of different false-belief tasks. Based on this kind of evidence, the received view is that children younger than 3.5 years old have not yet developed a sophisticated theory of mind that involves explicitly representing others' beliefs.

Given the high demands that these tasks put on language, one might argue that the standard false-belief task underestimates children's understanding of belief. In contrast, tasks that involve deception in social contexts may provide a more natural context for children to demonstrate their understanding of beliefs (Sodian, 2005). To illustrate the kinds of task used to investigate deception, imagine yourself in the following situation: You and a competitor are each allowed to select one item from among a set of alternatives, such as a voucher for a free pizza, a set of new pens, or an attractive coffee mug. You decide that the mug is most appealing. You have to mention your preference before either one of you selects, and unfortunately, the competitor selects first. You must first covertly tell the experimenter your preference (so the competitor does not know at this point), and then you tell your competitor which alternative you prefer. At first, you may tell both the experimenter and competitor your true preference. Your competitor will always choose what you say is your preference; thus, when you say you prefer the coffee mug, he chooses the coffee mug. Now, you play again, but with a new set of alternatives. On this trial, would you tell your competitor what you wanted most, or what you wanted least? Most adults would be deliberately deceptive and say they prefer an alternative that in fact they like the least. By doing so, they implant a false belief in the competitor and would end up with the alternative that they actually desire. As Peskin (1992) demonstrated, however, 3-year-olds almost never attempt to deceive a competitor, whereas older children did so readily. Peskin (1992) noted that "3-year-olds did not know to misinform or withhold information from an opponent. Although the children were frustrated again and again as their rival claimed their much desired sticker, they continued to reveal their true intentions" (p. 87). In fact, in a study by Russell, Mauther, Sharpe, and Tidswell (1991), 3-year-old children did not attempt to deceive their competitor even after 20 trials of the task! In line with the research using the false-belief task described above, these results suggest that at 3 years of age, children do not realize that other people can hold a false belief, whereas around the age of 4 years, children begin to understand that people's beliefs do not need to reflect reality, and hence they can use this knowledge about mental states to deliberately deceive others.

Appearance Versus Reality

The false-belief task and the deception task have several commonalities, so it may not be too surprising that if young children cannot do well on one that they could also not do well on the other. Thus, researchers have developed other tasks that could potentially provide converging evidence about children's understanding of how the mind operates. One intriguing task involves having children distinguish between reality and mere appearance. If you were shown a candle that was shaped like a bird, you would understand that this single object could both appear to be one thing (a bird) yet in reality be another (a candle). Understanding this difference requires that you understand how your mind operates, because you must realize that your own sight—that is, your perception—is responsible for the (apparent) similarity between the reality and the appearance of the object (Sodian, 2005).

Mystery BOX 10.1
Monsters, Witches, and Ghosts, Oh My!

Children engage in fantasy play from a young age: Bananas become telephones, blocks become skyscrapers, cushions turn into forests, shoe boxes are castles, and dolls become fairy princesses or fearsome dragons. With all this fantasy, one might wonder how seriously children take it all, and whether they can tell the imaginary from the real. Although Piaget thought that young children's reality boundaries were flexible, and the immaturity of the frontal lobes suggests a similar conclusion, a number of studies have shown that, when asked, even very young children can tell the difference between the real and the imagined.

A fascinating study on this issue suggests, however, that this conclusion may have its limits. Paul Harris and his colleagues (Harris, Brown, Mariott, Whittall, & Harmer, 1991) first asked children simple questions, such as whether a pencil that they could plainly see on the table, and touch if they wanted, was real; whether a pencil that they imagined when they closed their eyes was real; and whether a monster that wags its tail, a witch that flies in the sky, or a ghost that comes in the window (that they could see when they closed their eyes) was real. Although reality-monitoring skills do show a developmental progression (e.g., with 4-year-olds performing worse than older children) (Sussman, 2001), Harris et al.'s (1991) results speak favorably to children's abilities. In particular, by and large, the kids—both 3-year-olds and 6-year-olds—did pretty well, saying with few errors that the pencil was real, and that both the scary imaginary creatures and the images of the pencils and such were imaginary. The 3-year-olds they tested were a little worse than the 6-year-olds on the imaginary objects, but both age groups were highly accurate, and most of the kids made no mistakes at all. Furthermore, their judgments were only slightly worse when the experimenters had the kids imagine the supernatural objects interacting with them. But there was a hint of something else going on. When asked if the witch that flies in the sky "was chasing after you," a number of the children, both younger and older, confessed to feeling afraid, even though they still said that the witch was not real. Was this just pretended fear? Perhaps not. When the experimenters showed the kids two large empty boxes on the floor and asked them to imagine that there was a terrible, biting monster in one of them and a cute little finger-licking puppy in the other, and then asked the kids to put their finger in a hole in either box, few children chose to put the finger in the box with the biting monster. And if they were told (after having gotten the imaginary lick from the imaginary puppy) to put their finger in the other box, many kids wouldn't do it. And those who would do it decided to poke a stick in the hole rather than risk their finger. The children acted as if the imaginary animals were real. But perhaps they were just going along with what they perceived was the adults' pretending game?

(Continued)

(Continued)

    To see if such behavior was collusion with the experimenters in their pretend play, or whether the imaginary creatures provoked real fears, Harris et al. (1991)—in their final study—asked the children to imagine that a monster was in a box (or in a control group, that there was a cute little bunny in the box). The kids were given descriptions of the monster or bunny, and then shortly thereafter, they were asked about whether they were real. As usual, the children were able to accurately tell the experimenters that the monster (or bunny) was not real. But then the experimenter told the children that she needed to go away for a few minutes, to get a treat for them. The children were also told that, while waiting for the experimenter to come back, they could move around in the room, and do whatever they wanted. At this point, several of the younger children in the monster group broke down, and they refused to let the experimenter leave them alone with the monster. The experimenter, of course, stayed with the frightened children, reassuring them, and showing them that indeed the box was empty—no monster. But even for the children who allowed the experimenter to leave (in contrast to the collusion hypothesis), being left alone was apparently not a signal that the pretend game was over and that they could stop making believe. Instead, fears about the possible reality of the monster surfaced. Slightly more than half of the younger children, and only slightly fewer than half of the older children, confessed that while the experimenter was away they had seriously wondered whether a monster was hidden inside the box. And a number of the children indicated that even though imagined monsters were not real they might be able to *become real!* A number said that even though they, themselves, did not have the powers to generate a creature through pretense, such transmigration from the imaginary to the real could be possible.

    Certainly, children have an incredible ability for pretense even at an early age, which itself indicates that very young children are developing an ability to understand mental states (Leslie, 1987). The research by Harris et al. (1991) is provocative in suggesting that perhaps children's pretend play is more real than they say, and further understanding exactly how real they believe it is should be considered an important mystery for future research to resolve.

Flavell and his colleagues (for a review, see Flavell, 1993) have conducted numerous studies in which children are shown objects with multiple identities (e.g., a sponge made to look like a rock) and then are asked, "What is this object really?" and "What does this object look like?" As with the false-belief tasks, most 4-year-olds have no problem answering the questions correctly, whereas the majority of 3-year-olds answer them incorrectly and hence fail to differentiate between the reality of the object versus its appearance. That is, the 3-year-olds would tend to answer both questions in the same way, such as "rock and rock" or "sponge and sponge" (for a review and discussion about why appearance-reality tasks may somewhat underestimate children's abilities, see Hansen & Markman, 2005). Performance on appearance-reality tasks and false-belief tasks are correlated across children, and training children about belief (by having them report on their own and others' false beliefs) improves their performance on the appearance-reality task (Slaughter & Gopnik, 1996). These results suggest that children's theory of mind develops as a coherent system of thoughts about the mind, because as children pass (or are trained on) one theory-of-mind task, they tend to perform well on the others.

Theories About the Development of Theory of Mind

What maturational processes are responsible for the development of children's theory of mind? The 4-year-old child who now readily passes a false-belief task couldn't pass it just 6 months earlier—what happened developmentally to cause such a profound change in a child's understanding of how minds operate? Although a variety of theories have been proposed to explain the development of ToM, they can largely be separated into two general classes of theory (Sodian, 2005): those that claim a special mechanism is responsible for the development of theory of mind, and those that claim the development of a different—more general—ability is responsible. Let's consider an example from each class of theory.

The *modular* theory proposes that a special mechanism is specifically responsible for a child's theory of mind. As argued by Leslie (2005), a neurocognitive system may be devoted to theory of mind. If so, children's abilities to pass theory-of-mind tasks arise from innate neurological structures that mature from birth through early childhood. If a theory-of-mind module were innate, however, one might expect that children much younger than 3 and a half years old would be able to pass the theory-of-mind tasks. Consistent with this view, some researchers have argued that standard theory-of-mind tasks underestimate children's developing knowledge about the mind (Bloom & German, 2000). Even more impressive, other research has shown that even 6-month-old infants have some capacity for using metarepresentations (i.e., using an internal representation about another representation), and 15-month-old babies are able to pass a nonverbal form of the false-beliefs task (Onishi & Baillargeon, 2005). Such outcomes suggest that the precursors for a full-blown theory of mind are available well before 3 years of age (for a review, see Leslie, 2005). Even so, given that some researchers dispute that infants pass the nonverbal tests through the use of an implicit theory of mind (Ruffman & Perner, 2005), it is evident that whether an innate theory-of-mind module exists will be debated for some time.

The second class of theories suggests that more general mechanisms are responsible for children's developing ability to pass theory-of-mind tests. These general mechanisms are not specifically built for ToM but support the development of many other cognitive abilities. One prominent theory is that the development of executive functioning—the ability to inhibit irrelevant thoughts and/or to work with more than two thoughts at a time—is responsible for children's increasing abilities to pass theory-of-mind tasks from ages 3 to 5. Consider the standard false-belief task, illustrated in Figure 10.1 (see inside back cover). To complete this task, children must first remember that Max originally put the chocolate in the green cupboard, and they must also inhibit the interfering memory that the chocolate is now in the blue cupboard. Without the ability to consciously inhibit this interfering memory, children may find it difficult to respond correctly. To evaluate these possibilities, researchers have examined the relationship between children's ability to inhibit thought and performance on theory-of-mind tasks. As expected, across many different studies, the two abilities were correlated: Children who exhibited better executive functioning also were more likely to pass the theory-of-mind tasks (for reviews, see Moses, Carlson, & Sabbagh, 2005; Perner & Lang, 1999; Schneider, Lockl, & Fernandez, 2005). The strong relationship between executive (or self-) control and theory of mind is no longer in question. Why this relationship exists, however, is still a focus of debate: Does developing executive control allow children to pass theory-of-mind tasks, or does the development of the ability to form metarepresentations (i.e., theory of mind) contribute to children's executive control? According to Perner and Lang (1999), the data do not necessarily rule out either direction of causality. Instead, there may be "a functional interdependence of [theory of mind] and [executive functioning]. Better understanding of one's own mind provides better insights into how to exert self-control, and the exercise of self-control is one of the main grounds for building such an understanding" (p. 343). Given the multiplicity of theories that have arisen to explain the development of theory of mind (for others not discussed here, see Flavell, 2000; Sodian, 2005), no doubt discussion will continue concerning how children develop the ability to impute mental states onto themselves and others.

Development of Metamemory

As we've learned from other chapters, adult humans have rather impressive memory-monitoring abilities. They can accurately monitor their learning of new materials, as well as accurately predict whether they will recognize information that they cannot currently retrieve. The questions addressed in the next two sections focus on when these monitoring skills may arise. In particular, do nonhuman species demonstrate precursors of metacognitive monitoring skills? And, when do human children begin to demonstrate the metacognitive abilities so readily apparent in adults?

Metacognition in Nonhumans

It is often said that an adult chimpanzee is mentally like a human child of perhaps 3 or 4. If this were so, then one might expect chimps to have certain cognitive capabilities that are analogous to those seen in children. Such reasoning has led a number of researchers to wonder: Might chimps and other primates have metacognitive capabilities? The problem is that most metacognitive tasks (even those used with children) involve some degree of verbalization, and these capabilities are not available in other primates to any great extent. So the challenge in testing metacognition in animals other than humans is to find a task that would require metacognitive capabilities but would not require language.

A fascinating study on this topic was conducted by Josep Call (2005), who reasoned that if an animal knew that it did not know, it would seek information. Such information seeking was taken as an indication that the animals were metacognitive—that is, they could monitor what they did versus did not know. In his task, Call showed the chimps a treat being hidden in one of two tubes, so they could plainly see where it was hidden. In this case, the animal would go straight to the tube where the treat was placed. Alternatively, he let the chimp see that something was being hidden in one of the two tubes but he made sure that the chimp did not see which tube it was hidden in. Call found that when they could not know which tube the treat was hidden in, chimps (and orangutans) would look before they would try to get the treat—seeking information when they did not know. Other animals, such as dogs, did not do this information seeking prior to action.

Smith, Shields, and Washburn (2003) have also shown that nonhuman primates, as well as dolphins, show an uncertainty response. Instead of responding about whether a particular signal is present or absent, they instead choose a third "opt-out" option when the discrimination task is too difficult, and hence the animal cannot be assured that it will respond correctly and receive a reward versus respond incorrectly and be punished. They have interpreted animals' use of this opt-out response as meaning that the animals know when they are uncertain, and they believe that this expression of doubt is metacognitive in nature.

Both of these lines of research are fascinating and demonstrate the sophisticated nature of some nonhuman animals' behavior. Nevertheless, they have also provoked debates about whether the animals are really acting in a metacognitive fashion (e.g., Metcalfe, 2008) That is, perhaps their behavior can be explained by complex conditioning, or innate tendencies. Less controversial is the work of Robert Hampton, who has been studying Rhesus monkeys (see also Smith, Beran, Redford, & Washburn, 2006). Hampton (2001) used a task in which the to-be-remembered stimulus—a picture—was removed from view for a short interval before the monkey took a memory test. In the delay interval, the monkeys were given the choice to opt out (i.e., not receive the test) to get a smaller reward or to take the test for a larger reward, assuming, of course, that they respond correctly. The question Hampton asked was, Would the monkeys opt out more when they did not know the answer than when they did know it? Here's more specifically how his task worked: The monkeys were shown a picture on a computer screen. Then, in the basic task, the monkeys had to wait for up to 240 seconds before they were given that picture, on screen, in a random position, along with three other distracter pictures (which had been shown in other trials, but which were not the target on the current trial). The monkey had to touch the picture that had been presented (i.e., that matched the originally presented sample) to get a reward. This is a fairly standard memory test, and monkeys are well above chance on it. The metacognitive aspect that Hampton added was that before the four pictures were shown for the test, on two thirds of the trials, the monkey was allowed to choose one icon to take the test (and, if right, get a large reward, but if wrong get nothing), or to touch a different icon to opt out of taking the test and to receive a small, but sure, reward. On some trials, Hampton also just made the monkeys take the test without having a choice of whether they wanted to do so. Performance on these "forced-test" trials was compared to performance when the animal had chosen (or chosen not) to take the test. If the monkeys could truly rely on their monitoring of how well they remembered the to-be-recognized picture when they decided whether or not to be tested, they should perform better when they chose to take the test than when they were forced to take it.

This task was not just a conditioning task (which can be done by many other animals, including monkeys), because it was a genuine memory task in which, on each trial, the target among the four alternatives changed—so the monkey had to remember what had just happened. Also, because the judgment came when the stimuli were no longer present in the environment, the monkey had to examine his own mind or mental processes (not just what was there in the outside world) to come up with the choice. A crucial result was that when the monkeys chose to take the test, their memory performance was better than when they chose not to take it. This result indicates that the monkeys knew when they knew and when they didn't, and that they used this knowledge to control whether they would take the test or not—a truly metacognitive feat.

Kornell, Son, and Terrace (2007) followed up this work by asking Rhesus monkeys to make "bets" on whether they had been incorrect or correct when responding to a memory test they had just taken. If the monkeys knew they were correct, they should place a "high-risk" bet, because the payoff (which would later be converted into a reward) would be large. If they were incorrect, however, and took the "high-risk" bet, then they would not gain any payoff; thus, if they could accurately monitor that their response was likely to be incorrect, they should choose the "low-risk" bet (which would always yield a payoff, although a smaller one) so as to maximize gains. This task is illustrated in Figure 10.2 (shown inside the back cover), which shows a monkey studying a sample (far left), choosing the correct sample during the test, placing a "high-risk" bet, and then observing the large payoff. They found that the correlation between the monkeys' high-risk bets and the accuracy of their performance was well above chance, again indicating metacognition. Furthermore, this betting behavior was not a learned response to a particular contingency, because it transferred immediately to a true memory task, which was not included in the original training task.

We can conclude, then, that we are not alone among species in our metacognitive capability. Monkeys also have it, and given that they do, it's highly likely that once tested, we'll find that chimps and other great apes, and perhaps other highly intelligent animals like dolphins have it too.

Development of Memory Monitoring in Children

As we grow from infancy to adulthood, many cognitive changes occur that ultimately enable us to more effectively learn and solve problems. Whereas 5- and 6-year-old children may have many difficulties memorizing even relatively simple associations, by 12 years of age their learning abilities have substantially improved and continue to do so. Certainly, many factors may contribute to this developmental pattern, but our main interest here concerns metamemory. In particular, when do memory monitoring and control processes develop, and could they be responsible for any age-related improvements in learning and memory? In this section, we consider the growing literature on development of children's ability to monitor their ongoing learning and retrieval. If any of these metacognitive processes develop as we mature through childhood, such development may in part be responsible for why our learning and memory improves as well.

Global Judgments

To investigate children's ability to evaluate their performance, researchers have had them make global judgments in which they predicted how many to-be-remembered items they thought they would eventually remember. In one of the earliest studies, Flavell, Friedrichs, and Hoyt (1970) asked children in nursery school to the fourth grade to make global judgments about how well they would perform on a memory-span task. They were shown up to 10 pictures and were asked how many they would remember when all the pictures were covered. Across the entire range of grade, children were overconfident in that they predicted that they would recall more items than they actually could recall. Since this study, children's overconfidence in their memories has been demonstrated multiple times (for a review, see Schneider & Lockl, 2008).

One might argue, given that such a memory task would be novel to many (if not all) children, why would we expect them to accurately predict their performance on it? In the context of this question, what is even more astounding is that children's overconfidence is not eliminated after they receive practice on the task. For instance, Shin, Bjorklund, and Beck (2007) had kindergartners predict how many of 15 pictures they would be able to remember. After making this global judgment, they then were shown 15 pictures and had 2 minutes to study them. After a brief retention interval, they were asked to recall the names of the pictures they had just studied. As expected from earlier studies, their judgments made on the first trial were overconfident. More important, they repeated the judgment-study-test trials four more times—each time with a new set of pictures. Even though they had plenty of experience with this task, their judgments were equally overconfident across all five trials!

Mystery BOX 10.2
Does Overconfidence Have an Adaptive Function?

What is perhaps most fascinating about children's judgments of their knowledge is their extreme overconfidence, which goes beyond judging their competency at remembering. For instance, in what seems to be a rather simple task, Merriman and Bowman (1989) had 2- to 3-year olds play a word game. The experimenter would say a word, such as "cat," and the children merely had to say whether they knew what each word meant. For "cat" and "egg," the children confidently nodded their heads "yes." The more interesting trials were when the children were confronted with a nonsense word, such as "pilson" or "zav." Even though the children less often said "yes" to these words than to the familiar ones, they said that they knew them more often than they said that they did not know them. These researchers have even shown the same overconfidence in children's judgments of whether they can name objects. That is, when 3-year-olds were shown an object that was foreign to them (e.g., a gyroscope), they often replied that they knew what it was (Marazita & Merriman, 2004). In the context of physical activity, children are also overconfident in their abilities, believing they can jump farther or aim at targets better than they really can.

In much of this book, we have argued that such misplaced confidence (e.g., believing that you know something that you do not) can have a detrimental effect. And, in fact, in research with adults on self-regulated learning, it is evident that inaccurate monitoring can undermine their effectiveness of learning. But what about children's overconfidence? Could it be adaptive? Bjorklund and Green (1992) say "yes." These authors argue that "unrealistic optimism about their own abilities and an equally unrealistic evaluation of their behaviors give young children the opportunity to practice skills in situations in which accurate metacognition might discourage them from doing so" (p. 47). Although this reasoning may seem a bit counterintuitive at first, we suspect most parents would readily agree. In particular, overconfidence appears to help their children by keeping them engaged in difficult tasks: Their misplaced self-efficacy—the belief that they can accomplish any task—will ensure that they continue to persist on a task, even in the face of failure.

Although empirical evidence linking overconfidence to persistence on memory tasks is sparse, some benefits of overconfidence have been demonstrated. For instance, Shin et al. (2007) separated children into two groups based on their overconfidence on the first of two judgment-study-test trials: Those who showed high levels of overconfidence versus those who had lower levels of overconfidence. They found that increases in performance across trials were greater for children who showed high levels of initial overconfidence than for those showing low levels of overconfidence. These findings are consistent with the prediction from an adaptivity hypothesis, but further research is needed to replicate and extend them (for a review that extends beyond metacognition, see Bjorklund & Green, 1992).

Not all the evidence favors an adaptivity hypothesis. For instance, in the research on lexical and object ignorance introduced above, children who accurately say "no" to the unfamiliar words or objects tend to map novel words onto novel objects more reliably than children who are unaware of their ignorance (Marazita & Merriman, 2004; Merriman & Bowman, 1989). In terms of physical activity, children who are overconfident in their ability to perform physical tasks may be more likely to engage in them, but it is equally evident that they are more prone to accidental injury (Plumert, 1995; Plumert & Schwebel, 1997). Perhaps these overconfident—and potentially hospital bound—children are at a disadvantage in the short run, but maybe with further persistence they will end up being star athletes in the future. Moreover, overestimation of one's physical abilities is not metacognitive per se, so perhaps overconfidence in one's cognitive abilities is at times adaptive. Given the evidence to date, however, we decided to place the "adaptive nature of overconfidence" in a Mystery Box: The possibility of overconfidence having an adaptive function for children is fascinating, but much more research is needed to fully evaluate the credibility of the claim that overconfident children are the most likely to persist on cognitive tasks and to succeed.

Everyone agrees that children's judgments of their memory are overconfident, which has served to stimulate two questions. First, does this overconfidence have some adaptive function—that is, does it serve some purpose? We consider answers to this question in Mystery Box 10.2. Second, *why* are children so overconfident, even after experience performing a task? Schneider and his colleagues (described in Schneider & Lockl, 2008) evaluated two explanations for children's overconfidence. One possibility is that children just cannot accurately monitor their performance; that is, their retrospective confidence judgments about how well they have performed may be overconfident, which in turn could lead to overconfidence in predicting performance. They ruled this possibility out, because it turns out that participants in their study (4-, 6-, and 9-year olds) demonstrated good performance monitoring (see also Pressley, Levin, Ghatala, & Ahmad, 1987). Another possibility, called the *wishful-thinking* hypothesis, is that young children confuse their desires (or wishes) with what they expect to happen. So a child may predict that "I will recall all 15 of the items" because she wants to recall all 15. Consistent with this hypothesis, 4- and 6-years-olds did not differentiate between what they wished to get correct and how many items they expected to get correct.

In other studies evaluating the wishful-thinking hypothesis, experimenters ask children to predict their own performance and to predict how another child will do. If children's predictions are based on wishful thinking, then their predictions of other children's performance may show *less* overconfidence, because one might not expect children to hold such desires for others. In some cases, children's overconfidence is greater when they predicted their own performance than when they predicted others' performance (e.g., Stipek, Roberts, & Sanborn, 1984); however, this differential overconfidence is not always found (Schneider, 1998). Thus, wishful thinking may explain some of children's overconfidence, but it is unlikely to explain all of it.

Item-by-Item Judgments of Learning (JOLs)

The metamemory research described above mainly focused on global judgments, so the question arises as to whether children are good at evaluating their learning of individual items. In contrast to the massive literature on how adults judge their learning of individual items, very few studies are currently available on how children make item-by-item JOLs. We'll describe two particularly informative studies here, the first of which evaluated whether children use the same cues as older adults to make judgments of learning.

According to a cue-utilization approach, adults' JOLs are inferential in nature in that they infer how well they have learned a particular item based on any number of cues (for details, see Chapter 5). Two cues that are influential in adults' JOLs are the perceived ease of learning an item (JOLs increase with perceived ease) and the number of times an item has been presented for study (JOLs increase as study trials increase). Koriat and Shitzer-Reichert (2002) explored whether children in the second and fourth grades (roughly 7 and 9 years of age, respectively) would also be sensitive to these cues as they made JOLs. In particular, the children studied word pairs that were either normatively difficult to learn or normatively easy to learn; they studied these pairs across multiple trials, and they made an immediate JOL for each item during each study trial. Just like adults, children in both age groups made higher JOLs for the easy-to-learn pairs (versus the difficult-to-learn ones) and the magnitude of their JOLs increased across trials. Moreover, although relative JOL accuracy was somewhat greater for the older children in their first experiment, no age-related differences in relative accuracy were found in their second experiment.

In the first study examining children's ability to make delayed JOLs, Schneider, Visé, Lockl, and Nelson (2000) had kindergartners, second, and fourth graders participate in a standard JOL task, which involved making both immediate and delayed JOLs. The children studied pairs of unrelated concrete objects that were presented on colored picture cards, and they made immediate JOLs for half and delayed JOLs for the other half (for a primer on this method, see Chapter 5). After study-ing and judging the items, the stimulus of each pair was presented for paired-associate recall. The different age groups were equated on overall level of recall performance by giv-ing the kindergartners fewer items to study than the second graders, who studied fewer items than the fourth graders. Thus, any developmental trends in JOLs could not be attributed to differences in memory per se (for further discussion, see Box 3.1). Relative accuracy was measured by correlating each participant's JOLs with his or her recall per-formance, and means across the individual correlations are presented in Figure 10.3. Several outcomes are noteworthy. First, the accuracy of all groups tended to be above chance (i.e., as represented by a mean corre-

Wolfgang Schneider
Prolific contributor to our understanding of the development of metacognition

lation greater than zero). Second, all groups demonstrated the delayed-JOL effect, with accuracy being higher for delayed JOLs than for immediate JOLs. Third, and most important, age-related trends did not appear in rela-tive accuracy: The kindergartners were just as accurate as the older children, and everyone's delayed JOLs were highly accurate.

Thus, even though few studies have been conducted in this area, the exist-ing data converge on the conclusion that the ability to accurately monitor memory during encoding develops quite early in life. In fact, even kinder-gartners appear to have monitoring skills that are remarkably adult-like. Accordingly, one may ask, "Do children appear to use their monitoring to allocate study time in an effective manner?" The few studies that have inves-tigated this important issue suggest that effective allocation of study time does develop in early childhood. For instance, Dufresne and Kobasigawa (1989) had 6- to 12-year-old children study paired associates that were either easy to learn or relatively difficult to learn. Whereas the older children spent more time studying the relatively difficult pairs, the youngest children spent about equal amounts of time studying the easy and difficult pairs.

Schneider and Lockl (2008) described a study that investigated the rela-tionship between children's JOLs for paired associates made on one trial and their study-time allocation on a second trial. After self-paced study on the second trial, they were given a final test of paired-associate recall. Both 7- and 9-year-olds tended to spend more time studying items that they had orig-inally judged as being less well learned than those judged as more well

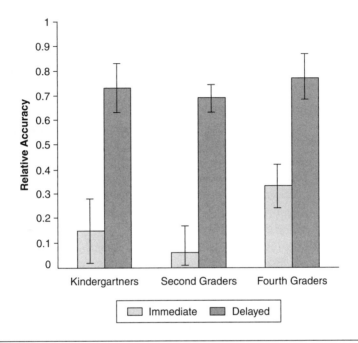

Figure 10.3   Relative Accuracy of Children's Item-by-Item Judgments of
               Learning

SOURCE: Adapted from Table 2 of Schneider, W., Visé, M., Lockl, K., and Nelson, T. O. (2000).
Developmental trends in children's memory monitoring. Evidence from a judgment-of-learning
task. *Cognitive Development, 15,* 115–134.

learned. This relationship, however, was stronger for 9-year-olds than for 7-year-olds. As important, those children who dedicated more time to studying the most difficult (versus easier) items also performed best on the final recall test. Thus, although developmental differences in monitoring accuracy do not appear to account for children's improvements in recall (even kindergartners are good monitors), the development of self-regulation skills (using accurate monitoring to control study) may partly account for memory improvements in childhood.

Feeling-of-Knowing (FOK) Judgments

Given that FOK judgments were the first metacognitive judgments to be systematically investigated in the field (beginning with Hart, 1965), it is not surprising that they were the first judgments to receive attention in the developmental literature. Although the earliest research demonstrated developmental increases in FOK accuracy, this work used methods that may have inadvertently put the youngest children at a disadvantage. In contrast, Butterfield, Nelson, and Peck (1988) used sophisticated measurement techniques—for example, examining accuracy using an intra-individual correlation between FOK judgments and recognition, as discussed in Chapter 3—to evaluate whether age-related increases occurred in FOK accuracy. The participants were 6-, 10-, and 18-year-old students. During an initial trial, participants had to orally define words until they failed to define 35 of them. Afterwards, participants made an FOK judgment for the words that they could not define and were later given a multiple-choice test for each one. Relative FOK accuracy for each age group was .37 for 6-year-olds, .23 for 10-year-olds, and .18 for 18-year olds.

In a follow-up study, Lockl and Schneider (2002) further explored developmental trends in FOK accuracy as well as the basis for the children's judgments. Seven- to 10-year-olds participated in an experiment very similar to that conducted by Butterfield et al. (1988). In contrast to the bulk of previous research, however, students made FOK judgments for words (a) that they defined correctly, (b) that they provided an incorrect definition for (i.e., commission error), and (c) that they did not provide any definition for (i.e., an omission error). Replicating Butterfield et al. (1988), they found no developmental trends in FOK accuracy. Moreover, the magnitude of children's FOK judgments was similar when they provided a correct definition versus a commission error, whereas the FOK judgments were higher for both of these classes of response than they were when the children made omission errors. These results support the accessibility hypothesis for FOK judgments. That is, just like adults, as long as children accessed information about a to-be-judged target (regardless of whether it was correct or incorrect), they felt their chances of recognizing the correct answer were higher than when they accessed nothing. As important, the lack of developmental trends in FOK accuracy suggests that memory monitoring at retrieval cannot account for the common developmental increases found in learning and memory.

Strategy Use

Imagine the number of ways that you could try to learn a simple list of words, such as "maple, bus, car, elm, table, train, chair, couch, birch, airplane, sofa, oak." You could just sit passively and read them all, but you could also attempt to repeat each one as often as possible, or even better, develop a story that ties them all together. You could even organize them by their category, if you realized that the list contained examples of trees, modes of transportation, and furniture. Using the latter strategies involves attempts to control your memory and hence these are metacognitive in nature. Such strategic behavior while learning can lead to dramatic improvements in memory when compared to just passively reading items that you want to remember (Richardson, 1998).

Given this link between strategy use and learning, it seems natural that many researchers have investigated whether increases in the use of strategies are responsible for the developmental trends that are consistently observed in learning. So, for instance, is learning the words above easier for a 7-year-old than for a 4-year-old because the 7-year-old uses effective strategies whereas the younger child would be more passive during study? The research conducted to answer this and many other related questions is vast and cannot be reviewed in any detail here (for a thorough analysis of this literature, see Schneider & Pressley, 1997). In the remainder of this section, we'll touch on some of the research that has led to relatively solid conclusions about the role of strategy use in the development of learning and memory.

Knowledge About Strategies

Some of the first research on metamemory development concerned the degree to which children knew about effective strategies that would help promote learning. In their classic monograph, Kreutzer, Leonard, and Flavell (1975) interviewed children in kindergarten, first, third, and fifth grades, with the aim to discover how much knowledge children have about their memory and learning. The interviews were extensive and involved asking the children questions about many aspects of memory, such as savings, decay from short-term memory, and the effects of mnemonic strategies. For instance, the following question was aimed at uncovering the children's knowledge of savings (i.e., that learning information—even if it is forgotten—makes relearning it easier): "Jim and Bill are in grade ___ [the participant's own grade was used to complete this sentence]. The teacher wanted them to learn the names of all the kinds of birds they might find in their city. Jim had learned them last year and then forgotten them. Bill had never learned them before. Do you think one of these boys would find it easier to learn the names of all the birds? Which one? Why?" (Kreutzer et al., 1975, p. 8). For the savings question, children across all grades were more likely to say that Jim would learn them more easily, although the older children were better at describing why. Based on their responses to questions like these, it was also evident that children of all ages (even many of the kindergartners) had intuitions that memories quickly decayed from short-term memory and that memory performance itself is influenced by the amount of study time and the number of items that one is trying to learn.

As far as children's knowledge about strategies, Kreutzer et al. (1975) asked children how they (or others) would go about remembering certain events or objects, such as how they would find a jacket that they had lost at school. Although the younger children—even kindergartners—recommended searching externally for the lost jacket, the third and fifth graders were more likely to recommend tactics that were more strategic, such as retracing one's steps or doing an ordered search for the lost jacket. Both of these tactics involve planning and reflection, which epitomize metacognitively driven regulation. As for the use of internal strategies, the children were also asked which of two girls would find it easier to remember a set of pictures (e.g., bed, tie, shoes, table, etc.): a girl who was merely shown the pictures or another girl who heard a story involving the pictures as she saw them (e.g., "A man gets out of *bed* and gets dressed, putting on his best *tie* and *shoes* . . . "). Only half the kindergartners correctly said that the story would make remembering the pictures easier, whereas the large majority of third and fifth graders realized the story would make remembering easier and provided an appropriate justification for why it would help.

Since Kreutzer et al.'s (1975) research, many others have established developmental trends in children's knowledge about strategy use. Such trends lead to two questions that we consider briefly in the next two sections: Can developmental trends in actual strategy use explain age-related improvements in memory performance? And, is the development of strategy knowledge related to the development of strategy use? The latter question is critical, because answering it in the affirmative would establish that children's metamemory knowledge per se is important for their control of memory.

Strategy Use and Its Effectiveness

It is evident that even preschoolers use some strategies to remember, such as when they are trying to locate a missing or hidden toy. Equally evident, however, is that the explicit application of strategies at encoding and retrieval becomes more prevalent as children progress through grade school. Let's take a look at an early research effort that captures the developmental trends in strategy use that have been consistently demonstrated over the past several decades. Ornstein, Naus, and Liberty (1975) investigated whether developmental trends occurred in the strategies children used to rehearse a list of to-be-remembered words. Third, sixth, and eighth graders were presented with 18 unrelated words, one at a time for 5 seconds per word. Most important, half the participants were asked to rehearse the words aloud. Immediately after presentation of the final word in the list, the students attempted to recall all of the words. Their main results are presented in Figure 10.4. First, inspect Panel A of the figure, which presents the percentage of words recalled as a function of serial position. Serial position is the order in which the words were presented for study, so that Serial Position (SP) 1 represents the first word presented, SP 2 represents the second word presented, and so forth. The pattern in the figure represents the classic serial position curve: Higher recall for the initial words (SP 1–4) versus those in the middle serial positions (SP 7–13) is called the *primacy effect* and is due to recall from long-term memory. Higher recall of the final words (SP 17 and 18) is called the *recency effect* and is often attributed to recall from short-term memory. Note the developmental trend in recall performance, with the primacy effect being larger for eighth graders than for sixth graders, which in turn is larger than the third graders' primacy effect.

A key question is, can these age-related increases in the primacy effect be due to differential strategy use? To answer this question, Ornstein et al. (1975) analyzed two aspects of the rehearsal protocols: (a) the number of times that the children rehearsed each word and (b) the number of items that were rehearsed in each rehearsal set. For total rehearsals (Figure 10.4, Panel B), the third graders rehearsed words overall less often than did the older students, especially in the primacy positions. As pointed out by Ornstein et al., however, total rehearsals cannot entirely explain the developmental trends shown in recall (Figure 10.4, Panel A), because the third graders did rehearse more often in the middle serial positions (SP 10–14, Panel B), yet they tended to recall fewer of these items (Panel A). The number of items rehearsed in each rehearsal set was more telling. This measure represents the number of *different* words that are rehearsed during the presentation of any given word. For instance, if the word "dog" is the first word presented, you could only rehearse "dog" (e.g., by repeating, dog, dog, dog. . .). When the next word is presented, however—let's say the word is "man"—during that rehearsal set you could continually repeat "man" or you could repeat both "dog" and "man." The first example (repeating only "dog" during its rehearsal set) represents one item rehearsed per a rehearsal set, whereas the latter example (repeating "dog" and "man" during the rehearsal set of "man") represents two items rehearsed during that rehearsal set. Rehearsing more items per set often benefits memory because it increases the chances that the words are integrated into larger chunks during encoding. As evident

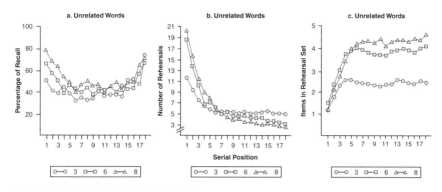

Figure 10.4   Mean percentage of unrelated items recalled (Panel A), mean number of rehearsals of items (Panel B), and mean number of different items in each rehearsal set (Panel C) as a function of serial position for third-, sixth-, and eighth-grade subjects in Experiment 1.

SOURCE: Ornstein, P. A., Naus, M. J., & Liberty, C. (1975). Rehearsal and organizational processes in children's memory. *Child Development, 46,* 818–830.

from Panel C in Figure 10.4, the third graders rehearsed substantially fewer items per rehearsal set. In a follow-up experiment that involved using related (and categorizable words), Ornstein et al. again found that third graders (versus sixth and ninth graders) were less strategic both in terms of rehearsing items together but also in terms of how much they clustered words within a category together at recall—two indices indicative of effective strategy use.

Given such developmental trends in strategy use, researchers have sought to more specifically identify younger children's strategy deficits. For instance, one form of deficiency, called a *production deficiency,* indicates that although younger children do not always spontaneously use effective strategies, when they are instructed to do so, they are capable of using them and benefit from them (for a review, see Schneider & Pressley, 1997). Another form of deficiency, called a *utilization deficiency,* is one in which even when children use an effective strategy, they do not benefit from it because they do not implement it well (Miller, 1994; Miller, Seier, Barron, & Probert, 1994). In a review of 30 years of research, Bjorklund, Miller, Coyle, and Slawinski (1997) describe multiple examples from the literature in which young children who are successfully trained to use a strategy show little or no benefit from using it. In fact, for the 76 conditions that they discuss, in 39 conditions children demonstrated utilization deficiencies and in 32 conditions they demonstrated production deficiencies (the remaining 5 were equivocal with respect to the form of deficiency). An intriguing possibility is that a utilization deficiency arises when children do not have enough mental resources to successfully execute a strategy, whereas when they do have enough mental resources they can execute it successfully and hence benefit from doing so. Given the importance of discovering when children will benefit from strategy training, understanding why one (versus the other) deficiency emerges will certainly continue to receive empirical scrutiny.

The Relationship Between Metamemory and Strategy Use

Given that both knowledge about strategies and the use of strategies develop in childhood, a natural conclusion would be that as children develop more sophisticated knowledge about strategies they are more likely to use them. Borkowski, Milstead, and Hale (1988) offer an eloquent version of this metamemory hypothesis: "When a child possesses a number of strategies together with knowledge about their various uses, he or she is able to make an *informed* judgment about strategy deployment" (p. 80). But are children who know more about strategies more likely to use effective ones? In an early study on this topic, Cavanaugh and Borkowski (1980) evaluated the metamemory knowledge of 178 children using the interview procedure developed by Kreutzer et al. (1975). The children included kindergartners, first, third, and fifth graders. After administering this interview, the children also completed several memory tasks, and their strategies and memory performance were measured. Collapsed across all participants, positive correlations were evident between metamemory knowledge and strategy use as well as between metamemory knowledge and memory performance. When computed within each grade level, however, the correlations were less impressive and were not always statistically different from zero. Thus, this evidence does provide some support for the metamemory hypothesis, although the support was not consistently strong.

Since the earliest research investigating the link between metamemory and strategy use, many more studies have been conducted and most of these converge on the conclusion that metamemory knowledge does predict strategic behavior, at least when we consider strategies used during simple learning tasks (Schneider & Pressley, 1997). Even with these tasks, however, it is also apparent that metamemory knowledge is not the only factor that accounts for when children will discover and effectively use strategies. According to Siegler and his colleagues (e.g., Crowley, Shrager, & Siegler, 1997; Siegler, 1999), both explicit metacognitions (involving monitoring and knowledge) and implicit memory-based associations contribute to children's discovery and use of strategies. More specifically, Siegler (1999) explains that "most models of [strategy] discovery can be classified into one of two categories: metacognitive or associative. Metacognitive models make discoveries through application of high level heuristics; associative models make discoveries by extracting among tasks, actions, and outcomes" (p. 433). In both cases, the idea is that with experience using various strategies, children (and people of all ages) learn about which strategies are most effective for certain tasks and hence are more likely to use them. For metacognitive models, this learning process is explicit and conscious, and studies by Pressley and his colleagues (Pressley, Levin, & Ghatala, 1984; Pressley, Ross, Levin, & Ghatala, 1984) have demonstrated that children can obtain consciously accessible information about strategy effectiveness as they experience using them. For associative models, if a particular strategy for a given task is successful, then an associative link between that strategy and task is strengthened in memory, which subsequently increases the chances the child will use the strategy for that task. In this case, learning about strategy effectiveness from task experience is largely implicit in that people are not consciously aware that the associations are being developed.

Siegler (1999) discusses models that are based either solely on metacognition or solely on associationism and concludes that both kinds of model have difficulties accounting for how children discover new strategies. Given that both accounts also have strengths, Shrager and Siegler (1998) proposed a hybrid model that combines both metacognitive and associationistic principles. This model, called SCADS for "Strategy Choice and Discovery Simulation," includes metacognitive processes, which operate on relevant data produced by the underlying associative (or cognitive) processes. More specifically, as SCADS uses a strategy, doing so produces information about the speed and success of each strategy, which is later used to select the most effective one for a particular task. This associative part of the model is supplemented by a metacognitive system that analyzes "the sequence of operators in existing strategies, identifies potential improvements, and recombines operators from existing approaches to form new strategies" (Siegler, 1999, p. 434). By combining both metacognitive and associationistic principles, SCADS was capable of simulating the development of strategy use that neither of the individual accounts could likely account for alone. SCADS highlights a theme that has arisen throughout this textbook, namely, that it is the mutual influence between metacognitive and cognitive processes that is responsible for how we think and behave when faced with many different tasks.

Relationship Between ToM and Metamemory

In this chapter, we've focused on the development of theory of mind and on the development of metamemory. Although one might expect that these two aspects of metacognition would develop in a lock-step fashion, metacognition itself is multifaceted and different processes likely rely on at least a subset of different neurological substrates. Moreover, theory-of-mind tasks and metamemory tasks differ in a variety of dimensions. One important difference is that theory-of-mind researchers investigate children's knowledge about mental states, whereas metamemory researchers investigate knowledge and processes relevant to task performance, such as metamemory knowledge and the use of task-relevant strategies. Moreover, theory-of-mind researchers tend to investigate younger children (from infancy to 5 years of age) than do metamemory researchers (6 years and older) (Schneider et al., 2005). Even with such differences in mind, the issue still arises as to whether development in one domain will predict development in the other.

To address this issue, Lockl and Schneider (2007) conducted a longitudinal study in which they tested 183 children on three separate occasions—at approximately 3 years, 4 years, and 5 years of age. A major question was, Would children who first began passing theory-of-mind tasks at an early age also be the first to develop sophisticated knowledge about how their memories operate? During the first two testing sessions, the children attempted to pass standard theory-of-mind tasks, such as the false-belief task (as illustrated in Figure 10.1 [inside the back cover]) and the appearance-reality task. During the final testing session at the age of 5, children's metamemory knowledge was evaluated using questions adapted from Kreutzer et al. (1975). For instance, one question involved asking the children to explain what they could do in the evening to make sure they would remember in the morning to take a pretzel to school for lunch. Besides responding to this open-ended question, they were told about two children who used different strategies— one child used a poor strategy (e.g., ask your little brother to help you remember), whereas the other child used a good strategy (e.g., hang your lunch bag over the front door). The children were asked which strategy they thought was best and why.

A major finding was that children's performance on the theory-of-mind tasks during the first test session positively correlated with their performance on the metamemory tasks 2 years later. This relationship was even stronger when performance on the theory-of-mind tasks administered during the second session was used to predict metamemory performance a year later. As impressive, Lockl and Schneider (2007) also administered measures of language ability during the first two testing sessions. Language is an essential cognitive tool for helping children represent mental states involved in passing theory-of-mind tasks, and in their study, individual differences in language ability were related both to theory-of-mind performance and to metamemory performance. Most important, the relationship between early development on theory-of-mind tasks and later metamemory performance was reliable even when individual differences in children's language ability were statistically controlled. According to Lockl and Schneider (2007), "These findings provide support for the hypothesis that early theory-of-mind competencies can be considered as a precursor of subsequent metamemory. More specifically, it seems as if the acquisition of the concept of representation might be a crucial step in children's development that in the end enables them to think about their own and other people's memories" (p. 164).

Summary

The multifaceted nature of metacognition may be most evident in the vast literature examining metacognitive development. In this literature, researchers have explored the degree to which early development influences children's theory of mind, their competencies at monitoring and controlling their learning and retrieval, their metamemorial knowledge, and their use of strategies to boost task performance. Children younger than 4 years of age have difficulties in passing theory-of-mind tasks that measure their explicit beliefs and understanding about mental states. Explanations for these developmental trends in theory of mind (and exactly when they begin to develop) are currently being heatedly debated and will likely generate a great deal of new research aimed at discovering the origins of mental representation.

Although research on monitoring has typically not shown developmental trends, the children in these studies were often older as compared to children participating in theory-of-mind studies, so one may wonder whether 3-year-olds (assuming they could be trained to make metacognitive judgments) would have above-chance accuracy at predicting their memory. Even children in fourth grade are highly overconfident in their learning and tend to underutilize effective strategies. Both of these metacognitive deficiencies may limit a child's skill at learning—if they are overconfident, they may prematurely stop studying, and if they do not use effective strategies, they certainly will perform more poorly than older children who do use them. Our discussion in this chapter merely scratches the surface of a massive and fascinating literature, but we hope it has served to introduce you to some of the most vital questions (and answers) in the field of metacognitive development.

DISCUSSION QUESTIONS

1. You're playing with a friend's nephew, Tristan, who is 5 years old. It dawns on you that it would be fun to find out if Tristan has developed a few of the basic metacognitive skills, so you devise some simple tests for him. Using two dolls, a small rubber ball, and some Play-Doh jars (with Play-Doh still inside), devise a task to measure Tristan's theory of mind, as measured both by false belief and by appearance reality. You get extra points if you use only the toys listed above! Do you think Tristan will pass the theory-of-mind (ToM) tasks? If he doesn't, based on theories of ToM development, why would you think he's having difficulties?

2. Research on the development of monitoring skills suggests that the accuracy of children's judgments is poor in some contexts yet good in others. The kinds of judgments and measures of accuracy, however, differ across these contexts. Compare and contrast the contexts in which children appear poor versus good at judging their learning and/or retrieval. Based on this comparison, how would you rate children's metacognitive monitoring abilities? Sophisticated or relatively unsophisticated? Why?

CONCEPT REVIEW

For the following questions, we recommend you write down the answers on a separate sheet in as much detail as possible, and then check them against the relevant material in the chapter.

1. What mental abilities are measured by theory-of-mind tasks?

2. What are two explanations for why 3-and-a-half-year-old children have difficulties passing theory-of-mind tasks, whereas most 6-year-old children would pass them with ease?

3. The development of which aspect of metacognition is most likely to account (at least partly) for developmental improvements in learning: on-line monitoring of learning individual items, monitoring of retrieval, or the use of strategies? Why?

4. What is the wishful-thinking hypothesis and how does it explain children's overconfidence? How might overconfidence be adaptive?

11

Older Adulthood

Tony has just reached his 75th birthday, and although he's been retired for some time now, he still is actively involved in his daily life and with his community. His interests have him pursuing new hobbies, such as bird-watching, and some of his community work involves conducting surveys of the variety and number of trees in local parks. These activities involve learning new information, such as memorizing the names of new birds and learning how to accurately identify various trees. In developed countries, staying active late in life is not at all unusual, because the average life expectancy has steadily increased since the early 1900s. In the United States, people born in 1900 could expect to live to about 40 years of age on average, whereas those born in 2000 can expect to live 75 years. The aging of America—and the world in general—will continue, with estimates indicating that in 2025, more than 25% of the U.S. population will be 85 years or older.

Given these demographics, a major goal of gerontological research has been to develop techniques to improve the chances that older adults stay mentally healthy late into life, so that they can continue to contribute to society—through taking on new jobs, volunteering in the community, helping their family with child care, and so on. Excellent mental health is important in ensuring happiness, autonomy, and a consistently high quality of life. Unfortunately, aging has detrimental effects on many aspects of cognitive functioning, such as attention, memory, learning, and problem solving, to name a few. For instance, in our example above, Tony may experience more difficulties learning tree names than he would have had when he was younger, so much so that he may complain about his poor memory and withdraw from activities that require new learning. In fact, memory complaints—which are a kind of metamemory self-assessment—are among the most common complaints made by older adults.

People's complaints are not entirely unfounded, because age-related deficits in learning new information are substantial. Compared to their younger adult counterparts, older adults in their 70s and 80s take considerably longer to learn and retrieve new associations (e.g., connecting a bird name with a bird) and lists of words and concepts (e.g., memorizing a grocery list) (for a broad overview, see Kausler, 1994). For instance, consider results from Dunlosky and Connor (1997). Although hundreds of studies have demonstrated age-related deficits in memory, this investigation is particularly relevant to metacognition because the participants made monitoring judgments and could control how they allocated study time—two metacognitive processes that we consider in more detail below. Most relevant now, younger and older adults studied paired associates (e.g., dog-spoon) during multiple study-test trials. During a trial, each pair was presented individually, and participants could spend as much time as they wanted studying it before moving on to the next. After studying all the pairs, each cue was represented (i.e., dog-?) and participants attempted to recall the correct response (i.e., spoon). The study-test trials were repeated three times. Percentage correct recall performance is presented across the three trials (filled symbols) in Figure 11.1. Although recall performance improved across trials for both age groups, the most striking outcome is that it took older adults three study trials to achieve the same level of performance younger adults achieved after only one trial!

Such dramatic age-related memory impairment has stimulated enormous effort to answer two fundamental questions, the first of which is relevant to theory and the second of which is applied. First, why does aging have a negative effect on learning and memory? Second, and perhaps even more relevant to our aging society, how can people compensate for such age-related memory impairment and become better learners? In the present chapter, we focus most closely on aging and memory, because the bulk of the research on metacognitive aging has focused on metamemory. This emphasis is perhaps not surprising, because metamemory processes are natural candidates for answering these fundamental questions about aging and memory.

Concerning the former question about theory, a possible answer from a metacognitive perspective is that aging also negatively influences metamemory, and it is this influence on metamemory that is responsible for older adults' difficulties in learning and retrieval. For instance, perhaps older adults do not accurately monitor ongoing learning and hence do not effectively regulate their learning. Concerning the latter, applied question, if older adults have deficits in metamemory, efforts to improve their metamemory

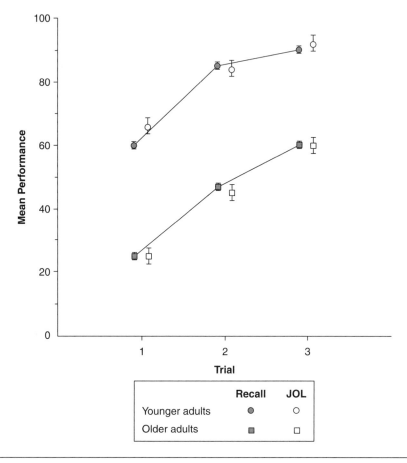

Figure 11.1   During a self-paced study task, older adults required three study trials to obtain the same level of recall performance that younger adults obtained after only one trial.

SOURCE: Dunlosky, J., and Connor, L. (1997). Age-related differences in the allocation of study time account for age-related differences in memory performance. *Memory and Cognition, 25,* 691–700.

may naturally lead to improved learning as well. If older adults do not apply effective mnemonic strategies to learn lists because they lack the knowledge about these strategies, perhaps they could be trained to use them effectively. To foreshadow, evidence reviewed in this chapter suggests that (a) with some notable exceptions, older adults' metamemory is largely intact and functions well, and (b) training older adults to take advantage of their intact metamemory abilities to better control their learning does help them to compensate for age-related memory impairment.

Much of the literature on metacognition in aging has used methods developed in the cognitive literature, so the themes previously described in this book will arise in this chapter on aging as well. Key questions about metacognitive aging include, Does aging in adulthood negatively affect judgment-of-learning (JOL) accuracy, and do older adults effectively use the output from monitoring to regulate their learning? In contrast to the bulk of cognitive literature, which mainly focuses on monitoring and control processes, early research on metacognitive aging explored age-related differences in *knowledge* about memory and memory self-efficacy. The driving issues were whether older adults just knew less about how to effectively learn new information (as measured by questionnaires) and whether they had less confidence that they could effectively learn. Accordingly, before moving on to the process-oriented measures of metamemory, we first consider research on older adults' beliefs and knowledge about memory.

Finally, research described in this chapter can serve as a model on how metacognitive methods and theory can be applied to a special population. That is, similar questions (and methods) can be used to explore the degree to which metacognitive deficits contribute to poor cognition and performance of any group, such as individuals with ADHD, frontal-lobe patients, patients with traumatic brain injury, and so forth. Of course, explaining these deficits is often not researchers' only goal, because many also want to discover how people can compensate for them. Accordingly, throughout the chapter, we also highlight some intervention research aimed at improving older adults' learning. Many of the same techniques that have helped older adults become more effective learners likely can benefit people of all ages, so as you read about various techniques to improve learning, think about how you might use them in your own life now, not just in the distant future.

What Do Older Adults Believe About Memory?

Some of the first—and most programmatic—research on aging and metamemory set out to assess people's beliefs about cognition by having them complete questionnaires. When Gilewski and Zelinski reviewed the area in 1986, 10 questionnaires were already being used, but two of them have been used most widely and will be highlighted here—the Metamemory in Adulthood (MIA) scale developed by Roger Dixon and David Hultsch (e.g., Dixon & Hultsch, 1983; Hultsch, Hertzog, & Dixon, 1987) and the Memory Functioning Questionnaire (MFQ) developed by Michael Gilewski and his colleagues (e.g., Gilewski & Zelinski, 1986; Gilewski, Zelinski, Schaie, & Thompson, 1983). Each questionnaire included many questions, which were analyzed to form a set of factors that best represented the constructs that various subsets of questions were measuring. For instance, the MIA includes 120 questions that measure eight factors. Some of these factors are presented in Table 11.1.

As shown in Table 11.1, the questions from the MIA and MFQ measure many aspects of metamemory knowledge and beliefs, such as a person's beliefs about (a) how memory functions in general (Task), (b) one's own memory abilities (Capacity), and (c) the degree to which memory abilities change across time (Change). Although the specific questions used in the MIA and the MFQ differ, they do include some overlapping factors; for instance, two factors from the MFQ are a general rating of how well one's

Table 11.1   Some Factors Assessed by Questions From the Metamemory in Adulthood (MIA) Scale and the Metamemory Functioning Questionnaire (MFQ)

Factor	Brief Description
MIA	
Strategy	Knowledge of one's learning abilities, such as the use of strategies to help their memory
Task	Knowledge about how memory functions in general
Capacity	Beliefs about one's own capacity to remember
Change	Beliefs about whether memory abilities change across time
Achievement	Perceived importance of having a good memory
MFQ	
General rating	Beliefs about how one's memory abilities depend on the problems encountered
Frequency of forgetting	How often various memory tasks (e.g., remembering names) present a problem
Retrospective functioning	Beliefs about how one's memory has changed across time
Mnemonics	Beliefs about how often one uses strategies to support remembering

SOURCE: Adapted from Hultsch, Hertzog, and Dixon (1987) and Gilewski and Zelinski (1986).

memory functions (analogous to "Capacity" in the MIA) and how one's memory is changing over time (analogous to "Change" in the MIA). These questionnaires have been used to answer two key questions, namely, Do adults of different ages have different metamemory knowledge and beliefs? And, as important, Are any of these age-related differences connected to people's actual memory ability, such as measured by a memory test in the laboratory or by memory performance in everyday life? The inspiration behind the latter question is simple: If older adults have overly negative beliefs about their memories, or if they have inaccurate knowledge about how memory operates, then their learning and memory may suffer. Older adults who believe their memories are in decline may avoid activities that involve memory or may not put as much effort into learning.

Older adults hold more negative views about memory than do younger adults. In a mammoth study, Hultsch et al. (1987) administered both the MIA and the MFQ to 793 adults ranging in age from 20 to 78 years. Although age-related differences were often more apparent on the MIA than on the MFQ, a relatively consistent picture emerged. In particular, age-related differences were most evident on two factors: Older adults believed that their capacity to learn was worse than younger adults' capacity to learn, and perhaps less surprising, older adults reported that in fact their memory had declined. Consistent with the conclusions, two decades of research investigating people's knowledge and beliefs about memory indicates that as compared to younger adults, (a) older adults tend to believe they have less ability to learn new materials (i.e., they have lower memory self-efficacy); (b) older adults believe their memories are declining more across time; and (c) older adults often feel they have less control over their learning and memory decline (Hertzog & Hultsch, 2000; Lachman, 2006).

Of course, these conclusions raise the question, If you believe your memory is becoming a problem as you grow older, is it really a problem? That is, when older adults are pessimistic about their memories, does that actually mean that they are having difficulty remembering? In a review of the earliest literature, Herrmann (1982) found that people's beliefs about their memories—as measured by memory questionnaires—show only a modest relationship with memory performance. People's beliefs are not very accurate.

One reason for the disconnect between people's beliefs and actual memory abilities is that their beliefs are influenced more by stereotypes of aging than by assessments of their actual memories. Recall Tony from our opening vignette: He may claim that his memory is deteriorating because our culture—from TV shows, advertisements, newspaper articles, and cartoons—often highlights the negative aspects of aging. Just turning 50 years old (which is relatively young given today's long life expectancies) is heralded by many as "going over the hill," as is evident by 50th birthday parties where people bring gifts that poke fun at how the celebrants will need to wear diapers in public or will soon forget their own names. Thus, Tony, and many others like him, may believe their memories are failing because of cultural stereotypes that our memories get worse as we age and not because they are accurately monitoring their own rate of decline. And although many people do have memory declines as they grow older, not everyone does, and the declines themselves often are much less than the extreme losses the stereotypes suggest. Consistent with this possibility, Lineweaver and Hertzog (1998) found that both older and younger adults have a general expectation that as people age they will have more difficulties with memory, whether that involves current or future control over memory functioning or in the ability to learn names, faces, or telephone numbers. Unfortunately, these stereotypes also are associated with different *reasons* for memory failures. In particular, Erber and her colleagues (Erber, 1989; Erber, Szuchman, & Rothberg, 1990) have shown that older and younger adults believe that younger adults' memory failures arise from lack of effort, whereas older adults' memory failures arise from a mental deficiency. The difficulty here is that the memory abilities of many older adults are relatively intact (and even superior to some of their younger adult counterparts), so their occasional memory failures may not be due to mental deficiencies per se.

The question arises as to whether people's beliefs arise entirely from stereotypes or whether they are at all based on an actual appraisal of memory functioning. Assume that one older adult believes his memory has declined rapidly over the past 6 years, whereas another older adult believes her memory has remained relatively intact over the past 6 years. Do these differences in belief partly reflect individual differences in true declines in memory, with the former adult showing greater decline in memory ability across time? Answering this question involves a longitudinal investigation, in which older adults' memory abilities and beliefs are assessed across time. Johansson, Allen-Burge, and Zarit (1997) examined older adults in their 80s and 90s, and they tested them twice across a 2-year span. They found that people's beliefs about memory decline were related to actual declines in memory across the 2-year interval, although the magnitude of this relationship was small (see also McDonald-Miszczak, Hertzog, & Hultsch, 1995; Valentijn et al., 2006). Thus, people's beliefs about their memories may be partly based on their assessments of their own idiosyncratic changes in memory across time. Even so, people's beliefs as they age are not highly related to actual memory decline, suggesting that other factors—such as culturally driven stereotypes—have a greater influence on our perceptions about how well our memory is functioning. As we discuss in Box 11.1, older adults' overly pessimistic beliefs about their ability to control their memory functioning have been the focus of many training programs that aim to induce optimistic beliefs about memory in hopes of improving memory functioning as well.

BOX 11.1
Improving Older Adults' Self-Efficacy Beliefs

Imagine two adults in their 70s: Betty, who is confident that she can accomplish almost any activity that involves her memory, and Sue, who is unsure of herself when it comes to using her memory to accomplish new activities. These differences in memory self-efficacy—which involve people's beliefs about their ability to use memory successfully in various situations—can have a noticeable impact on people's lives. For instance, even if Betty and Sue do not differ in their actual memory abilities, their differences in self-efficacy may induce Betty to embrace challenging activities that keep her mentally alert, such as Scrabble and Gin Rummy, whereas Sue may be unwilling to take on new activities that involve a memory burden (West & Berry, 1994).

Perhaps not surprisingly, older adults have lower memory self-efficacy (MSE) than do younger adults (Hultsch et al., 1987). Unfortunately, as foreshadowed above, older adults with low MSE tend to be less strategic in attacking memory problems, perhaps because they simply believe that it is not worth trying. A dramatic example of this relationship between MSE and strategy use was reported by Lachman and Andreoletti (2006). They had 116 participants between the ages of 60 and 83 take a test that measured their self-efficacy for accomplishing cognitive tasks. The participants also attempted to learn a list of 30 words that could be categorized (e.g., kinds of fruits and flowers) and were later given a recall test for the words. Their results were striking: Older adults with better self-efficacy were also more likely to use effective strategies to learn the list of words (e.g., associating the exemplars of each category), and these individuals in turn later remembered more of the list.

Given results like these and the fact that many older adults have low MSE, many intervention studies have been conducted to evaluate whether it is possible to boost older adults' MSE. The idea here is simply to make older adults realize that they are overly pessimistic and to make them believe that they in fact can use their memories successfully. For instance, Lachman and her colleagues (Lachman, 1991; Lachman, Weaver, Bandura, & Elliott, 1992) have developed various interventions that serve to restructure older adults' beliefs so that they no longer believe that memory decline is inevitable. In a meta-analysis of the entire memory-intervention literature, Floyd and Scogin (1997) reported that

(Continued)

(Continued)

these interventions have been successful, and that the best way to boost older adults' MSE involves a combination of (a) training directly aimed at changing their attitudes about memory along with (b) training them in skills to actually improve their memory. This news is very encouraging if one's aim is to enhance people's self-image of their memory abilities. Doing so may have the added benefit of turning an otherwise reluctant older adult into an individual who more willingly engages in activities that require memory and new learning.

Aging and Memory Monitoring

The evidence is clear: As we age, some of our mental abilities—which include learning new information, in particular—decline as we move into our 60s, 70s, and beyond. Of course, not everyone declines at the same rate: For some, the decline may be relatively steep whereas others may show relatively gradual (or even no) decline. Given the tight relationship between metamemory and memory, one might expect that older adults' metacognitive processes would also show similar declines, which in turn may actually be responsible for some of the age-related memory impairment. For instance, older adults may have difficulties accurately monitoring their progress while learning new materials. Perhaps as we age, we may be less able to make accurate judgments of learning. If so, this deficit in monitoring could undermine the effectiveness of older adults' self-regulated study. Likewise, deficits in feeling-of-knowing accuracy could disrupt the effectiveness of retrieval processes, which also could result in poorer memory performance.

Such possibilities have stimulated a great deal of research, which has sought to investigate whether aging in adulthood has a detrimental effect on metacognitive monitoring and control. In the next two sections, we briefly review the evidence relevant to judgments of learning and to FOK judgments.

Judgments of Learning

Global Judgments of Learning

In many investigations on aging and predictions of future performance, researchers had older adults and younger adults make a single prediction about the percentage of items they would correctly remember on a memory task. Calibration was then assessed by comparing this *global* prediction (global, because it referred to performance across the entire list globally) with actual memory performance. For instance, Bruce, Coyne, and Botwinick (1982) had older and younger adults study four lists, each of which included 20 words. Before beginning, all participants were shown a sample of the kinds of word that they would be studying. Prior to studying each list, they were asked to predict the number out of 20 that they would recall if they were allowed unlimited time to study the list. After making a prediction, they studied the words on a list at their own pace, and then attempted to recall all the words. In terms of calibration, the predicted percentage of word recall (mean global JOL) was similar for younger adults (57%) as compared to older adults (48%), whereas the percentage of correctly recalled words was substantially greater for younger adults (58%) than for older adults (37%). Thus, younger adults were almost perfectly calibrated, whereas older adults showed a great deal of overconfidence in what they recalled.

In a review of this and other research, Connor et al. (1997) concluded that the most common outcome from the literature was that older adults were overconfident whereas younger adults were less so. Nevertheless, they also noted some cases in which older adults showed better calibration for their global judgments. Why might these inconsistencies arise? In answering this question, Connor et al. noted an important pattern across studies. In the majority of cases, both younger and older adults' global judgments were anchored near the middle of the prediction scale; that is, both groups predicted that they would perform at about the 50% mark. Calibration of the judgments was better for whichever group *performed* at about the 50% mark. Thus, age-related differences here may not be due to differences in monitoring ability, but instead to age-related differences in recall performance.

To evaluate this possibility, Connor et al. (1997) conducted a series of experiments in which they manipulated the overall levels of *recall* performance. In particular, in Experiment 1, they used a standard procedure, in which recall performance was at about 50% for younger adults and substantially lower for older adults. In Experiment 2, everyone received an extra study trial on the items before the final test, so now recall performance was at about 50% for older adults and substantially higher for younger adults. If younger adults were just better at making these global judgments than were older adults, then in both cases, younger adults should have been accurate whereas older adults should still have been overconfident. In contrast, if the previous pattern of age-related differences in calibration were actually due to differences in recall performance, then (a) the typical pattern (overconfidence for older adults) should have occurred in Experiment 1, whereas (b) older adults should have shown excellent calibration in Experiment 2 (when their level of recall was near 50%) and younger adults should have shown underconfidence. Results from these experiments are presented in Figure 11.2, and they confirm the hypothesis that age-related differences in calibration are not due to differences in monitoring per se but instead were largely due to differences in recall performance. In particular, note that the mean judgments for both groups (in both experiments) hover near the 40 to 50% mark regardless of the level of recall performance. Thus, whichever group recalled near 50% had the best global judgment accuracy, and hence, older adults' apparent overconfidence demonstrated in some investigations certainly is not indicative of poor monitoring accuracy. In fact, as we'll see next, older adults' monitoring skills remain largely intact.

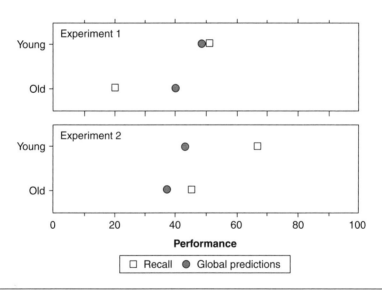

Figure 11.2   Mean global predictions and recall performance. Global predictions are consistently in the middle of the scale, regardless of whether recall performance is relatively low (Experiment 1) or is relatively high (Experiment 2). Thus, recall magnitude itself is driving age-related changes in calibration, not differences in monitoring.

SOURCE: Dunlosky, J., and Hertzog, C. (1998). Training programs to improve learning in later adulthood: Helping older adults educate themselves. In D. J. Hacker, J. Dunlosky, and A. Graesser (Eds.), *Metacognition in Educational Theory and Practice* (pp. 249–276). Hillsdale, NJ: Lawrence Erlbaum.

Item-by-Item Judgments of Learning

As with the experimental literature (Chapter 5), metacognitive aging research has also focused on the accuracy of people's item-by-item judgments of learning. For these JOLs, participants judge the likelihood that each item will be correctly remembered on the upcoming test, and then the JOLs are compared to actual performance across items (for a primer, see Chapter 3). Consider a classic study by Rabinowitz, Ackerman, Craik, and Hinchley (1982), who had participants study paired associates, which were presented individually at a rate of 10 seconds per pair. The to-be-studied list was composed of 60 pairs: 20 of the pairs were highly related (grass-cow), 20 had a medium relationship (wallet-cow), and 20 had a low relationship (airplane-cow). All participants were instructed to learn the pairs during study, so that they could recall the second member of a pair (cow) when later shown the first (grass-?). Half the participants were also told to study each pair by developing an image of the words in a pair interacting, such as a mental image of "a cow eating grass." After studying each pair, participants made an immediate JOL on a 1 to 10 scale, where lower values meant a low likelihood of correctly recalling the pair. After studying the pairs and making JOLs, each stimulus (e.g., grass-?) was presented again for the recall test.

Figure 11.3 presents the level of recall performance as a function of the level of prediction, where the scale values were collapsed into high (predictions 8–10), medium (4–7), and low (1–3) levels of predictions. Several outcomes are noteworthy. First, as expected, recall performance was higher for younger adults than for older adults, and those who were instructed to use imagery outperformed those who were instructed only to learn the pairs. Second, the predictions show above-chance relative accuracy: As the predictions decrease from high to low, so does the level of recall performance. Third, and most important, the shape of the curves is nearly identical for younger and older adults, suggesting that metacognitive monitoring during learning remains largely intact as we age in adulthood (see also Lovelace & Marsh, 1985).

Since this groundbreaking research, the optimistic conclusion—that aging spares monitoring of learning—has been even more closely scrutinized. Consider an experiment by Christopher Hertzog, who also has consistently reported age equivalence in the accuracy of JOLs (Hertzog & Hultsch, 2000). Younger and older adults studied lists that contained both related and unrelated word pairs—similar to those used by Rabinowitz et al. (1982). Relative accuracy was then computed by correlating each participant's JOLs with recall performance across different subsets of

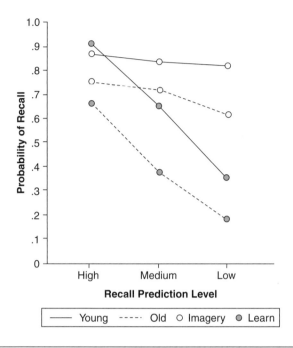

Figure 11.3   Recall performance (probability of recall) plotted as a function of recall prediction level (i.e., either high, medium, or low judgment of learning). Note that the shape of the curves is similar for older and younger adults.

SOURCE: Rabinowitz, J. C., Ackerman, B. P., Craik, F.I.M., and Hinchley, J. L. (1982). Aging and metamemory: The roles of relatedness and imagery. *Journal of Gerontology, 37,* 688–695.

pairs—either for related pairs alone, for unrelated pairs alone, or across all pairs. They found that older adults' relative accuracy was just as good as that of younger adults, regardless of the subset of pairs examined (Hertzog, Kidder, Powell-Moman & Dunlosky, 2002). Furthermore, Hertzog and his colleagues have investigated whether older adults would also receive as much benefit from delaying JOLs as do younger adults (for a primer on the delayed-JOL effect, see Chapter 5). Across several experiments, older adults demonstrated the delayed-JOL effect, and as important, older and younger adults' delayed JOLs attained the same high levels of relative accuracy.

In summary, the bulk of the research on aging and monitoring of memory during learning has shown that aging in adulthood does not disrupt the accuracy of monitoring. One implication of this optimistic conclusion is that perhaps older adults could be trained to use their intact monitoring skills to efficiently guide their learning and compensate for their declines in memory. We consider this possibility in Box 11.3.

Feeling-of-Knowing Judgments

Some of the first research on aging and metacognition was conducted to evaluate the degree to which aging in adulthood undermines FOK accuracy (e.g., see Lachman, Lachman, & Thronesbery, 1979). If older adults' FOKs are less accurate, such a deficit could in turn result in

Christopher Hertzog
Conducted groundbreaking research on aging in all facets of metacognition

deficiencies in the regulation of retrieval and in memory performance as well. Butterfield et al. (1988) had college students and older adults in their mid-60s attempt to answer general-knowledge questions such as, "Who wrote *Alice in Wonderland*?" After participants answered 12 questions incorrectly, they then made a FOK judgment for each one by making a yes/no prediction about whether they would select the correct answer from a number of alternatives. After the FOK judgments were made, participants took a seven-alternative recognition test for each of the questions. Relative accuracy was then measured by correlating each participant's FOK judgments with his or her own recognition performance across the 12 questions. Perhaps surprisingly, Butterfield et al. reported that the relative accuracy of the FOK judgments was as good for older adults (*Mean* gamma correlation = .54) as it was for younger adults (*M* = .51). Likewise, Marquié and Huet (2000) also found that older and younger adults achieved similar levels of relative FOK accuracy for general-knowledge questions as well as for questions concerning computer knowledge.

The lack of age-related deficits in relative FOK accuracy may seem surprising for two reasons. First, people with deficient frontal-lobe functioning often demonstrate poor FOK accuracy (Pannu & Kazniak, 2005). Thus, assuming that aging has a negative impact on the prefrontal cortex (Raz, 2000), one might expect older adults to have reduced FOK accuracy. Second, older adults often have difficulties retrieving sought-after ideas, which in turn may hinder their ability to evaluate what is stored in memory. Given these reasons, one may wonder, Why doesn't aging negatively influence FOK accuracy? One answer to this question was offered by Céline Souchay and her colleagues (Perrotin, Isingrini, Souchay, Clarys, & Taconnat, 2006; Souchay et al. 2000; Souchay, Moulin, Clarys, Taconnat, & Isingrini, 2007), who have argued that FOKs made for semantic information—for instance, memories for general facts learned long ago—may not be sensitive to subtle aging effects. Part of their argument is based on how people make FOK judgments. Recall from Chapter 4 that FOK judgments are heuristic based in that when making their judgments, people rely on inferences about how various cues are related to memory. For instance, when people cannot recall an answer to a general-knowledge question, they may rely on their domain familiarity to make the FOK judgment: An older adult may not recall who played the leading female role in the movie *Holiday*, yet being a movie buff, would make a high FOK judgment. For judging whether they have access to such semantic memories, it seems reasonable that older and younger adults have access to relevant cues (e.g., domain familiarity) that would accurately predict memory performance.

In contrast, Souchay et al. (2007) speculated that older adults might show deficits if instead they studied new items and were asked to make FOK judgments for those they could not recall. Their rationale was that older adults show major deficits in learning new materials—that is, they show a deficit in episodic memory. Thus, when older adults fail to recall a newly learned item, they may not even remember some cues (e.g., the specific context that the item was studied in) that could help them predict whether they could later recognize the correct answer. According to this rationale, aging will negatively influence the accuracy of FOK judgments for episodic memories. To evaluate this possibility, Souchay et al. (2007) had older and younger adults participate in two different FOK tasks, which were identical except for whether they involved semantic memory (as in previous FOK research) or episodic memory. For the semantic FOK task, the participants answered general-knowledge questions and made FOK judgments as per usual. For the episodic FOK task, the same participants first studied 40 paired associates (e.g., birthday-pipe) at a rate of 5 seconds per pair. After study, they were provided with each cue (i.e., birthday-?), and they were asked to recall the correct response and make a FOK judgment about whether they would recognize the correct response among multiple

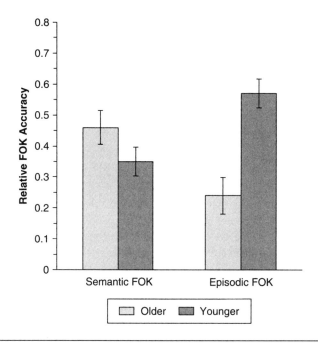

Figure 11.4   Relative FOK accuracy for semantic memory and for episodic memory. Error bars show standard errors of the mean.

SOURCE: Adapted from Souchay, C., Isingrini, M., and Espagnet, L. (2000). Aging, episodic memory feeling-of-knowing, and frontal functioning. *Neuropsychology, 14,* 299–309.

alternatives. Finally, a recognition test was administered, where each cue was presented with the correct answer and four alternatives.

Relative FOK accuracy is presented in Figure 11.4. As in previous research, no age-related differences occurred in relative FOK accuracy for the semantic memories—in fact, older adults performed slightly better than did younger adults. In contrast, however, FOK accuracy for the episodic task was reliably lower for older than younger adults (see also Souchay et al., 2000). In earlier work, Souchay et al. (2000) evaluated whether these age-related deficits in episodic FOK accuracy were related to deficits in frontal lobe functioning. To do so, they administered multiple tasks that presumably measure the integrity of the frontal lobes, and as expected, performance on these tasks was worse for older than younger adults. Most important, individual differences in frontal lobe functioning were found to completely account for the age deficits observed in episodic FOK accuracy (see also Perrotin et al., 2006). The important take-home message here is that aging does appear to negatively influence

FOK accuracy, and these deficits are apparently mediated by the negative influence age has on frontal lobe functioning.

Mystery BOX 11.2
Do Alzheimer's Patients Suffer From Monitoring Deficits?

Alzheimer's disease (AD) is a devastating form of dementia that involves the progressive degeneration of neural functioning. As life expectancy of individuals across the globe continues to rise, the prevalence of AD will grow as well. In fact, various estimates indicate that by the year 2050, the worldwide prevalence of AD will be somewhere between 50 and 100 million people! Even if the lower estimates are most accurate, we cannot deny that even this rise in AD represents a global epidemic that will have far-reaching consequences for the mental, physical, and financial well-being of AD patients, their caretakers, and society as a whole. Beyond its prevalence in the population, its effects on individuals are devastating. The cognitive symptoms—which become worse as the disease progresses—can include deficits in memory, attention, language, and social functioning. Deficits in memory are one of the first and most severe symptoms of AD (for a review, see Nebes, 1992), which suggests the possibility that AD patients will also suffer profound metamemory deficits. Of course, many AD patients do have some metamemory deficits, which can become dramatic as they progress into the final phases of the disease. As we describe next, however, whether AD leaves some monitoring processes intact is an important mystery—if the ultimate solution is that individuals with AD can monitor and evaluate their memories, they may be able to use these skills to compensate for some of their memory loss.

   During the initial onset of AD, many people are aware that their memory is suffering. Nevertheless, some AD patients say that their memories are still relatively good, but this lack of awareness may arise from depression instead of AD and may even reflect a person's attempt to deny the detrimental effects of the disease (McGlynn, 1998). To more closely scrutinize whether AD impairs memory monitoring and awareness, researchers have investigated AD patients' predictions of memory performance, such as global predictions and item-by-item JOLs. Early research reported that the calibration of AD patients' global predictions was very poor—perhaps surprisingly, they often dramatically overestimated their actual levels of performance (for reviews, see McGlynn, 1998; Moulin, 2002). Even such dramatic overestimation, however, does not definitively indicate that AD patients are unaware of their memory deficits, because the same kind of anchoring effects that are responsible for older adults' apparent overconfidence may also be responsible for AD patients' overconfidence (Moulin, 2002).

   Recent research on item-by-item JOLs by Moulin and his colleagues (e.g., Moulin, Perfect, & Jones, 2000; Moulin, Perfect, & Fitch, 2002) also illustrates the mystery about whether AD disrupts people's memory monitoring. On the one hand, AD patients' JOLs made during study are sensitive to item difficulty in that they are higher for normatively easy-to-remember words (e.g., sky) than difficult-to-remember words (e.g., hint). On the other hand, as compared to matched controls, AD patients' JOLs are insensitive to whether an item was studied once, twice, or three times. Thus, at times AD patients appear sensitive to factors that influence memory, whereas at other times they do not appear sensitive. Moulin (2002) argues that the sensitivity of AD patients' JOLs to item difficulty could result from their beliefs about memory (e.g., a belief that concrete words like "sky" are easier to remember than abstract words like "hint") and hence may not indicate that they can accurately monitor their memory. Nevertheless, a definitive solution is still needed for the intriguing mystery as to whether Alzheimer's disease can leave monitoring processes largely intact when at the same time it dramatically depletes memory and learning.

Source Monitoring

As discussed in Chapter 7, judging the source of a memory is often as important as having the memory itself. For instance, you may remember that "a new medication that you are thinking of taking has no significant side effects," but if you incorrectly remember that the source of this memory was from your doctor when in fact it came from a potentially misleading television advertisement, then you may make a bad decision about taking that medication. Unfortunately, a large number of studies have demonstrated that older adults have deficits in their source memory.

Spencer and Raz's (1995) review of the literature indicated that aging does negatively influence source memory as well as memory for context that was presented with the to-be-remembered items. Contextual memory refers to all the conditions (including the source) that are present while a to-be-remembered event is being learned. For instance, you may be asked to remember a series of pictures that are shown either in gray tones or in color, which are presented either by an artist or by a doctor. During the test, you would then be asked to remember whether a particular picture was presented during an experiment (the to-be-remembered event), but you also may be asked to remember who presented each picture (source memory) or whether the picture was originally presented in grey tones or in colors (perceptual context). As compared to younger adults, older adults have much more difficulty remembering the source and context of memories (for a review, see May, Rahhal, Berry, & Leighton, 2005). Why might older adults have more difficulties remembering the source and the context of a particular event? Let's briefly consider two possible explanations.

One broad explanation is simply that as we age in adulthood, we have more difficulties developing new associations (Naveh-Benjamin, Brav, & Levy, 2007). The idea is that because older adults have more difficulties developing new associations in general, of course they will have extra difficulties in associating the context (or source) with the focal to-be-remembered event. For explaining age-deficits in source memory, a provocative possibility was considered by May et al. (2005), who claim that the associative difficulty arises because as compared to younger adults, older adults are less likely to spontaneously attend to the contextual details of a particular event. Older adults would not spontaneously associate the context with the to-be-remembered event. Much evidence is consistent with this possibility. For instance, Glisky, Rubin, and Davidson (2001) had older and younger adults take part in a task in which they had to remember perceptual details (e.g., speakers' voices) during the criterion test. Most important, two types of encoding tasks were used: Some participants were not told to orient toward any specific detail of the to-be-remembered events, whereas other participants were directly instructed to orient to the source details. As expected, age-related deficits were evident in the former case, but older and younger adults remembered source equally well when they were oriented toward source during encoding. Thus, although older adults may not spontaneously orient toward source information, when they are told to do so, their source memory improves substantially.

Another explanation for why older adults may not always correctly identify source is because they do not use a strict criterion for identifying the correct source. For instance, let's say someone asked you whether your memory for a recent report of global warming (the event) came from a particular news reporter, Dan Rather (source). You may reply, yes it was "Dan Rather" merely because you are familiar with his name; in this case, however, a feeling of knowing for "Dan Rather" is a relatively lax criterion for making this decision. A stricter criterion would involve recalling the reporter who had discussed global warming from memory and then deciding whether the reporter was Dan Rather or someone else. Kristi Multhaup (1995) argued that older adults may sometimes use a lax criterion based on familiarity when making source judgments, which could result in errors. To evaluate this possibility, she used a false-fame task (as in Jacoby, Kelley, Brown, & Jasechko, 1989), which was also discussed in Chapter 7 on source monitoring. During an initial trial, participants pronounced non-famous names. Afterwards, they judged whether each name on a new list was famous or non-famous. This new list consisted of (a) the non-famous names that were pronounced on the initial trial, (b) new non-famous names that were not initially pronounced, and (c) famous names. The non-famous names that were pronounced on the first trial are misleading, because people's familiarity from initially pronouncing them can mislead them into thinking that some were in fact famous, and in fact, even younger adults more often judge as famous those non-famous names that were initially pronounced than those that were not initially pronounced, especially when tested at a delay. These false-fame errors partly arise because participants do not realize the source of the familiarity was that they had just pronounced the (non-famous) names on an initial trial.

Most important for our current interests, these false-fame effects are often larger for older adults than for younger adults. Could this age deficit arise because older adults rely more on familiarity when making the fame judgments? That is, as compared to younger adults, older adults may rely on familiarity more and be less likely to attempt to recollect the event in order to discover whether the familiarity arises (a) because the target was really famous or (b) because the target had been pronounced on an initial trial. Multhaup (1995) argued that encouraging older adults to use a stricter criterion to make the source decision could reduce the age deficits in the false-fame effect. Of course, if they were unable to recollect the previously pronounced names, merely shifting criterion would not work. To get participants to use a stricter criterion, all the possible sources (e.g., famous name, non-famous name pronounced earlier, or new non-famous name) were listed as participants made the source judgments, which may have encouraged them to recollect whether familiarity arose from actually being famous or from merely being pronounced. As expected, when both older and younger adults were given the possible sources as they judged fame, the false-fame effect itself was minimized and no different for older and younger adults.

In summary, a great deal of research has been conducted to both demonstrate and understand the age-related deficits that arise in source memory. The two mechanisms proposed to explain these deficits above—an associative deficit or use of a fallible familiarity criterion—may both contribute to the age deficits in source memory, and no doubt other mechanisms may be responsible as well (Johnson, 2005; Siedlecki, Salthouse, & Berish, 2005). Most exciting, the idea that older adults sometimes show deficits because they overly rely on familiarity and hence do not spontaneously (or exhaustively) attempt to recollect sources from memory—even though when encouraged they can do so—has led to innovative training.

Janine Jennings and her colleagues (Jennings & Jacoby, 2003; Jennings, Webster, Kleykamp, & Dagenbach, 2005) provided older adults with considerable training that forced them to recall the past to make correct memory decisions. Put differently, older adults obtained a lot of practice using a strict criterion—actual recall of a past event—in evaluating the source of their memories. This intervention technique boosted older adults' memory performance and helped them to make more accurate source discriminations. Thus, older adults can compensate for their apparent source-memory deficit.

Aging and Control of Learning and Retrieval

Consider again the recall data in Figure 11.1. The age-related deficits in recall (filled symbols) are enormous, even though study was self-paced. Also note the JOL magnitudes (empty symbols), which are means across individuals' delayed JOLs. What should be evident is that the calibration of the delayed JOLs is almost perfect, for both older and younger adults. Moreover, many experiments have shown that older adults' relative accuracy is unimpaired. Thus, the age-related deficits in learning cannot be explained by deficits in monitoring of learning, but the possibility still exists that older adults are deficient in how they regulate (or control) their memories.

Control of Learning

As compared to younger adults, older adults may have difficulties learning new information because they do not optimally control their study. Older adults may show deficient control of study in at least two ways: They may not apply the same effective strategies during study, and they may not use their monitoring to focus on those materials that need it most. We'll briefly discuss both possibilities in turn.

Application of Strategies

If you use inadequate strategies while trying to learn new information, you just aren't going to learn as much as someone who uses effective ones. For instance, in learning paired associates (e.g., dog-spoon), people's recall performance is better when they use interactive images to associate the words of a pair than when they merely repeat the words in a pair. Given that using poor strategies while studying can lead to poor memory performance, many studies have been conducted to evaluate whether older adults have a strategy *production deficiency*. A production deficiency means that as compared to younger adults, older adults do not spontaneously use effective strategies when studying. According to a production-deficiency account, however, if older adults were merely instructed to use effective strategies, they could do so effectively and their performance on memory tests would be substantially enhanced. For instance, when studying simple paired associates (e.g., dog-spoon) for an upcoming test (i.e., dog-?), younger adults often use a variety of effective strategies, such as interactive imagery (visualizing a small dog sitting in a huge spoon) or sentence generation (i.e., connecting the words in a sentence such as, "My dog licked my spoon every morning after breakfast"). These strategies boost performance considerably, as compared to merely repeating (or reading) the words during study (Richardson, 1998). The question arises, then, Do older adults use these same kinds of effective strategy—employed routinely by younger adults—when they study?

Early evidence suggested that older adults might have a minor production deficiency (Hulicka & Grossman, 1967). Overall the available evidence argues against the possibility that a production deficiency can entirely account for the difficulties older adults have in learning new materials (for a review, see Hertzog & Dunlosky, 2004). Even so, recent research by Naveh-Benjamin et al. (2007) dramatically demonstrates the contribution of production deficits. In particular, they had older and younger adults study paired associates (e.g., icebox-acrobat), and the adults were separated into one of three groups: (a) intentional learning, where participants were instructed to learn the pairs but they were not given any instructions about strategies; (b) associative strategy at encoding, where participants were strongly encouraged to learn the pairs by linking them with a sentence, which is an effective strategy for learning word pairs; and (c) associative strategy at encoding and retrieval, where participants were instructed to use the sentence strategy while studying as well as to use the sentences at test to help them remember the pairs. After studying, participants received two tests of recognition—one that measured whether they recognized each word of the pair (e.g., recognizing that they studied "icebox") and whether they recognized the associations (e.g., recognizing that "icebox" and "acrobat" were studied together).

According to a production-deficiency hypothesis, age-related differences should be largest for the uninstructed intentional-learning group (because older adults are not expected to use effective strategies spontaneously), whereas age-related differences should be much smaller for the other two groups. Age-related deficits were larger for associative recognition than for component recognition, indicating that older adults have particular difficulties producing new associations among words. Most important, these deficits were largest for the intentional learning groups and almost nonexistent for the groups who were instructed to use sentences to encode and retrieve pairs. These results provide definitive support for a production-deficiency hypothesis in older adults.

Another possibility is that even when older adults are strategic, the *quality* of their strategies is lacking. So, when studying "icebox-acrobat," an older adult may develop a sentence involving the two words in which the entities do not interact (e.g., "an icebox is sitting beside an acrobat"), whereas younger adults may develop a more effective sentence in which the two entities interact (e.g., "an acrobat is doing a handstand on an icebox"). The prevalent evidence, however, suggests this is not the case. Dunlosky, Hertzog, and Powell-Moman (2005) had older and younger adults study paired associates, and the participants were instructed to develop a sentence to link the two words of each pair in a meaningful fashion. A critical aspect of the procedure is that immediately after a pair had been studied, the participants reported the sentence that they had generated for the pair. As expected, both groups generated sentences for the majority of pairs. Most important, the sentences (which were reported during study) could be scored on multiple dimensions, so that age-related differences in their quality could be identified. The critical outcome was that older and younger adults' sentences were nearly identical on all key dimensions, such as the number of content words and the length of the sentences. Moreover, both age groups were equally likely to develop sentences that involved the words of a pair interacting. This evidence indicates that when older adults do use effective strategies, they are not deficient in their application of those strategies to learn simple materials.

Given that older adults do show some strategy deficiencies (as in Naveh-Benjamin et al., 2007), it raises the possibility that they will benefit from interventions aimed at training them to apply strategies effectively when learning new materials. In fact, a cottage industry has arisen to evaluate whether training older adults to use effective strategies (and giving them lots of practice using them) can boost their learning. A meta-analysis conducted by Verhaeghen, Marcoen, and Goossens (1992), which involved 31 different studies, revealed that such training programs were successful. In particular, older adults' learning benefits from training and practice using various mnemonic strategies, although the benefits of training do decrease with increasing age.

Allocation of Study Time

Even if older adults use effective strategies at study, they still may not allocate their study time in an efficient manner. For instance, perhaps because older adults believe they will forget much of what they learn, they may spend way too much time studying materials that they actually have learned well, which could slow their overall progress dramatically. This issue pertains to the allocation of study time, which was discussed in some detail in Chapter 5. Recall that allocation of study time is often assessed by examining the relationship between individuals' monitoring judgments and subsequent self-paced study time. The most common outcome is that younger adults spend more time studying materials that they judged have not been learned well than materials that they judged have already been learned well (Son & Metcalfe, 2000). Our question here is, Do older adults use the same strategy of allocating more time to the less well-known items?

To answer this question, Souchay and Isingrini (2004) had older adults (56 to 96 years old) and younger adults (20 to 31 years old) study 40 paired associates, which were presented at a rate of 5 seconds per pair. Afterwards, the cue for each pair was presented alone, and the participants attempted to recall the corresponding response. Participants then predicted whether they could later recognize the correct answer for each pair. On the next trial, they proceeded to study each pair again. For this trial, however, study was self-paced. After self-paced study, a final cued recall test was administered. As expected, final cued recall was greater for younger than older adults, which brings us to our focal question: Could this age-related deficit be attributed to how older adults allocated their study time? Each participant's metacognitive predictions were correlated with his or her subsequent self-paced study time. The mean correlation was substantially larger for younger adults (–.77) than for older adults (–.47), suggesting that older adults do not use their monitoring to the same degree to allocate study time (Souchay & Isingrini, 2004). Moreover, based on regression analyses, the authors demonstrated that the age-related differences in study-time allocation accounted for more than 60% of the age-related deficits in final recall performance.

Dunlosky and Connor (1997) reported the same outcomes in multi-trial learning. Namely, the correlation between JOLs and self-paced study was larger for younger than older adults. This age-related difference in the allocation of study time was even found when both age groups had the same level of recall performance prior to allocating their study time. That is, when both age groups needed to learn the same number of items, all of which were noun-noun pairs (e.g., dog-spoon) that were within everyone's ability to learn, older adults still allocated less time to the more difficult items. Moreover, these age-related differences in the allocation of study time statistically mediated some of the age-related deficits in learning that are depicted in Figure 11.1. Put differently, those older adults who allocated the least study time to the most difficult items (and spent more time studying the easier ones) ended up recalling fewer items, which suggests that their allocation of study time was inadequate. Other investigators have also reported that some age-related differences occur in study-time allocation as measured by the relationship between JOLs and self-paced study (e.g., Miles & Stine-Morrow, 2004). Nevertheless, such age-related deficits in the allocation of study time are not always found (Stine-Morrow, Shake, Miles, & Noh, 2006). In fact, in all cases where age-related deficits are present, it must be stressed that older adults do use monitoring to guide learning, but they just do not do so to the same degree as younger adults. For instance, in Souchay and Isingrini (2004), the mean correlation between older adults' predictions and self-paced study time was –.46, indicating that they do tend to allocate more study time to less well-learned items than to more well-learned items.

In summary, older adults may at times show some deficits in how they regulate their study, but overall they tend to allocate study time in a relatively effective manner. The good news here is obviously that when we are in our 70s and 80s, our monitoring and control of learning will be largely intact. Perhaps surprisingly, however, older adults sometimes fail to use their intact metacognitive skills when they are learning difficult materials (Murphy, Schmitt, Caruso, & Sanders, 1987). Such observations have led some researchers to explore the possibility that training older adults to use their (underutilized but intact) metacognitive skills could help them compensate for age-related deficits in learning. In Box 11.3, we describe these metacognitive-training interventions in more detail.

BOX 11.3
Training Adults to Monitor Learning

One of older adults' most impressive—and surprising—deficits in metacognitive control was demonstrated by Murphy et al. (1987). Their procedure was simple: Show each individual some pictures of objects to memorize, and then say, "Study these pictures until you can recall the names of each of the objects, and just tell us when you are ready to recall them." Take a moment and think about how you would attack this task. How would you know when to stop studying and tell the experimenter you are ready for the test? Younger adults in their late teens and early 20s all approached the problem in a similar way. Namely, they studied the pictures, and then before they said "ready for the test," they tested themselves to evaluate whether in fact they had learned them all. In contrast, many of the older adults did not self-test themselves, and in comparison to the younger adults, they studied much less and did poorly on the recall test. So the older adults did not use a skill—accurately monitoring their learning through self-testing—that they presumably could have used. Put differently, the older adults showed a production deficiency with respect to using an effective self-monitoring strategy to regulate their learning.

To further test a production deficiency account, Murphy et al. (1987) conducted a follow-up experiment in which one group of older adults was explicitly told to test their memory for the object names before they stopped studying. This group of older adults not only self-tested themselves, but they studied longer and obtained the same level of performance as uninstructed younger adults! Thus, merely telling older adults to use self-testing led to an immediate improvement in their self-regulation and learning. Inspired by these findings, a memory intervention was recently developed to train older adults to monitor their ongoing learning of paired associates by self-testing (Dunlosky, Kubat-Silman, & Hertzog, 2003). In particular, older adults were trained to study paired associates (e.g., bee-noodle) by associating them using interactive imagery (e.g., visualizing a bee slurping down a noodle) or by generating a sentence (e.g., A bee dances around a noodle). One group of older adults was also trained to self-test themselves as they studied by covering the response (i.e., noodle) and trying to recall it from memory. This delayed retrieval attempt is analogous to making delayed JOLs, which yield nearly perfect levels of monitoring accuracy. Moreover, if they recalled it, they were instructed to put it aside; but if they could not recall it, then they saved it to restudy later on. After training, a criterion test was administered in which everyone studied 40 pairs (for up to 20 minutes) and then attempted to recall the response for each pair (e.g., bee-?).

Several outcomes were noteworthy. First, as expected, performance on the criterion test was greater for the two groups that were trained to use associative strategies (both groups described above) than for a control group that received no training. Second, and most relevant here, criterion performance was also substantially greater for older adults who were also trained to self-test themselves than for those who were only trained associative strategies. Thus, by merely training older adults to evaluate their learning as they study, their efficiency of study and learning can easily be improved. Unfortunately, very few studies have examined the efficacy of training older adults to monitor their learning, so although the present findings are encouraging, much still needs to be learned about the strengths (and weaknesses) of monitoring interventions.

Control of Retrieval

As we discussed in Chapter 6 on retrospective confidence (RC) judgments, people can dynamically control their retrieval by recalling potential answers to a question and then judging the likelihood that each candidate answer is actually correct. At that point, if confidence for a candidate answer is above some threshold, then the candidate answer is reported (Koriat & Goldsmith, 1996). So imagine yourself playing a game of Trivial Pursuit and being asked the question, "What is the capital city of Australia?" You may overtly recall Sydney, Canberra, and Melbourne, but you also realize that it is important to get the answer right, so you decide that you will only report an answer if your confidence exceeds 90%. Although you are only 50% confident that Canberra and Melbourne are correct, you are almost sure (95%) that Sydney is the capital of Australia, so you report "Sydney." In this way, two factors can influence the *quality* of what you end up reporting aloud— that is, the proportion of items you *correctly* recalled out of all those that you report. First, the accuracy of your RC judgments will influence recall quality, because if you are inaccurate then you may report high-confidence answers that are incorrect. In fact, the example above illustrates this point, because "Sydney" is the incorrect answer but was reported due to inappropriate confidence. Second, your threshold for reporting answers can influence quality, because as the threshold becomes less stringent (e.g., moves from 90% to 50%), you would be more likely to report answers that are incorrect.

Based on this rationale, Kelley and Sahakyan (2003) investigated whether older adults have difficulties in controlling their retrieval of newly learned paired associates. They used methods developed by Koriat and Goldsmith (1996), so that older and younger adults could be compared on monitoring accuracy and quality of recall, among other components of self-regulated retrieval (for a refresher, see Chapter 6). Recall that an important aspect of these methods is that participants choose whether they report a candidate answer or not. For such free-report tests, the key measure of performance is the proportion of correctly recalled targets out of the number of targets reported, which has been referred to as *recall accuracy*. Recall accuracy was lower for older adults than for younger adults. More important, Kelley and Sahakyan (2003) linked this recall-accuracy deficit to age-related deficits in monitoring accuracy. For instance, in one condition, the relative accuracy of older adults' confidence judgments was only +.46, where the comparable value for younger adults was +.85. Thus, older adults apparently have more difficulties in accurately reporting only correct answers in part because they have some difficulties in monitoring the correctness of candidate answers (see also Dodson, Bawa, & Slotnick, 2007; Rhodes & Kelley, 2005). Whether older adults could further improve their performance on free-report tests by training them to more accurately monitor their memories provides an important applied issue for future research.

At this point, you may find the conclusions about how aging influences metacognitive monitoring somewhat confusing. Namely, research on JOLs suggests that no age-related deficits occur in monitoring, whereas research on RC judgments suggests that deficits in monitoring can occur. What such a pattern of outcomes indicates, however, is that the accuracy of metacognitive monitoring is multifaceted: Different processes are involved in monitoring learning (as measured by JOLs) than are involved in monitoring retrieval (as measured by RC judgments). So, aging may leave one form of monitoring intact (during learning) yet disrupt another form of monitoring (during retrieval). Why aging affects one kind of monitoring (and not the other) remains an important mystery to be solved by future research.

Summary

We began this chapter with a brief anecdote about Tony—a retiree who is faced with many new opportunities to engage in life that will ultimately challenge him to continue learning new information. For those who live long lives yet want to remain engaged, part of the challenge will be to overcome mild deficits that arise in the proficiency of learning. In the present chapter, we explored the degree to which deficits in metacognition contribute to these age-related deficits in memory and learning. Given the multifaceted nature of metacognition, it perhaps is not surprising that there is not just one answer to the question, Do older adults show deficits in metacognition?

Current evidence suggests that older adults are deficient in some aspects of metacognition but not in others. For instance, whereas older adults' on-line monitoring of encoding (as measured by JOLs) remains largely intact, they also appear to have a production deficiency with respect to spontaneously using the most effective strategies during learning and retrieval (Naveh-Benjamin et al., 2007). As important, research aimed at improving older adults' learning by helping them to use their intact metacognitive processes has been largely successful. Thus, even though we may have a few more difficulties learning and remembering as we grow older, the outlook is optimistic: We will be able to compensate for at least some of these difficulties through the judicious application of metacognition.

DISCUSSION QUESTION

1. Leslie is in her mid-70s, and although she is moving a bit more slowly than she did 20 years ago, she's generally in good physical health and has not shown any signs of losing her mental capabilities. Nevertheless, she has begun complaining about her memory. Why might she be complaining even if her memory isn't worse than it used to be? You want to evaluate whether her judgments about her memory are invalid. Develop a metacognitive task that might help you establish whether her judgments are inaccurate or whether her memory is poorer than typical 70-year-olds.

CONCEPT REVIEW

For the following questions, we recommend you write down the answers on a separate sheet in as much detail as possible, and then check them against the relevant material in the chapter.

1. Can changes in metamemory (either monitoring or control) explain the deficits in memory that can arise as people grow older?

2. What is self-efficacy? How can you boost people's low memory self-efficacy?

3. What is a production deficiency, and can it account for age-related deficits in memory performance? What is the evidence both for and against a production-deficiency hypothesis?

4. How might older adults use their intact metacognitive abilities to improve their memory and learning?

References

Adams, P. A., & Adams, J. K. (1958). Training in confidence judgments. *American Journal of Psychology, 71,* 747–751.

Ainsworth, S., & Burcham, S. (2007). The impact of text coherence on learning by self-explanation. *Learning and Instruction, 17,* 286–303.

Akehurst, L., Köhnken, G., Vrij, A., & Bull, R. (1996). Lay persons' and police officers' beliefs regarding deceptive behaviour. *Applied Cognitive Psychology, 10,* 461–471.

Alba, J. W., & Hasher, L. (1983). Is memory schematic? *Psychological Bulletin, 93,* 203–231.

Allwood, C. M., & Granhag, P. A. (1996). The effects of arguments on realism in confidence judgements. *Acta Psychologica, 91,* 99–119.

American Academy of Pediatrics. (2001). Media violence. *Pediatrics, 108,* 1222–1226.

American Psychological Association. (1996). Distinguished Scientific Award for the Applications of Psychology: Ann L. Brown. *American Psychologist, 51,* 309–311.

Anderson, J. C., Lowe, D. J., & Reckers, P. M. J. (1993). Evaluation of auditor decisions: Hindsight bias effects and the expectation gap. *Journal of Economic Psychology, 14,* 711–737.

Arbuckle, T. Y., & Cuddy, L. L. (1969). Discrimination of item strength at time of presentation. *Journal of Experimental Psychology, 81,* 126–131.

Arkes, H. R. (1991). Costs and benefits of judgment errors: Implications for debiasing. *Psychological Bulletin, 110,* 486–498.

Atkinson, R. C., & Shiffrin, R. (1968). Human memory: A proposed system and its control processes. In K. Spence & J. Spence (Eds.), *The psychology of learning and motivation* (Vol. 2, pp. 89–195). New York: Academic Press.

Azevedo, R., Cromley, J. G., Winters, F. I., Moos, D. C., & Greene, J. A. (2005). Adaptive human scaffolding facilitates adolescents' self-regulated learning and hypermedia. *Instructional Science, 33,* 381–412.

Baker, L., & Anderson, R. I. (1982). Effects of inconsistent information on text processing: Evidence for comprehension monitoring. *Reading Research Quarterly, 17,* 281–294.

Bandura, A. (1977). Self-efficacy: Toward a unifying theory of behavioral change. *Psychological Review, 84,* 191–215.

Bandura, A. (1997). *Self-efficacy: The exercise of control*. New York: Freeman.

Batchelder, W. H., & Riefer, D. M. (1990). Multinomial processing models of source monitoring. *Psychological Review, 97,* 548–564.

Bayen, U. J., Murnane, K., & Erdfelder, E. (1996). Source discrimination, item detection, and multinomial models of source monitoring. *Journal of Experimental Psychology: Learning, Memory, and Cognition, 22,* 197–215.

Bayen, U. J., Pohl, R. F., Erdfelder, E., & Auer, T. S. (2007). Hindsight bias across the life span. *Social Cognition, 25,* 83–97.

Beattie, G., & Coughlan, J. (1999). An experimental investigation of the role of iconic gestures in lexical access using the tip-of-the-tongue phenomenon. *British Journal of Psychology, 90,* 35–56.

Begg, I., Duft, S., Lalonde, P., Melnick, R., & Sanvito, J. (1989). Memory predictions are based on ease of processing. *Journal of Memory and Language, 28,* 610–632.

Begg, I., Vinski, E., Frankovich, L., & Holgate, B. (1991). Generating makes words memorable, but so does effective reading. *Memory & Cognition, 19,* 487–497.

Benjamin, A. S. (2005). Response speeding mediates the contributions of cue familiarity and target retrievability to metamnemonic judgments. *Psychonomic Bulletin & Review, 12,* 874–879.

Benjamin, A. S., & Bird, R. D. (2006). Metacognitive control of the spacing of study repetitions. *Journal of Memory and Language, 55,* 126–137.

Benjamin, A. S., & Bjork, R. A. (1996). Retrieval fluency as a metacognitive index. In L. M. Reder (Ed.), *Implicit memory and metacognition* (pp. 309–338). Hillsdale, NJ: Lawrence Erlbaum.

Benjamin, A. S., Bjork, R. A., & Schwartz, B. L. (1998). The mismeasure of memory: When retrieval fluency is misleading as a metamnemonic index. *Journal of Experimental Psychology: General, 127,* 55–68.

Benjamin, A. S., & Diaz, M. (2008). Measurement of relative metamnemonic accuracy. In J. Dunlosky & R. A. Bjork (Eds.), *Handbook of metamemory and memory* (pp. 73–94). New York: Taylor & Francis.

Benjamin, L. T., Cavell, T. A., & Shallenberger, W. R. (1984). Staying with initial answers on objective tests: Is it a myth? *Teaching of Psychology, 11,* 133–141.

Bentaleb, L. A., Beauregard, M., Liddle, P., & Stip, E. (2002). Cerebral activity associated with auditory verbal hallucinations: A functional Magnetic Resonance Imaging case study. *Journal of Psychiatry & Neuroscience, 27,* 110–115.

Bentall, R. P. (1990). The illusion of reality: A review and integration of psychological research on hallucinations. *Psychological Bulletin, 107,* 82–95.

Bereiter, C., & Scardamalia, M. (1987). *The psychology of writing composition.* Hillsdale, NJ: Lawrence Erlbaum.

Bjorklund, D. F., & Green, B. L. (1992). The adaptive nature of cognitive immaturity. *American Psychologist, 47,* 46–54.

Bjorklund, D. F., Miller, P. H., Coyle, T. R., & Slawinski, J. L. (1997). Instructing children to use memory strategies: Evidence of utilization deficiencies in memory training studies. *Developmental Review, 17,* 411–441.

Blakemore, S.-J. (2003). Deluding the motor system. *Consciousness and Cognition: An International Journal, 12,* 647–655.

Blakemore, S.-J., Wolpert, D., & Frith, C. (2000). Why can't you tickle yourself? *Neuroreport, 11,* 959–965.

Bloom, P., & German, T. P. (2000). Two reasons to abandon the false belief task as a test of theory of mind. *Cognition, 77,* B25–B31.

Boekaerts, M., Pintrich, P. R., & Zeidner, M. (2000). *Handbook of self-regulation.* San Diego, CA: Academic Press.

Bolles, R. C. (1993). *The story of psychology: A thematic history.* Pacific Grove, CA: Brooks/Cole.

Boring, E. G. (1929). *A history of experimental psychology.* New York: Appleton-Century.

Borkowski, J. G., Milstead, M., & Hale, C. (1988). Components of children's metamemory: Implications for strategy generalization. In F. E Weinert & M. Perlmutter (Eds.), *Memory development: Universal change and individual differences* (pp. 73–100). Hillsdale, NJ: Lawrence Erlbaum.

Brase, G. L., Cosmides, L., & Tooby, J. (1998). Individuation, counting, and statistical inference: The role of frequency and whole-object representations in judgment under uncertainty. *Journal of Experimental Psychology: General, 127,* 3–21.

Breen, N., Caine, D., & Coltheart, M. (2001). Mirrored-self misidentification: Two cases of focal onset dementia. *Neurocase, 7,* 239–254.

Brennen, T., Baguley, T., Bright, J., and Bruce, V. (1990). Resolving semantically-induced tip-of-the-tongue states for proper nouns. *Memory & Cognition, 18,* 339–347.

Brentano, F. (1995). *Psychology from an empirical standpoint.* London: Routledge. (Original work published 1874)

Brewer, N., & Burke, A. (2002). Effects of testimonial inconsistencies and eyewitness confidence on mock-juror judgments. *Law and Human Behavior, 26,* 353–364.

Brewer, W. F., & Sampaio, C. (2006). Processes leading to confidence and accuracy in sentence recognition: A metamemory approach. *Memory, 14,* 540–552.

Brewer, W. F., Sampaio, C., & Barlow, M. R. (2005). Confidence and accuracy in the recall of deceptive and nondeceptive sentences. *Journal of Memory and Language, 52,* 618–627.

Brincones, I., & Otero, J. (1994). Students' conceptions of the top-level structure of physics texts. *Science Education, 78,* 171–183.

Broadbent, D. E. (1958). *Perception and communication.* New York: Pergamon.

Brown, A. L. (1978). Knowing when, where, and how to remember: A problem of metacognition. In R. Glaser (Ed.), *Advances in instructional psychology* (pp. 367–406). New York: Halsted Press.

Brown, A. L., & Campione, J. C. (1996). Psychological theory and the design of innovative learning environments: On procedures, principles, and systems. In L. Schauble & R. Glaser (Eds.), *Innovations in learning: New environments for education* (pp. 289–325). Hillsdale, NJ: Lawrence Erlbaum.

Brown, A. L., & Smiley, S. S. (1977). Rating the importance of structural units of prose passages: A problem of metacognitive development. *Child Development, 48,* 1–8.

Brown, A. S. (1991). A review of the tip-of-the-tongue experience. *Psychological Bulletin, 109,* 204–223.

Brown, A. S., Brown, L. A., & Zoccoli, S. L. (2002). Repetition-based credibility enhancement of unfamiliar faces. *American Journal of Psychology, 115*(2), 199–209.

Brown, R., & McNeill, D. (1966). The "tip of the tongue" phenomenon. *Journal of Verbal Learning and Verbal Behavior, 5,* 325–337.

Bruce, P. R., Coyne, A. C., & Botwinick, J. (1982). Adult age differences in metamemory. *Journal of Gerontology, 37,* 354–357.

Bryant, F. B., & Brockway, J. H. (1997). Hindsight bias in reaction to the verdict in the O. J. Simpson criminal trial. *Basic and Applied Social Psychology, 19*(2), 225–241.

Burke, D. M., MacKay, D. G., Worthley, J. S., & Wade, E. (1991). On the tip of the tongue: What causes word finding failures in young and older adults? *Journal of Memory and Language, 30,* 542–579.

Butterfield, B., & Mangels, J. A. (2003). Neural correlates of error detections and correction in a semantic retrieval task. *Cognitive Brain Research, 17,* 793–817.

Butterfield, B., & Metcalfe, J. (2006). The correction of errors committed with high confidence. *Metacognition and Learning, 1,* 69–84.

Butterfield, E. C., Nelson, T. O., & Peck, V. (1988). Developmental aspects of the feeling of knowing. *Developmental Psychology, 24,* 654–663.

Call, J. (2005). The self and other: A missing link in comparative social cognition. In H. S. Terrace & J. Metcalfe (Eds.), *The missing link in cognition: Origins of self-reflective consciousness* (pp. 321–241). New York: Oxford University Press.

Campbell, J. D., & Tesser, A. (1983). Motivational interpretations of hindsight bias: An individual difference analysis. *Journal of Personality, 51,* 605–620.

Carr, M., & Jessup, D. L. (1995). Cognitive and metacognitive predictors of mathematics strategy use. *Learning and Individual Differences, 7,* 235–247.

Cassel, E. (2000, February). Behavioral science research leads to Department of Justice guidelines for eyewitness evidence. *Virginia Lawyer, 48,* 1–4.

Cavanaugh, J. C., & Borkowski, J. G. (1980). Searching for metamemory-memory connections: A developmental study. *Developmental Psychology, 16,* 441–453.

Cavanaugh, J. C., & Perlmutter, M. (1982). Metamemory: A critical examination. *Child Development, 53,* 11–28.

Chemers, M. M., Hu, L., & Garcia, B. F. (2001). Academic self-efficacy and first-year college student performance and adjustment. *Journal of Educational Psychology, 93,* 55–64.

Chi, M. T. H., & Bassok, M. (1989). Learning from examples via self-explanation. In L. B. Resnick (Ed.), *Knowing, learning, and instruction: Essays in honor of Robert Glaser.* Hillsdale, NJ: Lawrence Erlbaum.

Chi, M. T. H., Bassok, M., Lewis, M. W., Reimann, P., & Glaser, R. (1989). Self-explanations: How students study and use examples in learning to solve problems. *Cognitive Science, 13,* 145–182.

Chomsky, N. (1957). *Syntactic structures.* Oxford, UK: Mouton.

Cicero, M. T. (2001). *De oratore* [On the ideal orator]. (J. M. May & J. Wisse, Trans.). New York: Oxford University Press.

Clancy, S. A. (2005). *Abducted: How people come to believe they were kidnapped by aliens.* Cambridge, MA: Harvard University Press.

Conner, L. N. (2007). Cueing metacognition to improve researching and essay writing in a final year high school biology class. *Research in Science Education, 37*, 1–16.

Connor, L. T., Balota, D. A., & Neely, J. H. (1992). On the relation between feeling of knowing and lexical decision: Persistent threshold activation or topic familiarity? *Journal of Experimental Psychology: Learning, Memory, and Cognition, 18*, 544–554.

Connor, L. T., Dunlosky, J., & Hertzog, C. (1997). Age-related differences in absolute but not relative metamemory accuracy. *Psychology and Aging, 12*, 50–71.

Cosmides, L., & Tooby, J. (1996). Are humans good intuitive statisticians after all? Rethinking some conclusions from the literature on judgment under uncertainty. *Cognition, 58*, 1–73.

Costermans, J., Lories, G., & Ansay, C. (1992). Confidence level and feeling of knowing in question answering: The weight of inferential processes. *Journal of Experimental Psychology: Learning, Memory, and Cognition, 18*, 142–150.

Crowley, K., Shrager, J., & Siegler, R. S. (1997). Strategy discovery as a competitive negotiation between metacognitive and associative mechanisms. *Developmental Review, 17*, 462–489.

Cummins, C., Stewart, M. T., & Block, C. C. (2005). Teaching several metacognitive strategies together increases students' independent metacognition. In S. E. Israel, C. C. Block, K. L. Bauserman, & K. Kinnucan-Welsch (Eds.), *Metacognition in literacy learning: Theory, assessment, instruction, and professional development* (pp. 277–295). Hillsdale, NJ: Lawrence Erlbaum.

Cutler, B. L., Penrod, S. D., & Dexter, H. R. (1990). Juror sensitivity to eyewitness identification evidence. *Law and Human Behavior, 14*, 185–191.

Damasio, A. R., Graff-Radford, P. J., Eslinger, H., Damasio, H., & Kassel, N. (1985). Amnesia following basal forebrain lesions. *Archives of Neurology, 42*, 263–271.

Danziger, K. (1979). The positivist repudiation of Wundt. *Journal of the History of the Behavioral Sciences, 15*, 205–230.

Davachi, L., Mitchell, J. P., & Wagner, A. D. (2003). Multiple routes to memory: Distinct medial temporal lobe processes build item and source memories. *Proceedings From the National Academy of Sciences, 100*, 2157–2162.

De Corte, E., Verschaffel, L., & Op 'T Eynde, P. (2000). Self-regulation: A characteristic and a goal of mathematics education. In M. Boekaerts, P. R. Pintrich, & M. Zeidner (Eds.), *Handbook of self-regulation* (pp. 687–726). New York: Academic Press.

Delclos, V. R., & Harrington, C. (1991). Effects of strategy monitoring and proactive instruction on children's problem-solving performance. *Journal of Educational Psychology, 83*, 35–42.

DePaulo, B. M., & Pfeifer, R. L. (1986). On-the-job experience and skill at detecting deception. *Journal of Applied Social Psychology, 16*, 249–267.

Desoete, A., Roeyers, H., & De Clercq, A. (2003). Can offline metacognition enhance mathematical problem solving? *Journal of Educational Psychology, 95*, 188–200.

Dixon, R. A., & Hultsch, D. F. (1983). Structure and development of metamemory in adulthood. *Journal of Gerontology, 38*, 682–688.

Dodson, C. S., Bawa, S., & Slotnick, S. D. (2007). Aging, source memory, and misrecollections. *Journal of Experimental Psychology: Learning, Memory, and Cognition, 33,* 169–181.

Dodson, C. S., & Schacter, D. L. (2002). Aging and strategic retrieval processes: Reducing false memories with a distinctiveness heuristic. *Psychology and Aging, 17,* 405–415.

Dominowski, R. L. (1998). Verbalization and problem solving. In D. J. Hacker, J. Dunlosky, & A. C. Graesser (Eds.), *Metacognition in educational theory and practice* (pp. 25–45). Hillsdale, NJ: Lawrence Erlbaum.

Donndelinger, S. J. (2005). Integrating comprehension and metacognitive reading strategies. In S. E. Israel, C. C. Block, K. L. Bauserman, & K. Kinnucan-Welsch (Eds.), *Metacognition in literacy learning: Theory, assessment, instruction, and professional development* (pp. 241–260). Hillsdale, NJ: Lawrence Erlbaum.

Dougherty, M. R. P. (2001). Integration of the ecological and error models of overconfidence using a multiple-trace memory model. *Journal of Experimental Psychology: General, 130,* 579–599.

Dufresne, A., & Kobasigawa, A. (1989). Children's spontaneous allocation of study time: Differential and sufficient aspects. *Journal of Experimental Child Psychology, 47,* 274–296.

Dunlosky, J. (2004). Metacognition. In R. R. Hunt & H. C. Ellis, *Fundamentals of cognitive psychology* (7th ed., pp. 232–262). New York: McGraw-Hill.

Dunlosky, J., & Connor, L. (1997). Age-related differences in the allocation of study time account for age-related differences in memory performance. *Memory & Cognition, 25,* 691–700.

Dunlosky, J., Domoto, P. K., Wang, M.-L., Ishikawa, T., Roberson, I., Nelson, T. O., & Ramsay, D. S. (1998). Inhalation of 30% nitrous oxide impairs people's learning without impairing judgments of what will be remembered. *Experimental and Clinical Psychopharmacology, 6,* 77–86.

Dunlosky, J., & Hertzog, C. (1998). Training programs to improve learning in later adulthood: Helping older adults educate themselves. In D. J. Hacker, J. Dunlosky, & A. Graesser (Eds.), *Metacognition in educational theory and practice* (pp. 249–276). Hillsdale, NJ: Lawrence Erlbaum.

Dunlosky, J., Hertzog, C., & Powell-Moman, A. (2005). The contribution of mediator-based deficiencies to age differences in associative learning. *Developmental Psychology, 41,* 389–400.

Dunlosky, J., Kubat-Silman, A., & Hertzog, C. (2003). Training monitoring skills improves older adults' self-paced associative learning. *Psychology and Aging, 18,* 340–345.

Dunlosky, J., & Lipko, A. (2007). Metacomprehension: A brief history and how to improve its accuracy. *Current Directions in Psychological Science, 16,* 228–232.

Dunlosky, J., & Matvey, G. (2001). Empirical analysis of the intrinsic-extrinsic distinction of judgments of learning (JOLs): Effects of relatedness and serial position on JOLs. *Journal of Experimental Psychology: Learning, Memory, and Cognition, 27,* 1180–1191.

Dunlosky, J., & Nelson, T. O. (1992). Importance of the kind of cue for judgments of learning (JOL) and the delayed-JOL effect. *Memory & Cognition, 20,* 373–380.

Dunlosky, J., Rawson, K. A., & Middleton, E. (2005). What constrains the accuracy of metacomprehension judgments? Testing the transfer-appropriate-monitoring and accessibility hypotheses. *Journal of Memory and Language, 52,* 551–565.

Dunlosky, J., Serra, M., & Baker, J. M. C. (2007). Metamemory. In F. T. Durso (Sr. Ed.), *Handbook of applied cognition* (2nd ed., pp. 137–161). New York: Wiley.

Dunlosky, J., & Thiede, K. W. (1998). What makes people study more? An evaluation of factors that affect people's self-paced study and yield "labor-and-gain" effects. *Acta Psychologica, 98,* 37–56.

Dunlosky, J., & Thiede, K. W. (2004). Causes and constraints of the shift-to-easier-materials effect in the control of study. *Memory & Cognition, 32,* 779–788.

Dunning, D., Kerri, J., Ehrlinger, J., & Kruger, J. (2003). Why people fail to recognize their own incompetence. *Current Directions in Psychological Science, 12,* 83–87.

Efklides, A., & Chryssoula, P. (2005). Effects of mood on students' metacognition experiences. *Learning and Instruction, 15,* 415–431.

Ekman, P., & Friesen, W. V. (1969). The repertoire of nonverbal behavior: Categories, origins, usage, and coding. *Semiotica, 1,* 49–98.

Ekman, P., & O'Sullivan, M. (1991). Who can catch a liar? *American Psychologist, 46,* 913–920.

Erber, J. T. (1989). Young and older adults' appraisal of memory failures in young and older adult target persons. *Journals of Gerontology, 44,* P170–P175.

Erber, J. T., Szuchman, L. T., & Rothberg, S. T. (1990). Age, gender, and individual differences in memory failure appraisal. *Psychology and Aging, 5,* 600–603.

Erev, I., Wallsten, T. S., & Budescu, D. V. (1994). Simultaneous over- and underconfidence: The role of error in judgment processes. *Psychological Review, 101,* 519–527.

Ericsson, K. A., & Simon, H. A. (1980). Verbal reports as data. *Psychological Review, 87,* 215–251.

Ericsson, K. A., & Simon, H. A. (1984). *Protocol analysis: Verbal reports as data.* Cambridge: MIT Press.

Feinberg, T. E., & Shapiro, R. M. (1989). Misidentification-reduplication and the right hemisphere. *Neuropsychiatry, Neuropsychology, & Behavioral Neurology, 2,* 39–48.

Ferguson, S. A., Hashtroudi, S., & Johnson, M. K. (1992). Age differences in using source-relevant cues. *Psychology and Aging, 7,* 443–452.

Ferrell, W. R., & McGoey, P. J. (1980). A model of calibration for subjective probabilities. *Organizational Behavior and Human Performance, 26,* 32–53.

Fiedler, K. (1988). The dependence of the conjunction fallacy on subtle linguistic factors. *Psychological Research, 50,* 123–129.

Finn, B., & Metcalfe, J. (2007). The role of memory for past test in the under-confidence with practice effect. *Journal of Experimental Psychology: Learning, Memory, and Cognition, 33,* 238–244.

Finn, B., & Metcalfe, J. (2008). Judgments of learning are influenced by memory for past test. *Journal of Memory and Language, 58,* 19–34.

Fischhoff, B. (1975). Hindsight does not equal foresight. *Journal of Experimental Psychology, 1*, 288–299.

Fischhoff, B. (1982). Debiasing. In D. Kahneman, P. Slovic, & A. Tversky (Eds.), *Judgment under uncertainty: Heuristics and biases* (pp. 422–444). Cambridge, UK: Cambridge University Press.

Fischhoff, B., & MacGregor, D. (1982). Subjective confidence in forecasts. *Journal of Forecasting, 1*, 155–172.

Fisher, R. P., & Geiselman, R. E. (1992). *Memory enhancing techniques for investigative interviewing: The cognitive interview.* Springfield, IL: Charles C Thomas.

Fitzgerald, J., & Markham, L. (1987). Teaching children about revision in writing. *Cognition and Instruction, 4*, 3–24.

Flavell, J. H. (1963). *The developmental psychology of Jean Piaget.* New York: Van Nostrand.

Flavell, J. H. (1979). Metacognition and cognitive monitoring: A new area of cognitive-developmental inquiry. *American Psychologist, 34*, 906–911.

Flavell, J. H. (1993). The development of children's understanding of false belief and the appearance-reality distinction. *International Journal of Psychology, 28*, 595–604.

Flavell, J. H. (2000). Development of children's knowledge about the mental world. *International Journal of Behavioral Development, 24*, 15–23.

Flavell, J. H. (2004). Theory-of-mind development: Retrospect and prospect. *Merrill-Palmer Quarterly, 50*, 274–290.

Flavell, J. H., Friedrichs, A. G., & Hoyt, J. D. (1970). Developmental changes in memorization processes. *Cognitive Psychology, 1*, 324–340.

Floyd, M., & Scogin, F. (1997). Effects of memory training on the subjective memory functioning and mental health of older adults: A meta-analysis. *Psychology and Aging, 12*, 150–161.

Fox, S. G., & Walters, H. A. (1986). The impact of general versus specific expert testimony and eyewitness confidence upon mock juror judgment. *Law and Human Behavior, 10*(3), 215–228.

Fu, T., Koutstaal, W., Fu, C., Poon, L., & Cleare, A. J. (2005). Depression, confidence, and decision: Evidence against depressive realism. *Journal of Psychopathology and Behavioral Assessment, 27*, 243–252.

Fuchs, L. S., Fuchs, D., Prentice, K., Burch, M., Hamlett, C. L., Owen, R., & Schroeter, K. (2003). Enhancing third-grade students' mathematical problem solving with self-regulated learning strategies. *Journal of Educational Psychology, 95*, 306–315.

Funnell, M., Metcalfe, J., & Tsapkini, K. (1996). In the mind but not on the tongue: Feeling of knowing in an anomic patient. In L. M. Reder (Ed.), *Implicit memory and metacognition* (pp. 171–194). Mahwah, NJ: Lawrence Erlbaum.

Gardiner, J. M., Craik, F. I., & Bleasdale, F. A. (1973). Retrieval difficulty and subsequent recall. *Memory & Cognition, 1*, 213–216.

Garrett, M., & Silva, R. (2003). Auditory hallucinations, source monitoring, and the belief that "voices" are real. *Schizophrenia Bulletin, 29*, 445–457.

Gigerenzer, G. (1984). External validity of laboratory experiments: The frequency-validity relationship. *American Journal of Psychology, 97*, 185–195.

Gigerenzer, G. (1991). How to make cognitive illusions disappear: Beyond "heuristics and biases." In W. Stroebe & M. Hewstone (Eds.), *European Review of Social Psychology, 2,* 83–115. Chichester, UK: Wiley.

Gigerenzer, G. (1994). Why the distinction between single-event probabilities and frequencies is relevant for psychology (and vice versa). In G. Wright & P. Ayton (Eds.), *Subjective probability* (pp. 129–161). New York: Wiley.

Gigerenzer, G., Hoffrage, U., & Kleinbölting, H. (1991). Probabilistic mental models: A Brunswikian theory of confidence. *Psychological Review, 98,* 506–528.

Gigerenzer, G., Todd, P. M., & ABC Research Group. (1999). *Simple heuristics that make us smart.* New York: Oxford University Press.

Gilewski, M. J., & Zelinski, E. M. (1986). Questionnaire assessment of memory complaints. In L. W. Poon, B. Gurland, C. Eisdorfer, T. Crook, L. W. Thompson, A. Kaszniak, et al. (Eds.), *Handbook for clinical memory assessment of older adults* (pp. 93–107). Washington, DC: American Psychological Association.

Gilewski, M. J., Zelinski, E. M., Schaie, K. W., & Thompson, L. W. (1983). *Abbreviating the metamemory questionnaire: Factor structure and norms for adults.* Paper presented at the 91st annual meeting of the American Psychological Association, Anaheim, CA.

Gilovich, T., Griffin, D., & Kahneman, D. (Eds.). (2002). *Heuristics and biases: The psychology of intuitive judgment.* New York: Cambridge University Press.

Glenberg, A. M., & Epstein, W. (1987). Inexpert calibration of comprehension. *Memory & Cognition, 115,* 119–136.

Glenberg, A. M., Wilkinson, A. C., & Epstein, W. (1982). The illusion of knowing: Failure in the self-assessment of comprehension. *Memory & Cognition, 10,* 597–602.

Glisky, E. L., Rubin, S. R., & Davidson, P. S. R. (2001). Source memory in older adults: An encoding or retrieval problem? *Journal of Experimental Psychology: Learning, Memory, and Cognition, 27,* 1131–1146.

Gonzalez, R., & Nelson, T. O. (1996). Measuring ordinal association in situations that contain tied scores. *Psychological Bulletin, 119,* 159–165.

Greene, J. A., & Azevedo, R. (2007). A theoretical review of Winne and Hadwin's model of self-regulated learning: New perspectives and directions. *Review of Educational Research, 77,* 334–372.

Griffin, D., & Buehler, R. (1999). Frequency, probability, and prediction: Easy solutions to cognitive illusions? *Cognitive Psychology, 38,* 48–78.

Groninger, L. D. (1976). Predicting recognition during storage: The capacity of the memory system to evaluate itself. *Bulletin of the Psychonomic Society, 7,* 425–428.

Hacker, D. J. (1998a). Definitions and empirical foundations. In D. J. Hacker, J. Dunlosky, & A. C. Graesser (Eds.), *Metacognition in educational theory and practice* (pp. 1–24). Hillsdale, NJ: Lawrence Erlbaum.

Hacker, D. J. (1998b). Self-regulated comprehension during normal reading. In D. J. Hacker, J. Dunlosky, & A. C. Graesser (Eds.), *Metacognition in educational theory and practice* (pp. 165–191). Hillsdale, NJ: Lawrence Erlbaum.

Hacker, D. J., Bol, L., Horgan, D. D., & Rakow, E. A. (2000). Test prediction and performance in a classroom context. *Journal of Educational Psychology, 92,* 160–170.

Hacker, D. J., Bol, L., & Keener, M. C. (2008). Metacognition in education: A focus on calibration. In J. Dunlosky & R. A. Bjork (Eds.), *Handbook of metamemory and memory* (pp. 429–455). New York: Taylor & Francis.

Hampton, R. R. (2001). Rhesus monkeys know when they remember. *Proceedings of the National Academy of Sciences, 98,* 5359–5362.

Hancock, J. A., Moffoot, A. P. R., & O'Carroll, R. E. (1996). "Depressive realism" assessed via confidence in decision-making. *Cognitive Neuropsychiatry, 1,* 213–220.

Hansen, M. B., & Markman, E. M. (2005). Appearance questions can be misleading: A discourse-based account of the appearance-reality problem. *Cognitive Psychology, 50,* 233–263.

Hare, V. C., & Smith, D. C. (1982). Reading to remember: Studies of metacognitive reading skills in elementary school-aged children. *Journal of Educational Research, 75,* 157–164.

Harris, P. L., Brown, E., Mariott, C., Whittall, S., & Harmer, S. (1991). Monsters, ghosts, and witches: Testing the limits of fantasy-reality distinction in young children. *British Journal of Developmental Psychology, 9,* 105–123.

Hart, J. T. (1965). Memory and the feeling-of-knowing experience. *Journal of Educational Psychology, 56,* 208–216.

Hart, J. T. (1966). Methodological note on feeling-of-knowing experiments. *Journal of Educational Psychology, 57,* 347–349.

Hart, J. T. (1967). Memory and the memory-monitoring process. *Journal of Verbal Learning and Verbal Behavior, 6,* 685–691.

Hasher, L., Goldstein, D., & Toppino, T. (1977). Frequency and the conference of referential validity. *Journal of Verbal Learning and Verbal Behavior, 16,* 107–112.

Hayes, J. R., & Flower, L. (1980). Identifying the organization of writing processes. In L. W. Gregg & E. R. Steinberg (Eds.), *Cognitive processes in writing.* Hillsdale, NJ: Lawrence Erlbaum.

Herrmann, D. J. (1982). Know the memory: The use of questionnaires to assess and study memory. *Psychological Bulletin, 92,* 434–452.

Hertzog, C., & Dunlosky, J. (2004). Aging, metacognition, and cognitive control. *The Psychology of Learning and Motivation: Advances in Research and Theory, 45,* 215–251.

Hertzog, C., Dunlosky, J., Robinson, A. E., & Kidder, D. P. (2003). Encoding fluency is a cue used for judgments about learning. *Journal of Experimental Psychology: Learning, Memory, and Cognition, 29,* 22–34.

Hertzog, C., & Hultsch, D. F. (2000). Metacognition in adulthood and old age. In F. I. M. Craik (Ed.), *The handbook of aging and cognition* (2nd ed., pp. 417–466) Mahwah, NJ: Lawrence Erlbaum.

Hertzog, C., Kidder, D., Powell-Moman, A., & Dunlosky, J. (2002). Monitoring associative learning: What determines the accuracy of metacognitive judgments? *Psychology and Aging, 17,* 209–225.

Hicks, J. L., & Marsh, R. L. (1999). Attempts to reduce the incidence of false recall with source monitoring. *Journal of Experimental Psychology: Learning, Memory, and Cognition, 25,* 1195–1209.

Horn, J. L. (1989). Models of intelligence. In R. L. Linn (Ed.), *Intelligence: Measurement, theory, and public policy* (pp. 29–73). Urbana: University of Illinois Press.

Hothersall, D. (1995). *History of psychology* (3rd ed.). New York: McGraw-Hill.

Hubert, W., & de Jong-Meyer, R. (1989). Emotional stress and saliva cortisol response: Report on the workshop conference "Application of saliva in laboratory medicine." *Journal of Clinical Chemistry and Clinical Biochemistry, 27,* 235–237.

Hulicka, I. M., & Grossman, J. L. (1967). Age-group comparisons for the use of mediators in paired associate learning. *Journal of Gerontology, 22,* 46–51.

Hultsch, D. F., Hertzog, C., & Dixon, R. A. (1987). Age differences in metamemory: Resolving the inconsistencies. *Canadian Journal of Psychology/Revue Canadienne de Psychologie, 41,* 193–208.

Humphrey, G. (1951). *Thinking: An introduction to its experimental psychology.* New York: Wiley.

Hunt, R. R., & Ellis, H. C. (2004). *Fundamentals of cognitive psychology* (7th ed.). New York: McGraw-Hill.

Inbau, F. E., Reid, J. E., Buckley, J. P., & Jayne, B. P. (2001). *Criminal interrogations and confessions.* Gaithersburg, MD: Aspen.

Inhelder, B., & Piaget, J. (1958). Formal thought from the equilibrium standpoint. In *The growth of logical thinking from childhood to adolescence* (pp. 245–271). New York: Basic Books.

Israel, S. E., Block, C. C., Bauserman, K. L., & Kinnucan-Welsch, K. (Eds.). (2005). *Metacognition in literacy learning: Theory, assessment, instruction, and professional development.* Hillsdale, NJ: Lawrence Erlbaum.

Izaute, M., & Bacon, E. (2005). Specific effects of an amnesic drug: Effect of lorazepam on study time allocation and on judgment of learning. *Neuropsychopharmacology, 30,* 196–204.

Jacoby, L. L. (1991). A process dissociation framework: Separating automatic from intentional uses of memory. *Journal of Memory and Language, 30,* 513–541.

Jacoby, L. L. (1998). Invariance in automatic influences of memory: Toward a user's guide for the process-dissociation procedure. *Journal of Experimental Psychology: Learning, Memory, and Cognition, 24,* 3–26.

Jacoby, L. L., Kelley, C., Brown, J., Jasechko, J. (1989). Becoming famous overnight: Limits on the ability to avoid unconscious influences of the past. *Journal of Personality and Social Psychology, 56,* 326–338.

Jacoby, L. L., Woloshyn, V., & Kelley, C. M. (1989). Becoming famous without being recognized: Unconscious influences of memory produced by dividing attention. *Journal of Experimental Psychology: General, 118,* 115–125.

James, L. E., & Burke, D. M. (2000). Phonological priming effects on word retrieval and tip-of-the-tongue experiences in young and older adults. *Journal of Experimental Psychology: Learning, Memory, and Cognition, 26,* 1378–1391.

James, W. (1920). *The principles of psychology* (Vol. 1). American Science Series/ Advanced Courses. New York: Henry Holt.

Jameson, K. A., Narens, L., Goldfarb, K., & Nelson, T. O. (1990). The influence of near-threshold priming on metamemory and recall. *Acta Psychologica, 73,* 55–68.

Janowsky, J. S., Shimamura, A. P., & Squire, L. R. (1989). Memory and metamemory: Comparisons between frontal lobe lesions and amnesic patients. *Psycholobiology, 17,* 3–11.

Jennings, J. M., & Jacoby, L. L. (2003). Improving memory in older adults: Training recollections. *Neuropsychological Rehabilitation, 13,* 417–440.

Jennings, J. M., Webster, L. M., Kleykamp, B., & Dagenbach, D. (2005). Recollection training and transfer effects in older adults: Successful use of a repetition-lag procedure. *Aging, Neuropsychology, and Cognition, 12,* 278–298.

Johansson, B., Allen-Burge, R., & Zarit, S. H. (1997). Self-reports on memory functioning in a longitudinal study of the oldest old: Relation to current, prospective, and retrospective performance. *Journals of Gerontology: Series C: Psychological Sciences and Social Sciences, 52B,* P139–P146.

Johnson, M. K. (1983). A multiple-entry, modular memory system. In G. H. Bower (Ed.), *The psychology of learning and motivation: Advances in research and theory* (Vol. 17, pp. 81–123). New York: Academic Press.

Johnson, M. K. (2005). The relation between source memory and episodic memory: Comment on Siedlecki et al. *Psychology and Aging, 20,* 529–531.

Johnson, M. K., Foley, M. A., & Leach, K. (1988). The consequences for memory of imagining in another person's voice. *Memory & Cognition, 16,* 337–342.

Johnson, M. K., Hashtroudi, S., & Lindsay, D. S. (1993). Source monitoring. *Psychological Bulletin, 114,* 3–28.

Johnson, M. K., Hayes, S. M., D'Esposito, M., & Raye, C. L. (2000). Confabulation. In F. Boller & J. Grafman (Series Eds.) & L. S. Cermak (Vol. Ed.), *Handbook of neuropsychology: Vol. 2. Memory and its disorders* (2nd ed., pp. 383–407). Amsterdam: Elsevier Science.

Johnson, M. K., & Mitchell, K. J. (2002). Source monitoring. In J. H. Byrne (Ed.), *Learning and memory* (2nd ed., pp. 628–631). New York: Macmillan Reference USA.

Johnson, M. K., & Raye, C. L. (1981). Reality monitoring. *Psychological Review, 88,* 67–85.

Johnson, M. K., Raye, C. L., Wang, A. Y., & Taylor, T. H. (1979). Fact and fantasy: The roles of accuracy and variability in confusing imaginations with perceptual experiences. *Journal of Experimental Psychology: Human Learning and Memory, 5,* 229–240.

Jönsson, F. U., & Olsson, M. J. (2003). Olfactory metacognition. *Chemical Senses, 28,* 651–658.

Jungermann, H. (1983). The two camps on rationality. In R. W. Scholz (Ed.), *Decision making under uncertainty.* Amsterdam: Elsevier.

Juslin, P. (1993). An explanation of the hard-easy effect in studies of realism of confidence in one's general knowledge. *European Journal of Cognitive Psychology, 5,* 55–71.

Juslin, P., Olsson, H., & Björkman, M. (1997). Brunswikian and Thurstonian origins of bias in probability assessment: On the interpretation of stochastic components of judgment. *Journal of Behavioral Decision Making, 10,* 189–209.

Kassin, S. M., & Sukel, H. (1997). Coerced confessions and the jury: An experimental test of the "harmless error" rule. *Law and Human Behavior, 21,* 27–46.

Kausler, D. H. (1994). *Learning and memory in normal aging.* San Diego, CA: Academic Press.

Kelemen, W. L. (2000). Metamemory cues and monitoring accuracy: Judging what you know and what you will know. *Journal of Educational Psychology, 92,* 800–810.

Kelemen, W. L., & Creeley, C. E. (2001). Caffeine (4 mg/kg) influences sustained attention and delayed free recall but not memory predictions. *Human Psychopharmacology, 16,* 309–319.

Kelemen, W. L., & Weaver, C. A. (1997). Enhanced metamemory at delays: Why do judgments of learning improve over time? *Journal of Experimental Psychology: Learning, Memory, and Cognition, 23,* 1394–1409.

Kelley, C. M., & Jacoby, L. (2000). Recollection and familiarity: Process-dissociation. In E. Tulving & F. I. M. Craik (Eds.), *The Oxford handbook of memory* (pp. 215–228). New York: Oxford University Press.

Kelley, C. M., & Sahakyan, L. (2003). Memory, monitoring, and control in the attainment of memory accuracy. *Journal of Memory and Language, 48,* 704–721.

Kennedy, M. R. T., Carney, E., & Peters, S. M. (2003). Predictions of recall and study strategy decisions after diffuse brain injury. *Brain Injury, 17,* 1043–1064.

Keren, G. (1990). Cognitive aids and debiasing methods: Can cognitive pills cure cognitive ills? In J. Caverni, J. Fabre, & M. Gonzalez (Eds.), *Cognitive biases.* Oxford, UK: North-Holland.

Keren, G. (1991). Calibration and probability judgments: Conceptual and methodological issues. *Acta Psychologica, 77,* 217–273.

Kikyo, H., Ohki, K., & Miyashita, Y. (2002). Neural correlates for feeling-of-knowing: An fMRI parametric analysis. *Neuron, 36,* 177–186.

Kimball, D. R., & Metcalfe, J. (2003). Delaying judgments of learning affects memory, not metamemory. *Memory & Cognition, 31,* 918–929.

King, J. F., Zechmeister, E. B., & Shaughnessy, J. J. (1980). Judgments of knowing: The influence of retrieval practice. *American Journal of Psychology, 93,* 329–343.

Kinsbourne, M. (1995). Awareness of one's own body: An attentional theory of its nature, development, and brain basis. In J. Berm'dez, N. Eilan, & A. Marcel (Eds.), *The body and the self* (pp. 206–223). Cambridge: MIT Press.

Kintsch, W. (1988). *Comprehension: A paradigm for cognition.* Cambridge, UK: Cambridge University Press.

Kluwe, R. H. (1982). Cognitive knowledge and executive control: Metacognition. In D. R. Griffin (Ed.), *Animal mind—human mind.* (pp. 201–224). New York: Springer-Verlag.

Knoblich, G., Stottmeister, F., & Kircher, T. (2004). Self-monitoring in patients with schizophrenia. *Psychological Medicine, 34,* 1561–1569.

Köhnken, G. (1987). Training police officers to detect deceptive eyewitness statements: Does it work? *Social Behaviour, 2,* 1–17.

Kolers, P. A., & Palef, S. R. (1976). Knowing not. *Memory & Cognition, 4,* 553–558.

Koriat, A. (1993). How do we know that we know? The accessibility model of the feeling of knowing. *Psychological Review, 100,* 609–639.

Koriat, A. (1994). Memory's knowledge of its own knowledge: The accessibility account of the feeling of knowing. In J. Metcalfe & A. P. Shimamura (Eds.), *Metacognition: Knowing about knowing* (pp. 115–136). Cambridge: MIT Press.

Koriat, A. (1995). Dissociating knowing and the feeling of knowing: Further evidence for the accessibility model. *Journal of Experimental Psychology: General, 124*, 311–333.

Koriat, A. (1997). Monitoring one's own knowledge during study: A cue-utilization approach to judgments of learning. *Journal of Experimental Psychology: General, 126*, 349–370.

Koriat, A., & Goldsmith, M. (1996). Monitoring and control processes in the strategic regulation of memory accuracy. *Psychological Review, 103*, 490–517.

Koriat, A., & Levy-Sadot, R. (2001). The combined contributions of the cue-familiarity and accessibility heuristics to feelings of knowing. *Journal of Experimental Psychology: Learning, Memory, and Cognition, 27*, 34–53.

Koriat, A., Lichtenstein, S., & Fischhoff, B. (1980). Reasons for confidence. *Journal of Experimental Psychology: Human Learning and Memory, 6*, 107–118.

Koriat, A., Sheffer, L., & Ma'ayan, H. (2002). Comparing objective and subjective learning curves: Judgments of learning exhibit increased underconfidence with practice. *Journal of Experimental Psychology: General, 131*, 147–162.

Koriat, A., & Shitzer-Reichert, R. (2002). Metacognitive judgments and their accuracy: Insights from the processes underlying judgments of learning in children. In P. Chambres, M. Izaute, & P.-J. Marescaux (Eds.), *Metacognition: Process, function, and use* (pp. 1–18). Dordrecht, Netherlands: Kluwer Academic.

Kornell, N., & Metcalfe, J. (2006). "Blockers" do not block recall during tip-of-the-tongue states. *Metacognition and Learning, 1*, 248–261.

Kornell, N., Son, L. K., & Terrace, H. S. (2007). Transfer of metacognitive skills and hint seeking in monkeys. *Psychological Science, 18*, 64–71.

Kosslyn, S. M., Alpert, N. M., Thompson, W. L., Maljkovic, V., Weise, S. B., Chabris, C. F., et al. (1993). Visual mental imagery activates topographically organized visual cortex: PET investigations. *Journal of Cognitive Neuroscience, 5*, 263–287.

Kosslyn, S. M., & Thompson, W. L. (2000). Shared mechanisms in visual imagery and visual perception: Insights from cognitive neuroscience. In M. S. Gazzaniga (Ed.), *The new cognitive neurosciences* (2nd ed., pp. 975–985). Cambridge: MIT Press.

Kramarski, B., Mevarech, Z. R., & Arami, M. (2002). The effects of metacognitive instruction on solving mathematical authentic tasks. *Educational Studies in Mathematics, 49*, 225–250.

Kraut, R. E., & Poe, D. (1980). Behavioral roots of person perception: The deception judgments of customs inspectors and laymen. *Journal of Personality and Social Psychology, 39*, 784–798.

Kreutzer, M. A., Leonard, C., & Flavell, J. H. (1975). An interview study of children's knowledge about memory. *Monographs of the Society for Research in Child Development, 40*, 1–60.

Krinsky, R., & Nelson, T. O. (1985). The feeling of knowing for different types of retrieval failure. *Acta Psychologica, 58*, 141–158.

Kroll, N. E. A., & Kellicutt, M. H. (1972). Short-term recall as a function of covert rehearsal and of intervening task. *Journal of Verbal Learning and Verbal Behavior, 11*, 196–204.

Kroll, N. E. A., Knight, R. T., Metcalfe, J., Wolf, E., & Tulving, E. (1996). Cohesion failure as a source of memory illusions. *Journal of Memory and Language, 35*, 176–196.

Kruger, J., & Dunning, D. (1999). Unskilled and unaware of it: How difficulties in recognizing one's incompetence lead to inflated self-assessments. *Journal of Personality and Social Psychology, 77*, 1121–1134.

Kucan, L., & Beck, I. L. (1997). Thinking aloud and reading comprehension research: Inquiry, instruction, and social interaction. *Review of Educational Research, 67*, 271–299.

LaBine, S. J., & LaBine, G. (1996). Determinations of negligence and the hindsight bias. *Law and Human Behavior, 20*, 501–516.

Lachman, J. L., Lachman, R., & Thronesbery, C. (1979). Metamemory through the adult life span. *Developmental Psychology, 15*, 543–551.

Lachman, M. E. (1991). Perceived control over memory aging: Developmental and intervention perspectives. *Journal of Social Issues, 47*, 159–175.

Lachman, M. E. (2006). Perceived control over aging-related declines: Adaptive beliefs and behaviors. *Current Directions in Psychological Science, 15*, 282–286.

Lachman, M. E., & Andreoletti, C. (2006). Strategy use mediates the relationship between control beliefs and memory performance for middle-aged and older adults. *Journals of Gerontology: Series B: Psychological Sciences and Social Sciences, 61B*, P88–P94.

Lachman, M. E., Weaver, S. L., Bandura, M., & Elliott, E. (1992). Improving memory and control beliefs through cognitive restructuring and self-generated strategies. *Journals of Gerontology, 47*, P293–P299.

Lachman, R., Lachman, J. L., & Butterfield, E. C. (1979). *Cognitive psychology and information processing: An introduction.* Hillsdale, NJ: Lawrence Erlbaum.

Lane, S. M., Roussel, C. C., Villa, D., & Morita, S. K. (2007). Features and feedback: Enhancing metamnemonic knowledge at retrieval reduces source-monitoring errors. *Journal of Experimental Psychology: Learning, Memory, and Cognition, 33*, 1131–1142.

Leichtman, M., & Ceci, S. (1995). The effects of stereotypes and suggestions on preschoolers' reports. *Developmental Psychology, 31*, 568–578.

Le Ny, J.-F., Denhière, G., and Le Taillanter, D. (1972). Study-time of sentences as a function of their specificity and of semantic exploration. *Acta Psychologica, 37*, 43–53.

Leonesio, R. J., & Nelson, T. O. (1990). Do different metamemory judgments tap the same underlying aspects of memory? *Journal of Experimental Psychology: Learning, Memory, and Cognition, 16*, 464–470.

Leslie, A. M. (1987). Pretense and representation: The origins of "theory of mind." *Psychological Review, 94*, 412–426.

Leslie, A. M. (2005). Developmental parallels in understanding minds and bodies. *Trends in Cognitive Psychology, 9*, 459–462.

Lichtenstein, S., & Fischhoff, B. (1977). Do those who know more also know more about how much they know? *Organizational Behavior and Human Performance, 20,* 159–183.

Lichtenstein, S., & Fischhoff, B. (1980). *How well do probability experts assess probability?* (Decision Research Report 80-5). Eugene, OR: Decision Research.

Lichtenstein, S., Fischhoff, B., & Phillips, L. D. (1982). Calibration of probabilities: The state of the art to 1980. In D. Kahneman, P. Slovic, & A. Tversky (Eds.), *Judgment under uncertainty: Heuristics and biases* (pp. 306–334). Cambridge, UK: Cambridge University Press.

Lieberman, D. A. (1979). Behaviorism and the mind: A (limited) call for a return to introspection. *American Psychologist, 34,* 319–333.

Lin, L.-M., & Zabrucky, K. M. (1998). Calibration of comprehension: Research and implications for education and instruction. *Contemporary Educational Psychology, 23,* 345–391.

Lindsay, S., & Johnson, M. K. (1989). The eyewitness suggestibility effect and memory for source. *Memory & Cognition, 17,* 349–358.

Lindsay, S., & Johnson, M. K. (1991). Recognition memory and source monitoring. *Bulletin of the Psychonomic Society, 29,* 203–205.

Lineweaver, T. T., & Hertzog, C. (1998). Adults' efficacy and control beliefs regarding memory and aging: Seperating general from personal beliefs. *Aging, Neuropsychology, and Cognition, 5,* 264–296.

Lockl, L., & Schneider, W. (2002). Developmental trends in children's feeling-of-knowing judgements. *International Journal of Behavioral Development, 26,* 327–333.

Lockl, L., & Schneider, W. (2007). Knowledge about the mind: Links between theory of mind and later metamemory. *Child Development, 78,* 148–167.

Loftus, E. F. (1977). Shifting human color memory. *Memory & Cognition, 5,* 696–699.

Loftus, E. F., Coan, J. A., & Pickrell, J. E. (1996). Manufacturing false memories using bits of reality. In L. M. Reder (Ed.), *Implicit memory and metacognition* (pp. 195–220). Hillsdale, NJ: Lawrence Erlbaum. (Original work published 1979)

Loftus, E. F., & Hoffman, H. G. (1989). Misinformation and memory: The creation of memory. *Journal of Experimental Psychology: General, 118,* 100–104.

Loftus, E. F., & Ketcham, K. (1991). *Witness for the defense: The accused, the eyewitness, and the expert who puts memory on trial.* New York: St. Martin's Press.

Loftus, E. F., Miller, D. G., & Burns, H. J. (1978). Semantic integration of verbal information into a visual memory. *Journal of Experimental Psychology: Human Learning and Memory, 4,* 19–31.

Loftus, E. F., & Pickrell, J. E. (1995). The formation of false memories. *Psychiatric Annals, 25,* 720–725.

Lovelace, E. A. (1984). Metamemory: Monitoring future recallability during study. *Journal of Experimental Psychology: Learning, Memory, and Cognition, 10,* 756–766.

Lovelace, E. A., & Marsh, G. R. (1985). Prediction and evaluation of memory performance by young and old adults. *Journal of Gerontology, 40,* 192–197.

Maki, R. H. (1998). Predicting performance on text: Delayed versus immediate predictions and tests. *Memory & Cognition, 26,* 959–964.

Maki, R. H., & Berry, S. L. (1984). Metacomprehension of text material. *Journal of Experimental Psychology: Learning, Memory, and Cognition, 10,* 663–679.

Maki, R. H., & McGuire, M. J. (2002). Metacognition for text: Findings and implications for education. In T. J. Perfect & B. L. Schwartz (Eds.), *Applied metacognition* (pp. 39–67). New York: Cambridge University Press.

Mandler, G. (1967). Organization and memory. In K. W. Spence & J. T. Spence (Eds.), *The psychology of learning and motivation* (pp. 327–372). New York: Academic Press.

Mann, S., Vrij, A., & Bull, R. (2002). Suspects, lies and videotape: An analysis of authentic high-stakes liars. *Law and Human Behavior, 26,* 365–376.

Maril, A., Simons, J. S., Mitchell, J., Schwartz, B., & Schacter, D. L. (2003). Feeling-of-knowing in episodic memory: An event-related fMRI study. *NeuroImage, 18,* 827–836.

Markman, E. M. (1977). Realizing that you don't understand: A preliminary investigation. *Child Development, 48,* 986–992.

Markman, E. M. (1979). Realizing that you don't understand: Elementary school children's awareness of inconsistencies. *Child Development, 50,* 643–655.

Marquié, J. C., & Huet, N. (2000). Age differences in feeling-of-knowing and confidence judgments as a function of knowledge domain. *Psychology and Aging, 15,* 451–461.

Marsh, R. L., & Bower, G. H. (1993). Eliciting cryptomnesia: Unconscious plagiarism in a puzzle task. *Journal of Experimental Psychology: Learning, Memory, and Cognition, 19,* 673–688.

Marazita, J. M., & Merriman, W. E. (2004). Young children's judgment of whether they know names for objects: The metalinguistic ability it reflects and the processes it involves. *Journal of Memory and Language, 51,* 458–472.

Masson, M. E. J., & Rotello, C. M. (2008). *Bias in the Goodman-Kruskal gamma coefficient measure of discrimination accuracy.* Unpublished manuscript.

Masur, E. F., McIntyre, C. W., & Flavell, J. H. (1973). Developmental changes in apportionment of study time among items in a multitrial free recall task. *Journal of Experimental Child Psychology, 15,* 237–246.

Mather, M., Mitchell, K. J., Raye, C. L., Novak, D. L., Greene, E. J., & Johnson, M. K. (2006). Emotional arousal can impair feature binding in working memory. *Journal of Cognitive Neuroscience, 18,* 614–625.

May, C. P., Rahhal, T., Berry, E. M., & Leighton, E. A. (2005). Aging, source memory, and emotion. *Psychology and Aging, 20,* 571–578.

Mazzoni, G., & Nelson, T. O. (1995). Judgments of learning are affected by the kind of encoding in ways that cannot be attributed to the level of recall. *Journal of Experimental Psychology: Learning, Memory, and Cognition, 21,* 1263–1274.

McClelland, A. G. R., & Bolger, F. (1994). The calibration of subjective probabilities: Theories and models 1980–1994. In G. Wright & P. Ayton (Eds.), *Subjective probability* (pp. 453–482). Chichester, UK: Wiley.

McCloskey, M., & Zaragoza, M. (1985). Misleading postevent information and memory for events: Arguments and evidence against memory impairment hypotheses. *Journal of Experimental Psychology: General, 114,* 1–16.

McDonald-Miszczak, L., Hertzog, C., & Hultsch, D. F. (1995). Stability and accuracy of metamemory in adulthood and aging longitudinal analysis. *Psychology and Aging, 10,* 553–564.

McGlynn, S. M. (1998). Impaired awareness of deficits in a psychiatric context: Implications for rehabilitation. In D. J. Hacker, J. Dunlosky, & A. C. Graesser (Eds.), *Metacognition in educational theory and practice* (pp. 221–248). Mahwah, NJ: Lawrence Erlbaum.

McGuire, M. J., & Maki, R. H. (2001). When knowing more means less: The effects of fan on metamemory judgments. *Journal of Experimental Psychology: Learning, Memory, and Cognition, 27,* 1172–1179.

Meeter, M., & Nelson, T. O. (2003). Multiple study trials and judgments of learning. *Acta Psychologica, 113,* 123–132.

Merriman, W. E., & Bowman, L. L. (1989). The mutual exclusivity bias in children's word learning. *Monographs of the Society for Child Development, 54,* i–129.

Metcalfe, J. (1993). Novelty monitoring, metacognition, and control in a composite holographic associative recall model: Implications for Korsakoff amnesia. *Psychological Review, 100,* 3–22.

Metcalfe, J. (1994). A computational modeling approach to novelty monitoring, metacognition, and frontal lobe dysfunction. In J. Metcalfe & A. P. Shimamura (Eds.), *Metacognition: Knowing about knowing* (pp. 137–156). Cambridge: MIT Press.

Metcalfe, J. (2002). Is study time allocated selectively to a region of proximal learning? *Journal of Experimental Psychology: General, 131,* 349–363.

Metcalfe, J. (2008). Evolution of metacognition. In J. Dunlosky & R. A. Bjork (Eds.), *Handbook of metamemory and memory* (pp. 29–46). New York: Taylor & Francis.

Metcalfe, J., & Kornell, N. (2003). The dynamics of learning and allocation of study time to a region of proximal learning. *Journal of Experimental Psychology: General, 132,* 530–542.

Metcalfe, J., & Kornell, N. (2005). A region of proximal learning model of study time allocation. *Journal of Memory and Language, 52,* 463–477.

Metcalfe, J., Schwartz, B. L., & Joaquim, S. G. (1993). The cue-familiarity heuristic in metacognition. *Journal of Experimental Psychology: Learning, Memory, and Cognition, 19,* 851–861.

Miles, J. R., & Stine-Morrow, E. A. L. (2004). Adult age differences in self-regulated learning from reading sentences. *Psychology and Aging, 19,* 626–636.

Miller, G. A. (1962). *Psychology: The science of mental life.* New York: Harper & Row.

Miller, G. A., Galanter, E., & Pribram, K. H. (1960). *Plans and the structure of behavior.* New York: Henry Holt.

Miller, P. H. (1994). Individual differences in children's strategic behavior: Utilization deficiencies. *Learning and Individual Differences, 6,* 285–307.

Miller, P. H., Seier, W. L., Barron, K. L., & Probert, J. S. (1994). What causes a utilization deficiency? *Cognitive Development, 9,* 77–102.

Miner, A. C., & Reder, L. M. (1994). A new look at feeling of knowing: Its metacognitive role in regulating question answering. In J. Metcalfe & A. P. Shimamura (Eds.), *Metacognition: Knowing about knowing* (pp. 47–70). Cambridge: MIT Press.

Miozzo, M., & Caramazza, A. (1997). Retrieval of lexical-syntactic features in tip-of-the tongue states. *Journal of Experimental Psychology: Learning, Memory, and Cognition, 23,* 1410–1423.

Mitchell, K. J., & Johnson, M. K. (2000). Source monitoring: Attributing mental experiences. In E. Tulving & F. I. M. Craik (Eds.), *The Oxford handbook of memory* (pp. 179–195). New York: Oxford University Press.

Mitchell, K. J., Johnson, M. K., Raye, C. L., & Greene, E. J. (2004). Prefrontal cortex activity associated with source monitoring in a working memory task. *Journal of Cognitive Neuroscience, 16,* 921–934.

Morgan, C. A., III, Hazlett, G. A., Doran, A., Garrett, S., Hoyt, G., & Thomas, P., et al. (2004). Accuracy of eyewitness memory for persons encountered during exposure to highly intense stress. *International Journal of Law and Psychiatry, 27,* 265–279.

Morris, C. C. (1990). Retrieval processes underlying confidence in comprehension judgments. *Journal of Experimental Psychology: Learning, Memory, and Cognition, 16,* 223–232.

Moses, L. J., Carlson, S. M., & Sabbagh, M. A. (2005). On the specificity of the relation between executive function and children's theories of mind. In W. Schneider, R. Schumann-Hengsteler, & B. Sodian (Eds.), *Young children's cognitive development* (pp. 131–146). Hillsdale, NJ: Lawrence Erlbaum.

Moulin, C. J. A. (2002). Sense and sensitivity: Metacognition in Alzheimer's disease. In T. J. Perfect & B. L. Schwartz (Eds.), *Applied metacognition* (pp. 197–223). New York: Cambridge University Press.

Moulin, C. J. A., Perfect, T. J., & Fitch, F. (2002). Metacognitive processes at encoding. In P. Chambres, M. Izaute, & P.-J. Marescaux (Eds.), *Metacognition: Process, function and use* (pp. 35–48.) Dordrecht, Netherlands: Kluwer Academic.

Moulin, C. J. A., Perfect, T. J., & Jones, R. W. (2000). Evidence for intact memory in Alzheimer's disease: Metamemory sensitivity at encoding. *Neuropsychologia, 38,* 1242–1250.

Multhaup, K. S. (1995). Aging, source, and decision criteria: When false fame errors do and do not occur. *Psychology and Aging, 10,* 492–497.

Murnane, K., & Bayen, U. J. (1996). An evaluation of empirical measures of source identification. *Memory & Cognition, 24,* 417–428.

Murphy, M. D., Schmitt, F. A., Caruso, M. J., & Sanders, R. E. (1987). Metamemory in older adults: The role of monitoring in serial recall. *Psychology and Aging, 2,* 331–339.

Musch, J. (2003). Personality differences in hindsight bias. *Memory, 11,* 473–489.

Musch, J., & Wagner, T. (2007). Did everybody know it all along? A review of individual differences in hindsight bias. *Social Cognition, 25,* 64–82.

Myers, M., & Paris, S. G. (1978). Children's metacognitive knowledge about reading. *Journal of Educational Psychology, 70,* 680–690.

Naveh-Benjamin, M., Brav, T. K., & Levy, O. (2007). The associative memory deficit of older adults: The role of strategy utilization. *Psychology and Aging, 22,* 202–208.

Nebes, R. D. (1992). Cognitive dysfunction in Alzheimer's disease. In F. I. M. Craik & T. A. Salthouse (Eds.), *The handbook of aging and cognition* (pp. 373–446). Hillsdale, NJ: Lawrence Erlbaum.

Neisser, U. (1967). *Cognitive psychology.* New York: Appleton-Century-Crofts.

Nelson, T. O. (1984). A comparison of current measures of the accuracy of feeling-of-knowing predictions. *Psychological Bulletin, 95,* 109–133.

Nelson, T. O. (1996). Consciousness and metacognition. *American Psychologist, 51,* 102–116.

Nelson, T. O., & Dunlosky, J. (1991). When people's judgments of learning (JOLs) are extremely accurate at predicting subsequent recall: The "delayed-JOL effect." *Psychological Science, 2,* 267–270.

Nelson, T. O., Gerler, D., & Narens, L. (1984). Accuracy of feeling of knowing judgments for predicting perceptual identification and relearning. *Journal of Experimental Psychology: General, 113,* 282–300.

Nelson, T. O., Graf, A., Dunlosky, J., Marlatt, A., Walker, D., & Luce, K. (1998). Effect of acute alcohol intoxication on recall and on judgments of learning during the acquisition of new information. In G. Mazzoni & T. O. Nelson (Eds.), *Neuropsychology of metacognition* (pp. 161–180). Hillsdale, NJ: Lawrence Erlbaum.

Nelson, T. O., & Leonesio, R. J. (1988). Allocation of self-paced study time and the "labor-in-vain effect." *Journal of Experimental Psychology: Learning, Memory, and Cognition, 14,* 676–686.

Nelson, T. O., & Narens, L. (1990). Metamemory: A theoretical framework and new findings. In G. H. Bower (Ed.), *The psychology of learning and motivation* (Vol. 26, pp. 125–173). New York: Academic Press.

Nelson, T. O., & Narens, L. (1994). Why investigate metacognition? In J. Metcalfe & A. P. Shimamura (Eds.), *Metacognition: Knowing about knowing* (pp. 1–26). Cambridge: MIT Press.

Neuman, Y., & Schwarz, B. (1998). Is self-explanation while solving problems helpful? The case of analogical problem-solving. *British Journal of Educational Psychology, 68,* 15–24.

Newell, A., & Simon, H. A. (1972). *Human problem solving.* Englewood Cliffs, NJ: Prentice Hall.

Nietfeld, J. L., Cao, L., & Osborne, J. W. (2006). The effect of distributed monitoring exercises and feedback on performance, monitoring accuracy, and self-efficacy. *Metacognition and Learning, 1,* 159–179.

Nisbett, R., & Wilson, T. (1977). Telling more than we can know: Verbal reports on mental processes. *Psychological Review, 84,* 231–259.

Ofir, C., & Mazursky, D. (1997). Does a surprising outcome reinforce or reverse the hindsight bias? *Organizational Behavior and Human Decision Processes, 69,* 51–57.

Onishi, K., & Baillargeon, R. (2005). Do 15-month-old infants understand false beliefs? *Science, 308,* 255–258.

Ornstein, P. A., Naus, M. J., & Liberty, C. (1975). Rehearsal and organizational processes in children's memory. *Child Development, 46,* 818–830.

Oskamp, S. (1965). Overconfidence in case study judgments. *Journal of Consulting Psychology, 29,* 261–265.

Otero, J. (1998). Influence of knowledge activation and context on comprehension monitoring of science texts. In D. J. Hacker, J. Dunlosky, & A. C. Graesser (Eds.), *Metacognition in educational theory and practice* (pp. 145–164). Hillsdale, NJ: Lawrence Erlbaum.

Otero, J., & Kintsch, W. (1992). Failures to detect contradictions in a text: What readers believe versus what they read. *Psychological Science, 3,* 229–235.

Paivio, A. (1969). Mental imagery in associative learning and memory. *Psychological Review, 76,* 241–263.

Palinscar, A. S., & Brown, A. L. (1984). Reciprocal teaching of comprehension-fostering and comprehension-monitoring activities. *Cognition and Instruction, 1,* 117–175.

Pannu, J. K., & Kaszniak, A. W. (2005). Metamemory experiments in neurological populations: A review. *Neuropsychology Review, 15,* 105–130.

Paris, S. G., & Paris, A. H. (2001). Classroom applications of research on self-regulated learning. *Educational Psychologist, 36,* 89–101.

Paris, S. G., Wasik, B. A., & Turner, J. C. (1991). The development of strategic readers. In R. Barr, M. Kamil, P. Mosenthal, & P. D. Pearson (Eds.), *Handbook of reading research* (2nd ed., pp. 609–640). New York: Longman.

Pashler, H., Bain, P. M., Bottge, B. A., Graesser, A., Koedinger, K., McDaniel, M., & Metcalfe, J. (2007). *Organizing instruction and study to improve student learning* (NCER 2007-2004). Washington, DC: National Center for Education Research, Institute of Education Sciences, U.S. Department of Education.

Perfect, T. J., & Stark, L. J. (2008). Tales from the crypt . . . omnesia. In J. Dunlosky & R. A. Bjork (Eds.), *Handbook of metamemory and memory* (pp. 285–314). New York: Taylor & Francis.

Perner, J. (2000). Memory and theory of mind. In E. Tulving & F. I. M. Craik (Eds.), *The Oxford handbook of memory* (pp. 297–312). New York: Oxford University Press.

Perner, J., & Lang, B. (1999). Development of theory of mind and executive control. *Trends in Cognitive Science, 3,* 337–344.

Perrotin, A., Isingrini, M., Souchay, C., Clarys, D., & Taconnat, L. (2006). Episodic feeling-of-knowing accuracy and cued recall in the elderly: Evidence for double dissociation involving executive functioning and processing speed. *Acta Psychologica, 122,* 58–73.

Peskin, J. (1992). Ruse and representations: On children's ability to conceal information. *Developmental Psychology, 28,* 84–89.

Pintrich, P. R. (2000). The role of goal orientation in self-regulated learning. In M. Boekaerts, P. R. Pintrich, & M. Zeidner (Eds.), *Handbook of self-regulation* (pp. 451–502). New York: Academic Press.

Pintrich, P. R., Marx, R., & Boyle, R. (1993). Beyond cold conceptual change: The role of motivational beliefs and classroom contextual factors in the process of conceptual change. *Review of Educational Research, 63,* 167–199.

Plumert, J. M. (1995). Relations between children's overestimation of their physical abilities and accident proneness. *Developmental Psychology, 31,* 866–876.

Plumert, J. M., & Schwebel, D. C. (1997). Social and temperamental influences on children's overestimation of their physical abilities: Links to accidental injuries. *Journal of Experimental Child Psychology, 67,* 317–337.

Pohl, R. F., & Gawlik, B. (1995). Hindsight bias and the misinformation effect: Separating blended recollections from other recollection types. *Memory, 3,* 21–55.

Premack, D., & Woodruff, G. (1978). Does the chimpanzee have a theory of mind? *Behavioral and Brain Sciences, 4,* 515–526.

Pressley, M., & Afflerbach, P. (1995). *Verbal protocols of reading: The nature of constructively responsive reading.* Mahwah, NJ: Lawrence Erlbaum.

Pressley, M., Levin, J. R., & Ghatala, E. S. (1984). Memory strategy monitoring in adults and children. *Journal of Verbal Learning and Verbal Behavior, 23,* 270–288.

Pressley, M., Levin, J. R., Ghatala, E. S., & Ahmad, M. (1987). Test monitoring in young grade school children. *Journal of Experimental Child Psychology, 43,* 96–111.

Pressley, M., Ross, K. A., Levin, J. R., & Ghatala, E. S. (1984). The role of strategy utility knowledge in children's strategy decision making. *Journal of Child Psychology, 38,* 491–504.

Pressley, M., Van Etten, S., Yokoi, L., Freebern, G., & Van Meter, P. (1998). The metacognition of college studentship: A ground theory approach. In D. J. Hacker, J. Dunlosky, & A. C. Graesser (Eds.), *Metacognition in educational theory and practice* (pp. 347–366). Hillsdale, NJ: Lawrence Erlbaum.

Prins, F. J., Veenman, M. V. J., & Elshout, J. J. (2006). The impact of intellectual ability and metacognition on learning: New support for the threshold of problematicity theory. *Learning and Instruction, 16,* 374–387.

Puncochar, J. M., & Fox, P. W. (2004). Confidence in individual and group decision making: When "two heads" are worse than one. *Journal of Educational Psychology, 96,* 582–591.

Rabinowitz, J. C., Ackerman, B. P., Craik, F. I. M., & Hinchley, J. L. (1982). Aging and metamemory: The roles of relatedness and imagery. *Journal of Gerontology, 37,* 688–695.

Ranganath, C., Yonelinas, A. P., Cohen, M. X., Dy, C. J., Tom, S. M., & D'Esposito, M. (2003). Dissociable correlates of recollection and familiarity within the medial temporal lobes. *Neuropsychologia, 42,* 2–13.

Raz, N. (2000). Aging of the brain and its impact on cognitive performance: Integration of structural and functional findings. In F. I. M. Craik & T. A. Salthouse (Eds.), *The handbook of aging and cognition* (2nd ed., pp. 1–90). Mahwah, NJ: Lawrence Erlbaum.

Read, J. D. (1996). From a passing thought to a false memory in 2 minutes: Confusing real and illusory events. *Psychonomic Bulletin & Review, 3,* 105–111.

Reber, R., & Schwarz, N. (1999). Effects of perceptual fluency on judgments of truth. *Consciousness and Cognition: An International Journal, 8,* 338–342.

Reder, L. M. (1987). Strategy selection in question answering. *Cognitive Psychology, 19,* 90–138.

Reder, L. M. (1988). Strategic control of retrieval strategies. In G. Bower (Ed.), *The psychology of learning and motivation* (Vol. 22, pp. 227–259). San Diego, CA: Academic Press.

Reder, L. M., & Ritter, F. E. (1992). What determines initial feeling of knowing? Familiarity with question terms, not with the answer. *Journal of Experimental Psychology: Learning, Memory, and Cognition, 18,* 435–451.

Rhodes, M. G., & Kelley, C. M. (2005). Executive processes, memory accuracy, and memory monitoring: An aging and individual difference analysis. *Journal of Memory and Language, 52,* 578–594.

Richardson, J. T. E. (1998). The availability and effectiveness of reported mediators in associative learning: A historical review and an experimental investigation. *Psychonomic Bulletin & Review, 5,* 597–614.

Robbins, S. B., Lauver, K., Le, H., Davis, D., Langley, R., & Carlstrom, A. (2004). Do psychosocial and study skill factors predict college outcomes? A meta-analysis. *Psychological Bulletin, 130,* 261–288.

Roediger, H. L., & McDermott, K. B. (1995). Creating false memories: Remembering words not presented in lists. *Journal of Experimental Psychology: Learning, Memory, and Cognition, 21,* 803–814.

Rosenshine, B., & Meister, C. (1994). Reciprocal teaching: A review of the research. *Review of Educational Research, 64,* 479–530.

Rosenthal, D. M. (1998). A theory of consciousness. In N. Block, O. Flanagan, & G. Guzeldere (Eds.), *The nature of consciousness* (pp. 729–753). Cambridge: MIT Press.

Rotello, C. M., & Macmillan, N. A. (2006). Remember-know models as decision strategies in two experimental paradigms. *Journal of Memory and Language, 55,* 479–494.

Ruffman, T., & Perner, J. (2005). Do infants really understand false belief? *Trends in Cognitive Sciences, 9,* 462–463.

Russell, J., Mauther, N., Sharpe, S., & Tidswell, T. (1991). The "windows task" as a measure of strategic deception in preschoolers and autistic subjects. *British Journal of Developmental Psychology, 9,* 331–349.

Sanna, L. J., Schwarz, N., & Small, E. M. (2002). Accessibility experiences and the hindsight bias: I knew it all along versus it could never have happened. *Memory & Cognition, 30,* 1288–1296.

Schacter, D. L. (1996). *Searching for memory: The brain, the mind, and the past.* New York: Basic Books.

Schacter, D. L., & Worling, J. R. (1985). Attribute information and the feeling-of-knowing. *Canadian Journal of Psychology/Revue Canadienne de Psychologie, 39,* 467–475.

Schneider, W. (1998). Performance prediction in young children: Effects of skill, metacognition, and wishful thinking. *Developmental Science, 1,* 291–297.

Schneider, W., & Lockl, K. (2008). Procedural metacognition in children: Evidence for developmental trends. In J. Dunlosky & R. A. Bjork (Eds.), *Handbook of metamemory and memory* (pp. 391–409). New York: Taylor & Francis.

Schneider, W., Lockl, K., & Fernandez, O. (2005). Interrelationships among theory of mind, executive control, language development, and working memory in young children: A longitudinal analysis. In W. Schneider, R. Schumann-Hengsteler, & B. Sodian (Eds.), *Young children's cognitive development* (pp. 239–258). Hillsdale, NJ: Lawrence Erlbaum.

Schneider, W., & Pressley, M. (1997). *Memory development between two and twenty* (2nd ed.). Hillsdale, NJ: Lawrence Erlbaum.

Schneider, W., Visé, M., Lockl, K., & Nelson, T. O. (2000). Developmental trends in children's memory monitoring. Evidence from a judgment-of-learning task. *Cognitive Development, 15,* 115–134.

Schnyer, D., Verfaellie, M., Alexander, M., LaFleche, G., Nicholls, L., & Kaszniak, A. W. (2004). A role for right medial prefrontal cortex in accurate feeling-of-knowing judgments: Evidence from patients with lesions to frontal cortex. *Neuropsychologia, 42,* 957–966.

Schoenfeld, A. H. (1985). *Mathematical problem solving.* Orlando, FL: Academic Press.

Schoenfeld, A. H. (1987). What's all the fuss about metacognition? In A. H. Shoenfeld, (Ed.), *Cognitive science and mathematics education* (pp. 189–216). Hillsdale, NJ: Lawrence Erlbaum.

Schooler, J. W. (2002). Re-representing consciousness: Dissociations between experience and meta-consciousness. *Trends in Cognitive Sciences, 6,* 339–344.

Schraw, G., Potenza, M. T., & Nebelsick-Gullet, L. (1993). Constraints on the calibration of performance. *Contemporary Educational Psychology, 18,* 455–463.

Schunk, D. H., & Ertmer, P. A. (2000). Self-regulation and academic learning: Self-efficacy and enhancing interventions. In M. Boekaerts, P. R. Pintrich, & M. Zeidner (Eds.), *Handbook of self-regulation* (pp. 631–649). New York: Academic Press.

Schwartz, B. L. (1999). Sparkling at the end of the tongue: The etiology of tip-of-the-tongue phenomenology. *Psychonomic Bulletin & Review, 6,* 379–393.

Schwartz, B. L. (2002). *Tip-of-the-tongue states: Phenomenology, mechanism, and lexical retrieval.* Mahwah, NJ: Lawrence Erlbaum.

Schwartz, B. L., & Metcalfe, J. (1992). Cue familiarity but not target retrievability enhances feeling-of-knowing judgments. *Journal of Experimental Psychology: Learning, Memory, and Cognition, 18,* 1074–1083.

Schwartz, B. L., & Metcalfe, J. (1994). Methodological problems and pitfalls in the study of human metacognition. In J. Metcalfe & A. P. Shimamura (Eds.), *Metacognition: Knowing about knowing* (pp. 93–114). Cambridge: MIT Press.

Schwartz, B. L., & Smith, S. M. (1997). The retrieval of related information influences tip-of-the-tongue states. *Journal of Memory and Language, 36,* 68–86.

Shatz, M. A., & Best, J. B. (1987). Students' reasons for changing answers on objective tests. *Teaching of Psychology, 14,* 241–242.

Shaw, J. S., & McClure, K. A. (1996). Repeated postevent questioning can lead to elevated levels of eyewitness confidence. *Law and Human Behavior, 20,* 629–653.

Shergill, S. S., Brammer, M. J., Williams, S. C. R., Murray, R. M., & McGuire, P. K. (2000). Mapping auditory hallucinations in schizophrenia using functional Magnetic Resonance Imaging. *Archives of General Psychiatry, 57,* 1033–1038.

Shimamura, A. P. (2008). A neurocognitive approach to metacognitive monitoring and control. In J. Dunlosky & R. A. Bjork (Eds.), *Handbook of metamemory and memory* (pp. 373–390). New York: Taylor & Francis.

Shimamura, A. P., & Squire, L. R. (1986). Memory and metamemory: A study of the feeling-of-knowing phenomenon in amnesic patients. *Journal of Experimental Psychology: Learning, Memory, and Cognition, 12,* 452–460.

Shin, H., Bjorklund, D. F., & Beck, E. F. (2007). The adaptive nature of children's overestimation in a strategic memory task. *Cognitive Development, 22,* 197–212.

Shrager, J., & Siegler, R. S. (1998). SCADS: A model of children's strategy choices and strategy discoveries. *Psychological Science, 9,* 405–410.

Siedlecki, K. L., Salthouse, T. A., & Berish, D. E. (2005). Is there anything special about the aging of source memory? *Psychology and Aging, 20,* 19–32.

Siegfried, M. (2004). Modeling associative recognition: A comparison of two-high-threshold, two-high-threshold signal detection, and mixture distribution models. *Journal of Experimental Psychology: Learning, Memory, and Cognition, 30,* 83–97.

Siegler, R. S. (1999). Strategic development. *Trends in Cognitive Sciences, 3,* 430–435.

Siegler, R. S. (2002). Microgenetic studies of self-explanations. In N. Granott & J. Parziale (Eds.), *Microdevelopment: Transition processes in development and learning* (pp. 31–58). New York: Cambridge University Press.

Sikström, S., & Jönsson, F. (2005). A model for stochastic drift in memory strength to account for judgments of learning. *Psychological Review, 112,* 932–950.

Sitko, B. M. (1998). Knowing how to write: Metacognition and writing instruction. In D. J. Hacker, J. Dunlosky, & A. C. Graesser (Eds.), *Metacognition in educational theory and practice* (pp. 93–115). Hillsdale, NJ: Lawrence Erlbaum.

Skinner, B. F. (1957). *Verbal behavior.* New York: Appleton-Century-Crofts.

Slaughter, V., & Gopnik, A. (1996). Conceptual coherence in the child's theory of mind: Training children to understand belief. *Child Development, 67,* 2967–2988.

Slotnick, S. D., & Dodson, C. S. (2005). Support for a continuous (single-process) model of recognition memory and source memory. *Memory & Cognition, 33,* 151–170.

Smith, J. D., Beran, M. J., Redford, J. S., & Washburn, D. A. (2006). Dissociating uncertainty responses and reinforcement signals in the comparative study of uncertainty monitoring. *Journal of Experimental Psychology: General, 135,* 282–297.

Smith, J. D., Shields, W. E., & Washburn, D. A. (2003). The comparative psychology of uncertainty monitoring and metacognition. *Behavioral and Brain Sciences, 26,* 317–373.

Smith, S., & Blankenship, S. E. (1989). Incubation effects. *Bulletin of the Psychonomic Society, 27,* 311–314.

Smith, S., Brown, J. M., & Balfour, S. P. (1991). TOTimals: A controlled experimental method for studying tip-of-the-tongue states. *Bulletin of the Psychonomic Society, 29,* 445–447.

Sodian, B. (2005). Theory of mind—The case for conceptual development. In W. Schneider, R. Schumann-Hengsteler, & B. Sodian (Eds.), *Young children's cognitive development* (pp. 95–130). Hillsdale, NJ: Lawrence Erlbaum.

Soll, J. B. (1996). Determinants of overconfidence and miscalibration: The roles of random error and ecological structure. *Organizational Behavior and Human Decision Processes, 65,* 117–137.

Son, L. K., & Kornell, N. (2008). Research on the allocation of study time: Key studies from 1890 to the present (and beyond). In J. Dunlosky & R. A. Bjork (Eds.), *Handbook of metamemory and memory* (pp. 333–351). New York: Taylor & Francis.

Son, L. K., & Metcalfe, J. (2000). Metacognitive and control strategies in study-time allocation. *Journal of Experimental Psychology: Learning, Memory, and Cognition, 26,* 204–221.

Son, L. K., & Metcalfe, J. (2005). Judgments of learning: Evidence for a two-stage process. *Memory & Cognition, 33,* 1116–1129.

Son, L. K., & Sethi, R. (2006). Metacognitive control and optimal learning. *Cognitive Science, 30,* 759–774.

Souchay, C., & Isingrini, M. (2004). Age-related differences in the relation between monitoring and control of learning. *Experimental Aging Research, 30,* 179–193.

Souchay, C., Isingrini, M., & Espagnet, L. (2000). Aging, episodic memory feeling-of-knowing, and frontal functioning. *Neuropsychology, 14,* 299–309.

Souchay, C., Moulin, C. J. A., Clarys, D., Taconnat, L., & Isingrini, M. (2007). Diminished episodic memory awareness in older adults: Evidence from feeling-of-knowing and recollection. *Consciousness and Cognition: An International Journal, 16,* 769–784.

Spellman, B. A., & Bjork, R. A. (1992). When predictions create reality: Judgments of learning may alter what they are intended to assess. *Psychological Science, 3,* 315–316.

Spencer, W. D., & Raz, N. (1995). Differential effects of aging on memory for content and context: A meta-analysis. *Psychology and Aging, 10,* 527–539.

Sprangenberg, K. B., Wagner, M. T., & Bachman, D. L. (1998). Neuropsychological analysis of a case of abrupt onset mirror sign following a hypotensive crisis in a patient with vascular dementia. *Neurocase, 4,* 149–154.

Squire, L. R. (1986). Mechanisms of memory. *Science, 232,* 1612–1619.

Stine-Morrow, E. A. L., Shake, M. C., Miles, J. R., & Noh, S. R. (2006). Adult age differences in the effects of goals on self-regulated sentence processing. *Psychology and Aging, 21,* 790–803.

Stipek, D. J., Roberts, T. A., & Sanborn, M. E. (1984). Preschool-age children's performance expectations for themselves and another child as a function of the incentive value of success and the salience of past performance. *Child Development, 55,* 1983–1989.

Stone, E. R., & Opel, R. B. (2000). Training to improve calibration and discrimination: The effects of performance and environmental feedback. *Organizational Behavior and Human Decision Processes, 83,* 282–309.

Stone, N. J. (2000). Exploring the relationship between calibration and self-regulated learning. *Educational Psychology Review, 12,* 437–475.

Stuss, D. T. (1991). Disturbance of self awareness after frontal system damage. In G. P. Prigatano & D. L. Schacter (Eds.), *Awareness of deficit after brain injury* (pp. 63–83). New York: Oxford University Press.

Suddendorf, T., & Whiten, A. (2001). Mental evolution and development: Evidence for secondary representation in children, great apes, and other animals. *Psychological Bulletin, 127,* 629–650.

Sussman, A. L. (2001). Reality monitoring of performed and imagined interactive events: Developmental and contextual effects. *Journal of Experimental Child Psychology, 79,* 115–138.

Taraban, R., Maki, W. S., & Rynearson, K. (1999). Measuring study time distributions: Implications for designing computer-based courses. *Behavior Research Methods, Instruments & Computers, 31,* 263–269.

Tenney, E. R., MacCoun, R. J., Spellman, B. A., & Hastie, R. (2007). Calibration trumps confidence as a basis for witness credibility. *Psychological Science, 18,* 46–50.

Terrace, H. S., & Metcalfe, J. (Eds.). (2005). *The missing link in cognition: Origins of self-reflective consciousness.* New York: Oxford University Press.

Thiede, K. W. (1999). The importance of monitoring and self-regulation during multi-trial learning. *Psychonomic Bulletin & Review, 6,* 662–667.

Thiede, K. W., & Dunlosky, J. (1994). Delaying students' metacognitive monitoring improves their accuracy at predicting their recognition performance. *Journal of Educational Psychology, 2,* 290–302.

Thiede, K. W., & Dunlosky, J. (1999). Toward a general model of self-regulated study: An analysis of selection of items for study and self-paced study time. *Journal of Experimental Psychology: Learning, Memory, and Cognition, 25,* 1024–1037.

Thompson, R., Emmorey, K., & Gollan, T. H. (2005). "Tip of the fingers" experiences by deaf signers. *Psychological Science, 16,* 856–860.

Tinklepaugh, O. L. (1928). An experimental study of the representative factors of monkeys. *Journal of Comparative Psychology, 8,* 197–236.

Tolman, E. C. (1932). *Purposive behavior in animals and men.* New York: The Century Co.

Tulving, E., & Craik, F. I. M. (2000). *The Oxford handbook of memory.* New York: Oxford University Press.

Tulving, E., & Madigan, S. A. (1970). Memory and verbal learning. In P. H. Mussen & M. R. Rosenzweig (Eds.), *Annual review of psychology.* Palo Alto, CA: Annual Reviews.

Tulving, E., Schacter, D. L., and Stark, H. A. (1982). Priming effects in word-fragment completion are independent of recognition memory. *Journal of Experimental Psychology: Learning, Memory, and Cognition, 8,* 336–142.

Tulving, E., & Thomson, D. M. (1973). Encoding specificity and retrieval processes in episodic memory. *Psychological Review, 80*, 352–373.

Tversky, A., & Kahneman, D. (1974). Judgment under uncertainty: Heuristics and biases. *Science, 185*, 1124–1131.

Tversky, A., & Kahneman, D. (1982). Judgments of and by representatives. In D. Kahneman, P. Slovic, & A. Tversky (Eds.), *Judgment under uncertainty: Heuristics and biases* (pp. 84–98). New York: Cambridge University Press.

Underwood, B. J. (1966). Individual and group predictions of item difficulty for free-recall learning. *Journal of Experimental Psychology, 71*, 673–679.

Valentijn, S. A. M., Hill, R. D., Van Hooren, S. A. H., Bosma, H., Van Boxtel, M. P. J., Jolles, J., & Ponds, R. W. H. M. (2006). Memory self-efficacy predicts memory performance: Results from a 6-year follow-up study. *Psychology and Aging, 21*, 165–172.

Veenman, M. V. J., & Beishuizen, J. J. (2004). Intellectual and metacognitive skills of novices while studying texts under conditions of text difficulty and time constraint. *Learning and Instruction, 14*, 621–640.

Veenman, M. V. J., Kok, R., & Blöte, A. W. (2005). The relation between intellectual and metacognitive skills in early adolescence. *Instructional Science, 33*, 193–211.

Verhaeghen, P., Marcoen, A., & Goossens, L. (1992). Improving memory performance in the aged through mnemonic training: A meta-analytic study. *Psychology and Aging, 7*, 242–251.

Vesonder, G. T., & Voss, J. F. (1985). On the ability to predict one's own responses while learning. *Journal of Memory and Language, 24*, 363–376.

Wade-Stein, D., & Kintsch, E. (2004). Summary street: Interactive computer support for writing. *Cognition and Instruction, 22*, 333–362.

Wallsten, T. S. (1996). An analysis of judgment research analyses. *Organizational Behavior and Human Decision Processes, 65*, 220–226.

Watson, J. B. (1913). Psychology as the behaviorist views it. *Psychological Review, 20*, 158–177.

Watson, J. B. (1925). *Behaviorism*. New York: Norton.

Wegner, D. M., Sparrow, B., & Winerman, L. (2004). Vicarious agency: Experiencing control over the movements of others. *Journal of Personality and Social Psychology, 86*, 838–848.

Wegner, D. M., & Wheatley, T. (1999). Apparent mental causation: Sources of the experience of will. *American Psychologist, 54*, 480–492.

Wellman, H. M., Cross, D., & Watson, J. (2001). Meta-analysis of theory-of-mind development: The truth about false belief. *Child Development, 72*, 655–684.

West, R. L., & Berry, J. M. (1994). Age declines in memory self-efficacy: General or limited to particular tasks and measures? In J. D. Sinnott (Ed.), *Interdisciplinary handbook of adult lifespan learning*. Westport, CT: Greenwood.

Whitty, C. W. M., & Lewin, W. (1957). Vivid day-dreaming: An unusual form of confusion following anterior cingulectomy in man. *International Journal of Neurology, 5*, 72–76.

Wimmer, H., & Perner, J. (1983). Beliefs about beliefs: Representation and constraining function of wrong beliefs in young children's understanding of deception. *Cognition, 13,* 103–128.

Winne, P. H., & Hadwin, A. F. (1998). Studying as self-regulated learning. In D. J. Hacker, J. Dunlosky, & A. C. Graesser (Eds.), *Metacognition in educational theory and practice* (pp. 277–304). Hillsdale, NJ: Lawrence Erlbaum.

Wong, R. M. F., Lawson, M. J., & Keeves, J. (2002). The effects of self-explanation training on students' problem solving in high-school mathematics. *Learning and Instruction, 12,* 233–262.

Woodruff, C. C., Hayama, H., and Rugg, M. D. (2006). Electrophysiological dissociation of the neural correlates of recollection and familiarity. *Brain Research, 1100,* 125–135.

Woodworth, R. S. (1921). *Psychology: A study of mental life.* New York: Henry Holt.

Yaniv, I., & Meyer, D. E. (1987). Activation and metacognition of inaccessible stored information: Potential bases for incubation effects in problem solving. *Journal of Experimental Psychology: Learning, Memory, and Cognition, 13,* 187–205.

Yates, F. A. (1997). *The art of memory.* London: Pimlico.

Yonelinas, A. P. (1994). Receiver operating characteristics in recognition memory: Evidence for a dual-process model. *Journal of Experimental Psychology: Learning, Memory, and Cognition, 20,* 1341–1354.

Yonelinas, A. P., Otten, L. J., Shaw, K. N., & Rugg, M. D. (2005). Separating the brain regions involved in recollection and familiarity in recognition memory. *Journal of Neuroscience, 25,* 3002–3008.

Zaragoza, M. S., & Mitchell, K. J. (1996). Repeated exposure to suggestion and the creation of false memories. *Psychological Science, 7,* 294–300.

Zimmerman, B. J. (2000). Attaining self-regulation: A social-cognitive perspective. In M. Boekaerts, P. R. Pintrich, & M. Zeidner (Eds.), *Handbook of self-regulation* (pp. 13–39). New York: Academic Press.

Zimmerman, B. J. (2001). Theories of self-regulated learning and academic achievement: An overview and analysis. In B. J. Zimmerman & D. H. Schunk (Eds.), *Self-regulated learning and academic achievement* (2nd ed., pp. 1–38). Hillsdale, NJ: Lawrence Erlbaum.

Zimmerman, B. J., & Schunk, D. H. (2001). *Self-regulated learning and academic achievement* (2nd ed.).

Zuckerman, M., DePaulo, B. M., & Rosenthal, R. (1981). Verbal and nonverbal communication of deception. In L. Berkowitz (Ed.), *Advances in experimental social psychology* (Vol. 14, pp. 2–59). New York: Academic Press.

Author Index

ABC Research Group, 139
Ackerman, B. P., 275
Adams, J. K., 127
Adams, P. A., 127
Afflerbach, P., 216, 218
Ahmad, M., 249
Ainsworth, S., 224
Akehurst, L., 188
Alba, J. W., 157
Alexander, M., 80
Allen-Burge, R., 270
Allwood, C. M., 125
Alpert, N. M., 14
American Academy of Pediatrics, 183
Anderson, J. C., 196
Anderson, R. I., 220
Andreoletti, C., 271
Ansay, C., 64
Arami, M., 228
Arbuckle, T. Y., 91, 93, 115
Arkes, H. R., 124
Atkinson, R. C., 25-27, 29, 101
Auer, T. S., 193
Azevedo, R., 204, 230

Bachman, D. L., 161
Bacon, E., 99
Baguley, T., 78
Baillargeon, R., 242
Baker, J. M. C., 39
Baker, L., 220
Balfour, S. P., 76
Balota, D. A., 61-62, 64
Bandura, A., 204
Bandura, M., 271
Barlow, M. R., 138
Barron, K. L., 257
Bassok, M., 222
Batchelder, W. H., 154
Bauserman, K. L., 216
Bawa, S., 290
Bayen, U. J., 148, 154, 193
Beattie, G., 78
Beauregard, M., 160
Beck, E. F., 247-248

Beck, I. L., 218
Begg, I., 93, 105, 110
Beishuizen, J. J., 229
Benjamin, A. S., 50, 70, 104, 106, 115
Benjamin, L. T., 209
Bentaleb, L. A., 160
Bentall, R. P., 157
Beran, M. J., 245
Bereiter, C., 224-225
Berish, D. E., 283
Berry, E. M., 281-282
Berry, J. M., 271
Berry, S. L., 109
Best, J. B., 209
Bird, R. D., 115
Bjork, R. A., 102, 106
Bjorklund, D. F., 247-248, 257
Björkman, M., 136
Blakemore, S.-J., 158-159, 161
Blankenship, S. E., 73
Bleasdale, F. A., 106
Block, C. C., 216, 221
Bloom, P., 242
Blöte, A. W., 229
Boekaerts, M., 201
Bol, L., 96, 207, 210-211
Bolger, F., 120, 130
Bolles, R. C., 12
Boring, E. G., 12
Borkowski, J. G., 258
Bosma, H., 270
Botwinick, J., 273
Bower, G. H., 156
Bowman, L. L., 248-249
Boyle, R., 205
Brammer, M. J., 160
Brase, G. L., 134
Brav, T. K., 282, 285-286, 291
Breen, N., 162
Brennen, T., 78
Brentano, F., 14, 15
Brewer, N., 186
Brewer, W. F., 138-139
Bright, J., 78
Brincones, I., 218

Broadbent, D. E., 22
Brockway, J. H., 191
Brown, A. L., 33, 213-215
Brown, A. S., 30-31, 72, 190
Brown, E., 240-241
Brown, J., 282
Brown, J. M., 76
Brown, L. A., 190
Brown, R., 73
Bruce, P. R., 273
Bruce, V., 78
Bryant, F. B., 191
Buckley, J. P., 188
Budescu, D. V., 130, 137
Buehler, R., 134
Bull, R., 188
Burch, M., 228
Burcham, S., 224
Burke, A., 186
Burke, D. M., 73-75, 79
Burns, H. J., 172
Butterfield, B., 176
Butterfield, E. C., 19, 64, 253, 277

Caine, D., 162
Call, J., 244
Campbell, J. D., 192-193
Campione, J. C., 214
Cao, L., 211
Carlson, S. M., 243
Caramazza, A., 75
Carlstrom, A., 205
Carney, E., 99
Carr, M., 227
Caruso, M. J., 288-289
Cassel, E., 178-179
Cavanaugh, J. C., 33, 258
Cevell, T. A., 209
Ceci, S., 174-175
Chabris, C. F., 14
Chemers, M. M., 205
Chi, M. T. H., 222
Chomsky, N., 21
Chryssoula, P., 230
Cicero, M. T., 9-10
Clancy, S. A., 176
Clarys, D., 278-279
Cleare, A. J., 122-123
Coan, J. A., 174
Cohen, M. X., 165
Coltheart, M., 162
Comte, A., 12, 13
Conner, L. N., 226
Connor, L. T., 55, 61-62, 64, 99, 265, 273, 287
Cosmides, L., 134
Costermans, J., 64
Coughlan, J., 78
Coyle, T. R., 257
Coyne, A. C., 273

Craik, F. I. M., 13, 106, 275
Creeley, C. E., 99
Cromley, J. G., 230
Cross, D., 238
Crowley, K., 259
Cuddy, L. L., 91, 93, 115
Cummins, C., 221
Cutler, B. L., 185

Dagenbach, D., 283
Damasio, A. R., 157
Damasio, H., 157
Danziger, K., 12
Davachi, L., 165
Davidson, P. S. R., 282
Davis, D., 205
De Clercq, A., 228
Delclos, V. R., 212
De Corte, E., 227-228
De Jong-Meyer, R., 183
Denhière, G., 112
DePaulo, B. M., 188
Desoete, A., 228
Dexter, H. R., 185
D'Esposito, M., 157, 165
Diaz, M., 50
Dixon, R. A., 267, 269, 271
Dodson, C. S., 150, 154-155, 290
Dominowski, R. L., 224
Domoto, P. K., 99
Donndelinger, S. J., 221
Doran, A., 184
Dougherty, M. R. P., 130, 136
Dufresne, A., 251
Duft, S., 93, 105
Dunlosky, J., 39, 55, 97-100, 105, 107-108, 110, 113-114, 116, 265, 273, 276, 285-287, 289
Dunning, D., 207
Dy, C. J., 165

Efklides, A., 230
Ehrlinger, J., 207
Ekman, P., 187-189
Ellis, H. C., 19-20, 22
Elliott, E., 271
Elshout, J. J., 229
Emmorey, K., 78
Epstein, W., 109-110
Erber, J. T., 270
Erdfelder, E., 148, 154, 193
Erev, I., 130, 137
Ericsson, K. A., 29, 31
Ertmer, P. A., 206
Eslinger, H., 157
Espagnet, L., 80, 278-279

Feinberg, T. E., 161
Ferguson, S. A., 147

Fernandez, O., 243, 260
Ferrell, W. R., 130
Fiedler, K., 134
Finn, B., 94, 96-97
Fischhoff, B., 52, 120, 123-127, 191
Fisher, R. P., 179
Fitch, F., 280
Fitzgerald, J., 226
Flavell, J. H., 1, 31-34, 111, 237, 241, 243, 247, 254-255, 258, 260
Flower, L., 224-225
Floyd, M., 271
Foley, M. A., 149
Fox, P. W., 127, 129
Fox, S. G., 186
Frankovich, L., 110
Freebern, G., 230
Friedrichs, A. G., 31, 247
Friesen, W. V., 187
Frith, C., 161
Fu, C., 122-123
Fu, T., 122-123
Fuchs, D., 228
Fuchs, L. S., 228
Funnell, M., 75

Galanter, E., 23, 25
Garcia, B. F., 205
Gardiner, J. M., 106
Garrett, M., 158
Garrett, S., 184
Gawlik, B., 194
Geiselman, R. E., 179
Gerler, D., 70, 87
German, T. P., 242
Ghatala, E. S., 249, 259
Gide, A., vii
Gigerenzer, G., 51, 129, 134-136, 139, 190
Gilewski, M. J., 267-268
Gilovich, T., 131-132
Glaser, R., 222
Glenberg, A. M., 109-110
Glisky, E. L., 282
Goldfarb, K., 61
Goldsmith, M., 140-142, 289, 290
Goldstein, D., 189-190
Gollan, T. H., 78
Gonzalez, R., 50
Goossens, L., 286
Gopnik, A., 242
Graf, A., 99
Graff-Radford, P. J., 157
Granhag, P. A., 125
Green, B. L., 248
Greene, E. J., 148, 164
Greene, J. A., 204, 230
Griffin, D., 131-132, 134
Groninger, L. D., 93
Grossman, J. L., 285

Hacker, D. J., 33, 96, 207, 210-211, 215
Hadwin, A. F., 115, 201, 204, 213, 216, 230-231
Hale, C., 258
Hamlett, C. L., 228
Hampton, R. R., 245
Hancock, J. A., 123
Hansen, M. B., 242
Hare, V. C., 219
Harmer, S., 240-241
Harrington, C., 212
Harris, P. L., 240-241
Hart, J. T., 30, 31, 34, 37, 39, 60-61, 87, 91, 252
Hasher, L., 157, 189-190
Hashtroudi, S., 147, 149
Hastie, R., 187
Hayama, H., 155
Hayes, J. R., 224-225
Hayes, S. M., 157
Hazlett, G. A., 184
Hermann, D. J., 269
Hertzog, C., 55, 99, 105, 267, 269-271, 273, 275-276, 285-286, 289
Hicks, J. L., 177
Hill, R. D., 270
Hinchley, J. L., 275
Hoffman, H. G., 172
Hoffrage, U., 51, 135-136, 139
Holgate, B., 110
Horgan, D. D., 96, 207, 210
Horn, J. L., 229
Hothersall, D., 18-19
Hoyt, J. D., 31, 247
Hoyt, G., 184
Hu, L., 205
Hubert, W., 183
Huet, N., 64, 277
Hulicka, I. M., 285
Hultsch, D. F., 267, 269-271, 275
Humphrey, G., 17
Hunt, R. R., 19-20, 22

Inbau, F. E., 188
Ishikawa, T., 99
Isingrini, M., 80, 278-279, 287-288
Israel, S. E., 216
Izaute, M., 99

Jacoby, L. L., 151, 153-156, 282-283
James, L. E., 75
James, W., 14, 71-73
Jameson, K. A., 61
Janowsky, J. S., 53, 80-81
Jasechko, J., 282
Jayne, B. P., 188
Jennings, J. M., 283
Jessup, D. L., 227
Joaquim, S. G., 65-67, 76
Johansson, B., 270

Johnson, M. K., 146-151, 157, 163, 175, 177, 283
Jolles, J., 270
Jones, R. W., 280
Jönsson, F., 78, 103
Jungermann, H., 129
Juslin, P., 136

Kahneman, D., 129-132, 134, 194
Kassel, N., 157
Kassin, S. M., 195
Kaszniak, A. W., 80-81, 278
Kausler, D. H., 265
Keener, M. C., 211
Keeves, J., 224
Kelemen, W. L., 99, 103
Kelley, C. M., 151, 156, 282, 290
Kellicut, M. H., 26, 29
Kennedy, M. R., T., 99
Keren, G., 51, 120, 123, 132
Kerri, J., 207
Ketcham, K., 118-119
Kidder, D. P., 105, 276
Kikyo, H., 81
Kimball, D. R., 102
King, J. F., 93
Kinnucan-Welsch, K., 216
Kinsbourne, M., 160
Kintsch, E., 226
Kintsch, W., 216, 218-219
Kircher, T., 159
Kleinbölting, H., 51, 135-136, 139
Kleykamp, B., 283
Kluwe, R. H., 33
Knight, R. T., 165
Knoblich, G., 159
Kobasigawa, A., 251
Köhnken, G., 188
Kok, R., 229
Kolers, P. A., 85
Koriat, A., 48, 64, 67-71, 94, 96, 106-108,
       124-125, 140-142, 250, 289-290
Kornell, N., 48, 72-73, 111, 114, 246
Kosslyn, S. M., 14
Koutstaal, W., 122-123
Kramarski, B., 228
Kraut, R. E., 188
Kreutzer, M. A., 254-255, 258, 260
Krinsky, R., 64
Kroll, N. E. A., 27, 29, 165
Kruger, J., 207
Kubat-Silman, A., 289
Kucan, L., 218
Külpe, O., 16,

LaBine, G., 196
LaBine, S. J., 196
Lachman, J. L., 19, 22, 277
Lachman, M. E., 269, 271
Lachman, R., 19, 22, 277
LaFleche, G., 80

Lalonde, P., 93, 105
Lane, S. M., 178
Lang, B., 243
Langley, R., 205
Lauver, K., 205
Lawson, M. J., 224
Le, H., 205
Leach, K., 149
Leichtman, M., 174-175
Leighton, E. A., 281-282
Le Ny, J.-F., 112
Leonard, C., 254-255, 258, 260
Leonesio, R. J., 92-93, 111-113
Leslie, A. M., 241-243
Le Taillanter, D., 112
Levin, J. R., 249, 259
Levy, O., 282, 285-286, 291
Levy-Sadot, R., 70-71
Lewin, W., 157
Lewis, M. W., 222
Liberty, C., 255-257
Lichtenstein, S., 52, 120, 123-127
Liddle, P., 160
Lieberman, D. A., 26-27, 29
Lin, L.-M., 110
Lindsay, S., 147, 149, 152, 177
Lineweaver, T. T., 270
Lipko, A., 110
Lockl, K., 243, 247, 249-251, 253, 260-261
Loftus, E. F., 118-119, 172-174, 193
Lories, G., 64
Lovelace, E. A., 93, 275
Lowe, D. J., 196
Luce, K., 99

Ma' ayan, H., 94, 96
MacCoun, R. J., 187
MacGregor, D., 125
MacKay, D. G., 73-74, 79
MacMillan, N. A., 154
Madigan, S. A., 37
Maki, R. H., 105, 109-110
Maki, W. S., 113
Maljkovic, V., 14
Mangels, J. A., 64, 176
Mann, S., 188
Marazita, J. M., 248-249
Marbe, K., 16
Marcoen, A., 286
Maril, A., 81
Markham, L., 226
Markman, E. M., 31, 213, 218, 242
Marlatt, A., 99
Marquié, J. C., 64, 277
Mariott, C., 240-241
Marsh, G. R., 275
Marsh, R. L., 156, 176
Marx, R., 205
Masson, M. E. J., 50
Masur, E. F., 111

Mather, M., 148
Matvey, G., 108, 110
Mauther, N., 239
May, C. P., 281-282
Mazursky, D., 196
Mazzoni, G., 96
McClelland, A. G. R., 120, 130
McCloskey, M., 194
McClure, K. A., 181
McDermott, K. B., 177, 198
McDonald-Miszczak, L., 270
McGlynn, S. M., 280
McGoey, P. J., 130
McGuire, M. J., 105, 110
McGuire, P. K., 160
McIntyre, C. W., 111
McNeill, D., 73
Meeter, M., 96
Meister, C., 215
Melnick, R., 93, 105
Merriman, W. E., 248-249
Metcalfe, J., 37, 48, 54-55, 65-67, 72-73, 75-76, 79-80, 94, 96-97, 102, 104, 111, 113-114, 165, 176, 245, 287
Mevarech, Z. R., 228
Meyer, D. E., 61-62
Miles, J. R., 288
Mill, J. 14
Miller, D. G., 172
Miller, G. A., 22-23, 25
Miller, P. H., 257
Milstead, M., 258
Miner, A. C., 69-70, 80, 84
Miozzo, M., 75
Mitchell, K. J., 146, 148-149, 164, 172
Mitchell, J., 81
Mitchell, J. P., 165
Miyashita, Y., 81
Moffoot, A. P. R., 123
Moos, D. C., 230
Morgan, C. A., III, 184
Morita, S. K., 178
Morris, C. C., 106
Moses, L. J., 243
Moulin, C. J. A., 278, 280-281
Multhaup, K. S., 177, 282-283
Murnane, K., 148, 154
Murphy, M. D., 288-289
Murray, R. M., 160
Musch, J., 193
Myers, M., 219, 221

Narens, L., 4-5, 10, 25, 39, 61, 70, 87, 115, 215
Naus, M. J., 255-257
Naveh-Benjamin, M., 282, 285-286, 291
Nebelsick-Gullet, L., 210
Nebes, R. D., 280
Neely, J. H., 61-62, 64
Neisser, U., 22

Nelson, T. O., 4-5, 10, 12-13, 25, 39, 50, 61, 64, 70, 87, 92-93, 96-100, 111-113, 115, 215, 250, 252, 277
Neuman, Y., 224
Newell, A., 25
Nicholls, L., 80
Nietfeld, J. L., 211
Nisbett, R., 27-29
Noh, S. R., 288
Novak, D. L., 148

O' Carroll, R. E., 123
Ofir, C., 196
Ohki, K., 81
Olsson, H., 136
Olsson, M. J., 78
Onishi, K., 242
Opel, R. B., 126, 127
Op T' Eynde, P., 227, 228
Ornstein, P. A., 255, 256, 257
Osborne, J. W., 211
Oskamp, S., 180
O' Sullivan, M., 188-189
Otero, J., 218-219
Otten, L. J., 165
Owen, R., 228

Paivio, A., 22
Palef, S. R., 85
Palinscar, A. S., 214-215
Pannu, J. K., 81, 278
Paris, A. H., 221
Paris, S. G., 216, 219, 221
Peck, V., 253, 277
Penrod, S. D., 185
Perfect, T. J., 156, 280
Perlmutter, M., 33
Perner, J., 236-238, 243
Perrotin, A., 278-279
Peskin, J., 238
Peters, S. M., 99
Pfeifer, R. L., 188
Phillips, L. D., 120, 123
Piaget, J., 32-33
Pickrell, J. E., 172-174
Pintrich, P. R., 201, 205
Plumert, J. M., 249
Poe, D., 188
Pohl, R. F., 193-194
Ponds, R. W. H. M., 270
Poon, L., 122-123
Potenza, M. T., 210
Powell-Moman, A., 276, 286
Premack, D., 237
Prentice, K., 228
Pressley, M., 216, 218, 230, 249, 254, 257-259
Pribam, K. H., 23, 25
Prins, F. J., 229
Probert, J. S., 257
Puncochar, J. M., 127-128

Rabinowitz, J. C., 275
Raganath, C., 165
Rahhal, T., 281-282
Rakow, E. A., 96, 207, 210
Raye, C. L., 148-149, 157, 164, 175
Raz, N., 278, 281
Read, J. D., 177
Reber, R., 190
Reckers, P. M. J., 196
Reder, L. M., 65, 69-70, 80, 82-84, 86-87
Redford, J. S., 245
Reid, J. E., 188
Reimann, P., 222
Rhodes, M. G., 290
Richardson, J. T. E., 254, 285
Riefer, D. M., 154
Ritter, F. E., 83-84
Robbins, S. B., 205
Roberson, I., 99
Roberts, T. A., 250
Robinson, A. E., 105
Roediger, H. L., 177, 198
Roeyers, H., 228
Rosenshine, B., 215
Rosenthal, D. M., 6
Rosenthal, R., 188
Ross, K. A., 259
Rotello, C. M., 50, 154
Rothberg, S. T., 270
Roussel, C. C., 178
Rubin, S. R., 282
Ruffman, T., 243
Rugg, M. D., 155, 165
Russell, J., 239
Rynearson, K., 113

Sabbagh, M. A., 243
Sahakyan, L., 290
Salthouse, T. A., 283
Sampaio, C., 138
Sanborn, M. E., 250
Sanders, R. E., 288-289
Sanna, L. J., 196
Sanvito, J., 93, 105
Scardamalia, M., 224-225
Schacter, D, L., 68, 81, 146, 150, 153
Schaie, K. W., 268
Schmitt, F. A., 288-289
Schneider, W., 99, 243, 247, 249-251,
    253-254, 257-258, 260-261
Schnyer, D., 80
Schoenfeld, A. H., 226-228
Schooler, J. W., 6
Schraw, G., 210
Schroeter, K., 228
Schunk, D. H., 115, 201, 206
Schwartz, B. L., 1, 54-55, 65-67, 74,
    76-79, 81, 106
Schwarz, B., 224
Schwarz, N., 190, 196

Schwebel, D. C., 249
Scogin, F., 271
Seier, W. L., 257
Serra, M., 39
Sethi, R., 116
Shake, M. C., 288
Shallenberger, W. R., 209
Shapiro, R. M., 161
Sharpe, S., 239
Shatz, M. A., 209
Shaughnessy, J. J., 93
Shaw, J. S., 181
Shaw, K. N., 165
Sheffer, L., 94, 96
Shergill, S. S., 160
Shields, W. E., 244
Shimamura, A. P., 53, 79-81
Shin, H., 247-248
Shrager, J., 259
Shriffrin, R., 25-27, 29, 101
Shitzer-Reichert, R., 250
Siedlecki, K. L., 283
Siegfried, M., 154
Siegler, R. S., 222-223, 259
Sikström, S., 103
Silva, R., 158
Simon, H. A., 25, 29, 31
Simons, J. S., 81
Sitko, B. M., 225-226
Skinner, B. F., 21
Slawinski, J. L., 257
Slaughter, V., 242
Slotnick, S. D., 154-155, 290
Small, E. M., 196
Smiley, S. S., 214
Smith, D. C., 219
Smith, J. D., 244-245
Smith, S.M., 73, 76-77
Sodian, B., 237-239, 242-243
Soll, J. B., 136
Son, L. K., 104, 111, 113, 116, 246, 287
Souchay, C., 80, 278-279, 287
Sparrow, B., 162
Spellman, B. A., 102, 187
Spencer, W. D., 281
Sprangenberg, K. B., 161
Squire, L. R., 2, 53, 79-81
Stark, H. A., 153
Stark, L. J., 156
Stewart, M. T., 221
Stine-Morrow, E. A. L., 288
Stip, E., 160
Stipek, D. J., 250
Stone, E. R., 126-127
Stottmeister, F., 159
Stuss, D. T., 157
Suddendorf, T., 237
Sukel, H., 195
Sussman, A. L., 240
Szuchman, L. T., 270

Taconnat, L., 278-279
Taraban, R., 113
Taylor, T. H., 149
Tenney, E. R., 187
Terrace, H. S., 37, 246
Tesser, A., 192-193
Thiede, K. W., 55, 112-114, 116
Thomas, P., 184
Thompson, D. M., 146
Thompson, L. W., 268
Thompson, R., 78
Thompson, W. L., 14
Thronesbery, C., 22, 277
Tidswell, T., 239
Tinklepaugh, O. L., 20, 21
Todd, P. M., 139
Tolman, E. C., 20-21
Tom, S. M., 165
Tooby, J., 134
Toppino, T., 189-190
Tsapkini, K., 75
Tulving, E., 13, 37, 146, 153, 165
Turner, J. C., 216
Tversky, A., 129-132, 134, 194

Underwood, B. J., 91

Valentijn, S. A. M., 270
Van Boxtel, M. P. J., 270
Van Etten, S., 230
Van Hooren, S. A. H., 270
Van Meter, P., 230
Veenman, M. V. J., 229
Verfaellie, M., 80
Verhaeghen, P., 286
Verschaffel, L., 227-228
Vesonder, G. T., 93-94
Villa, D., 178
Vinski, E., 110
Visé, M., 250
Voss, J. F., 93-94
Vrij, A., 188

Wade, E., 73-74, 79
Wade-Stein, D., 226
Wagner, A. D., 165
Wagner, M. T., 161
Wagner, T., 193
Walker, D., 99
Wallsten, T. S., 52, 130, 137

Walters, H. A., 186
Wang, A. Y., 149
Wang, M.-L., 99
Washburn, D. A., 244-245
Wasik, B. A., 216
Watson, J., 238
Watson, J. B., 18-19, 34
Weaver, C. A., 103
Weaver, S. L., 271
Webster, L. M., 283
Wegner, D. M., 162
Weise, S. B., 14
Wellman, H. M., 238
West, R. L., 271
Wheatley, T., 162
Whiten, A., 237
Whittall, S., 240-241
Whitty, C. W. M., 157
Wilkinson, A. C., 109
Williams, S. C. R., 160
Wilson, T., 27-29
Wimmer, P. H., 237-238
Winerman, L., 162
Winne, P. H., 115, 201, 204, 213, 216, 230-231
Winters, F. I., 230
Wolf, E., 165
Woloshyn, V., 151
Wolpert, D., 161
Wong, R. M. F., 224
Woodruff, C. C., 155
Woodruff, G., 237
Woodworth, R. S., 12, 15
Worling, J. R., 68
Worthley, J. S., 73-74, 79
Wundt, W., 12

Yaniv, I., 61-62
Yates, F. A., 10
Yokoi, L., 230
Yonelinas, A. P., 154, 165

Zabrucky, K. M., 110
Zaragoza, M. S., 172, 194
Zarit, S. H., 270
Zechmeister, E. B., 93
Zeidner, M., 201
Zelinski, E. M., 267-268
Zimmerman, B. J., 115, 201
Zoccoli, S. L., 190
Zuckerman, M., 188

Subject Index

Abbey memory system, 10-11
Academic achievement, 205
Accuracy, see Judgment accuracy
Adaptivity of overconfidence, 248-249
Allocation of study time,
   see Self-paced study
Alzheimer's disease, 280-281
American Sign Language, 78-79

Behaviorism, 18-22
Bias, *see* Calibration

Calibration curves, *see* Judgment accuracy
Calibration, *see also* Judgment accuracy
   calibration index, 52-53
   retrospective-confidence judgments, 119-121
   self-regulated learning, 207-211
Changing test answers, 209-210
Childhood development, *see also* Memory
   development
   false memories, 173-176
   feeling of knowing, 252-253
   judgments of learning, 250-252
   metamemory knowledge, 254,
      255, 258, 260-261
   strategy use, 254, 258-259
   theory of mind, 236-243
   wishful-thinking hypothesis, 249-250
Cognition, 3
Comprehension monitoring:
   error detection, 31, 218-220
   judgment of learning, 218
   models of, 215-217
   reciprocal teaching and, 215
   self explanation, 222-224
   strategies and, 219-224
   think-aloud protocols, 218
   writing and, 226
Computer metaphor, 22
Comte's paradox, 11-15
Confabulation, *see also* false memories
   confidence, 174-175
   source monitoring, 156-157

Confidence accuracy:
   childhood development and, 247-250
   ecological approaches, 133-139
   eyewitness testimony, 176-179
   hybrid models, 136
Confidence judgments, *see also* Retrospective
   confidence judgments
   cognitive interview, 178-179
   courtroom witnesses and, 185-187
   education and, 211
   event-related potentials, 176-177
   false memories and, 172-176
   lie detection and, 187-189
   manipulation of, 180-182
Control:
   definition of, 3-6
   example, 25
   measurement of, 38-44
   questions about, 44
Cryptomnesia, 156
Cue utilization:
   extrinsic cues, 108
   intrinsic cues, 108
   judgments of learning,
      106-110, 250-252
   mnemonic cues, 108

Debiasing techniques:
   generating reasons, 124-125
   group confidence, 127-129
   performance feedback, 126-127
   process-oriented modifications, 124
   response-oriented modifications, 124
Delayed-JOL effect, 97-104
   child development and, 250-252
   method, 97-98
   Minds-on activity, 116-117
   monitoring-retrieval assumption, 100
   monitoring-dual-memories (MDM)
      hypothesis, 100-103
   older adulthood and, 276
   self-fulfilling-prophecy (SFP)
      hypothesis, 102-104

Depression:
  depressive-realism hypothesis, 121-123
  selective-processing hypothesis, 121-123
  source monitoring, 148-149
Dolphins, *see* Nonhuman metacognition

Ease of learning (EOL) judgments:
  definition of, 40-41, 90
  relationship to other judgments, 91-92
  self-paced study and, 111
Ease-of-processing hypothesis, 105-106
Error correction, *see* Comprehension
    monitoring
Explicit memory:
  source judgments, 153
  strategy use by children, 254, 258-259
Event-related potential, 176-177
Eyewitness memory, *see* also Confidence
    judgments
  confidence accuracy, 176-179
  cortisol levels and, 184-185
  jury decisions and, 185-187
  Trier social stress test, 184
  traumatic stress, 183-185

False-fame effect, 151-152, 282-283
False memories:
  childhood and, 173-176
  confidence judgments, 172-176
  false-fame effect, 151-152, 282-283
  Minds-on Activity, 198-199
  older adulthood and, 282-283
Feeling of knowing (FOK):
  child development and, 252-253
  collection and analysis, 44-57
  cue familiarity, 63-70, 76, 83
  definition of, 40-42, 60
  domain familiarity, 64, 278
  lexical decision and FOK, 62
  heuristic-based accounts, 62-69
  mathematics, 83-86
  older adulthood and, 277-280
  priming, 65
  recall-judge-recognition paradigm (RJR),
    60, 74, 87
  relationship to other judgments, 91-92
  target-accessibility
    hypothesis, 67-71
  target-strength account, 61-62, 67
Feeling of knowing (FOK) and control
    processes:
  game-show paradigm, 82
  retrieval termination, 84-87
  strategy selection, 82-84
Feeling of knowing and neuroscience:
  functional Magnetic Resonance Imaging, 81
  frontal lobes, 53-54, 79-81, 279-280
  Korsakoff syndrome and, 79-80
  prefrontal cortex, 81
  temporal lobe, 80

Functional Magnetic Resonance Imaging:
  feeling of knowing, 81
  source monitoring, 165
Forward model, *see* Reality-monitoring deficits
Frontal lobes, 53-54, 79-81, 279-280

Hard-easy effect, 51-52, 120-121, 123-124
Heurisitics:
  anchoring-and-adjustment heuristic, 131-132
  availability heuristic, 131
  conjunction fallacy, 131
  definition of, 63
  feeling of knowing and judgment of
    learning, 62-69
  judgments of learning, 105-106
  representative heuristic, 131
  retrospective confidence
    judgments, 130-133
  source monitoring, 146-147, 158
Hindsight bias:
  anchoring effect, 193-194
  court cases and, 194-196
  courtroom testimony and, 191-192
  definition of, 172
  examples of, 191, 194-197
  malpractice and, 195-196
  memory view, 193
  personal needs view, 192-193

Imageless thought, *see* Introspection
Implicit memory:
  source judgments, 153
  strategy use in children, 259
Information processesing, 4-6, 22
Intelligence, 228-229
International Association for
    Metacognition, viii
Introspection:
  concurrent, 12-14
  contemporary, 26-31
  imageless thought, 16-17
  trained, 12, 18
  retrospective, 14-15
  shortcomings, 15-19
Item selection, *see* Self-paced study

Judgment accuracy:
  measurement of, 92-93
  measurement pitfalls, 54-56
  gamma correlation, 47, 50, 92-93
  calibration, 47, 49
  calibration curve, 51-53
  relative accuracy, 47, 49
Judgments of learning (JOL):
  Alzheimer's disease and, 280-281
  childhood development and, 250-252
  collection and analysis, 44-57
  comprehension monitoring, 218
  cue utilization, 106-110, 250
  definition of, 40-42, 90

delayed-JOL effect, 97-104
drugs and, 99
ease of learning, 250
ease-of-processing hypothesis, 105-106
global judgments, 95-96, 247-250,
    272-274, 280
heuristic-based accounts, 105-106
older adulthood and, 272-277
relationship to other judgments, 91-92
retrieval-fluency hypothesis, 106
self-paced study and, 43, 57
study-test trials and accuracy, 94-97, 108
underconfidence-with-practice effect,
    94-97, 107
Judgments of learning (JOLs) and control
    processes:
discrepancy-reduction model, 113-114
functional role of, 110-112
region-of-proximal-learning hypothesis,
    114-115

Korsakoff syndrome:
feeling of knowing, 79-80
source monitoring, 157

Lie detection, see Lying
Life expectancy, 264
Long-term memory, 2, 27, 101-103, 140, 142,
    219, 225, 256
Lying:
accuracy and detection of, 188
confidence and, 188-189
courtroom testimony and, 187-189
deception cues, 187
frequency-validity relationship, 189-190
leakage cues, 187

Mathematics:
feeling of knowing, 83-86
math self efficacy, 228
self regulation of, 226-228
Memory beliefs, see also Older adulthood
relation to memory, 269
stereotypes and, 270
Memory development:
associative model, 259
effective strategy use, 255-259
metamemory hypothesis, 258-259
strategy choice and discovery
    simulation, 259
production deficiency, 257-258
strategy knowledge, 254-255
utilization deficiency, 257-258
Memory functioning questionnaire, 267-269
Memory training, 283-284, 286, 288-289
Metacognition:
definitions of, vii, 1, 3, 32
example, 1-2, 3
Metacognitive experiences, 32
Metacognitive framework, 4-6, 42-43

Metacognitive knowledge:
childhood development, 254, 255, 259, 260-261
definition of, 2, 3, 32
example, 3, 10
older adulthood, 267-272
Metacomprehension, 218-219
Meta-level, see Metacognitive framework
Metamemory development:
feeling of knowing, 252-253
global judgments, 247-250
judgments of learning, 250-252
overconfidence, 247-250
wishful-thinking hypothesis, 249-250
Metamemory framework, 40
Metamemory in Adulthood (MIA) scale, 267-269
Metamemory knowledge, see Metacognitive
    knowledge
Method of loci, 10
Mirror sign, see Reality-monitoring deficits
Modal model of memory,
    see Stage model of memory
Monitoring:
definition of, 3-6
measurement of, 38-44
questions about, 44
Monitoring accuracy, see Judgment accuracy
Monitoring-dual-memories (MDM) hypothesis:
definition of, 100-101
empirical evidence for, 100-103
Monkeys, see Nonhuman metacognition
Multinomial modeling, 148

Nonhuman metacognition:
chimpanzees, 244
dogs, 244
dolphins, 244-245
monkeys, 20-21, 245-246
Norm of study, 112

Object-level, see Metacognitive framework
Older adulthood:
Alzheimer's disease, 280-281
associative-deficit hypothesis, 282
false-fame effect, 283
feeling of knowing, 277-280
frontal-lobe functioning, 279-280
improving self efficacy, 271-272
judgments of learning, 272-277
memory beliefs, 267-272
memory training, 283-284, 286, 288-289
production deficiency, 284-285
self-paced study, 265-266
source judgments, 281-284
Overconfidence, see also Debiasing techniques
effect, 120-121

Piaget, J., 32-33
Prefrontal cortex:
feeling of knowing and, 80-81
source monitoring and, 164

Primacy effect, 256
Primates, *see* Nonhuman metacognition
Production anomia, 75
Production deficiency:
  childhood development and, 257-258
  older adulthood and, 284-285

Reading, 213-224, see also Comprehension
    monitoring
  constructively responsive reading, 216
  think-aloud protocols, 218
Reality monitoring:
  childhood development and, 240-241
  definition of, 156
  schizophrenia, 157-161, 164
  source monitoring, 156
Reality-monitoring deficits, 162-164
  forward model, 159-161
  mirror sign, 161-162
Recall-judge-recognition (RJR) method, 30,
    60, 64, 74, 87
Recency effect, 256
Reflex arc, 20
Relative accuracy, *see* Judgment accuracy
Retrieval termination:
  definition of, 40-42
  feeling of knowing, 84-87
  older adulthood and, 289-291
Retrospective confidence (RC) judgments:
  accuracy of, 120-129
  collection and analysis, 44-57
  debiasing techniques, 124-127
  definition of, 40-41, 118
  depressive-realism hypothesis, 121-123
  false memories and, 177
  group confidence, 127-129
  hard-easy effect, 51-52. 120-121, 123-124
  heuristics and biases, 130-133
  metacognition and, 138-139
  overconfidence effect, 120-121, 123-124
  performance feedback, 126-127
  retrieval termination, 140-143, 289-291
  selective-processing hypothesis, 122-123
Retrospective confidence and ecological
    approaches:
  frequency judgments, 133-134
  hybrid models, 136-137
  probabilistic mental models, 135-136, 139
  validity of, 134-136
Retrospective judgments and control
    processes, 139-143
Resolution, *see* Relative accuracy

Schizophrenia, *see* Reality monitoring
Search duration, *see* Retrieval termination
Self efficacy:
  academic self efficacy scale, 206
  academic achievement, 205
  definition of, 204
  improving, 271-272

math, 228
  self-regulated learning and, 115, 204-206
Self explanation, 222-224
Self-fulfilling-prophecy (SFP) hypothesis,
    102-104
Self-paced study, *see also* JOLs and control
    processes
  collection and analysis, 44-57
  item selection, 40-41
  judgments of learning and, 43, 57, 111-115
  older adulthood, 265-266, 286-289
  shift-to-easier-materials effect, 114
  termination of study, 40-41
Self-regulated learning and monitoring:
  calibration of, 207, 210-211
  confidence judgments and, 211
  student training, 212
  test preparation, 212
Self-regulated learning models:
  COPES model, 201-204
  comprehension and reading, 215-217
  monitoring and control processes, 202-204
  self-efficacy and, 204-206
  writing, 224-226
Short-term memory, 26, 101-103, 254-256
Simonides, 9-10
Source monitoring, *see also* Reality
    monitoring
  cryptomnesia, 156
  definition of, 40-41, 145
  emotion and imagery, 148-149
  false memories and, 177
  familiarity-based, 151-156, 165
  heuristics and, 158
  measurement of, 147-148
  multiple-entry modular memory system,
    149-151
  older adulthood and, 281-284
  recollection-based, 151-156, 165
  single-process model, 154-155
  source monitoring, 146, 154-155
  source similarity, 147-148
Source monitoring and neuroscience:
  confabulation, 156-157
  fMRI, 165
  frontal lobe, 165
  hippocampus, 165
  Korsakoff amnesia, 157
  prefrontal cortex, 164-165
  schizophrenia and, 157-161
  temporal lobe, 165
Stage model of memory, 26-27, 100-102
Strategy selection, 40-41, 82-84, 254, 258-259
Summary Street, 226

Termination of study, *see* Self-paced study
Test-operate-test-exit (TOTE) unit:
  definition of, 23-25
  relation to metacognitive framework, 25
Test taking, *see* Changing test answers

Theory of mind (ToM):
    appearance vs. reality, 239-242
    definition of, 236
    deception and, 238-239
    false beliefs task, 237-239
    metamemory and, 260-261
    reality-monitoring, 240-241
Theory of mind theories:
    executive functioning, 243
    modular theory, 242
Tip-of-the-tongue state:
    American sign language and, 78-79
    accessibility hypothesis, 77
    blockers, 72-73

cue familiarity, 76
definition of, 1, 30, 74
feeling of knowing, 71-79
resolving TOT states, 78-79
TOTimals, 76-77
Training:
    memory, 283-284, 286, 288-289
    metacognitive, 211-212

Watson, J. B., 18-19
Writing, 224-226
    knowledge telling, 225
    knowledge transforming, 225
    Summary Street, 226

About the Authors

John Dunlosky, Ph.D., is a Professor of Psychology at Kent State University (Ph.D. from University of Washington). He has contributed empirical and theoretical work on memory and metacognition, including theories of self-regulated learning and metacomprehension. Since his postdoctoral training at Georgia Institute of Technology, he has explored the metacognitive capabilities of older adults and has recently extended this research to grade-school children. A major aim of his research program is to develop techniques for improving the effectiveness of people's self-regulated learning across the life span. A fellow of the Association for Psychological Science, he is a founder of the International Association for Metacognition. He also serves as an Associate Editor for the *Journal of Experimental Psychology: Learning, Memory, and Cognition;* on the editorial boards of *Journal of Educational Psychology* and *Metacognition and Learning;* and has edited several books on metacognition.

Janet Metcalfe, Ph.D., is a Professor of Psychology and of Neurobiology and Behavior at Columbia University (Ph.D. from University of Toronto). She has contributed both empirical and theoretical work on memory and motivation, including a model of human memory called CHARM (composite holographic associative recall model), and the Hot-Cool framework of delay of gratification and impulse control. In addition, for the past 10 years, she has conducted studies applying principles of cognitive science to enhance learning with college students and with at-risk inner-city children. Current research centers on how people—both children and adults—know what they know, that is, their metacognitive skills and abilities, and whether they use these abilities efficaciously—for effective self-control. A fellow of the Association for Psychological Science and the Society for Experimental Psychology, she serves on the editorial boards of *Psychological Review*, *Psychological Bulletin*, and *Metacognition and Learning*, and has edited several books on metacognition.